I0754882

LOVE THEE,

NOTRE DAME

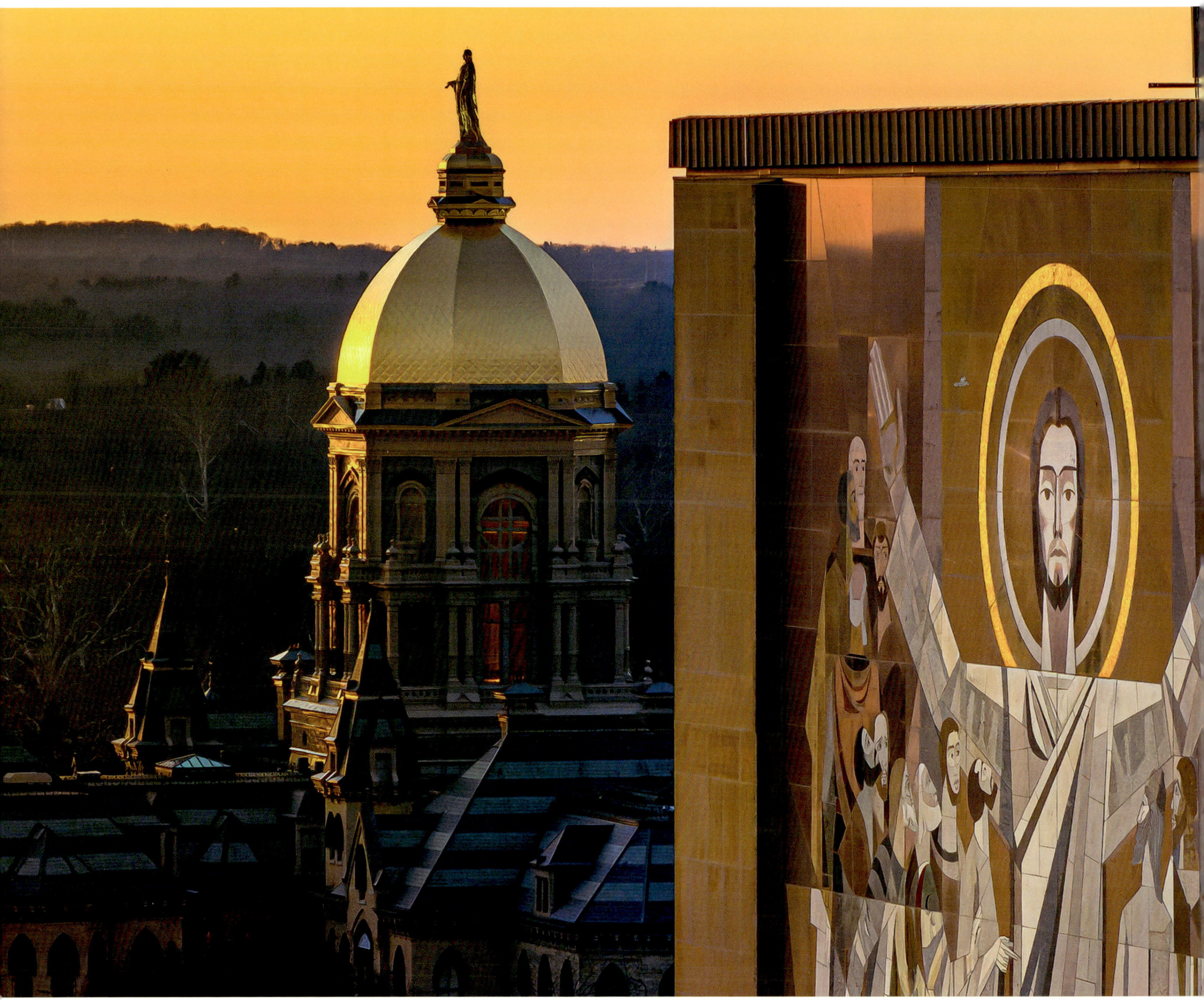

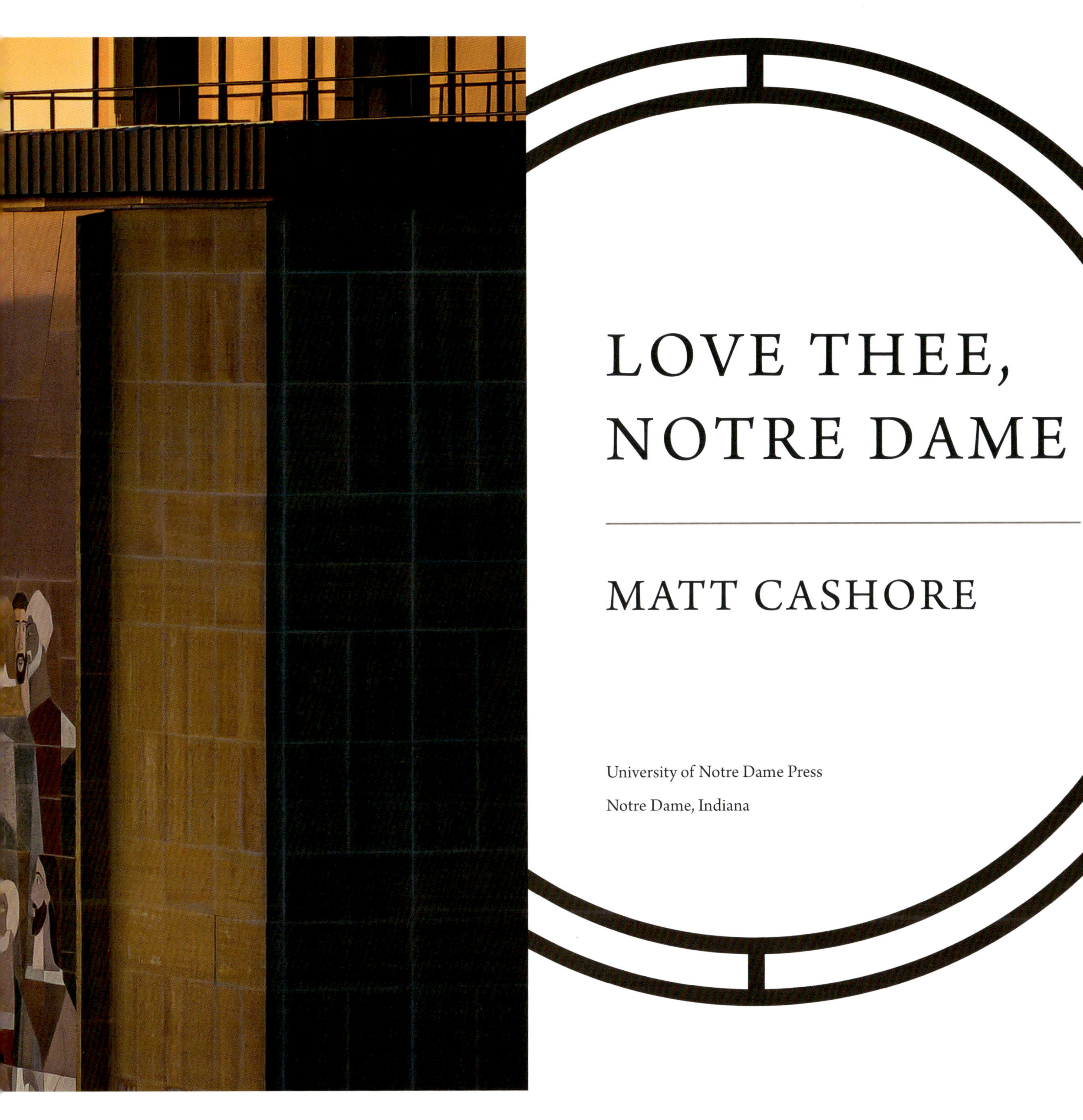

LOVE THEE, NOTRE DAME

MATT CASHORE

University of Notre Dame Press

Notre Dame, Indiana

Published by the University of Notre Dame Press
Notre Dame, Indiana 46556
undpress.nd.edu

Printed in Canada

Library of Congress Control Number: 2025934550

ISBN: 978-0-268-21025-0 (Hardback)
ISBN: 978-0-268-21032-8 (WebPDF)

GPSR Compliance Inquiries:
Mare Nostrum Group B.V., Mauritskade 21D, 1091 GC Amsterdam, The Netherlands
gpsr@mare-nostrum.co.uk | Phone: +44 (0)1423 562232

TO MARIA AND MADELINE

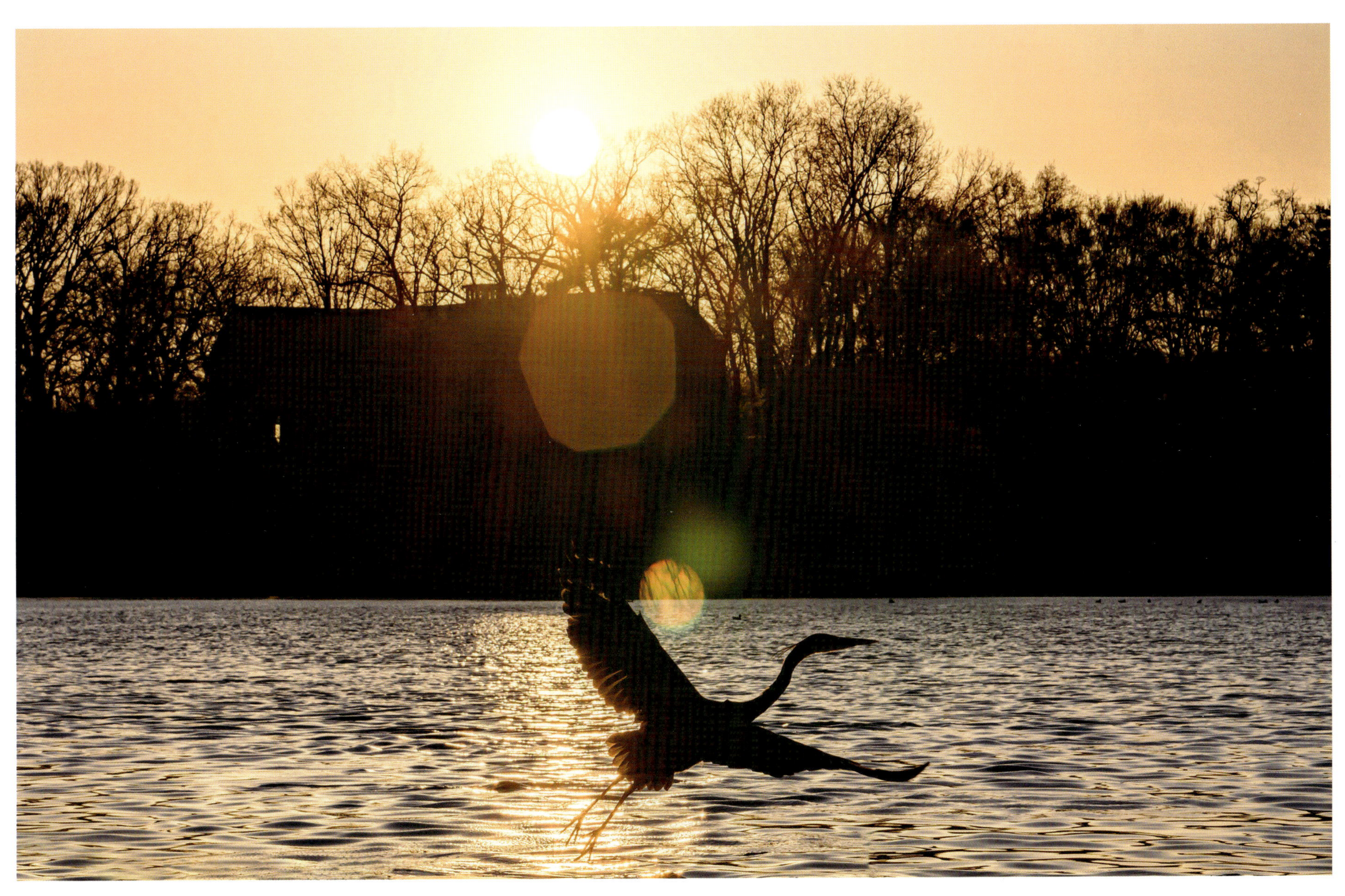

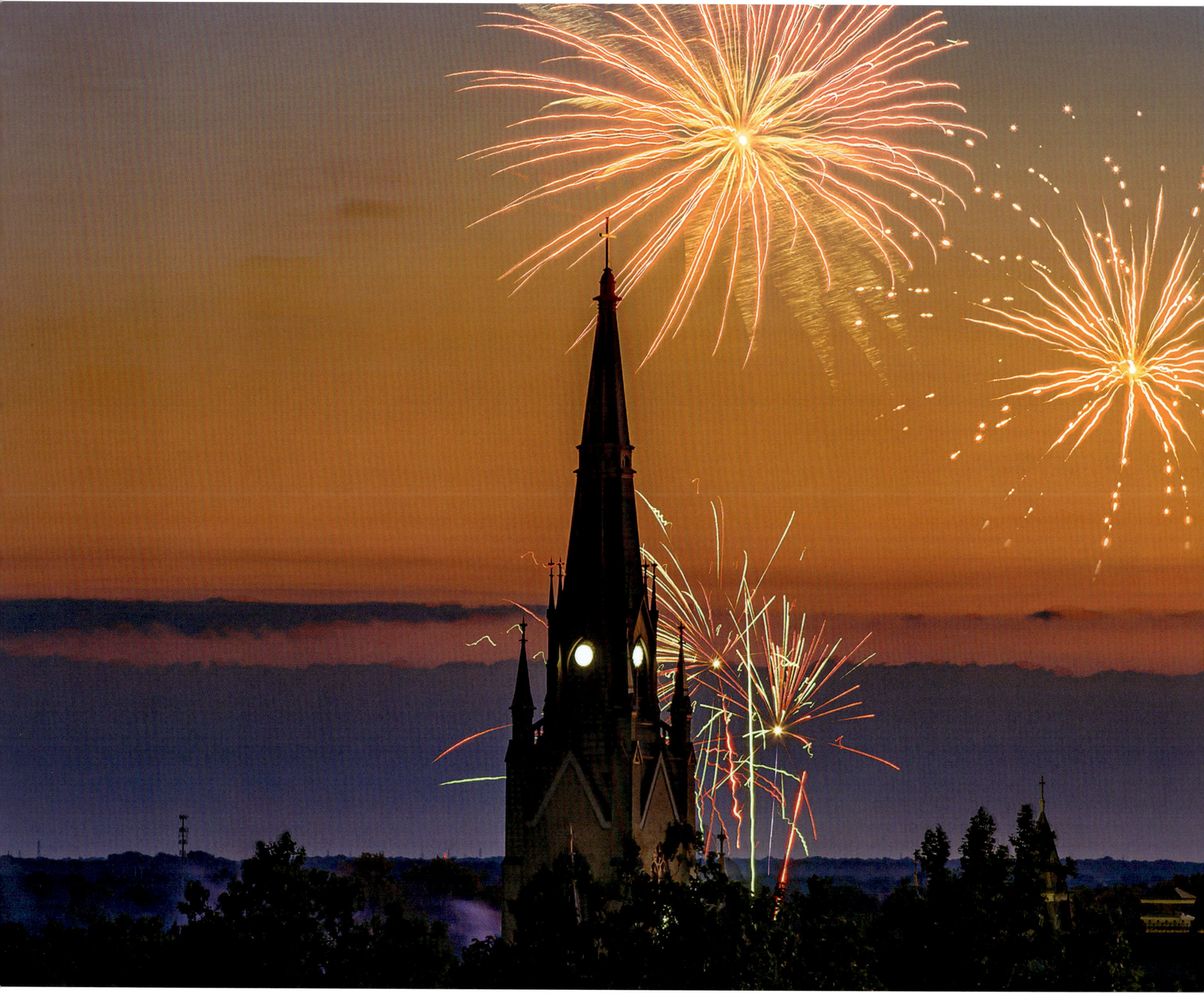

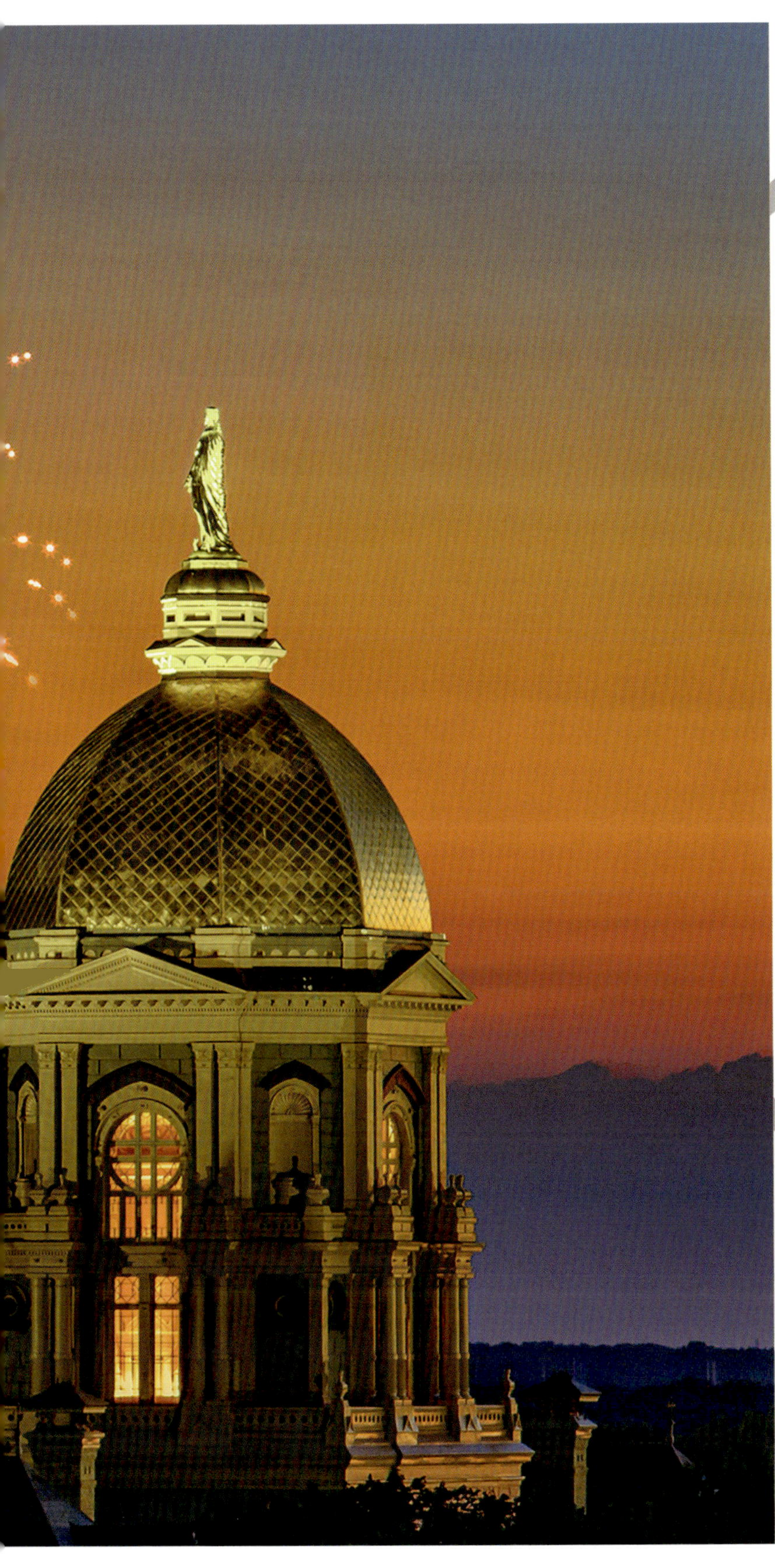

CONTENTS

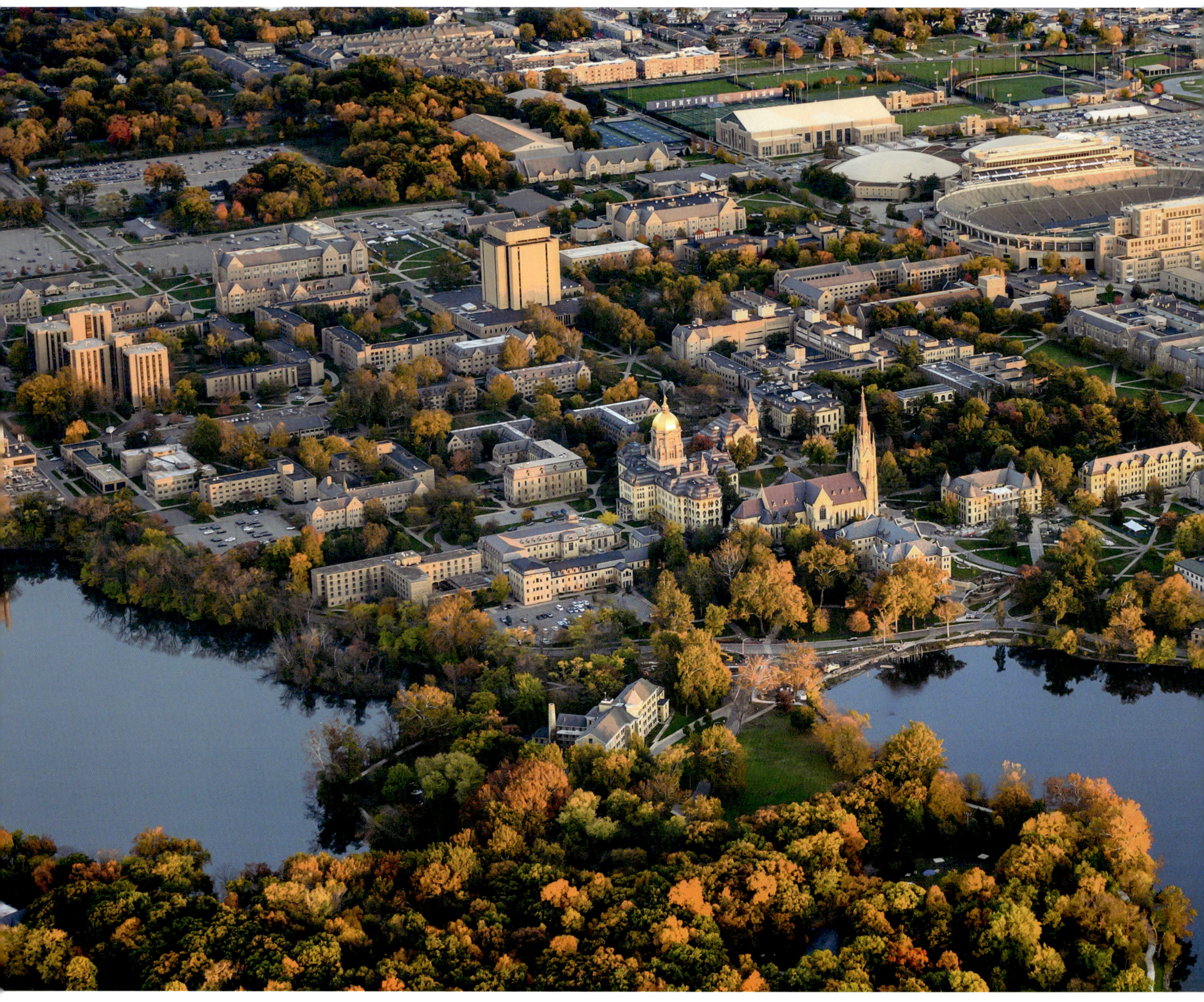
FIGHTING IRISH

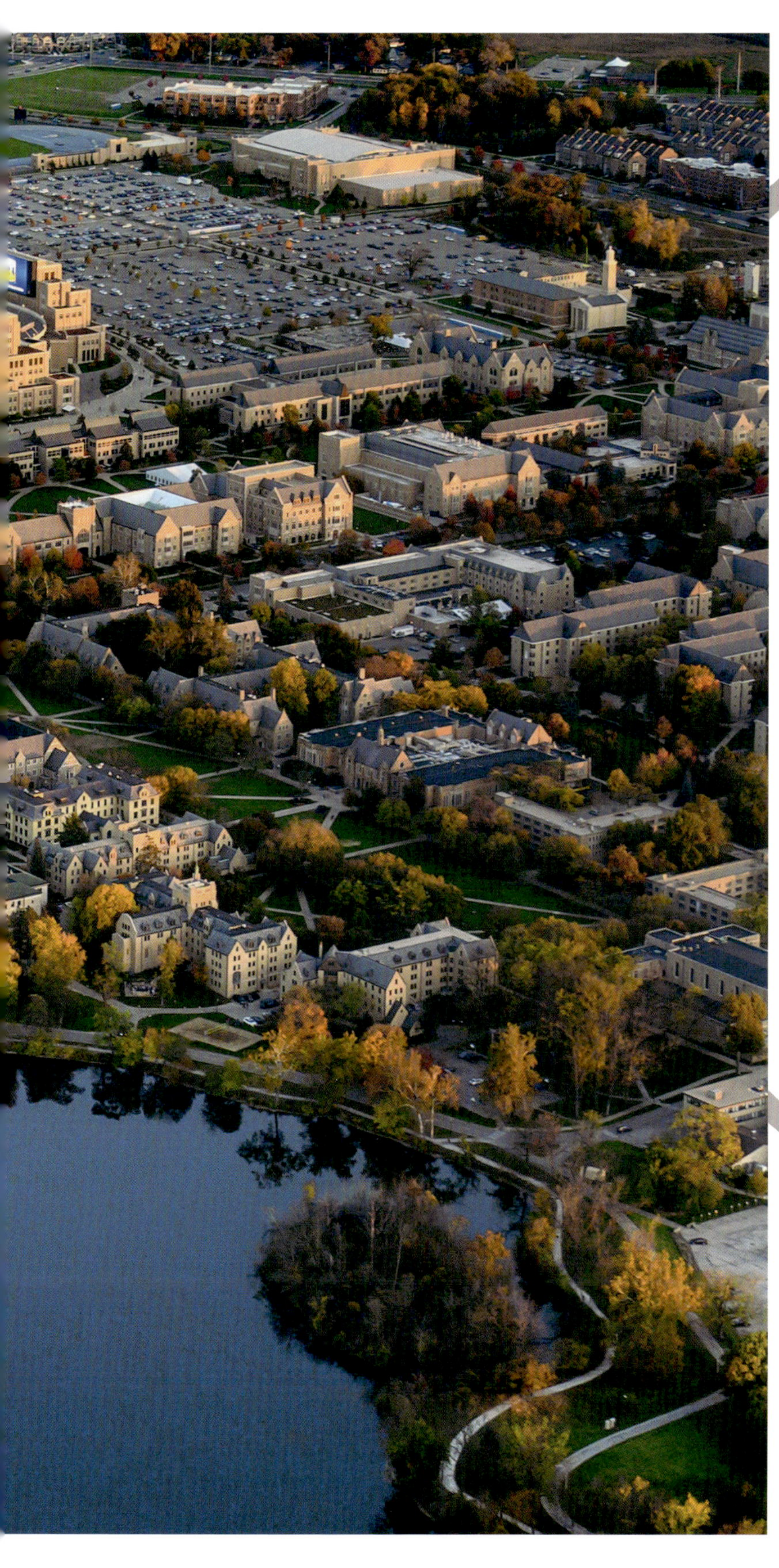

INTRODUCTION

It's not "where?"

It's "when."

I get asked somewhat regularly for information on vantage points for photos of the Notre Dame campus. The honest truth is I have no secret spots. Yes, in my role as a university photographer, on occasion I get access to rooftops, off-limits places, and campus nooks and crannies, but for the most part the photos in this book are made in spots anyone can easily walk to. I just do it at the right time.

Paraphrasing a photographer friend: I'm an adequately proficient technician of a camera who is willing to get up early, stand around in inconvenient weather, come away with nothing . . . and try again. Photography rewards persistence.

How did I start?

The short answer is: yearbook. Here's the long answer: My childhood career ambition was to go to the Air Force Academy and become a pilot. Genetics voted no in the form of nearsightedness.

Okay, then.

I remember sitting in a study hall freshman year of high school (Pius X, Lincoln, Nebraska, if you're curious) when someone came in and handed out the school newspaper. I remember thinking, "Huh? There's a school newspaper? Cool. I wanna do that."

I wasn't a photographer at first. In fact, I vaguely recall my first attempt at taking photos for the paper was an unqualified failure. But I definitely remember being curious about the darkroom in the back corner of the newspaper office, with the prints hanging to dry on a clothesline and the cool red light and trays of murky, smelly liquid. Coincidentally my high school required all students to take at least one fine arts class—and photography was an option. I had a chance at the trifecta of checking off a graduation requirement, improving my contributions to the school newspaper, and learning how the darkroom worked. You needed to supply your own SLR camera for the photo class, and my dad bought me a used Minolta SRT101 from the local camera store.

But black and white darkroom work isn't for the impatient. Make a mistake and there's no "undo" button. Start over. Film, paper, and chemicals cost money. Developing and printing took hours. Mistakes were expensive and demotivating. You were either all-in or quickly out.

Like I said earlier: Photography rewards persistence.

Turned out I was persistent enough to get adequately good enough to get encouragement from teachers and peers. I was all-in. It was tricky but measurable. Predictable but ephemeral.

If I had to name a "breakthrough" moment, it happened, coincidentally enough, at the Air Force Academy the summer before my senior year of high school. Even though I knew at that point I was going to apply to Notre Dame, I attended a summer camp at the Academy. One night a moonrise behind the iconic Air Force Academy chapel caught my eye, and I took a somewhat unauthorized excursion away from my group to make a photo. I got the "when" slightly wrong and the moon was overexposed (I'd learn a lot more in later years about photographing the moon), but it was the first time I had a specific vision and—more or less—got it on film.

It was probably around that time that I first had the conscious thought of wanting to do photography for a career. In the pre-internet days I had no idea there were any number of colleges that specialized in photography and photojournalism: Western Kentucky, Ohio University, Syracuse, Ball State, even the University of Nebraska right in my hometown, just to name a few. *Not* on that list? The University of Notre Dame. But that worked out to my advantage eventually.

When I arrived at Notre Dame in August of 1990, my cousin Amy Cashore '92 had already recruited me to work on the yearbook. I photographed my own freshman orientation. The yearbook started me down the road as a photographic

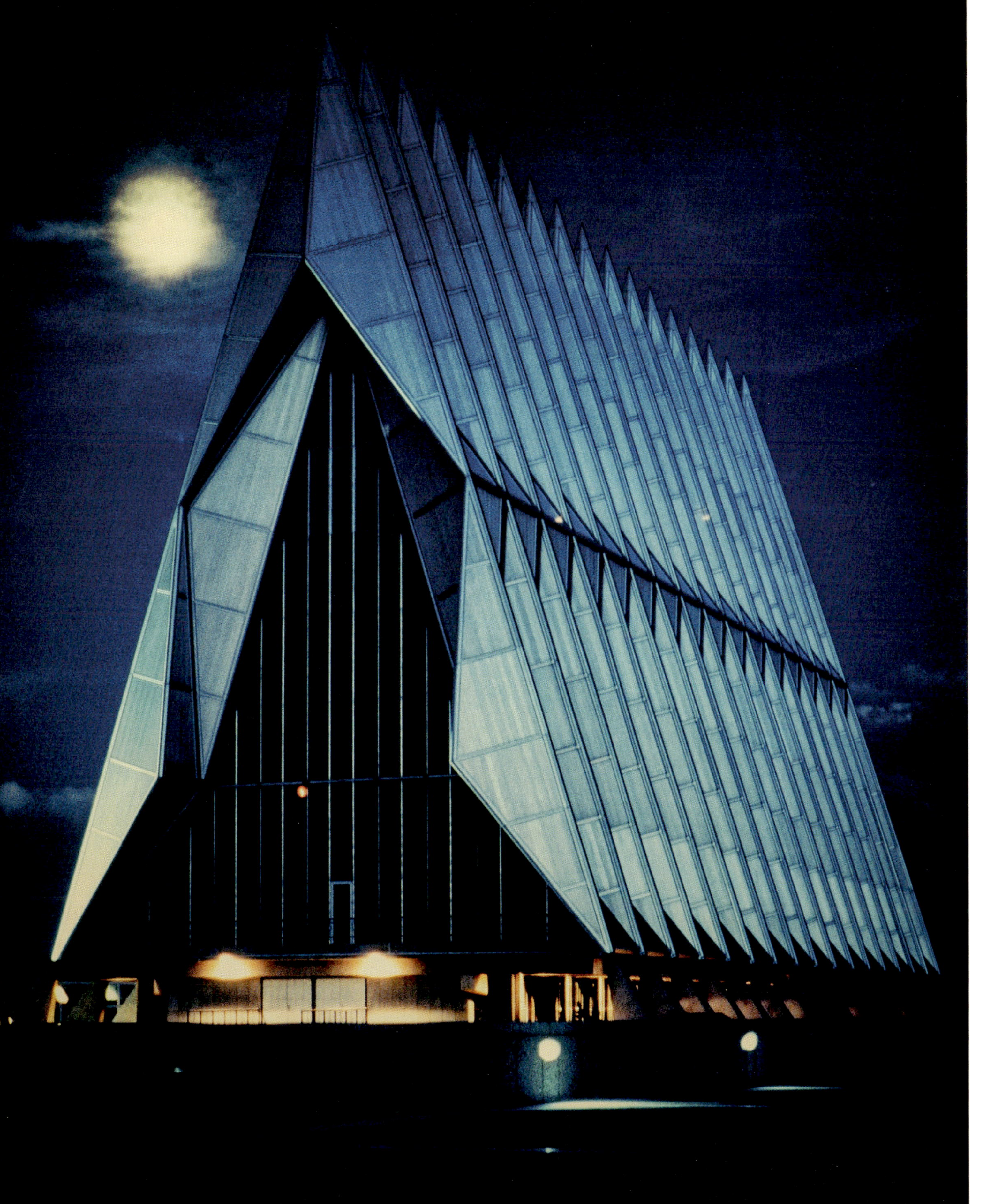

generalist. It was an early version of the job I have now. We had a small darkroom on the third floor of LaFortune Student Center. Officially we weren't allowed to stay in the building past 2 am, but sometimes there was too much to get done and I needed to keep cranking away. I played a little game of hide-and-seek with the student building monitors. Not sure if I was a good hider or if they were indifferent seekers, but I usually "won" and all-nighters in the yearbook darkroom were definitely part of my college experience. Until the early 2000s, Notre Dame owned the NBC affiliate TV station on the edge of campus: WNDU-TV. Notre Dame students could do internships for class credit. I wished Notre Dame owned a newspaper instead of a TV station, but a journalism internship at a TV station was better than no journalism internship at all. I learned to shoot and edit video, and, as luck would have it, when newspapers weren't offering me a job, WNDU did. I was the wee-hours-of-the-morning photojournalist/editor. Go in around 3 am, chase crimes, fires, weather, or whatever, and get done around noon. That left me all afternoon to do odd jobs for *Notre Dame Magazine* and others on campus. Eventually, I did enough work for Notre Dame that someone in Accounts Payable must have said, "Just hire him, already." And in 2007, they did.

So after all these years—two regildings, two presidential inaugurations, seven football coaches—isn't the tank empty? Haven't I exhausted all possible views of the Dome?

Isn't it . . . *boring*? Nope.

The question I get asked almost as much is what is my favorite thing to photograph. The answer is: "Everything." Being a university photographer is a perfect job for a generalist. There's a smidge of everything to do: landscapes, sports, portraits, feature photos, news photos . . . I'm rarely bored. There are, I'll admit, not as many, "Huh . . . never seen *that* before . . ." moments, but those still happen. And even when I have seen

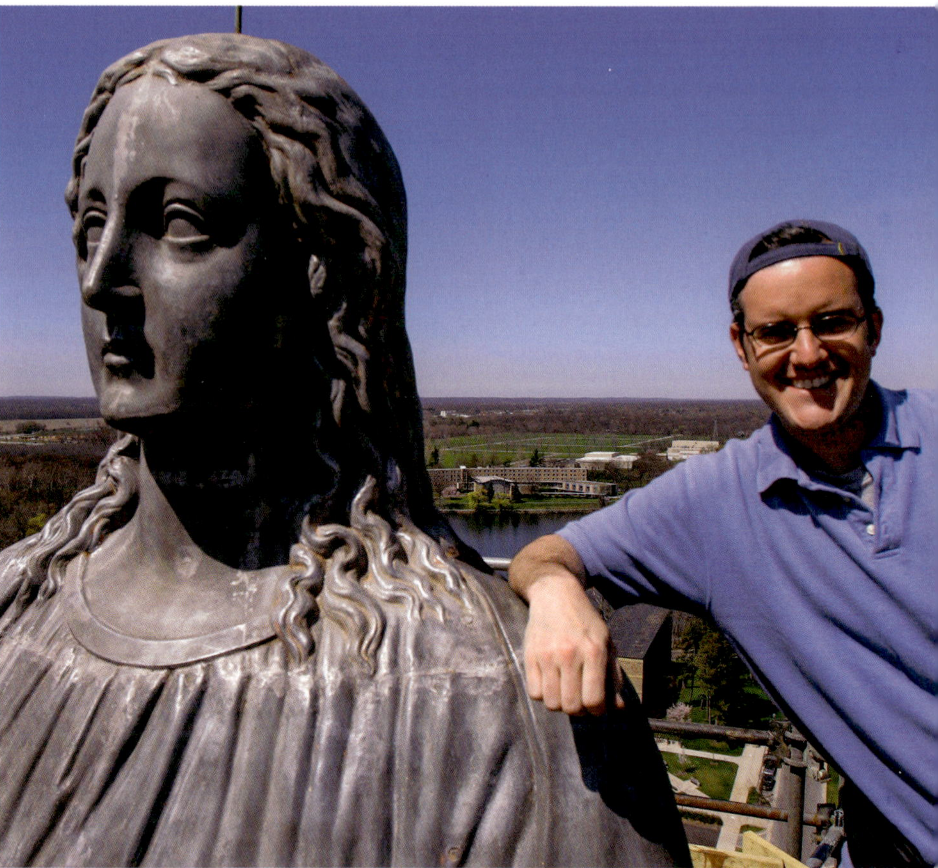

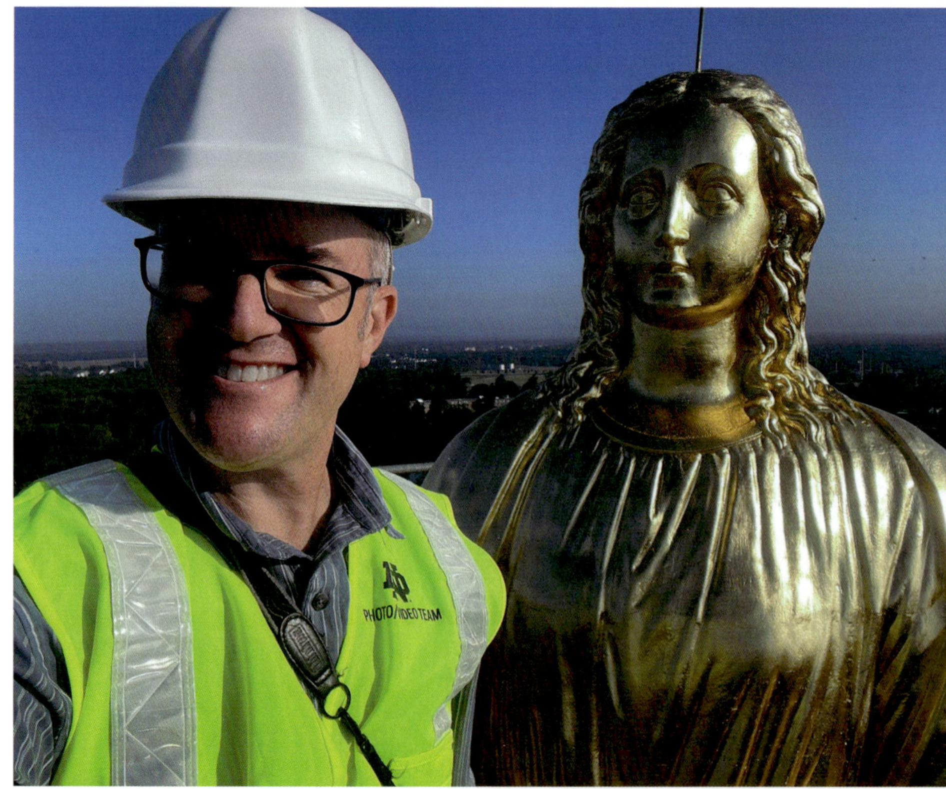

The author atop the Golden Dome during regildings in 2005 (photo by Ed Cohen of *ND Magazine*) and 2023 (author selfie).

it before, there might be a chance to share it in a new, different, and better way.

What makes a good photo?

Returning to the "where vs. when" at the start of this text: With a few exceptions, the most critical element in a good photo is good light. After all, "photography" literally translated means "drawing with light." The better the light, the better the drawing, right?

But "good light" doesn't necessarily mean "bright light." Think of paintings by Caravaggio or Rembrandt, with their pools of light and heavy shadows. The light has a shape and a direction. Good light in nature is usually at the extreme beginning and end of the day when the sun is low on the horizon and diffused—what people often refer to as "the golden hour."

In addition to light, there is composition. There are historically accepted rules on composition—"rule of thirds," "golden ratio," etc.—but of course artistic rules are practically by definition meant to be broken. The one thing I'd include in composition that's not breakable is a good background. Usually that means a nice sky or uninterrupted color or texture.

When an iconic subject like the Golden Dome combines with perfect light and a dramatic background like a moonrise or passing storm clouds, it all adds up to what I call "The Magic." I didn't have a name for it at the time, but that's what I had with the Air Force Academy chapel: Iconic subject, great light, and a dramatic background, and that's why my job today never gets boring, because the feeling of capturing The Magic is just as satisfying today as it was thirty-six years ago.

The good and bad part about The Magic is that it can't be scheduled. So I often describe what I do as "chasing The Magic." If it was predictable, anyone could do it, and it wouldn't be as magical. And I usually have to be ready before it happens or it's over by the time I can get the right lens or get to the perfect spot.

Yes, there are apps that will tell you exactly where the moon will be in what phase, and there are astonishingly accurate weather forecasts and sunset and sunrise times are consistently knowable. Many who have spent a winter at Notre Dame joke (or maybe not . . .) that they wish Father Sorin had left Vincennes and gone south instead of north, but he had the good luck to go north to a place with four very distinct seasons that is also downwind of Lake Michigan, with its unpredictable influence on the local meteorology. So that's how we might have a downpour immediately followed by calm winds and crystal blue skies. While campus's storm drains are momentarily overwhelmed, there's an opportunity for some nice reflections. I have ten, maybe fifteen minutes before the overcast comes back or the puddles drain away or something else changes and The Magic goes away. And even though it seems at times like campus is always covered in snow, there's really only a brief window where it's unblemished before being plowed and walked on, turning into what I call "snirt" (a combination of "snow" and "dirt"). That same weather that makes this region . . . inconvenient . . . is in large part what makes it possible to photograph the same place for thirty-plus years and come away with something slightly different each time.

Years of walking campus has given me a pretty good idea of "where." Certain spots might as well have signs that say "MAKE A PICTURE HERE." The way the trees on Main Quad perfectly frame the Main Building, for example. The tricky part is the "when." That Main Quad view will always look nice . . . but it won't always be magic.

And lastly, it helps a lot if the main subject of the photo has meaning to the viewer: maybe a loved one, a pet, or an important place or thing.

And this is where I get a big assist from Notre Dame.

Alumni, fans, friends . . . a lot of people identify with, have important memories and life events associated with, or are inspired by the Notre Dame campus. Yes, this is my job and it has job things, but it's rewarding to get an email, a social media comment, or have a conversation where someone says,

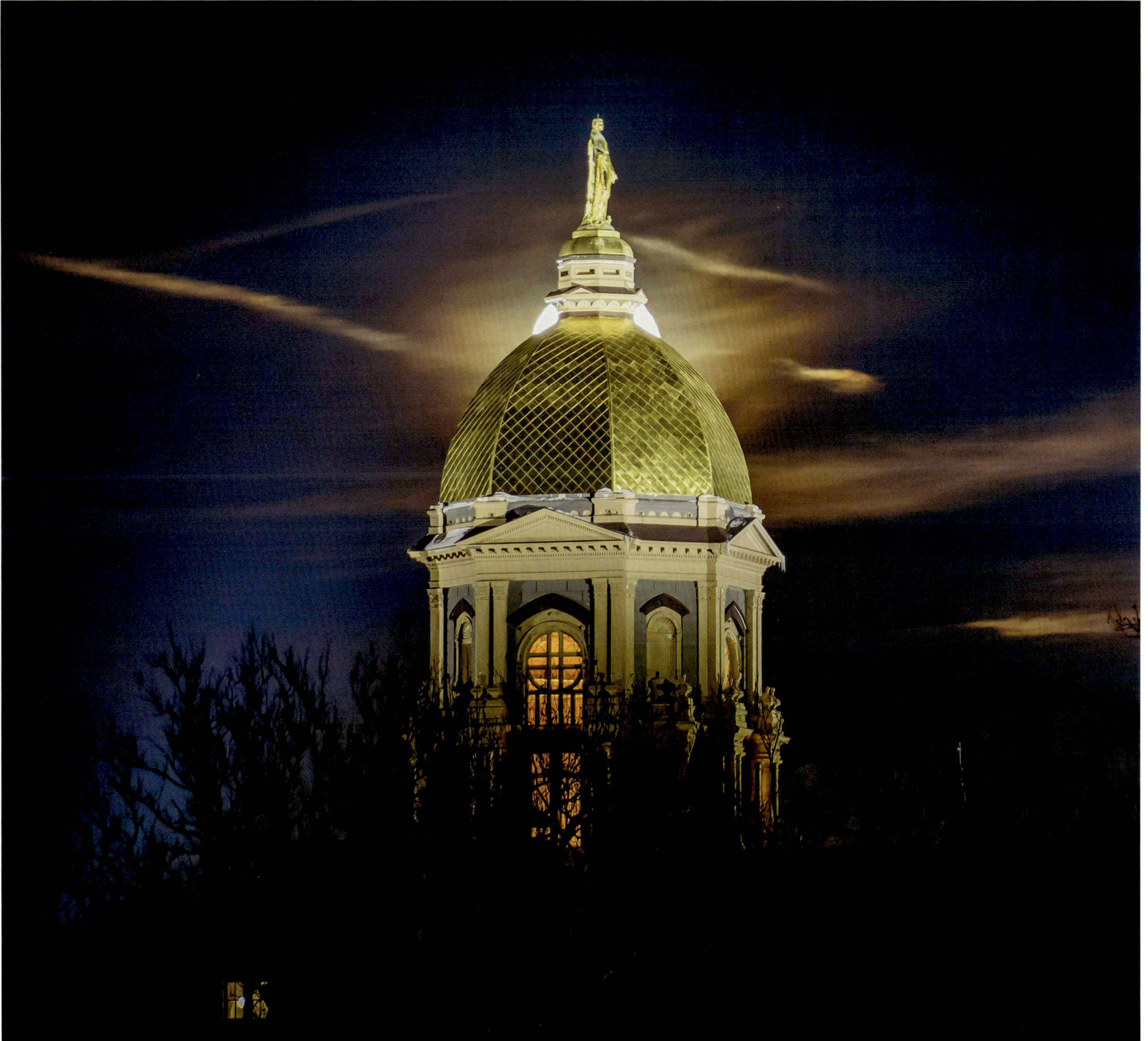

"Your photos keep me connected to campus," or "That's the spot I proposed to my wife," or something else that tells me a photo made a personal connection.

As a final thought on this collection: I often say, "My boss is Notre Dame Archives seventy-five years from now." I think of my role for Notre Dame as a historian. Even though the classic view down Notre Dame Avenue is largely the same from one decade to the next, campus is always changing.

One year at reunion, a group of alumni stopped me and asked for directions to the Morris Inn. They were standing right in front of it! It just looked substantially different from the last time they'd seen it. The ordinary every day is always changing. Walk by a building a thousand times and you don't notice it until one day it's replaced with a new building and suddenly you can't remember what it looked like before. I hope I can adequately show what Notre Dame looked like and capture the spirit of this time for future archivists.

CHARACTERS IN THE STORY

It's a thirty-five-year story. Here are some of the characters from that story. I can't possibly name everyone, so with apologies to those I don't have space to name, here are a few:

Bruce Harlan—Notre Dame's first university photographer from 1949 until 1992. He showed me there was such a job as university photographer. Funny enough, though, I messed up the only assignment I ever did for Bruce. I never worked for him again, but we remained friendly.

David Bergman—We never actually met until decades later. David was the photo editor of the University of Miami yearbook and showed me how high the bar could be for college yearbook photography.

Ted Genoways—A roommate during college summers, Ted started a student magazine at Nebraska Wesleyan University, and even though I wasn't a Wesleyan student, I *was* conveniently located. Working for Ted gave me some key opportunities to stretch my skills at a formative time.

Mark Alstott—When I came to South Bend, one of the first places I went was Gene's Camera Store, where I first met Mark. He was a combo of cheerleader and tech support. These days you can just Google, "How do I do this? What gadget do I need to do that?" Those days, you couldn't. Mark was my Google.

Kerry Temple, Don Nelson, Julie Ettl, and the rest of the staff at *Notre Dame Magazine*—If I had to name only one career catalyst it would be *ND Magazine*. They saw some yearbook photos that looked competent enough to ask the kid who made 'em to do a few portraits for the magazine. That started a ball rolling that's thankfully still going thrity-plus years later.

Tim Prister—Another career catalyst. Called one day in my junior year of Notre Dame needing a few baseball photos for "Blue and Gold Illustrated." Little did I know I'd crisscross the country with Tim photographing Notre Dame Football for over twenty-five years.

Joe Raymond—My definition of a mentor: Someone who cares that I care.

My wife, Maria—Who could be home while I ran around campus at all hours.

My parents—For never saying "You wanna do *what*? Get a real job!"

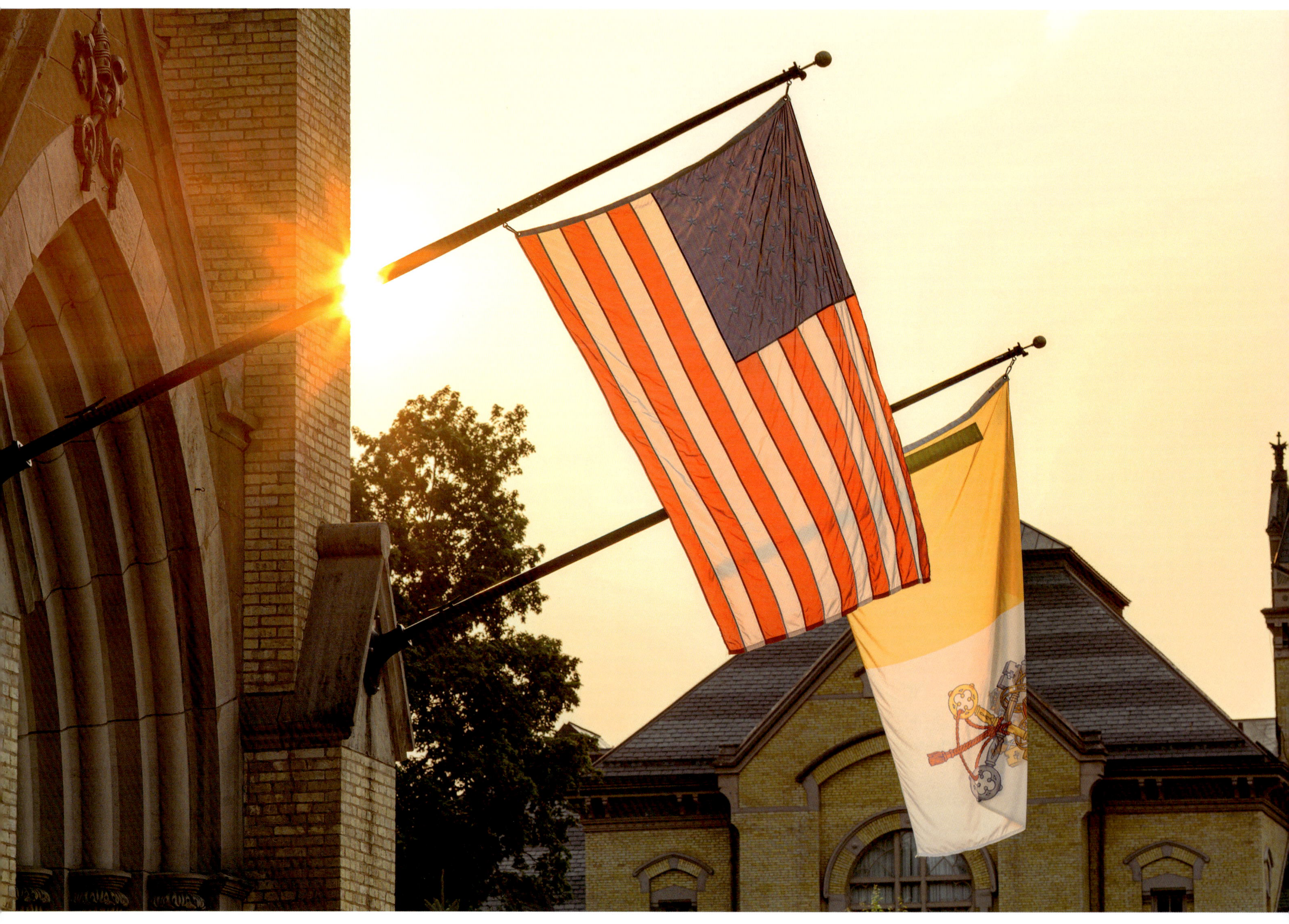

LOVE THEE,

NOTRE DAME

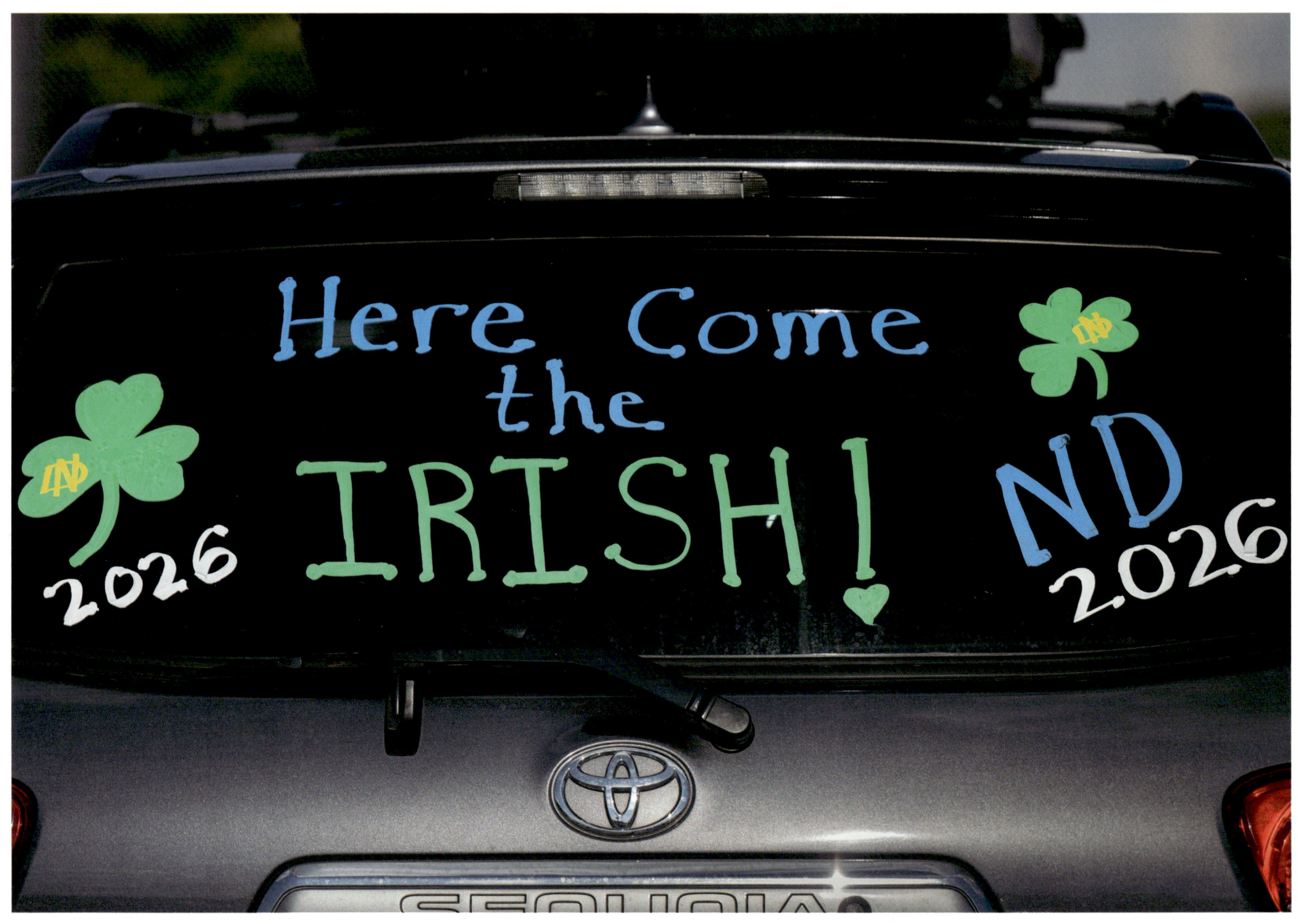

Move-in at Flaherty Hall, Nikon Z6II, 130mm, 1/5000 f2.8, ISO100

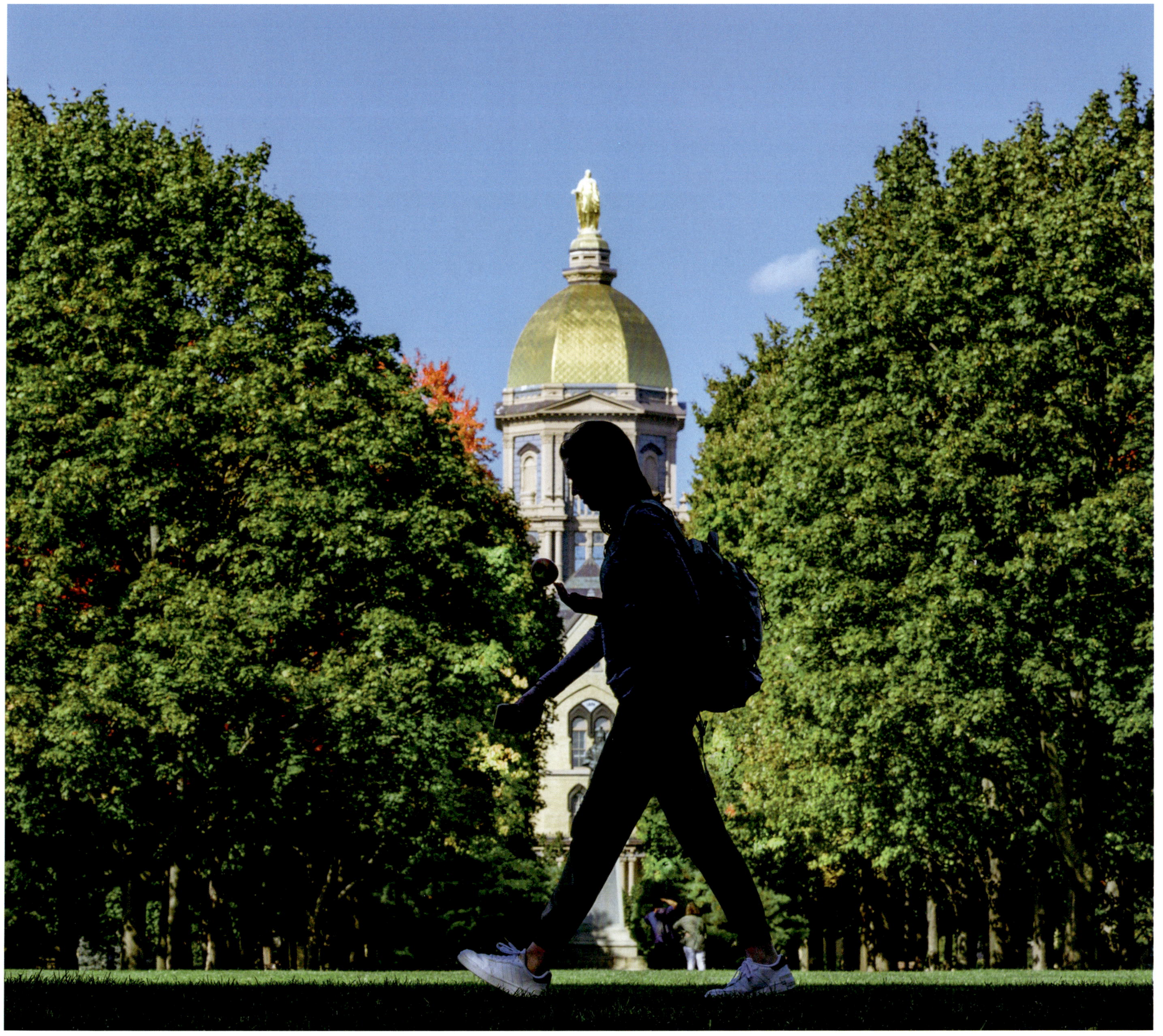

Main Quad, Nikon Z6II, 92mm, 1/800 f16, ISO800

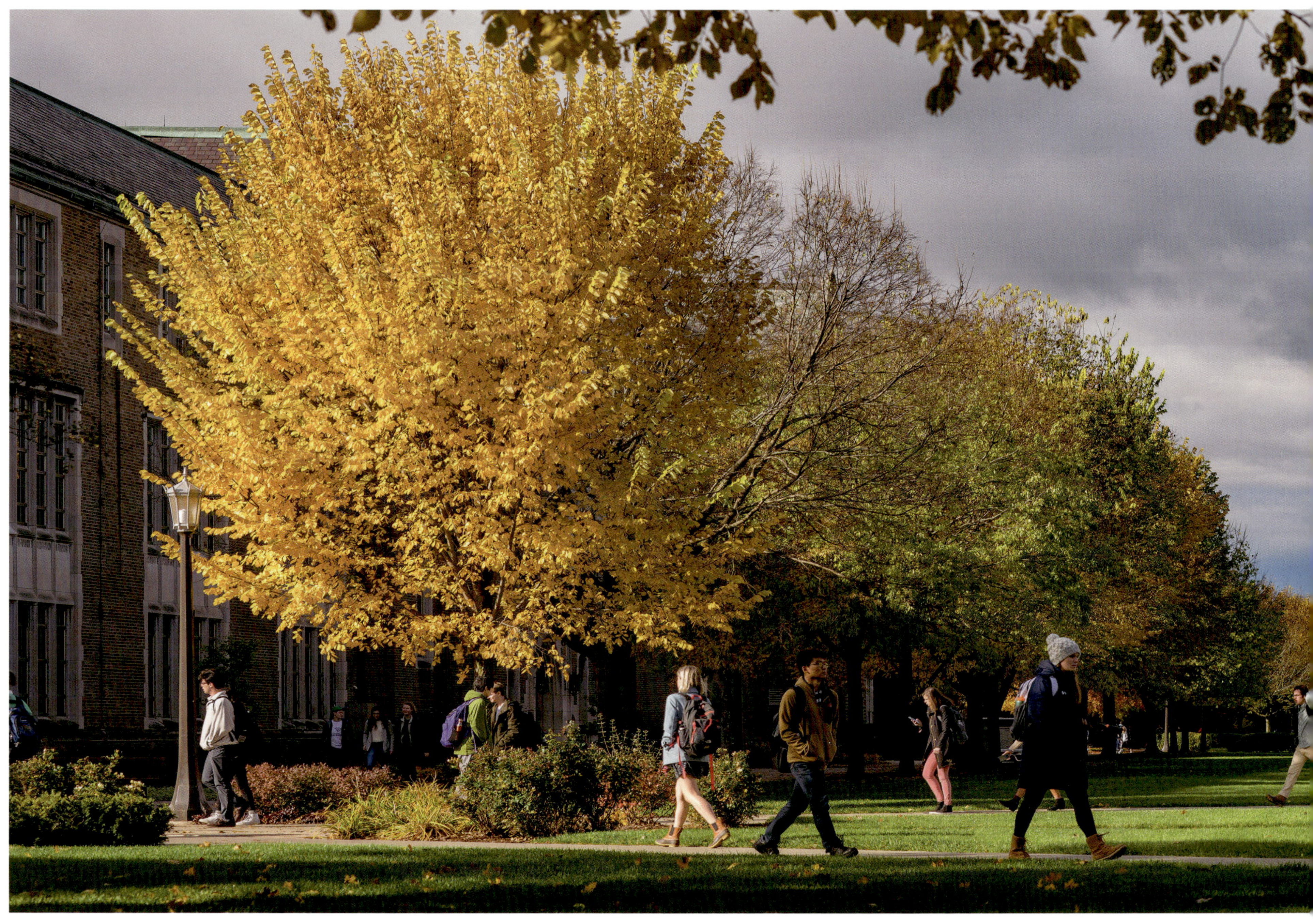

It helps to know where and how a photo will be used. This photo was made to be displayed nearly life-size in Duncan Student center, so simply cropping a regular-size frame into a panorama wouldn't have the image quality necessary. The most common solution for high-resolution panoramas is a multiframe stitched image. Take small sections of the entire scene and software will find and match the overlapping edges. You can make a total composite image orders of magnitude bigger than anything that can be done in-camera. It's easy for landscapes and architecture where nothing moves. When there are people—and they're moving—you can end up with the same person in multiple places, or a random leg or arm that the frame stitching didn't catch. I spent a good deal of time on this one manually fixing those problem spots, and whenever I'm in Duncan Student Center and see this photo I spend a minute or two double-checking my work!

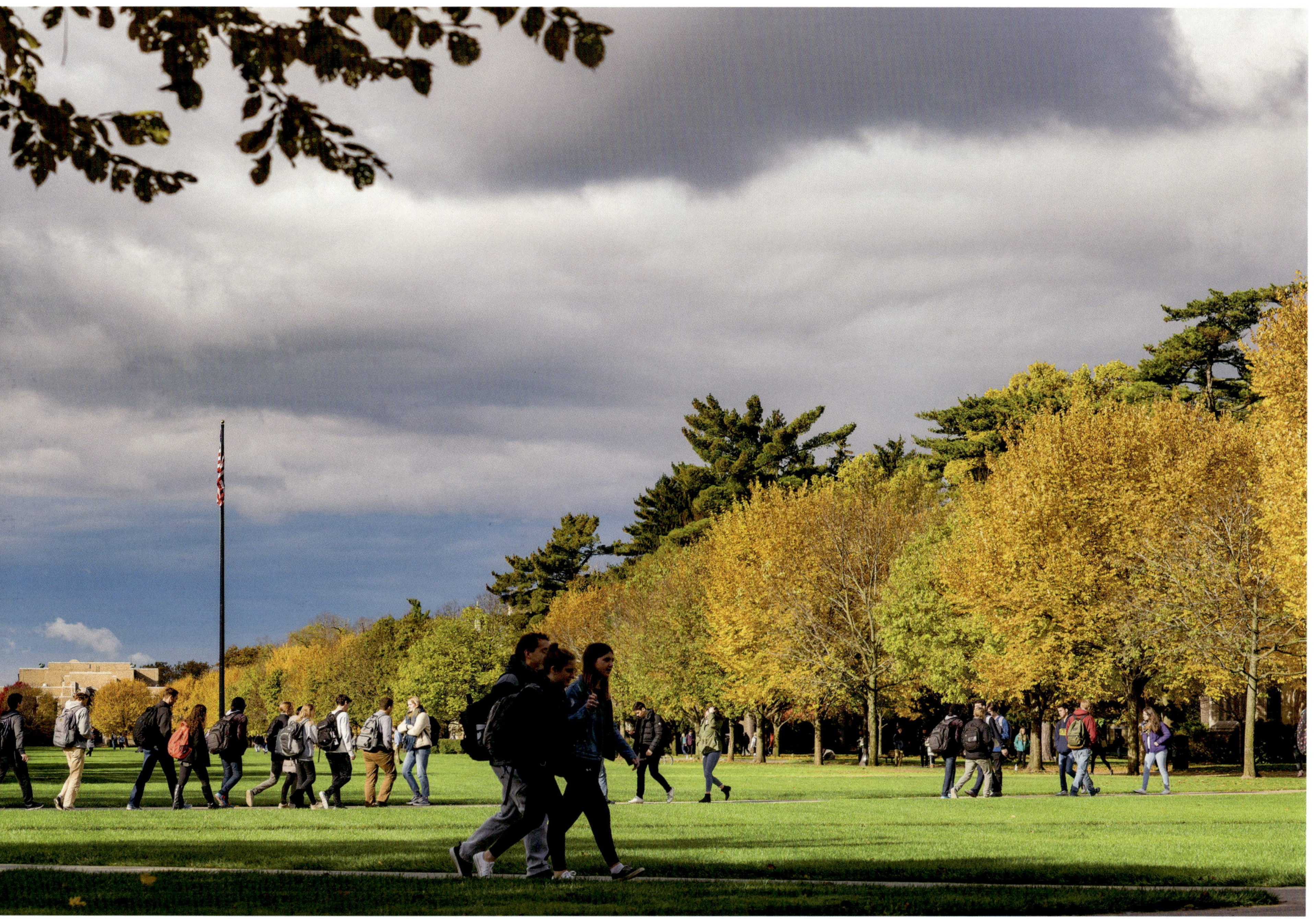

South Quad, Nikon Z7, 50mm, 1/250 f8, ISO125, stitched panorama

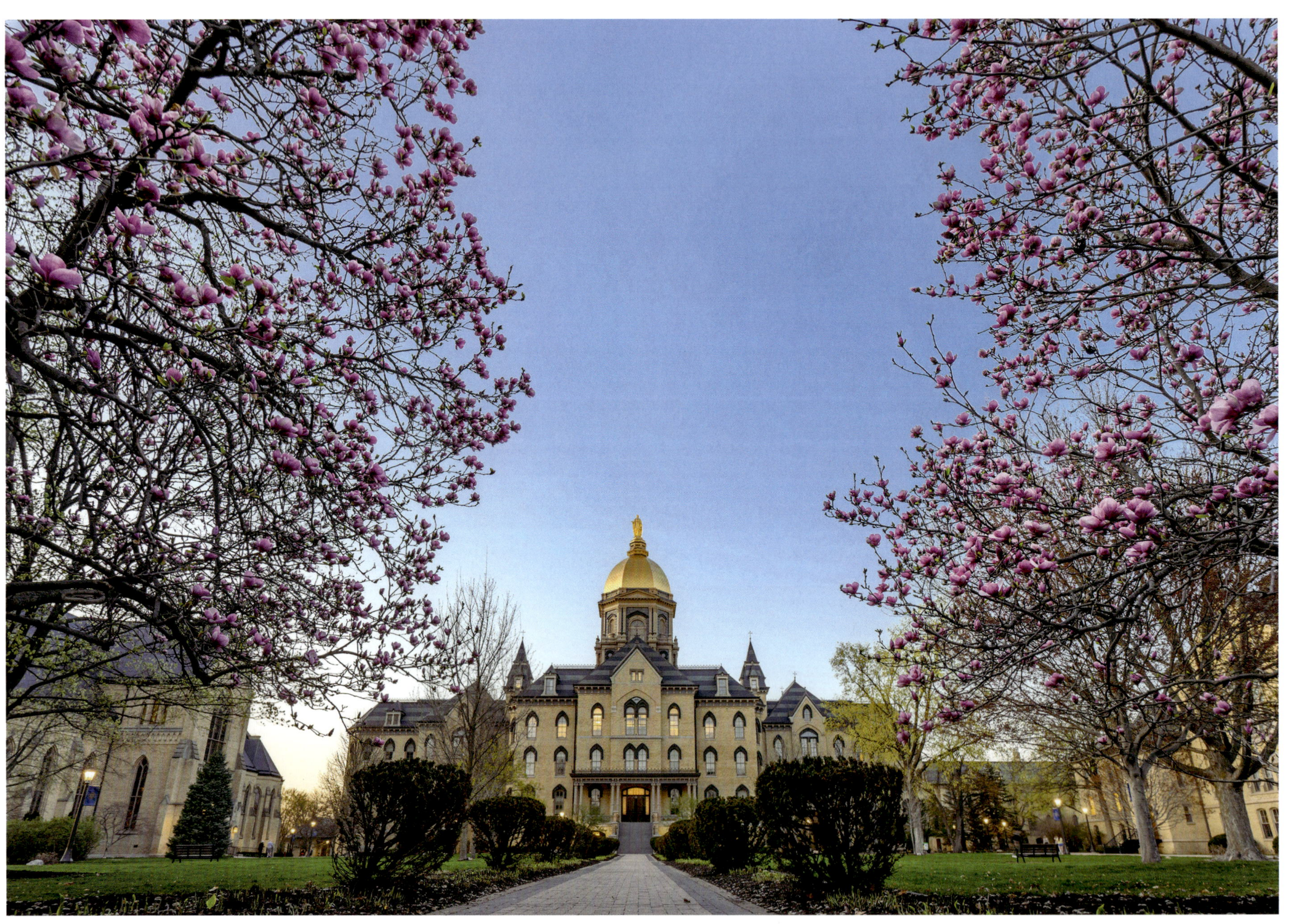

Main Building, Nikon Z9, 17mm, 1/4 f5.6, ISO64

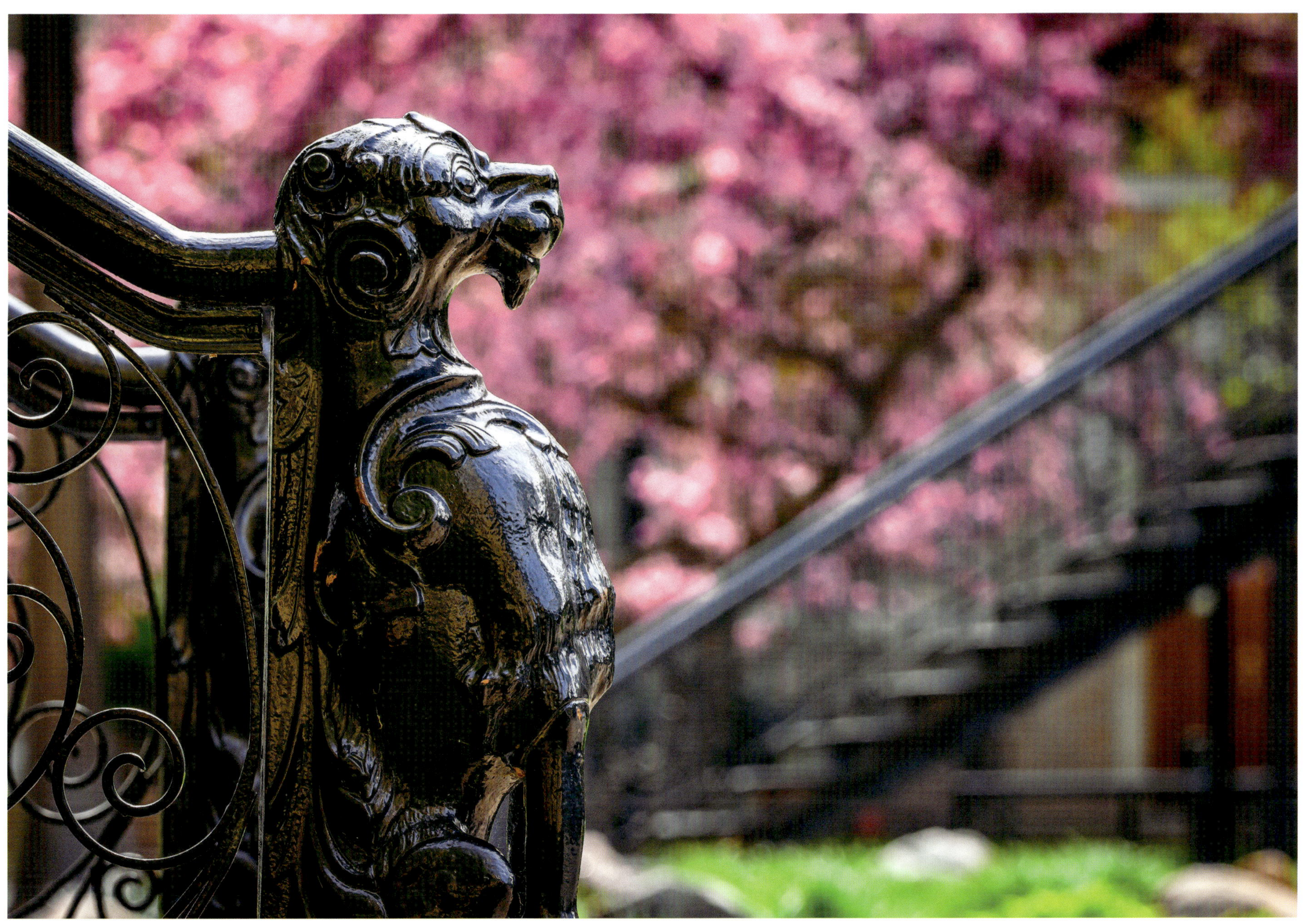

Decorative stairs on Main Building, Nikon Z7II, 200mm, 1/25 f9, ISO64

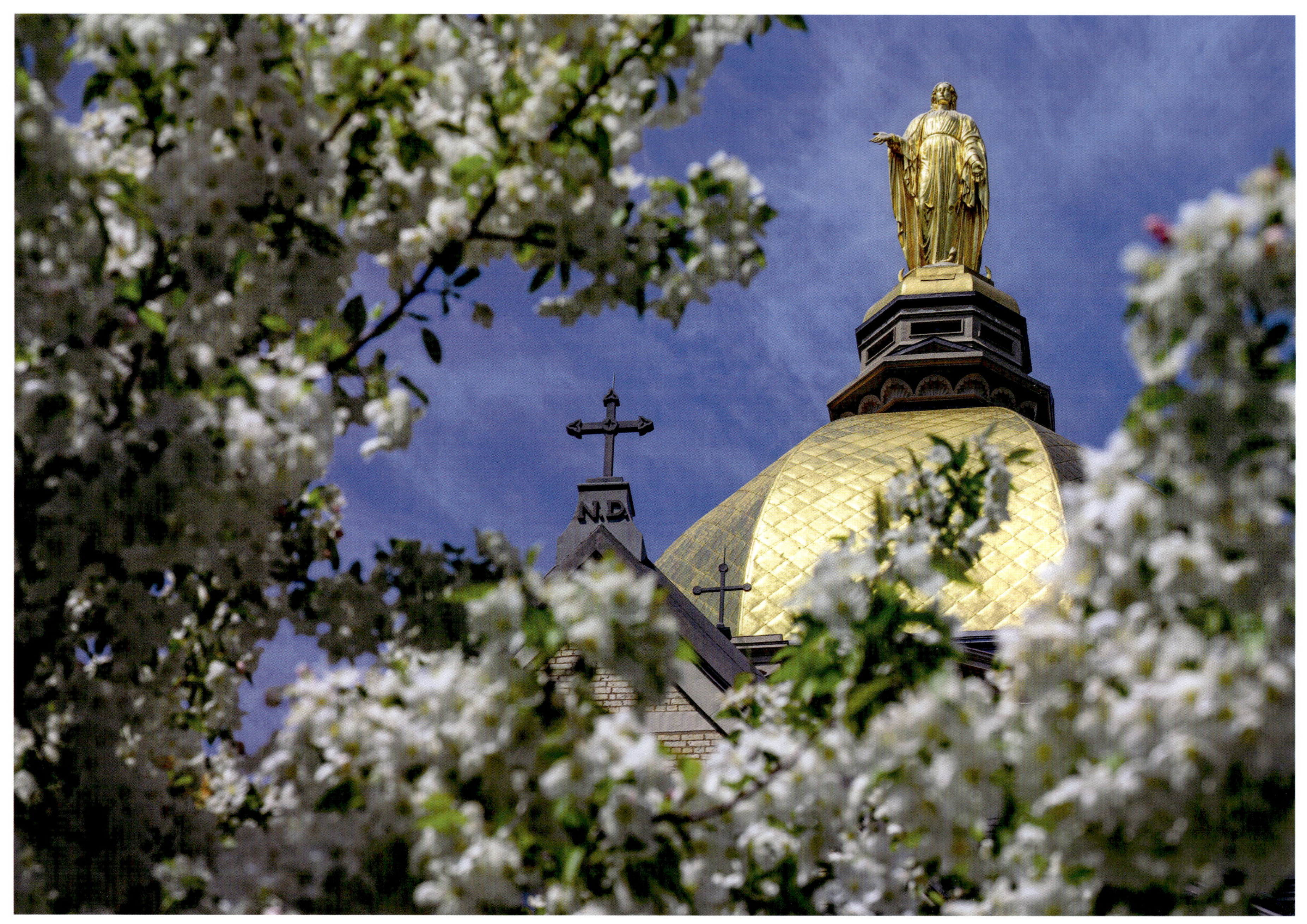

Main Quad in spring, Nikon Z7II, 97mm, 1/160 f14, ISO64

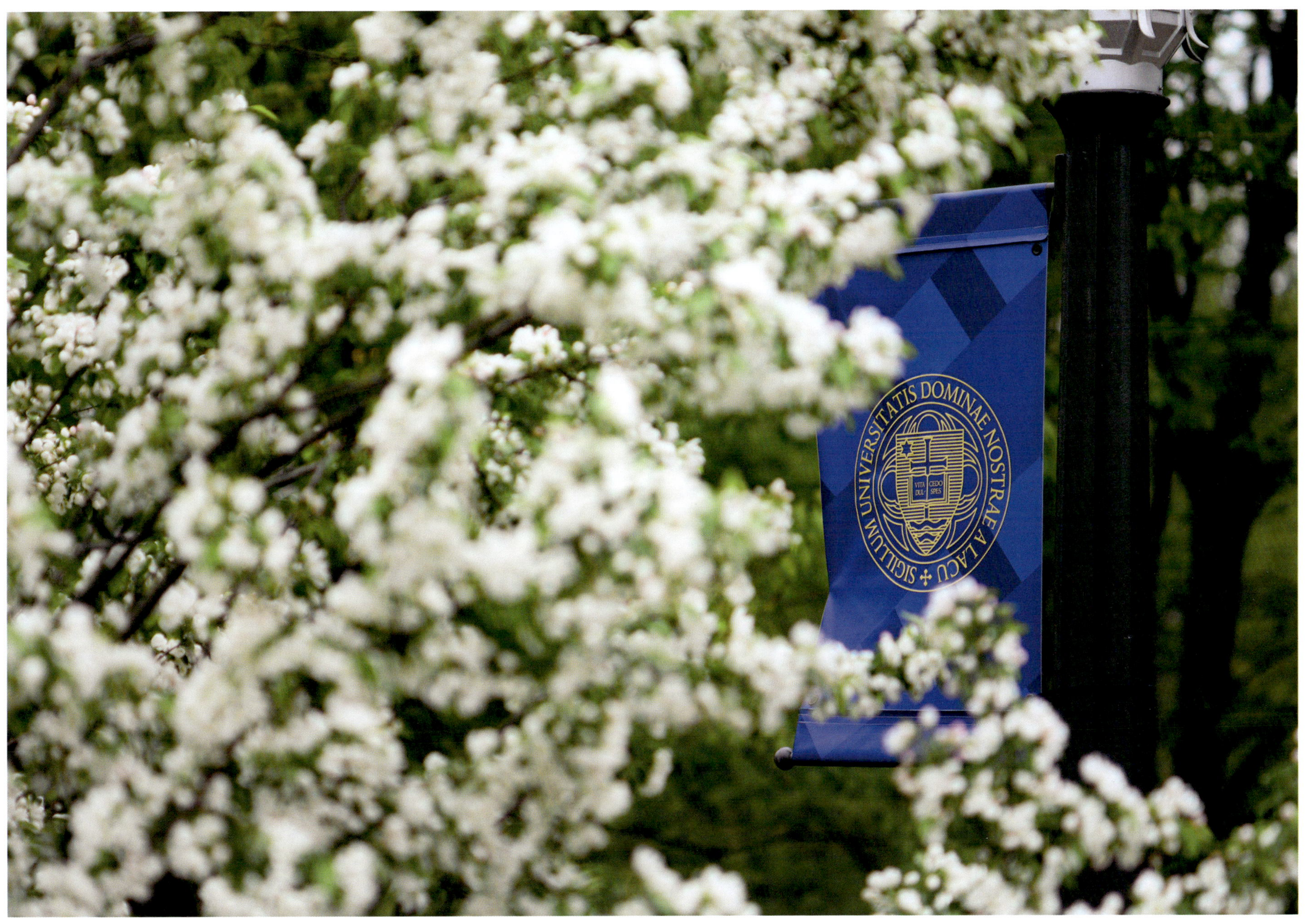

Near the main circle, Nikon Z6, 135mm, 1/320 f2.8, ISO200

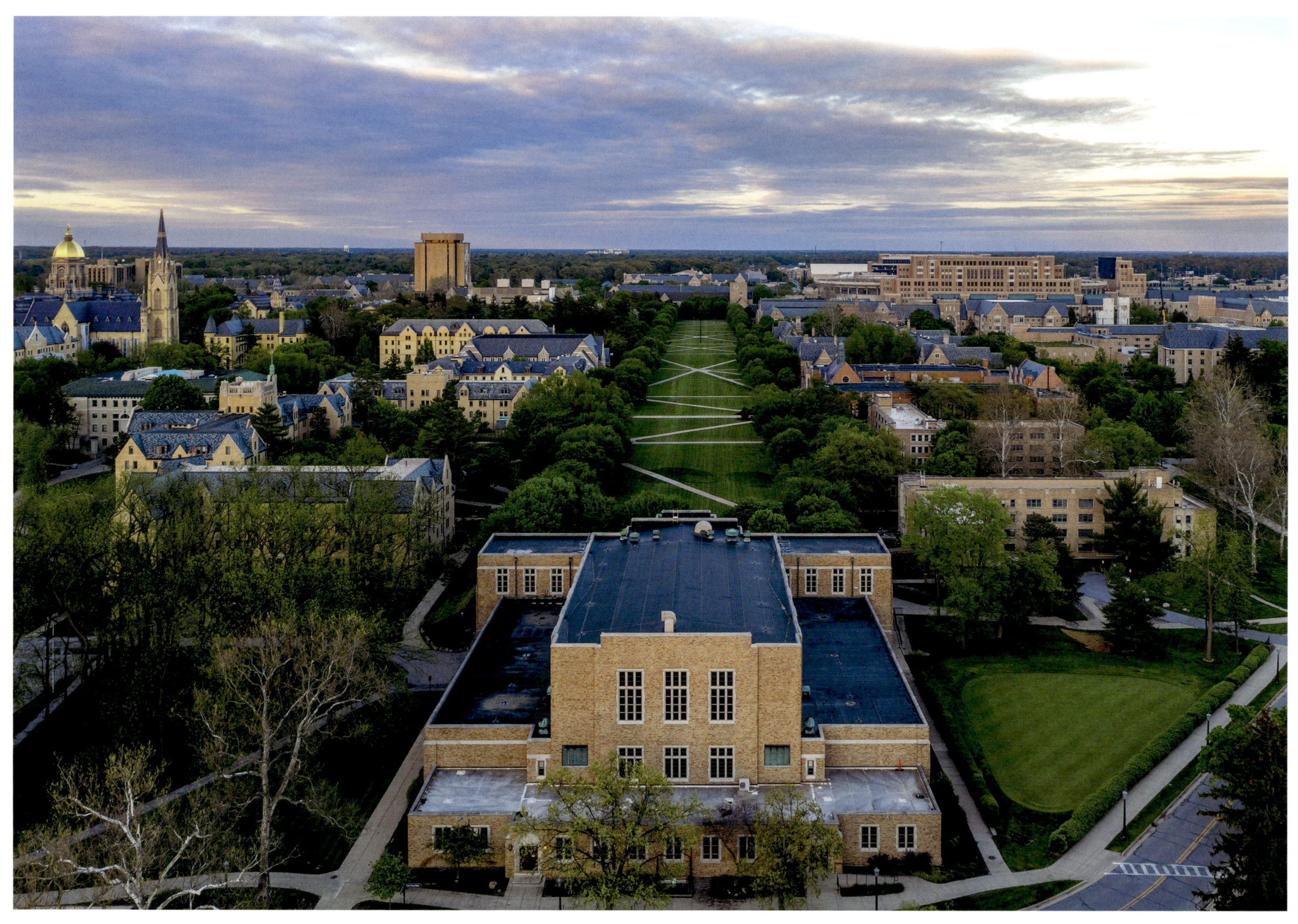

Over Rockne Memorial looking east, Mavic 2 Pro drone, 24mm equivalent, 1/120 f4, ISO100

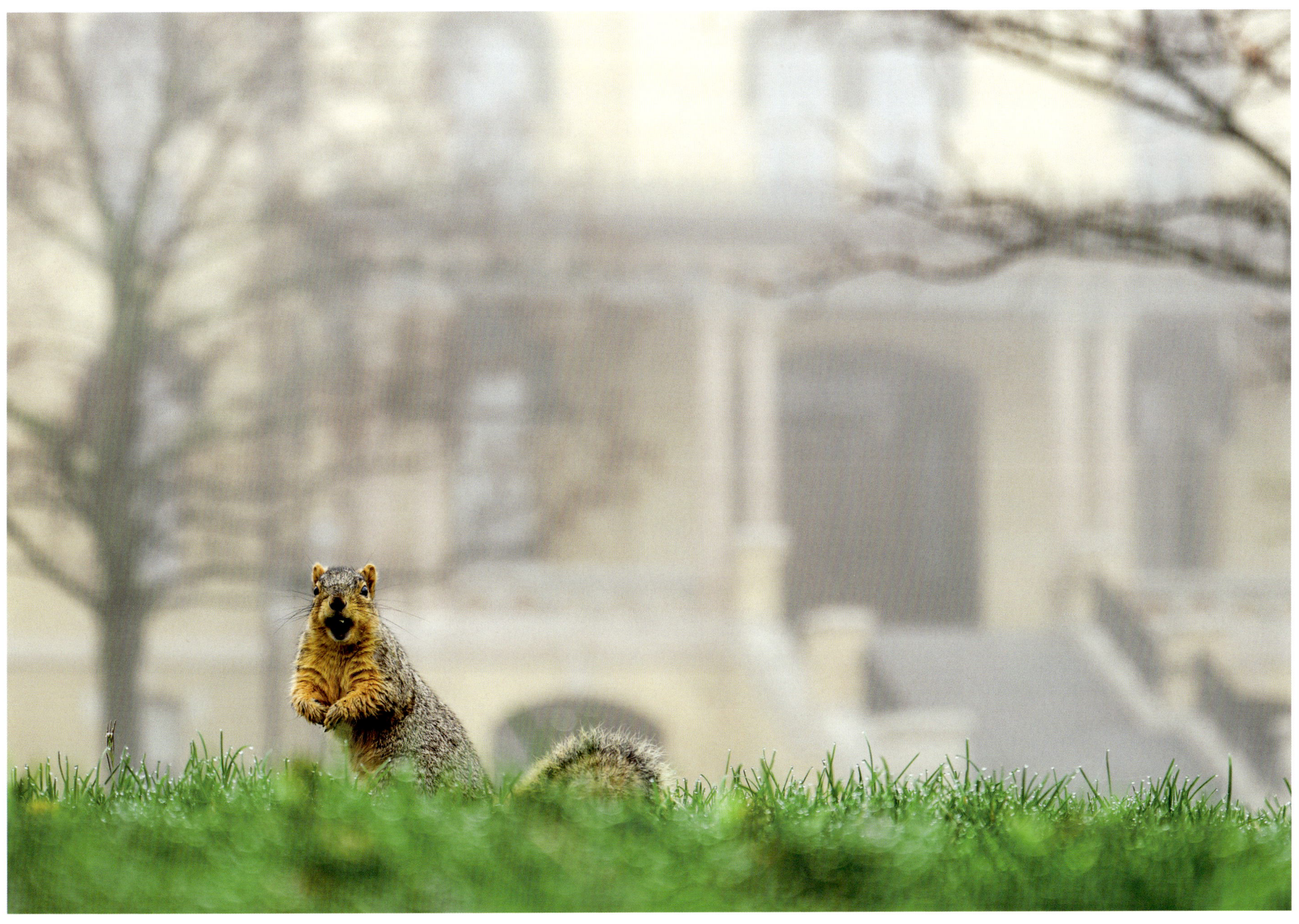

Squirrel in front of Main Building, Nikon Z7, 70mm, 1/100 f3.2, ISO64

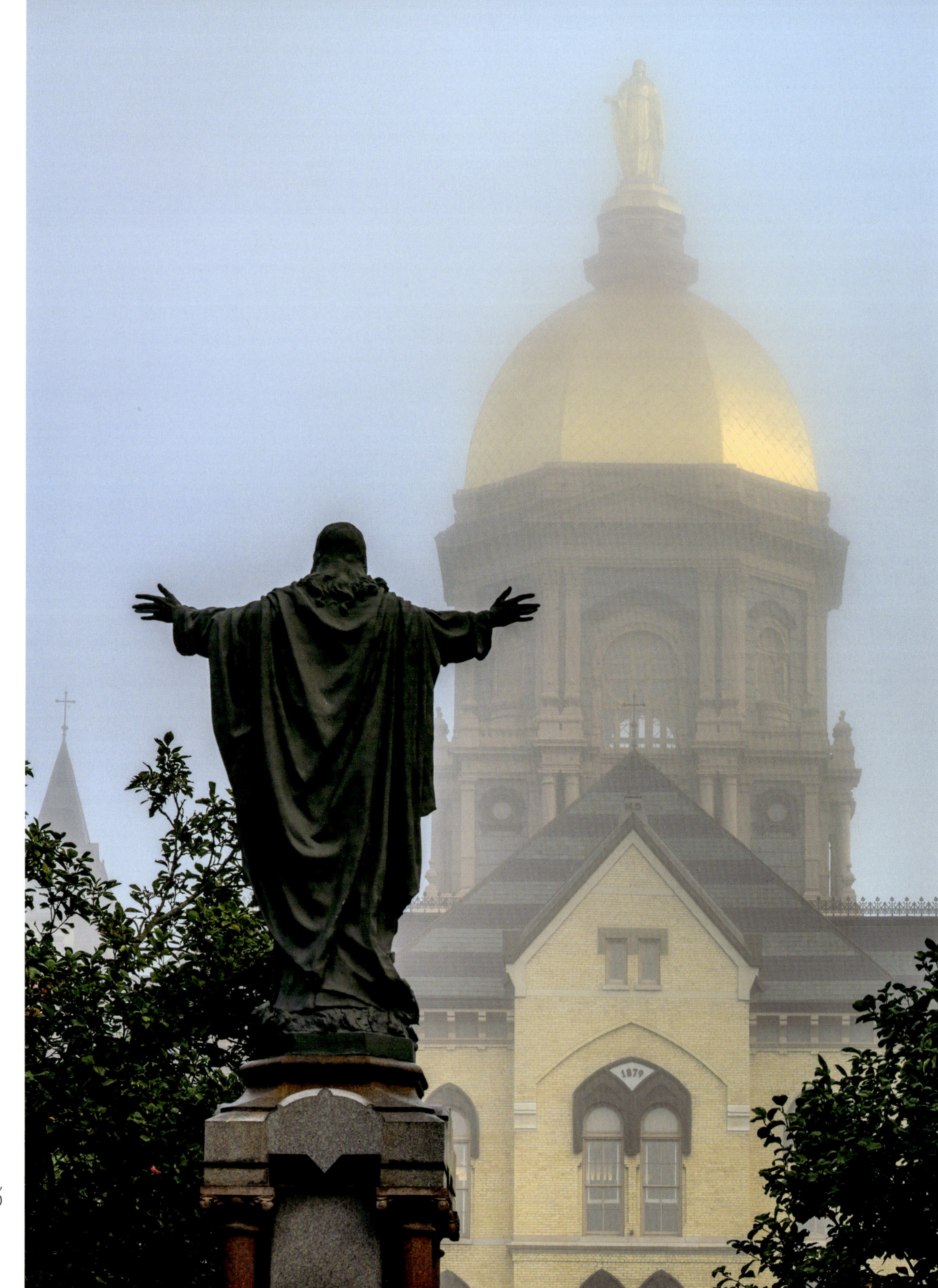

Main Quad Jesus statue,
Nikon Z7II, 135mm, 1/30 f22, ISO500

Statues on campus are great visual anchor points. Over the years the trees might get bigger or replanted, the buildings might change, but the statue stays the same, giving viewers of the photo an anchor point they're familiar with regardless of how campus looked when they were students or visited in a different season. Plus, statues are great in that they always hold still for me and they don't have to hurry off to a meeting!

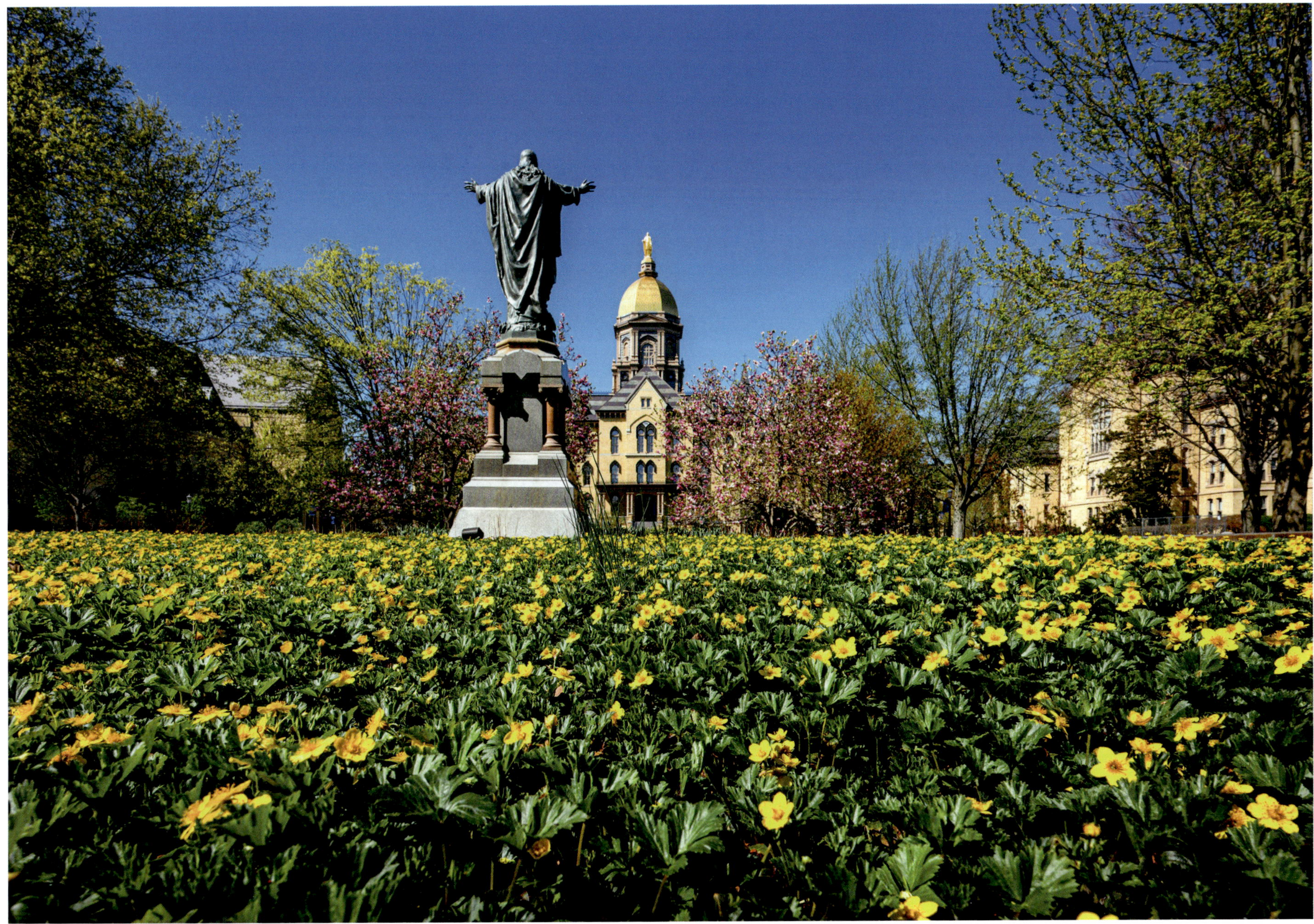

Planter around the Main Quad Jesus statue, Nikon Z6II, 17mm, 1/160 f13, ISO100

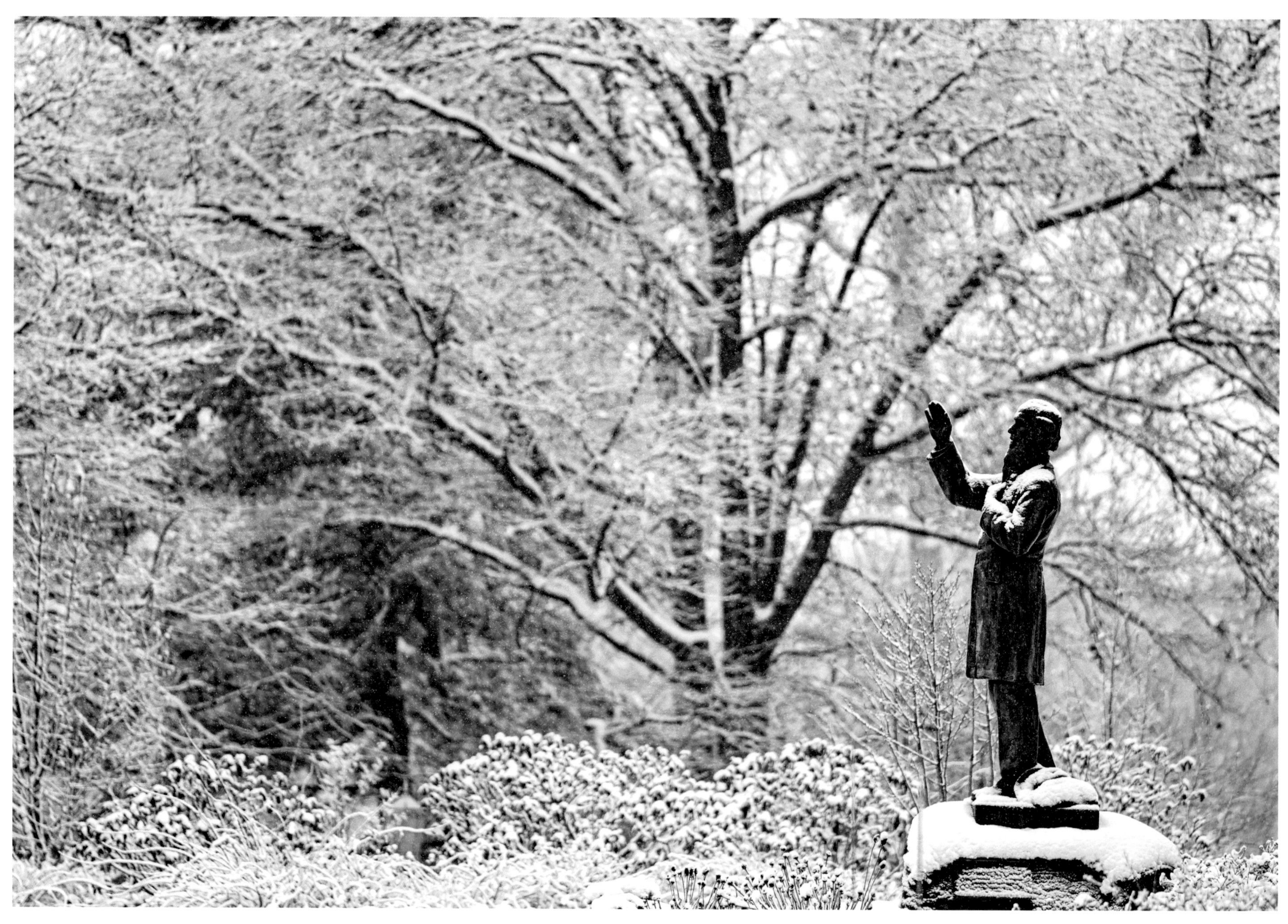

"Fair Catch Corby" in front of Corby Hall, Nikon Z9, 200mm, 1/1600 f2.8, ISO250

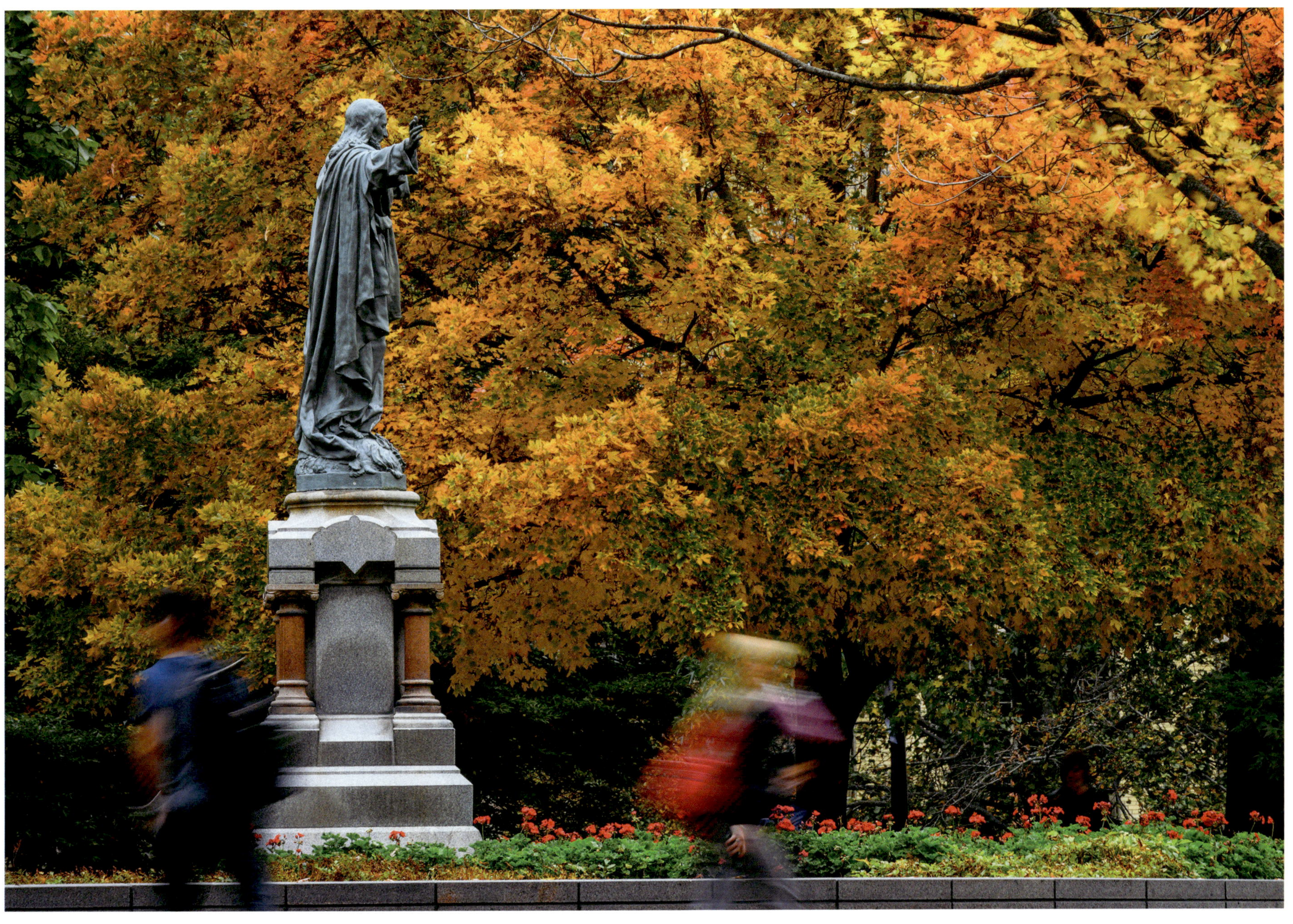

Main Quad Jesus statue, Nikon Z6II, 180mm, 1/5 f16, ISO100

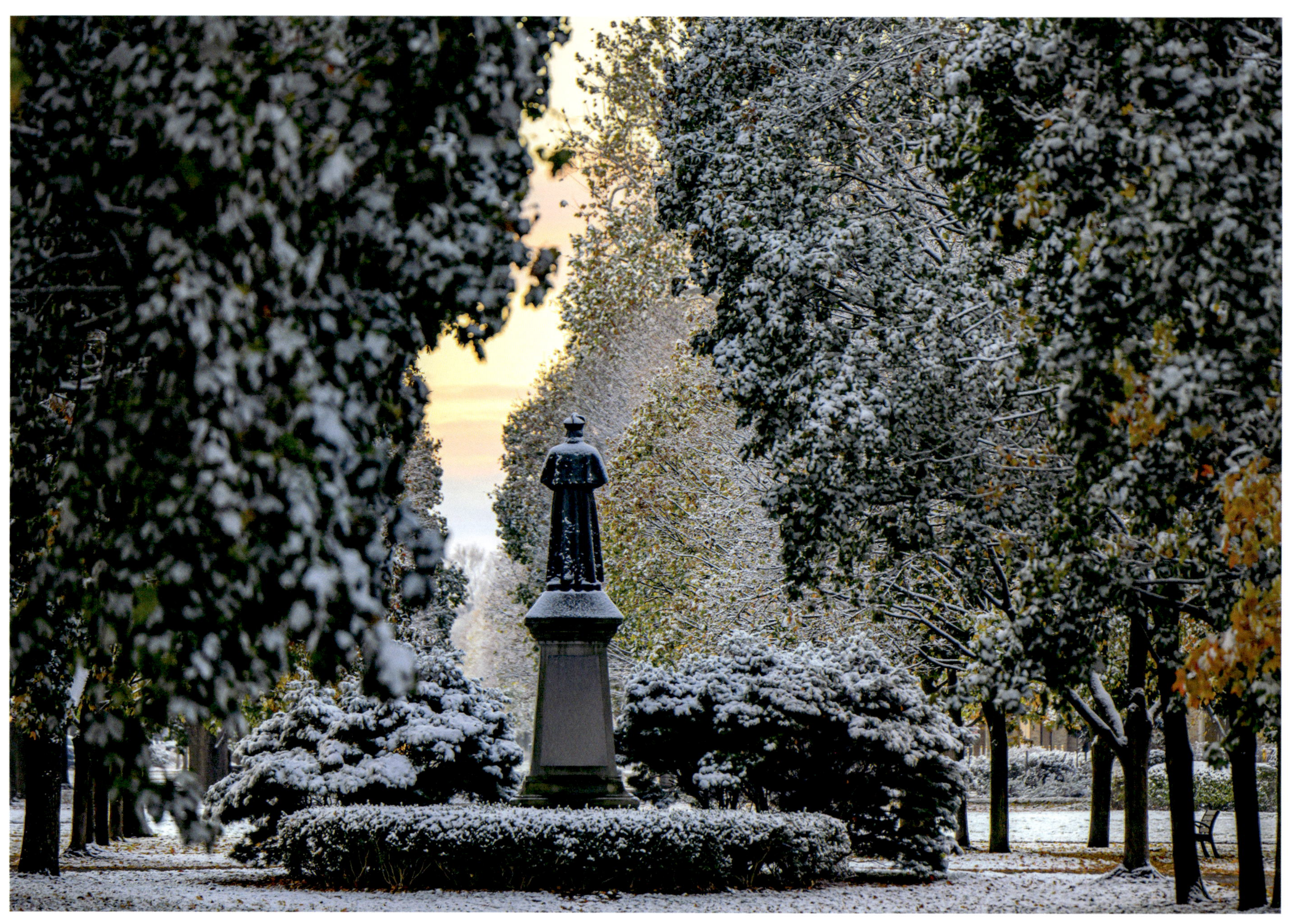

Statue of Fr. Sorin on Main Quad, Nikon Z6II, 180mm, 1/320 f2.8, ISO400

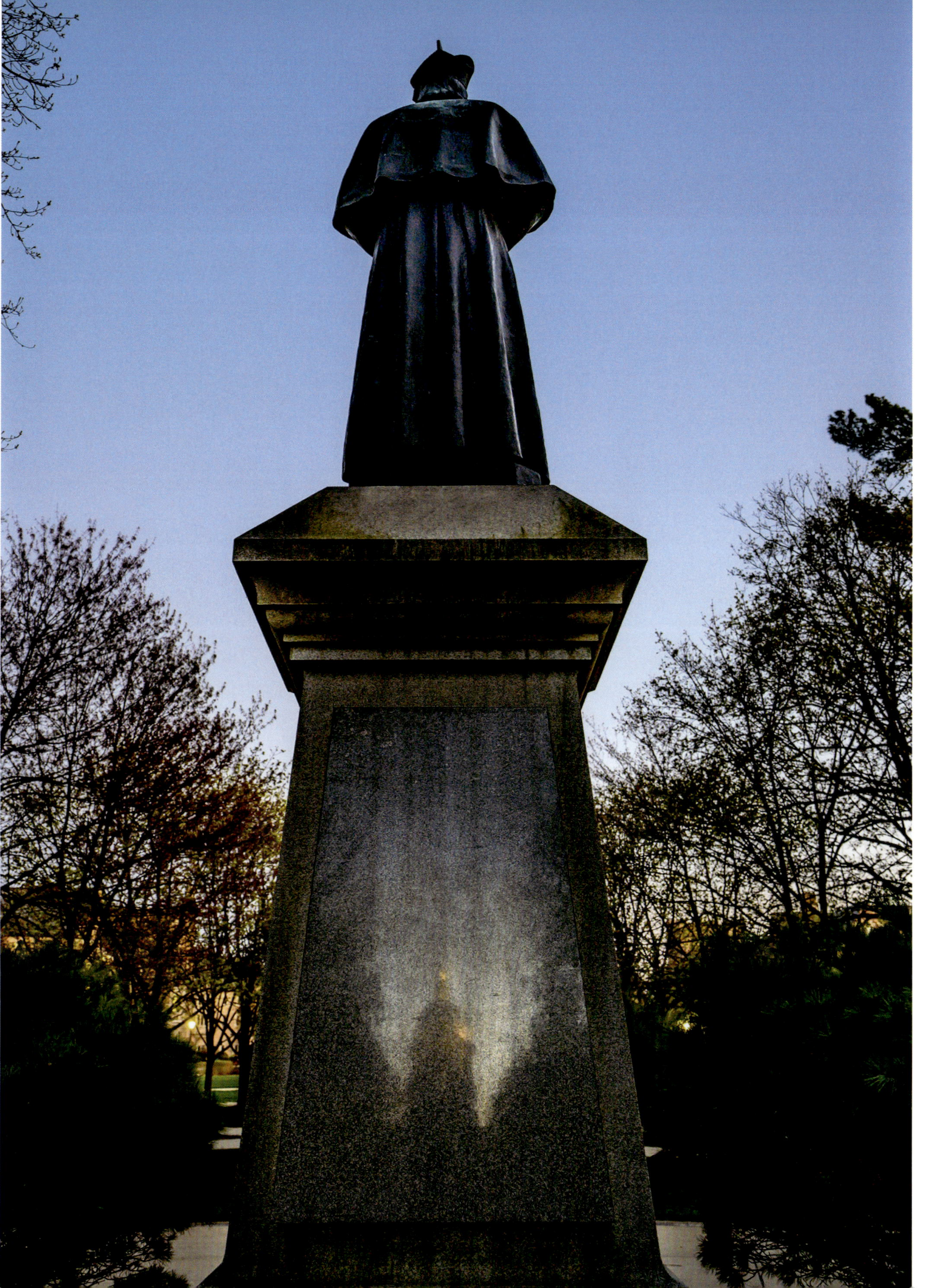

Main Building reflected in the Sorin Statue pedestal, Nikon Z6, 24mm, 1/8 f5, ISO400

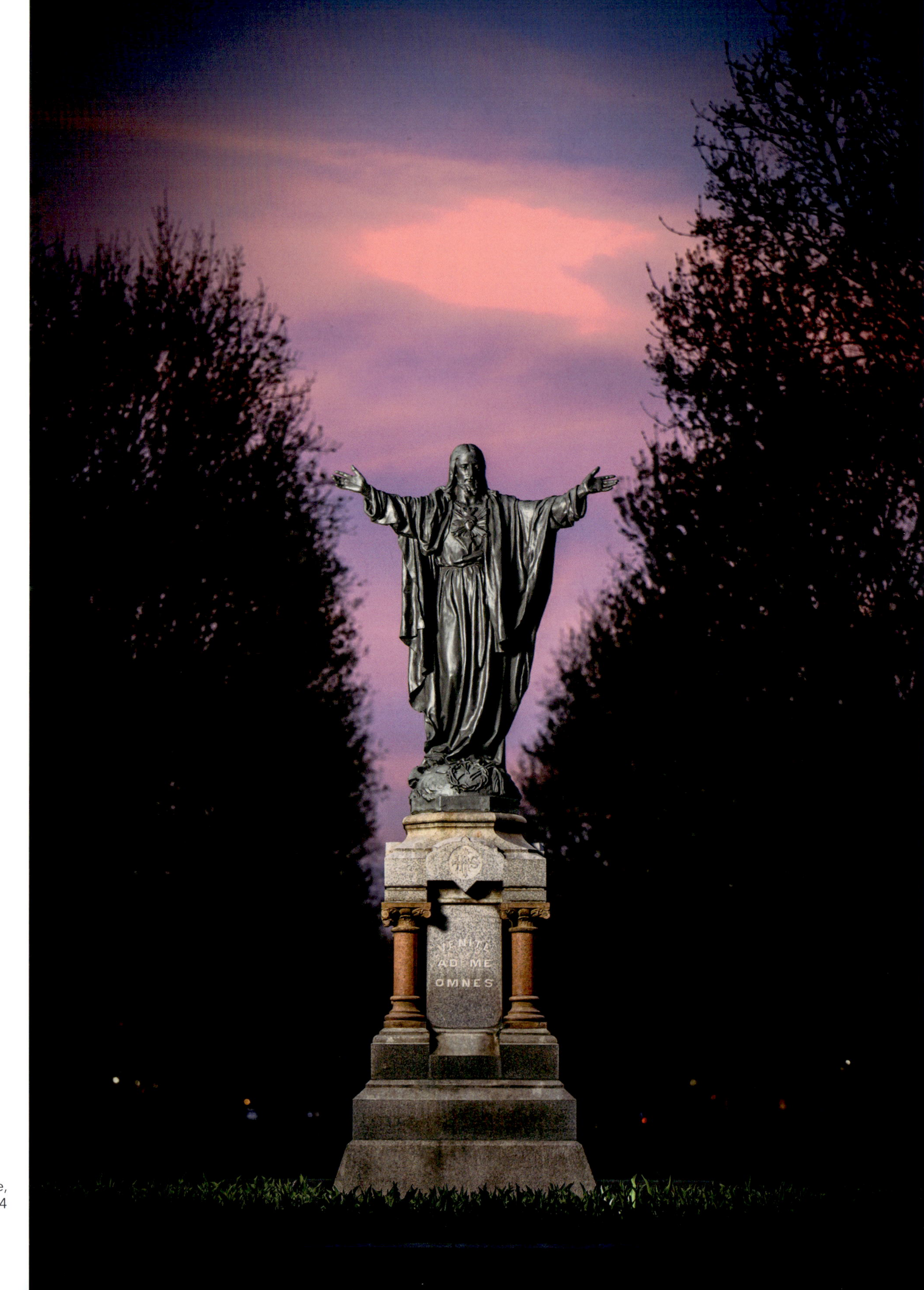

Main Quad Jesus statue,
Nikon Z8, 86mm, 1/80 f2.8, ISO64

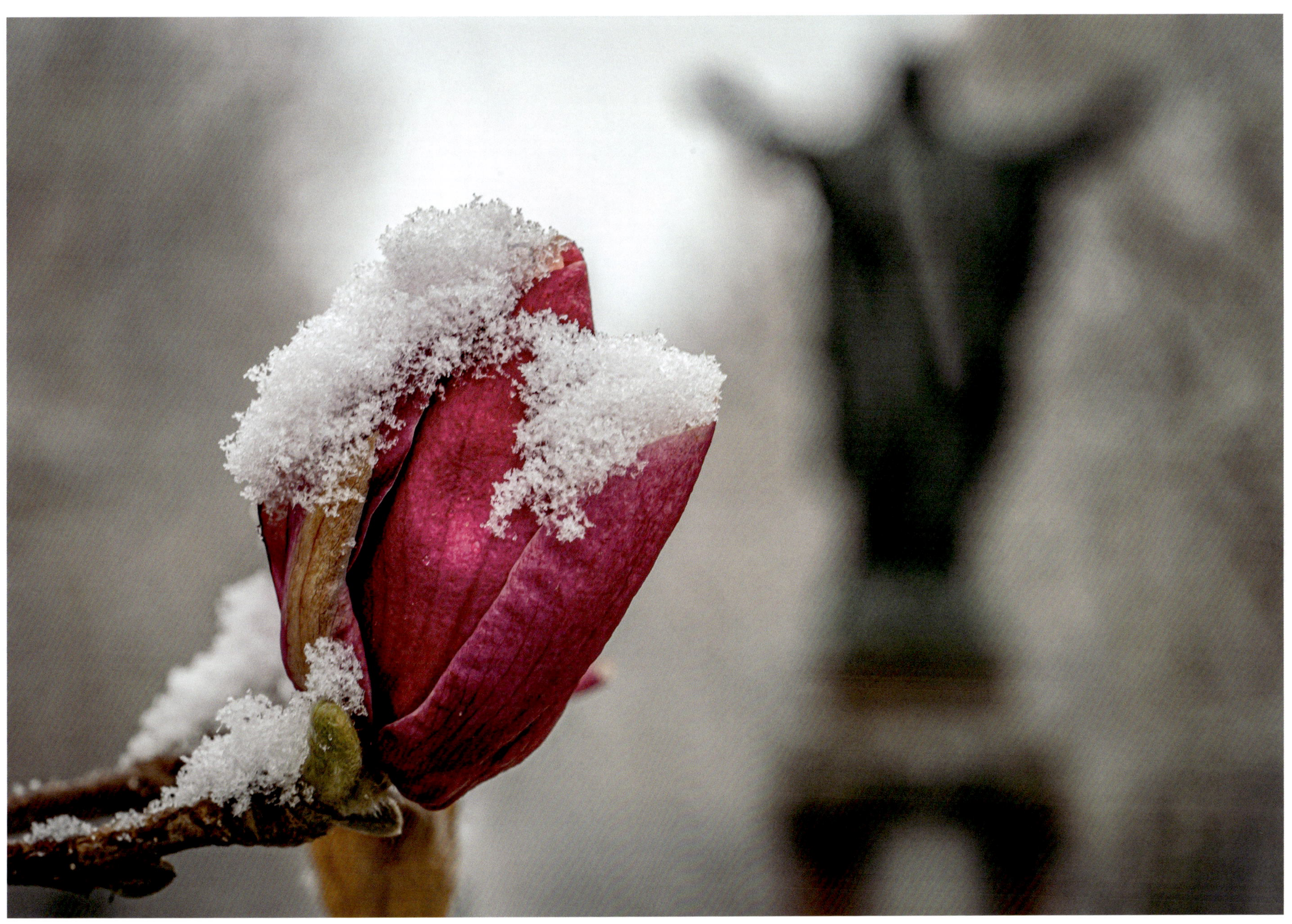

Magnolia tree on Main Quad, Nikon Z6II, 120mm, 1/30 f20, ISO800

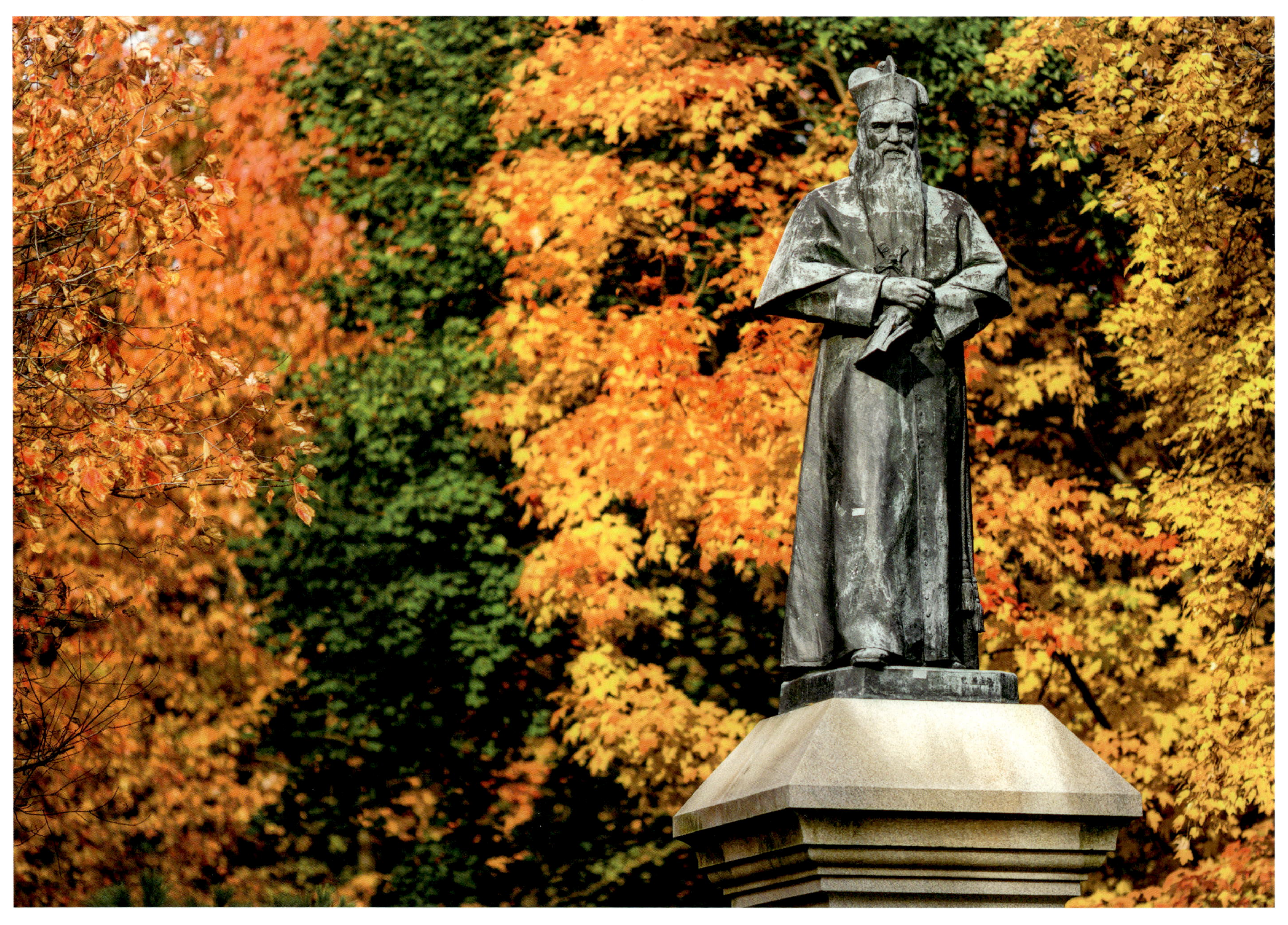

Main Quad Sorin statue, Nikon Z7, 135mm, 1/1000 f2, ISO64

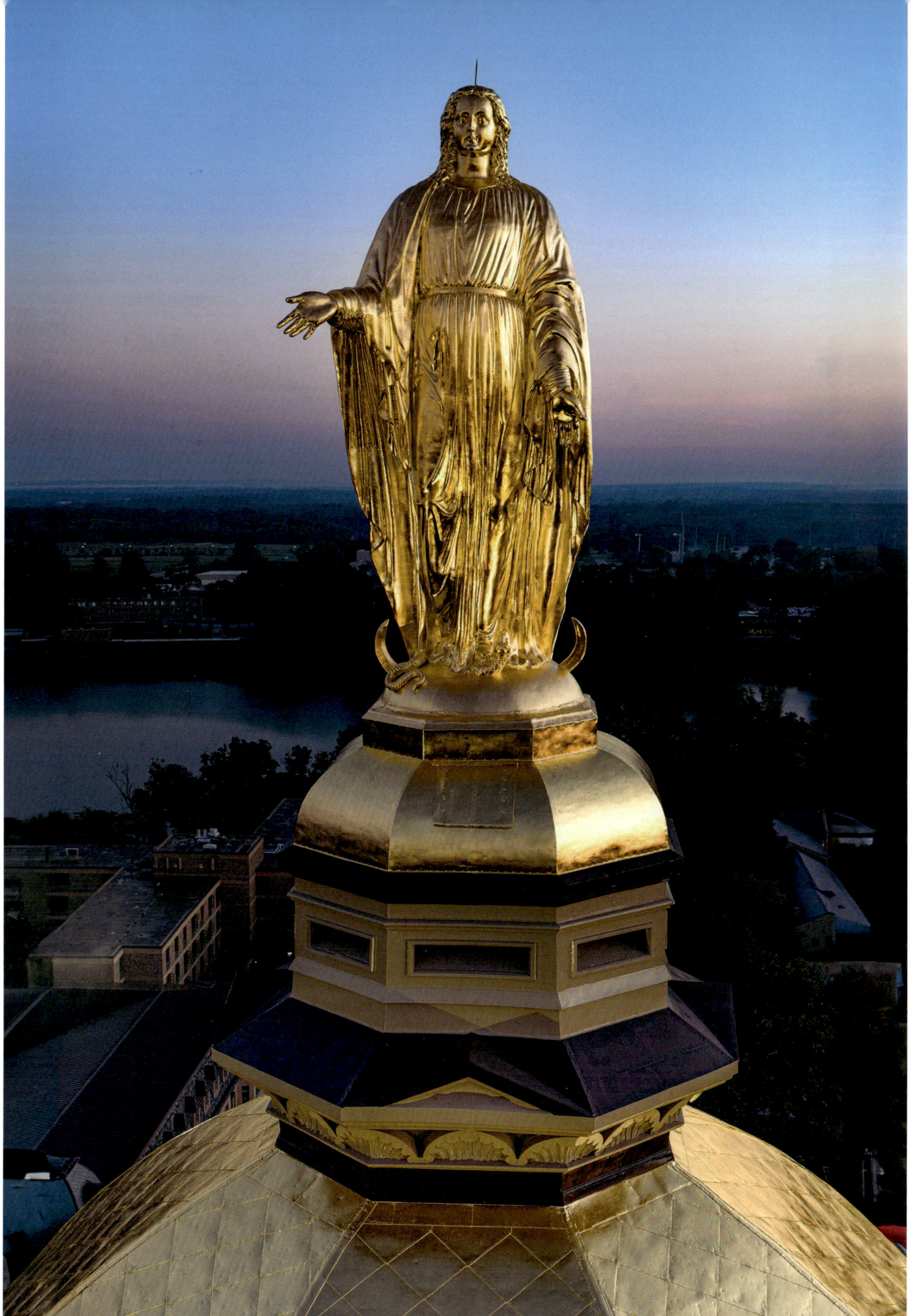

Aerial just after 2023 regilding, Mavic 3 Pro drone, 28mm equivalent, 1/30 f2.8, ISO100

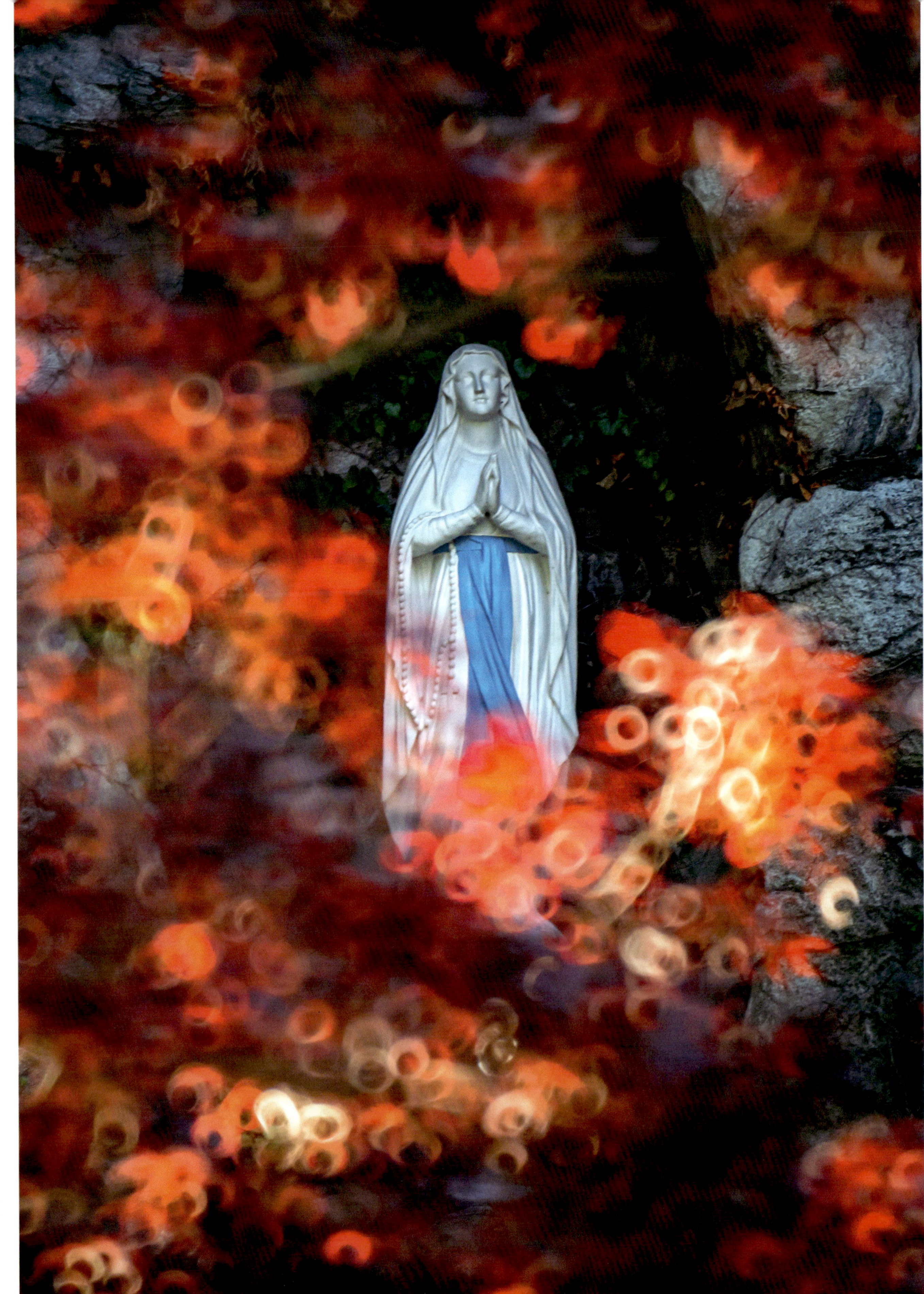

Statue of Mary at the Grotto,
Nikon D5, 500mm mirror lens, 1/250 f8, ISO800

There is arguably no place on campus more meaningful to people than the Grotto. Moments of challenge, celebration, grief, or gratitude will often result in lighting a candle and spending a moment in prayer or meditation. Notre Dame undergraduates begin and end their time on campus with class visits to the Grotto. Like campus as a whole, the Grotto visuals have changed. Long ago the candles were uncontained, and the candle wax drippings added really interesting texture—and fire risk, so that understandably had to change. The view of the Dome through the trees gets better and worse as the trees grow and get trimmed or removed. And true to the opening sentence of the book, the key to the best photos of the Grotto is "when." Dawn or dusk shows off the landscape but also allows the candles to make a warm glow.

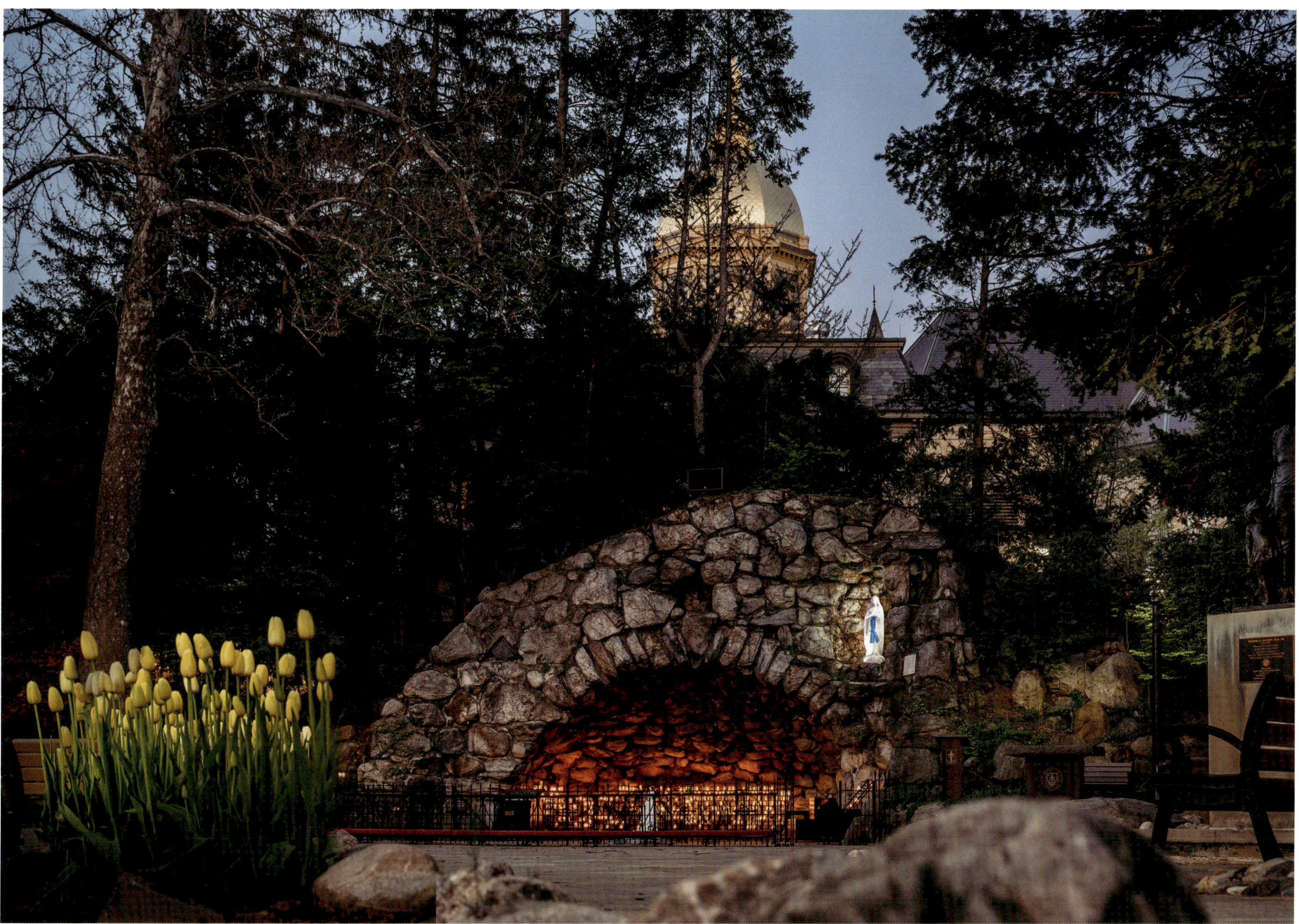

Grotto of Our Lady of Lourdes, Nikon Z6, 43mm, 1/2.5 f5, ISO100

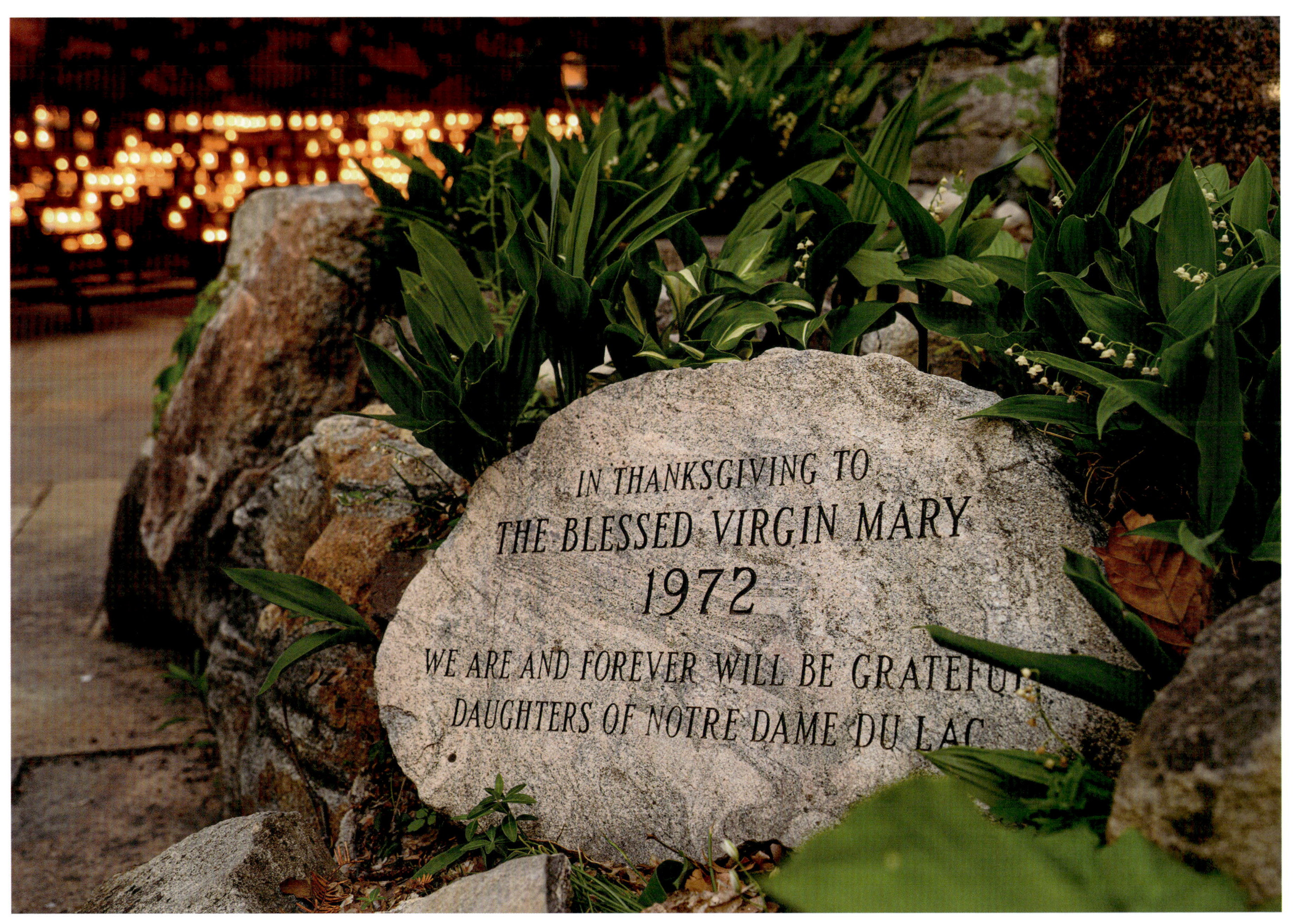

Rock commemorating the admission of women undergraduate students at the Grotto, Nikon Z7II, 35mm, 1/8 f4, ISO250

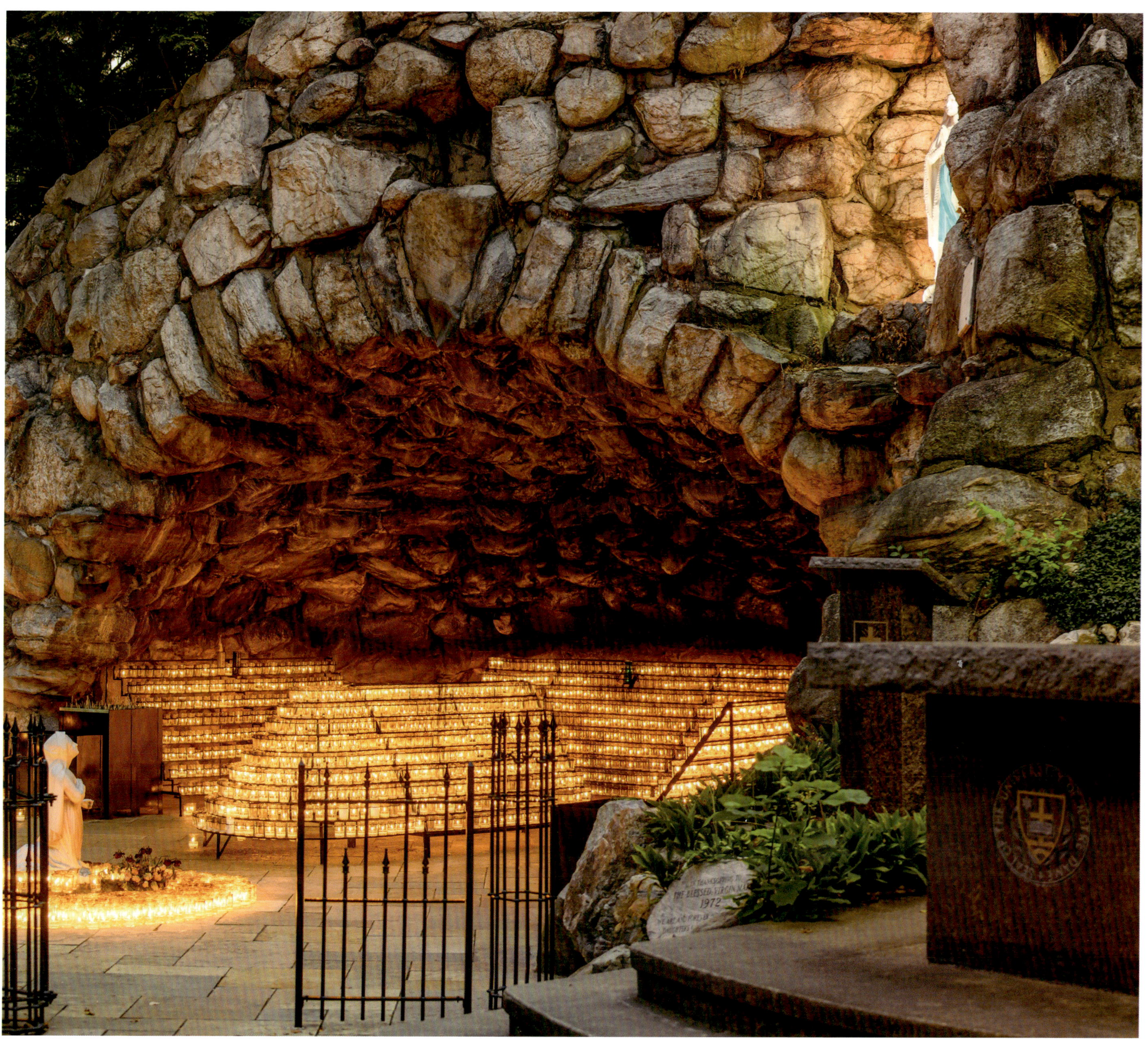

Grotto candles on Welcome Weekend, Nikon D850, 70mm, 1/15 f4, ISO500

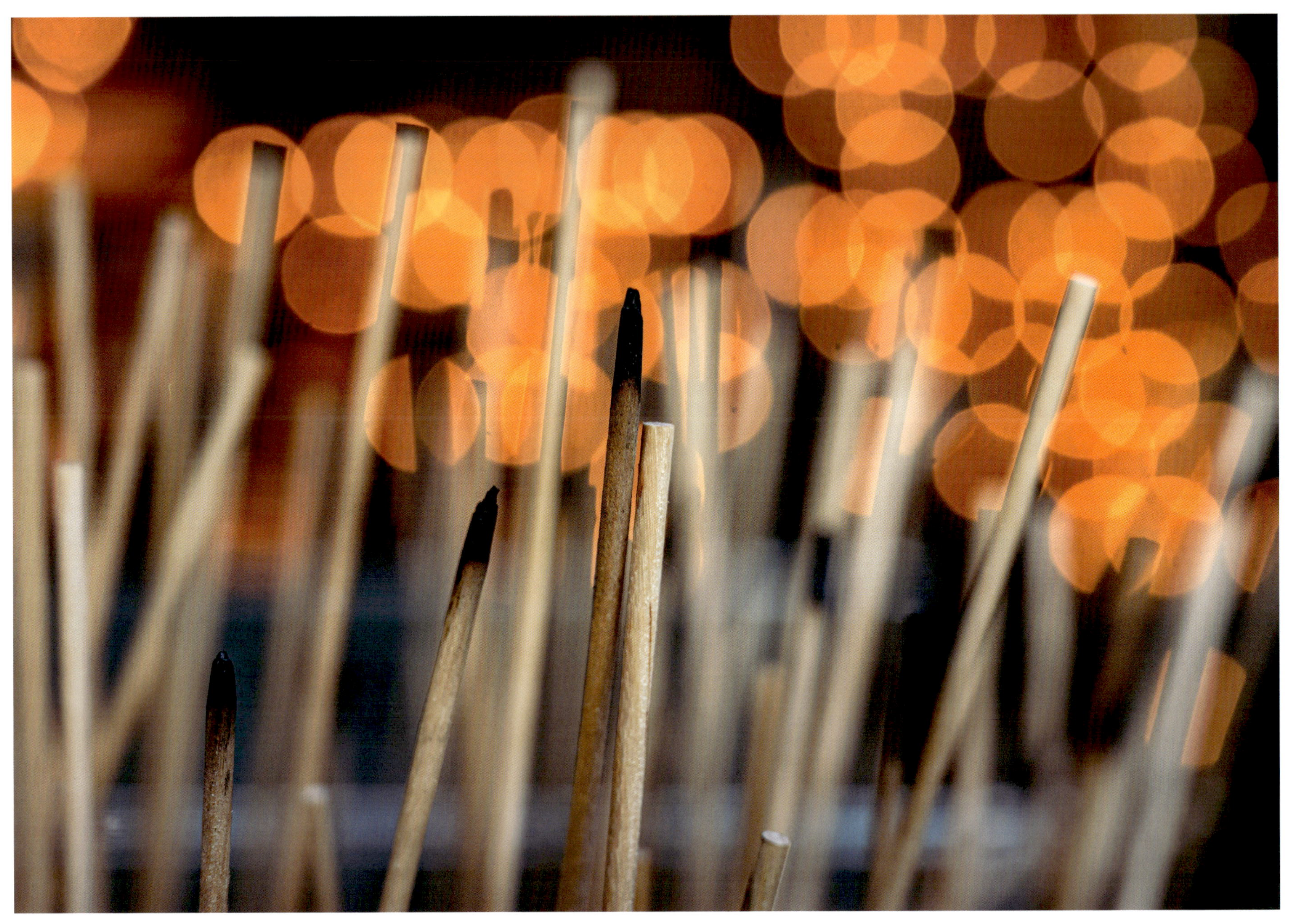

Candle lighting sticks at the Grotto, Nikon Z7, 70mm, 1/80 f5, ISO500

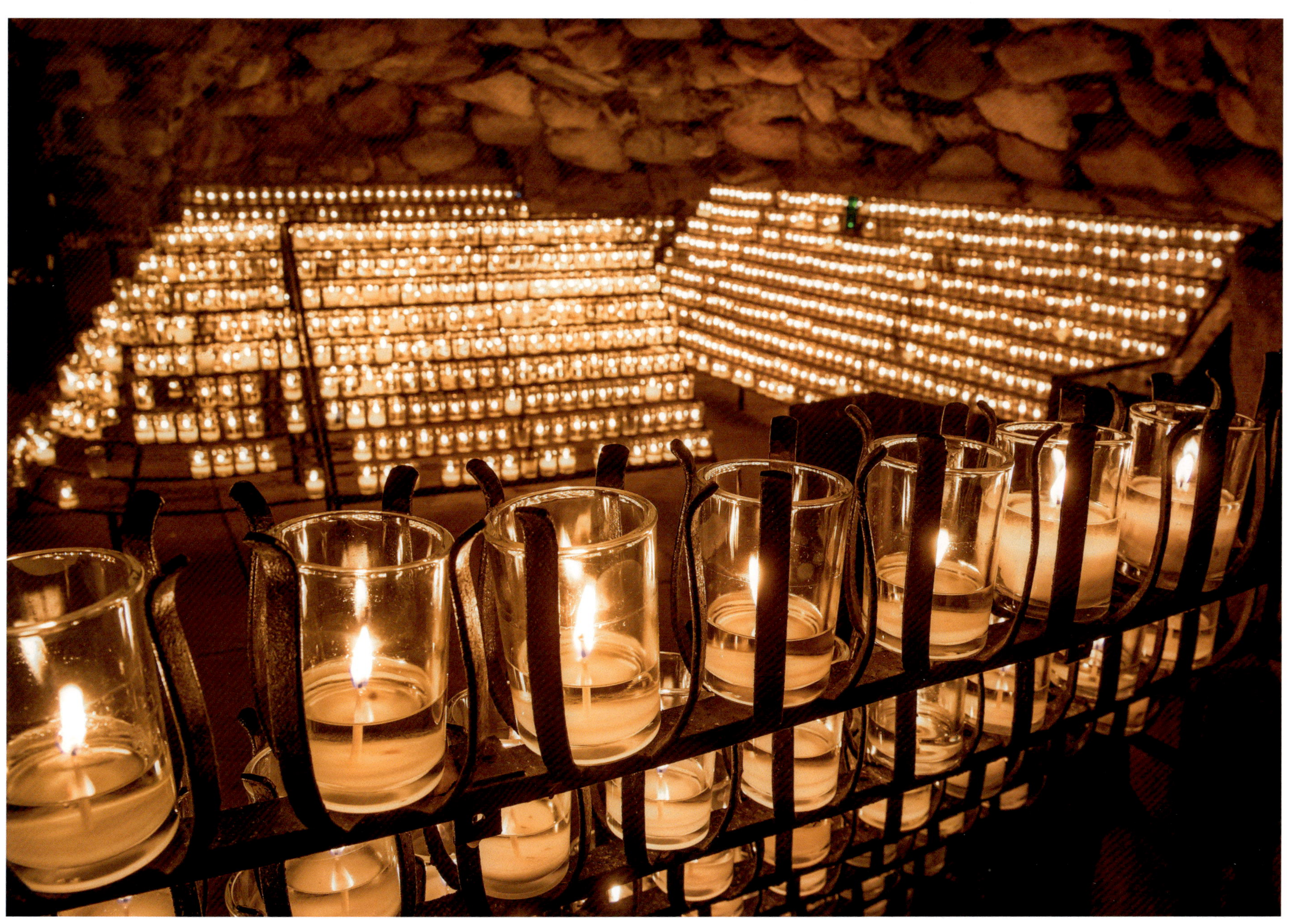

Candles on a football weekend, Nikon D5, 24mm, 1/10 f10, ISO1250

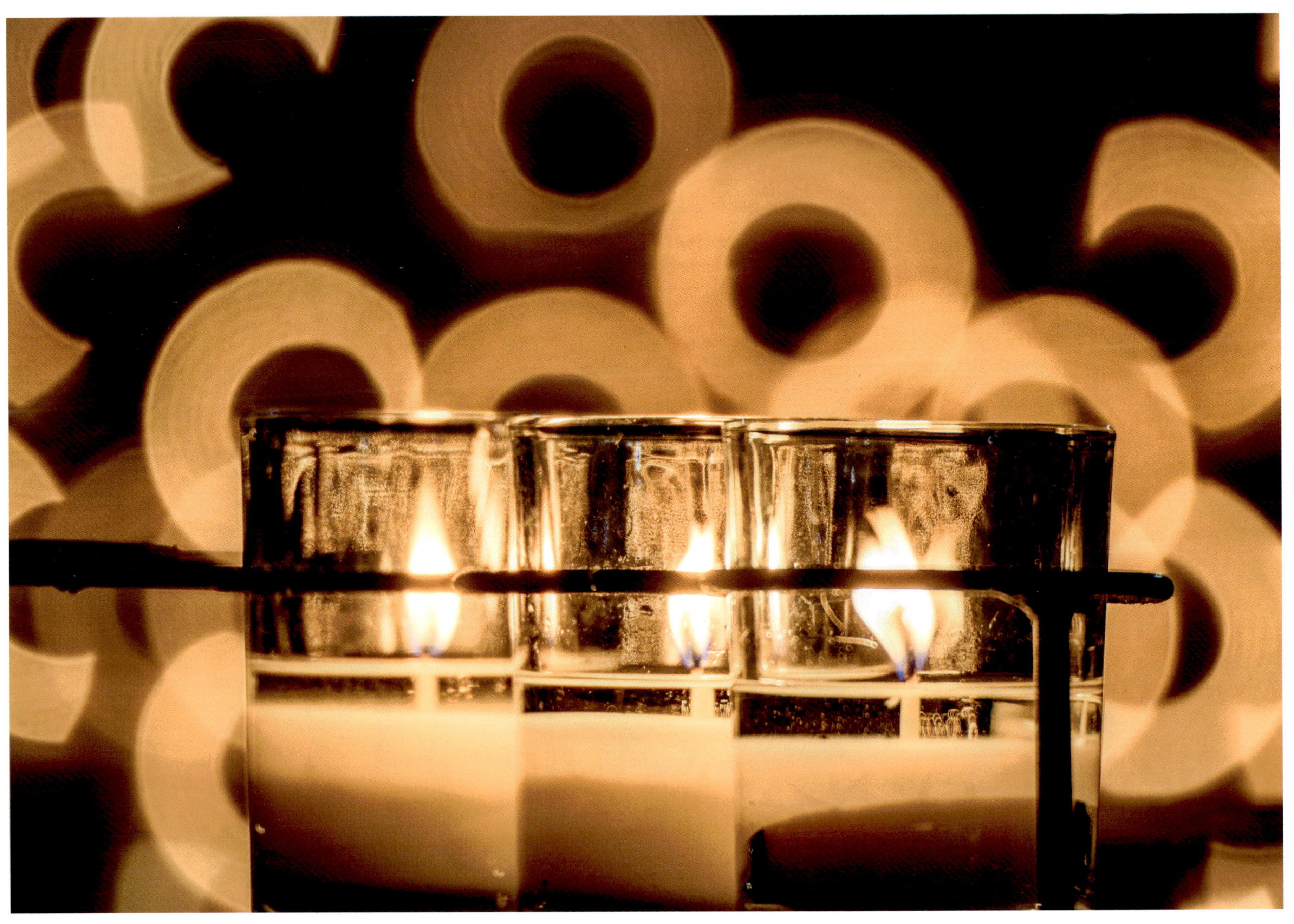

Detail of Grotto candles, Nikon D5, 500mm mirror lens, 1/8 f8, ISO400

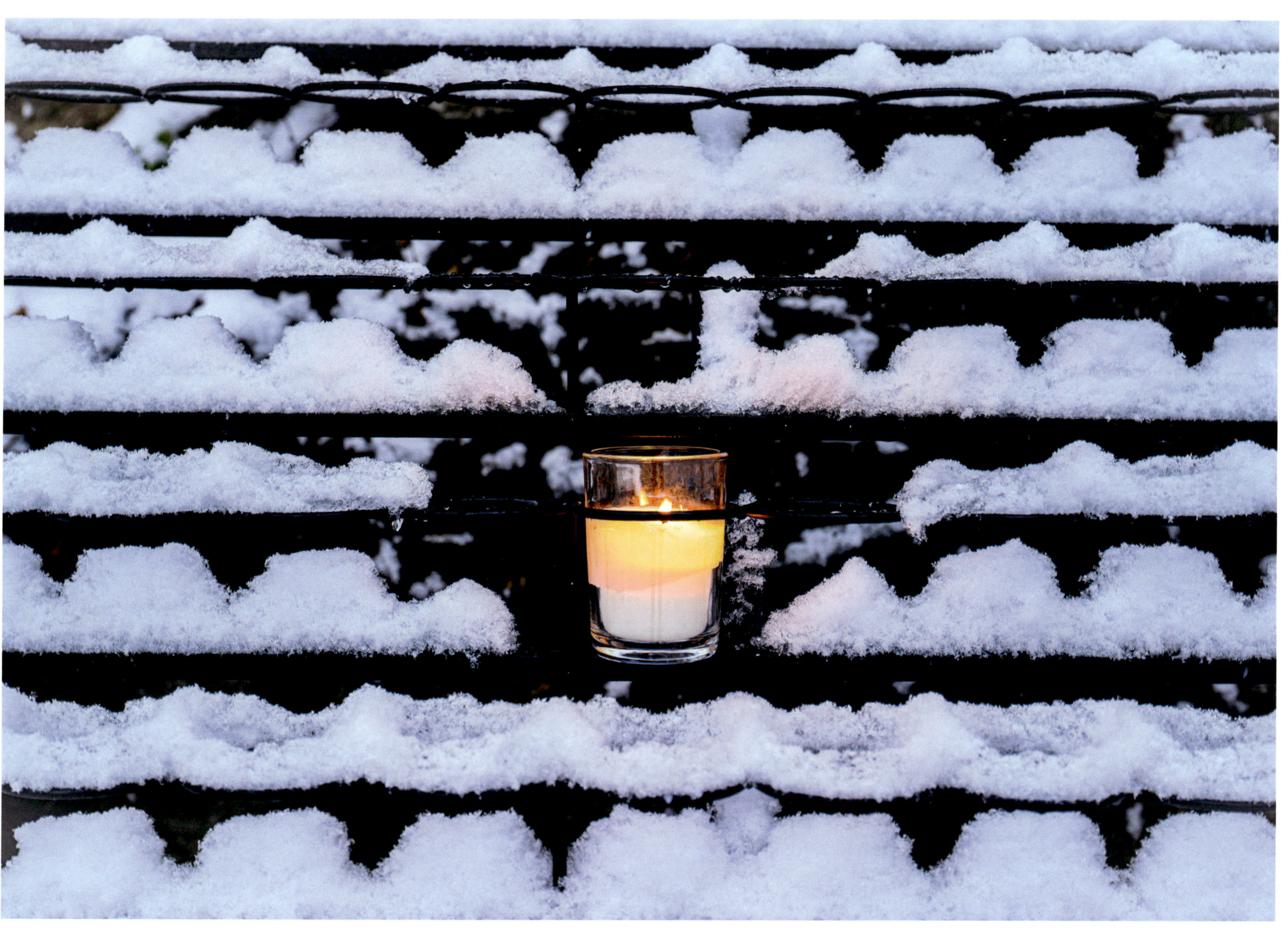

A lone candle on a snowy rack at the Grotto, Nikon Z6, 43mm, 1/30 f5.6, ISO320

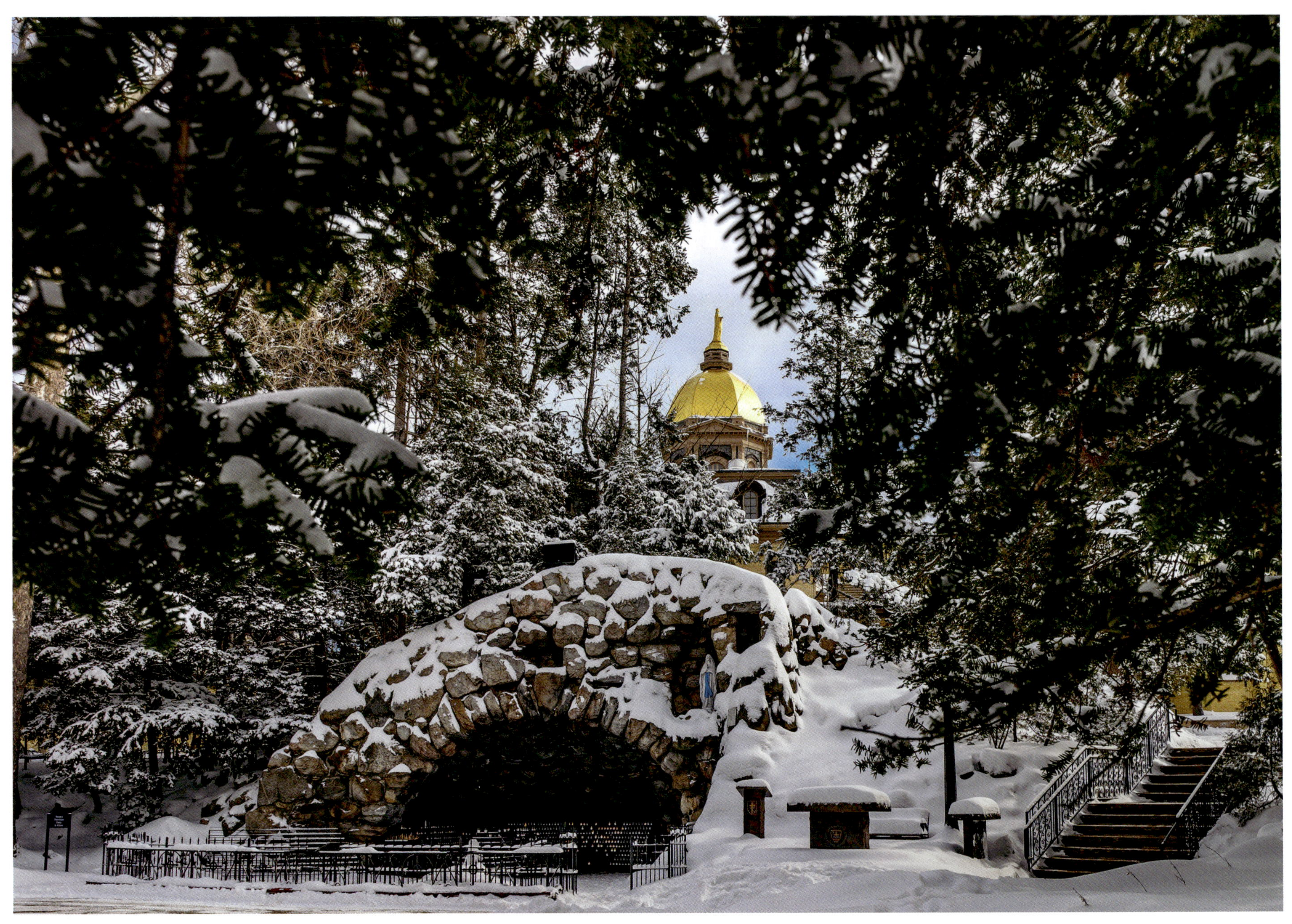

The Grotto in winter, Nikon Z6, 24mm, 1/320 f10, ISO100

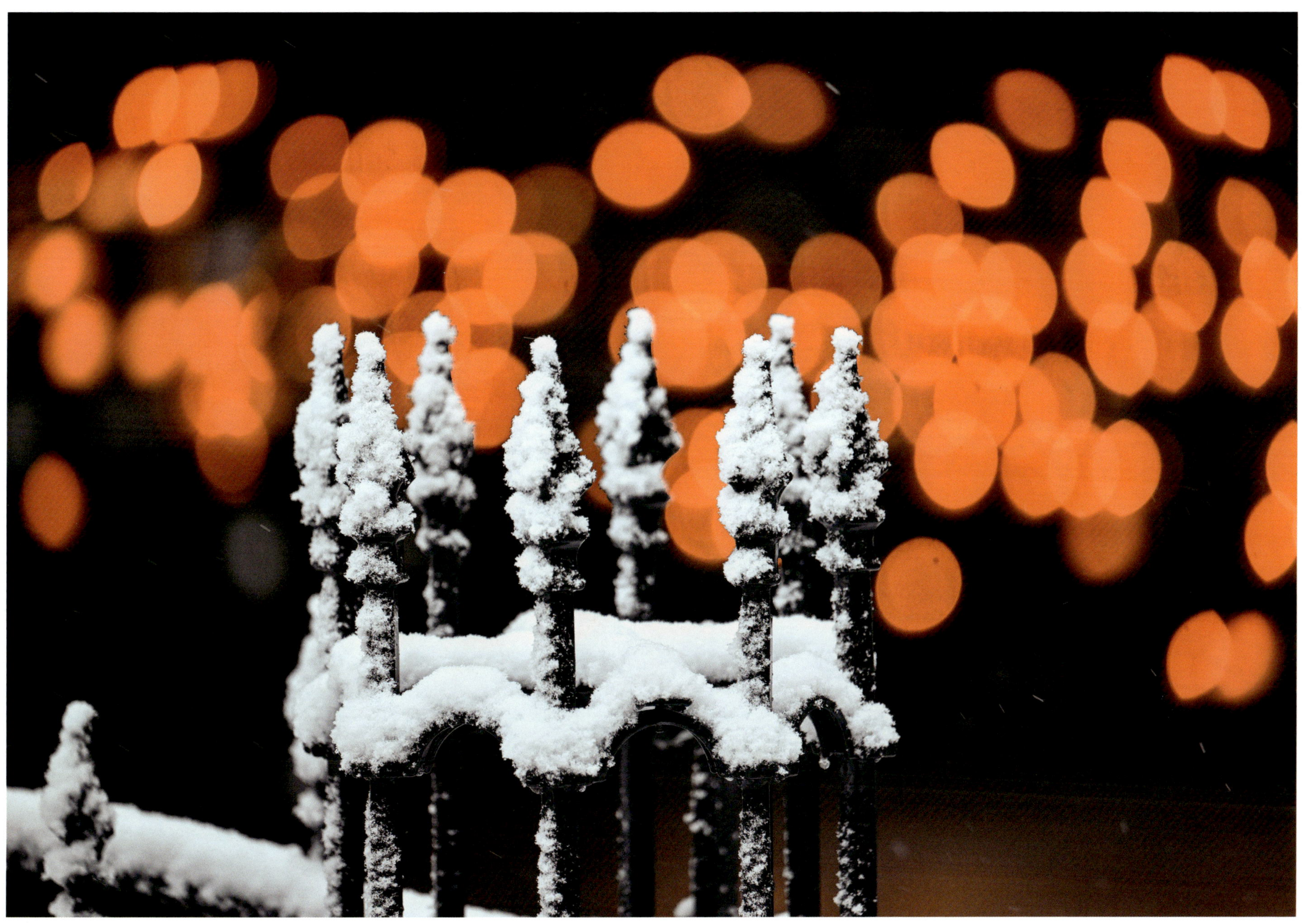

The decorative fence at the Grotto, Nikon Z9, 200mm, 1/160 f2.8, ISO400

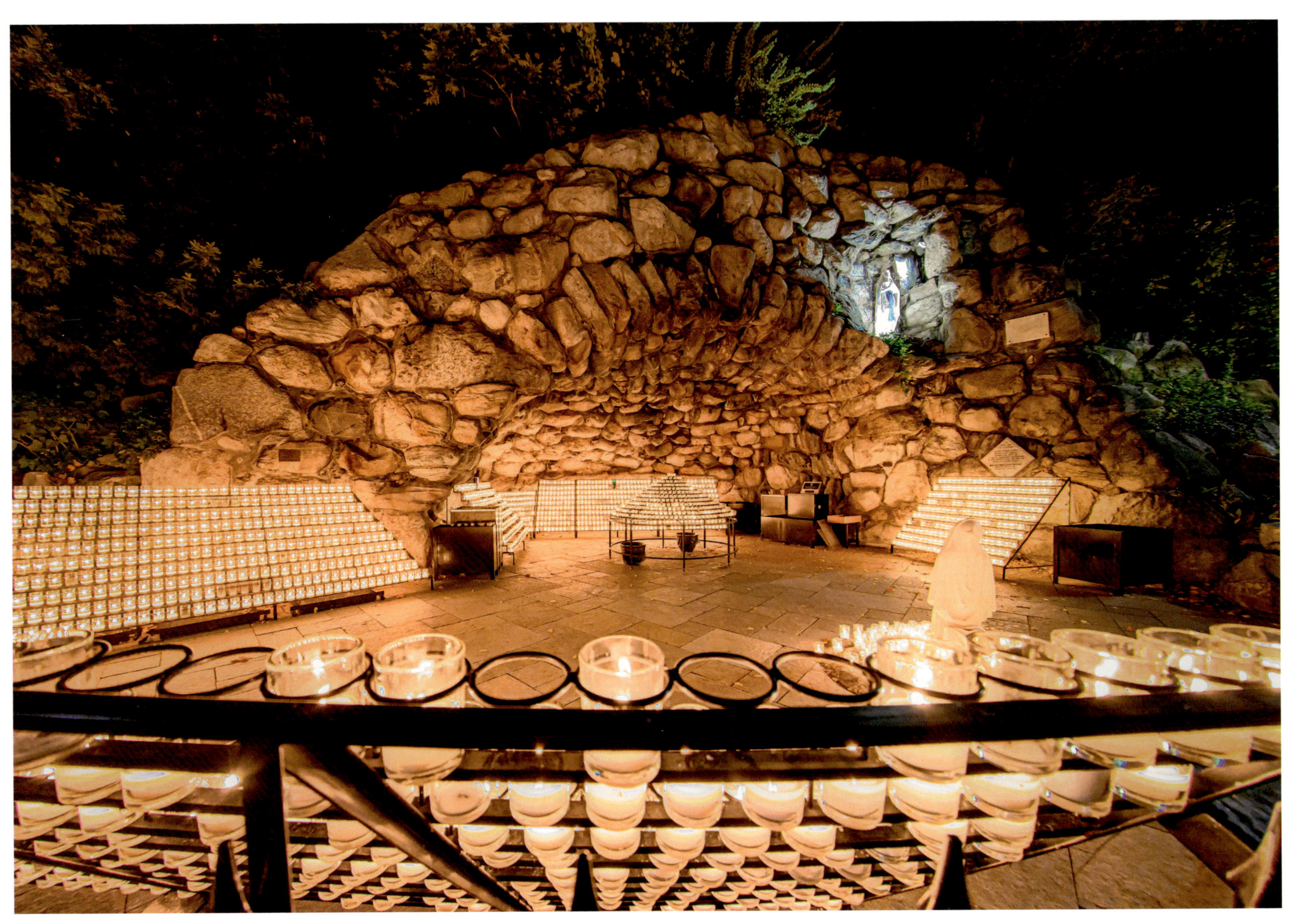

Grotto candles, Nikon Z7II, 14mm, 1/10 f5, ISO1600

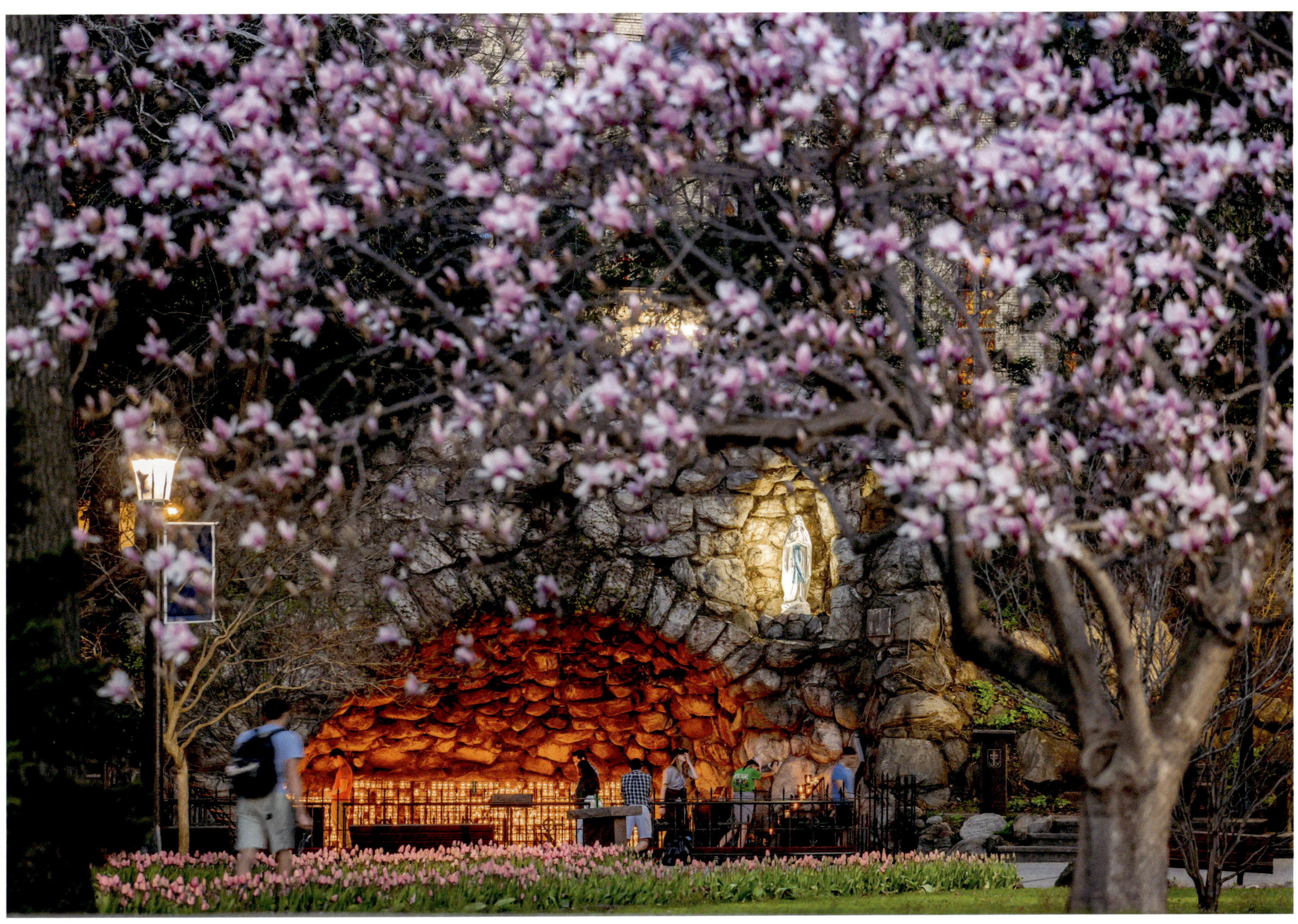

The Grotto seen from Saint Mary's Lake in spring, Nikon D850, 160mm, 1/10 f5.6, ISO800

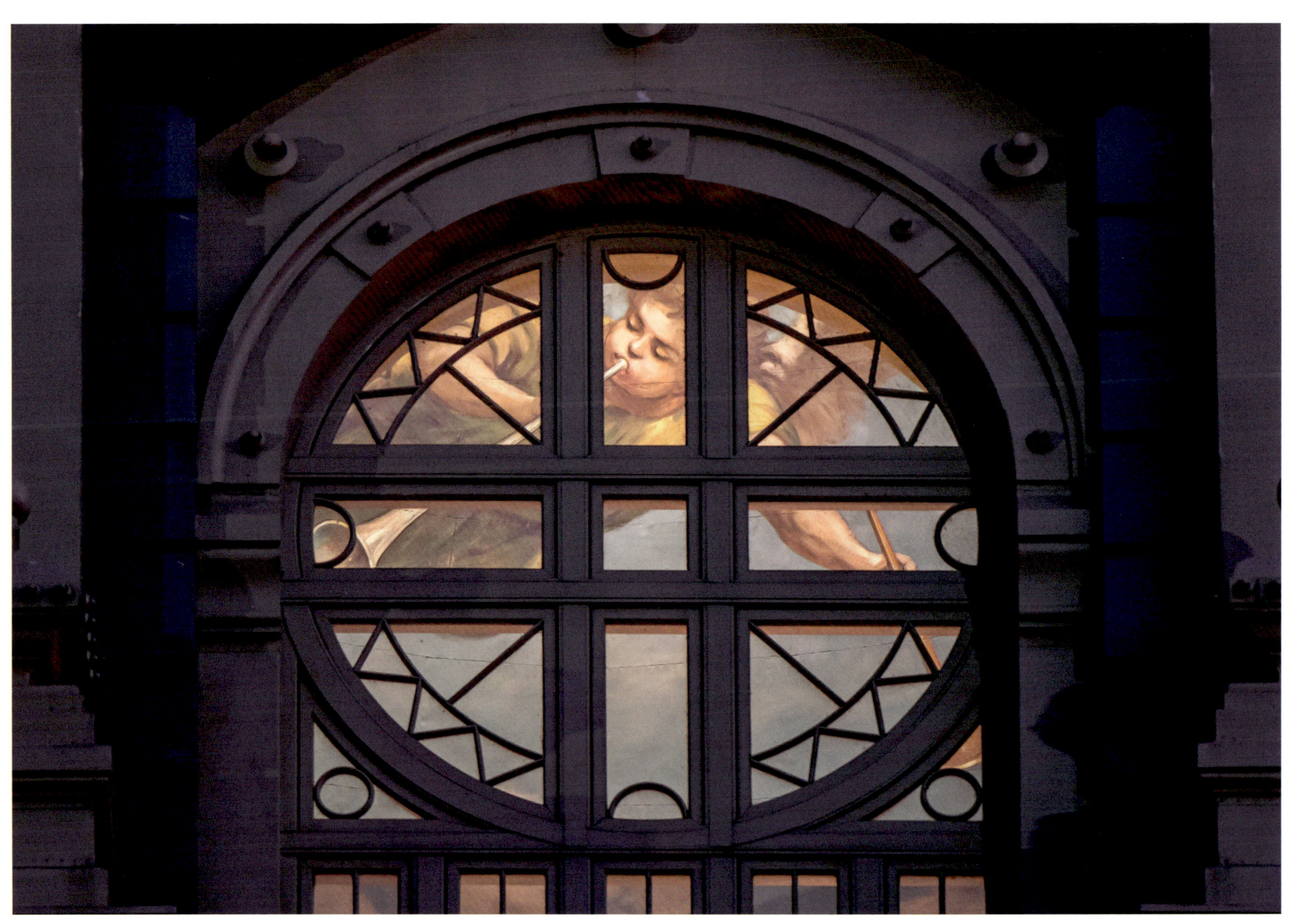

Looking into the Main Building rotunda from the north side of the building, Nikon D500, 300mm, 1/60 f4, ISO800

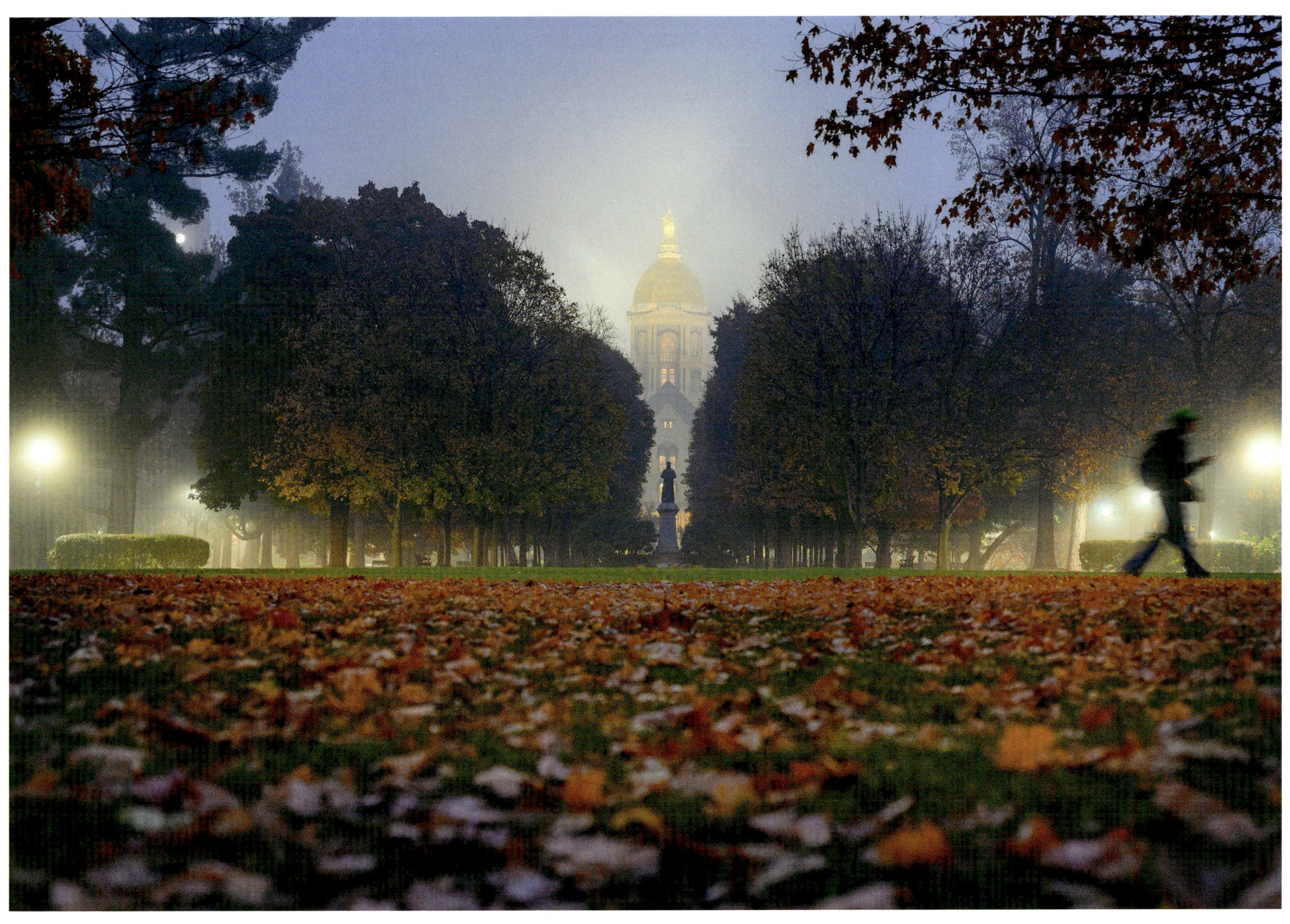

Main Quad on Halloween morning, Nikon Z6II, 51mm, 1/10 f4, ISO3200

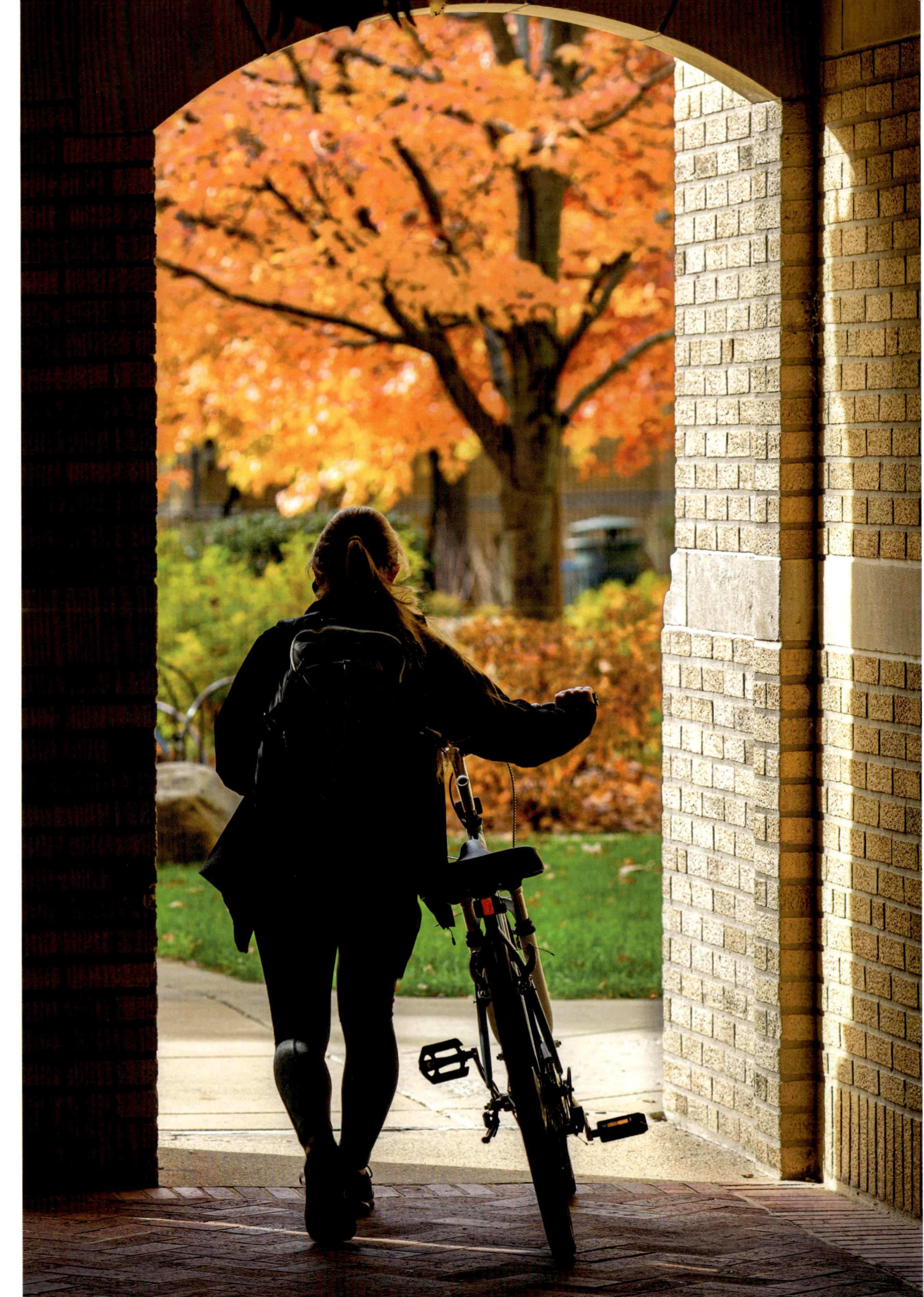

Howard Hall arch,
Nikon Z7, 135mm, 1/80 f4.5, ISO64

In the first week of photo class, students will learn about the classic rules of composition such as "rule of thirds" or "frame-within-a-frame." They're the rules because they work! But of course, rules are always meant to be broken.

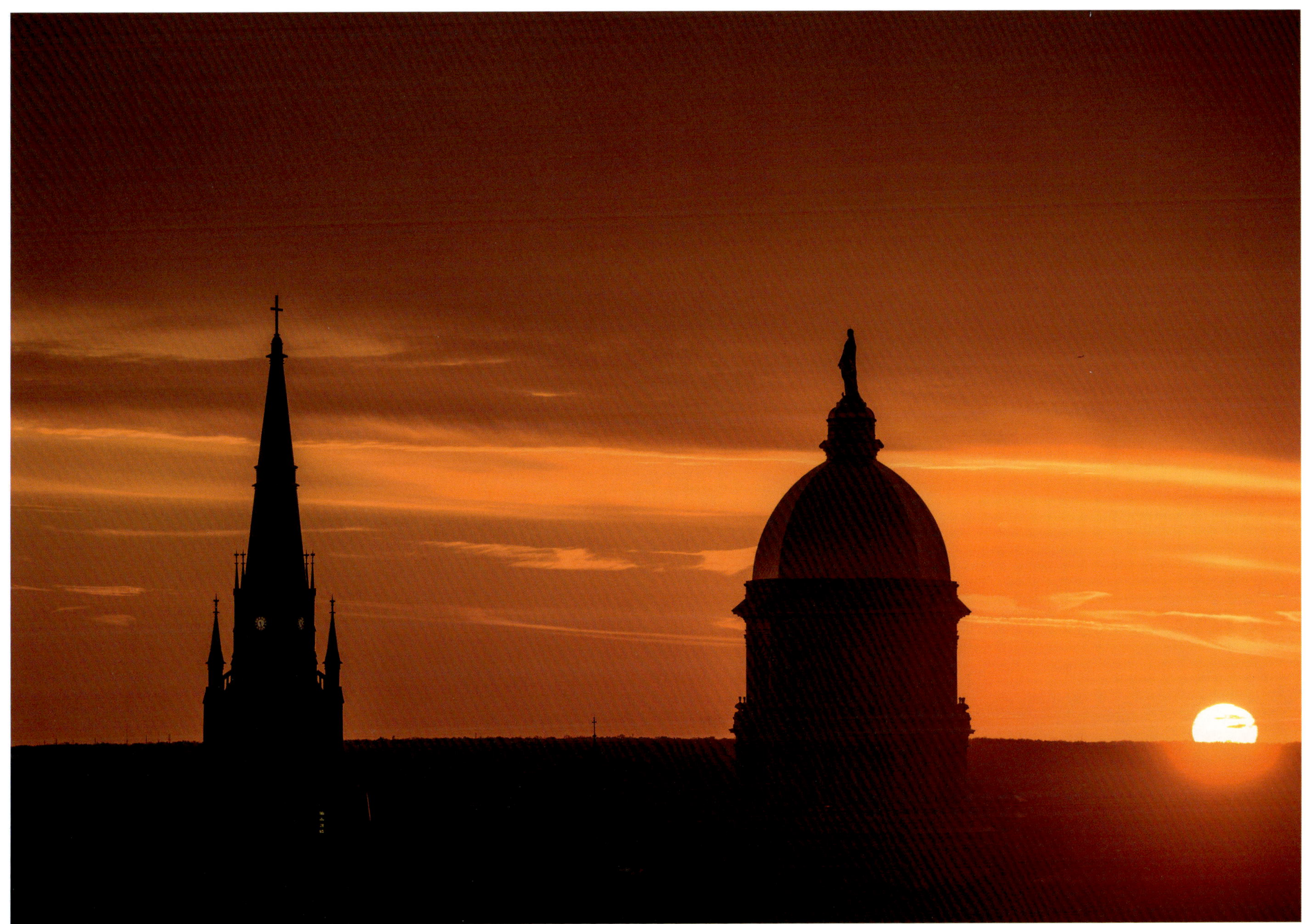

Sunset from the top floor of Grace Hall, Nikon D850, 175mm, 1/640 f5.6, ISO125

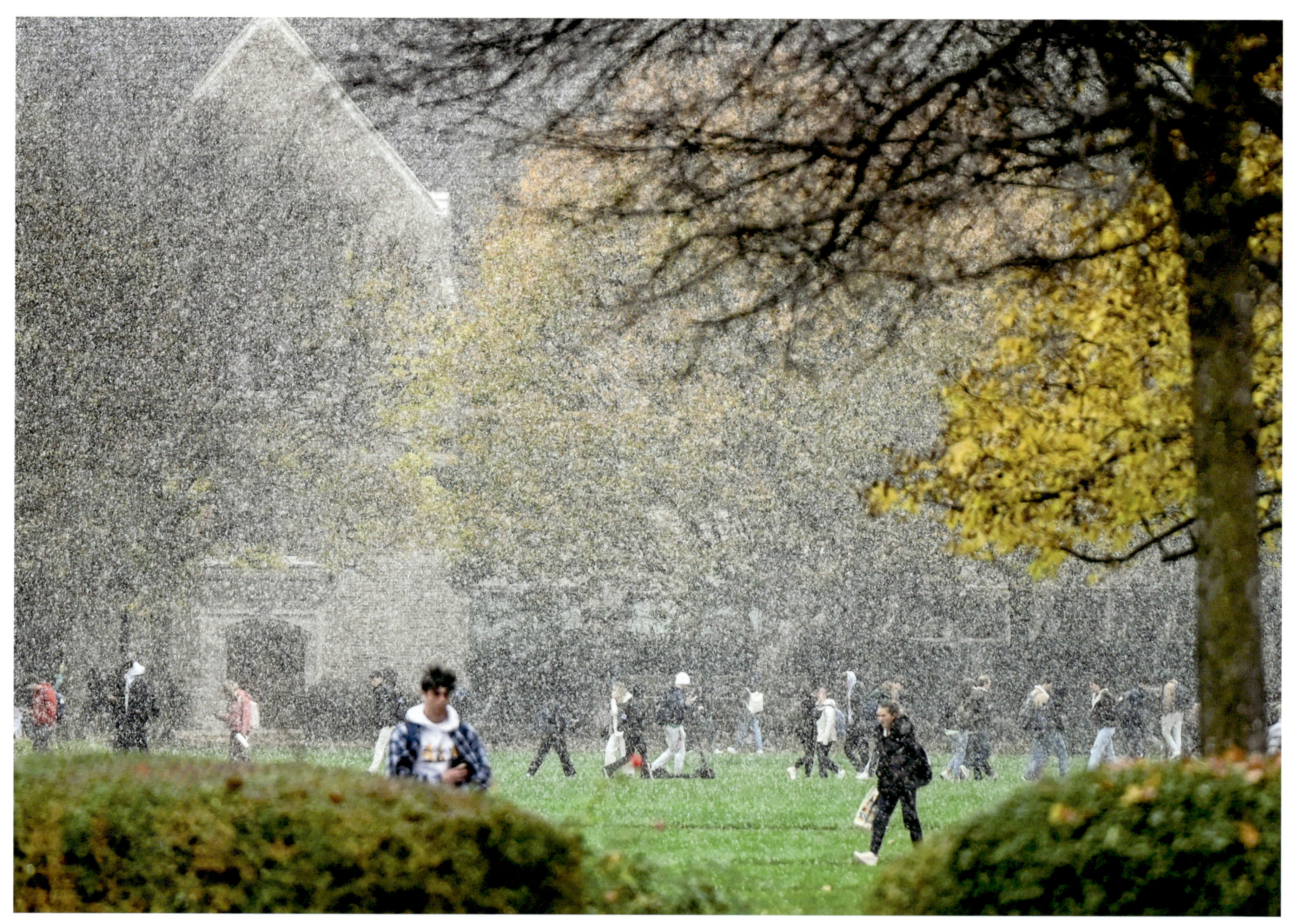

Fall snow flurries on South Quad, Nikon Z6II, 180mm, 1/2000 f2.8, ISO800

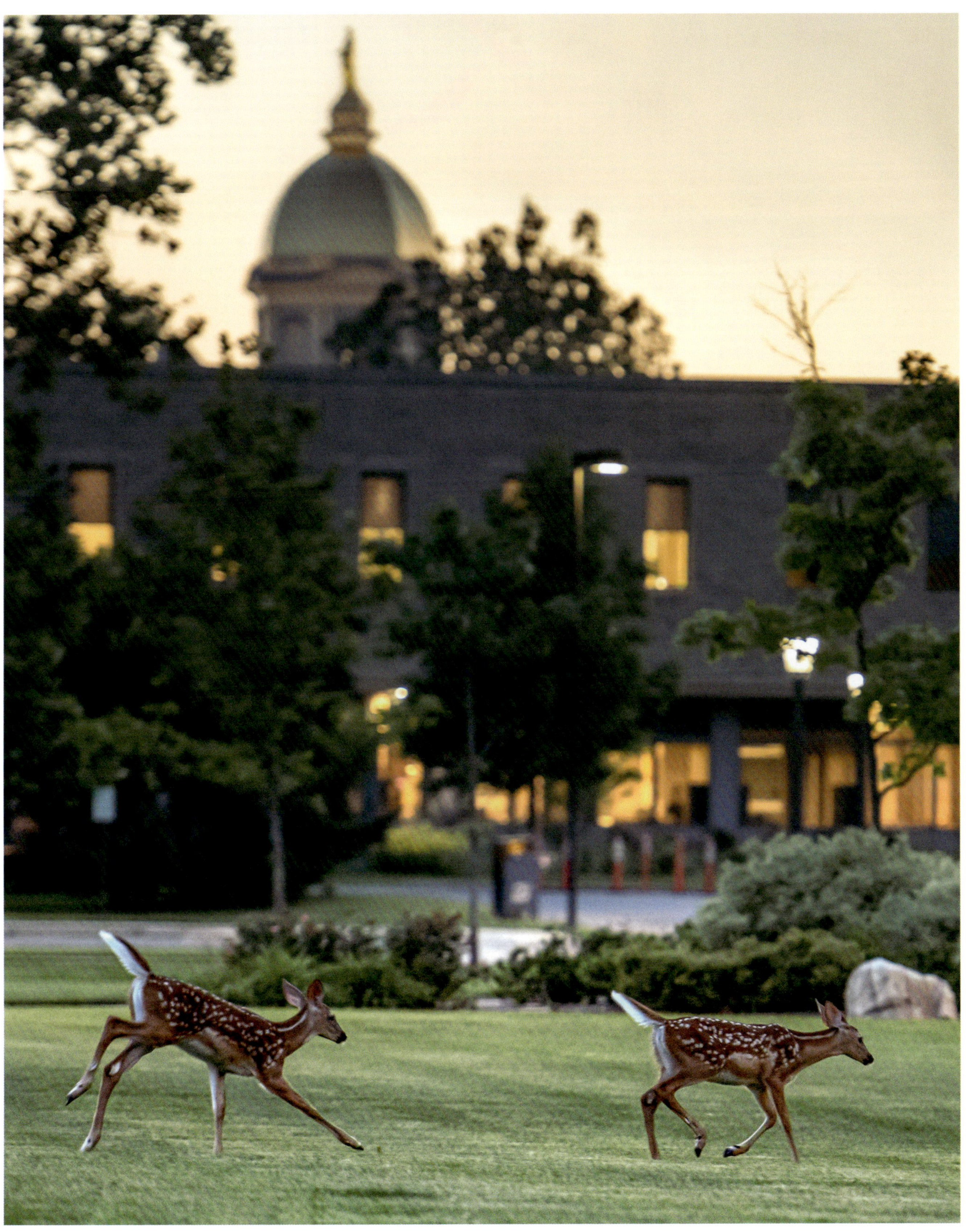

Deer near Hesburgh Library,
Nikon D5, 160mm, 1/160 f2.8, ISO3200

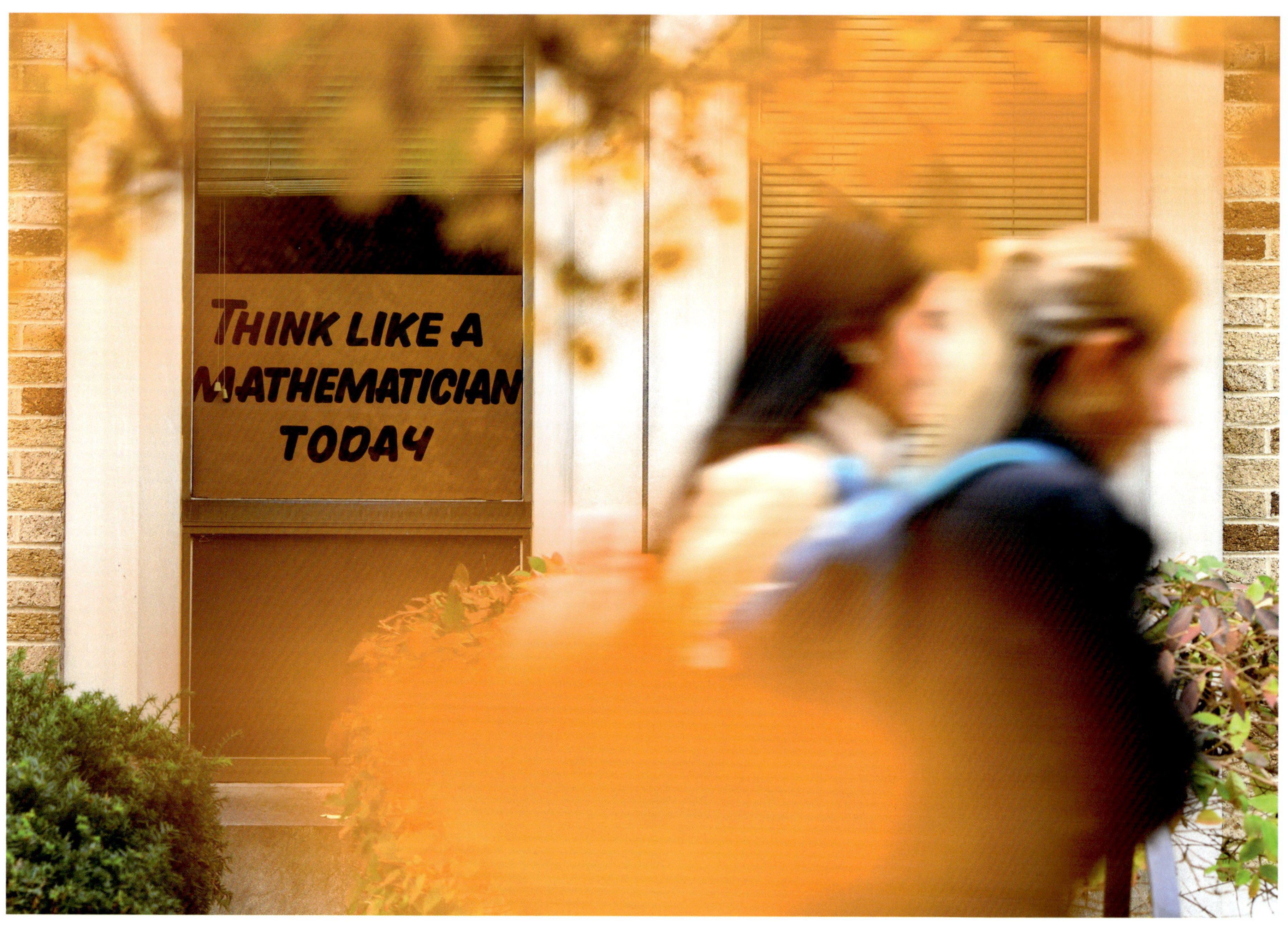

Hayes-Healy Hall, Nikon Z8, 135mm, 1/40 f4.5, ISO64

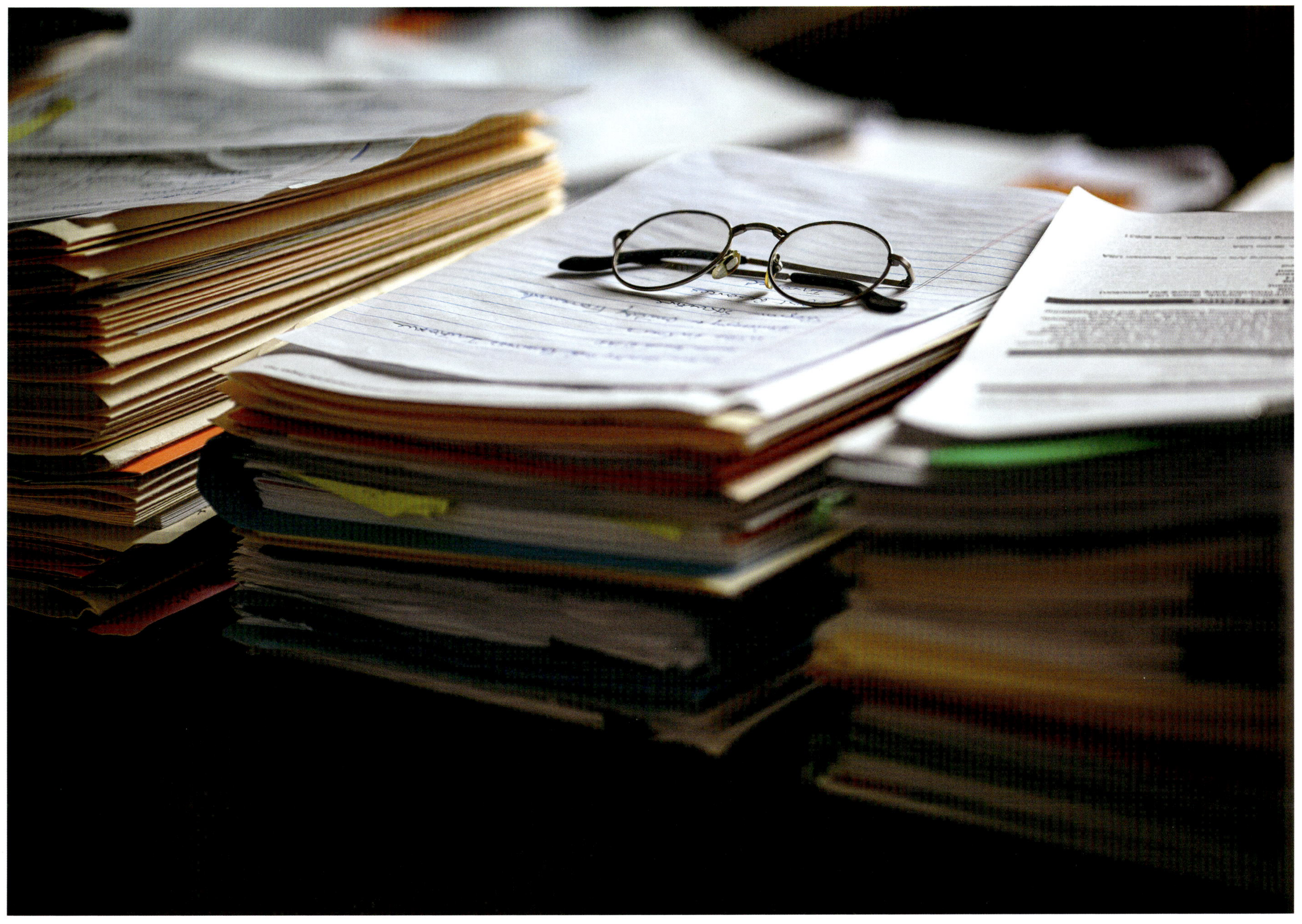

Faculty office in Jenkins-Nanovic Hall, Nikon Z9, 135mm, 1/250 f2, ISO1000

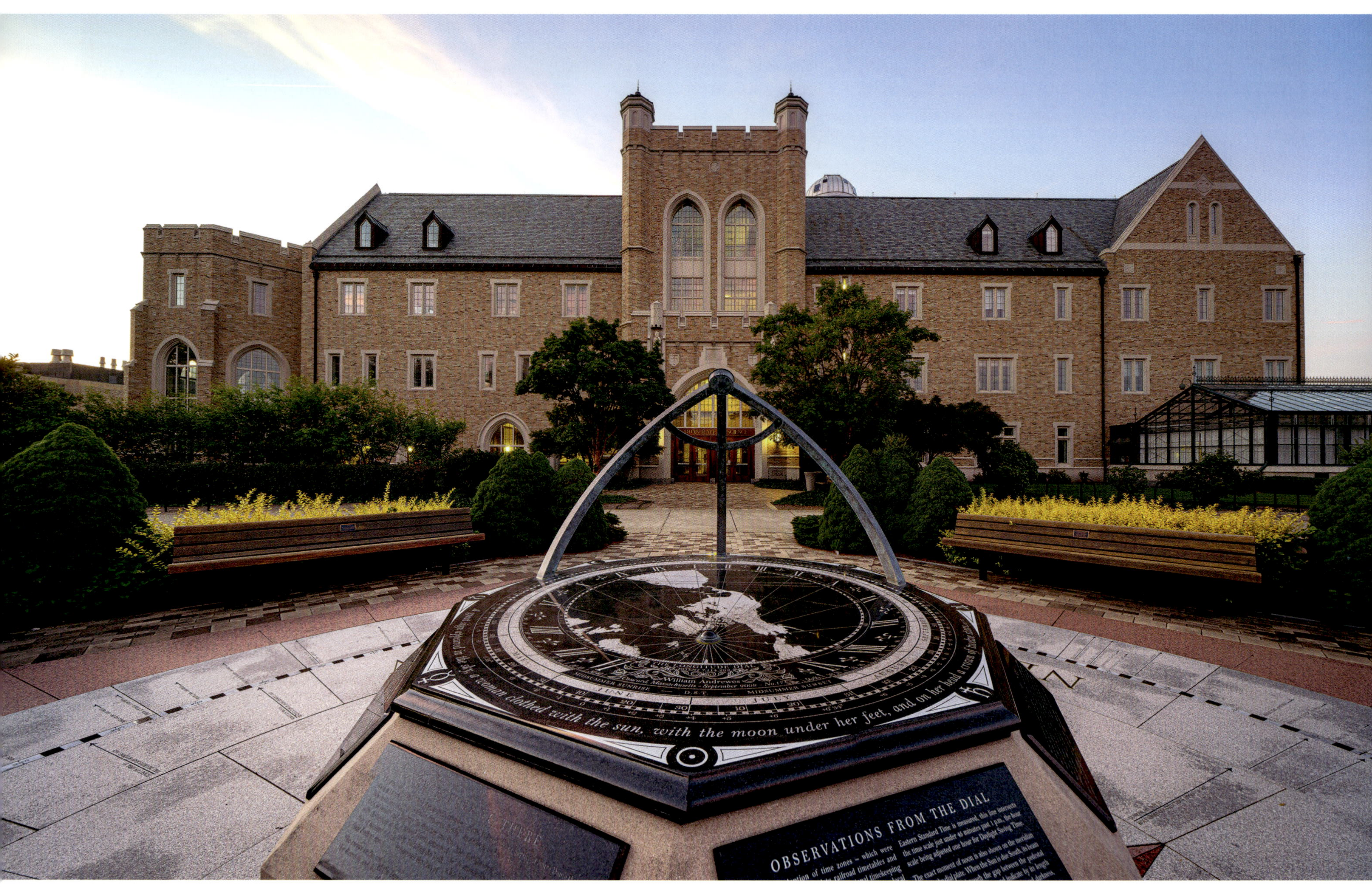

Facade of Jordan Hall of Science, Fuji GFX50R, 17mm, 1/4 f14, ISO100

I'm a big fan of architecture and I think Fr. Sorin was, too. Campus is a combination of many styles and trends over nearly two centuries. O'Shaughnessy and Hesburgh Library were built within ten years of each other. They don't seem alike at first, but there are similarities.

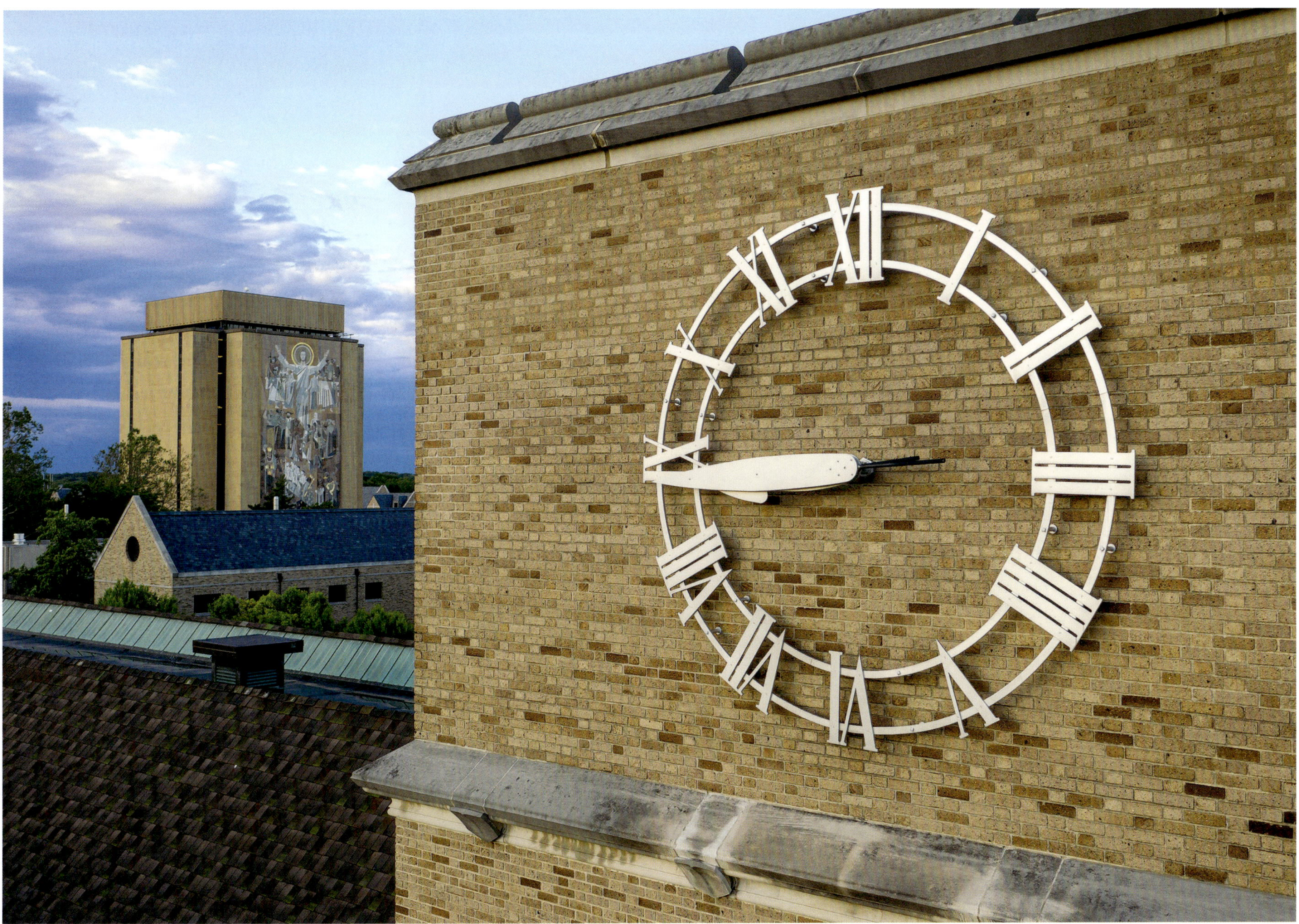

O'Shaughnessy Hall clock tower, Mavic 2 Pro drone, 24mm equivalent, 1/80 f4, ISO100

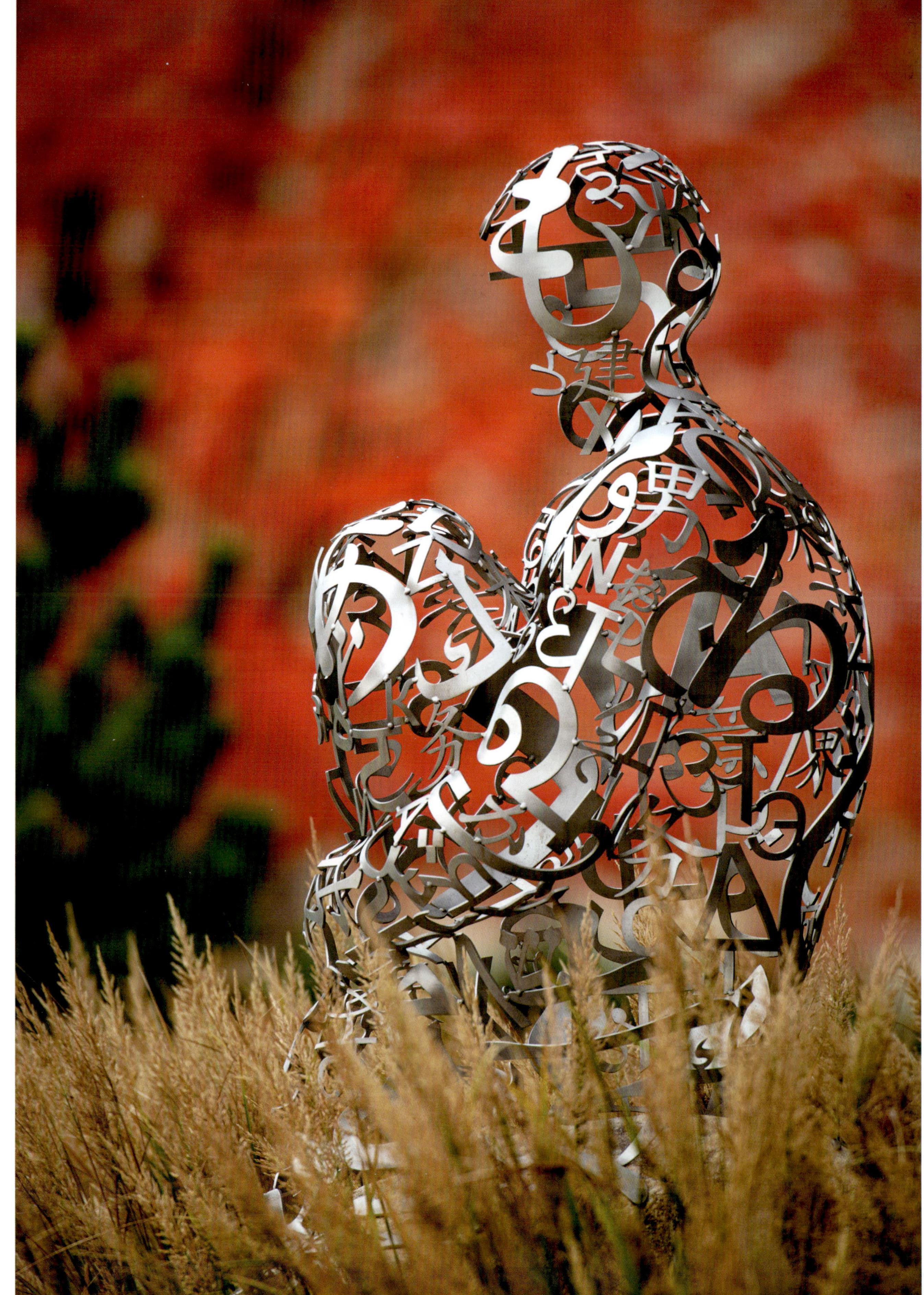

Sculpture in front of Snite Art Museum,
Nikon D850, 600mm, 1/200 f4, ISO80

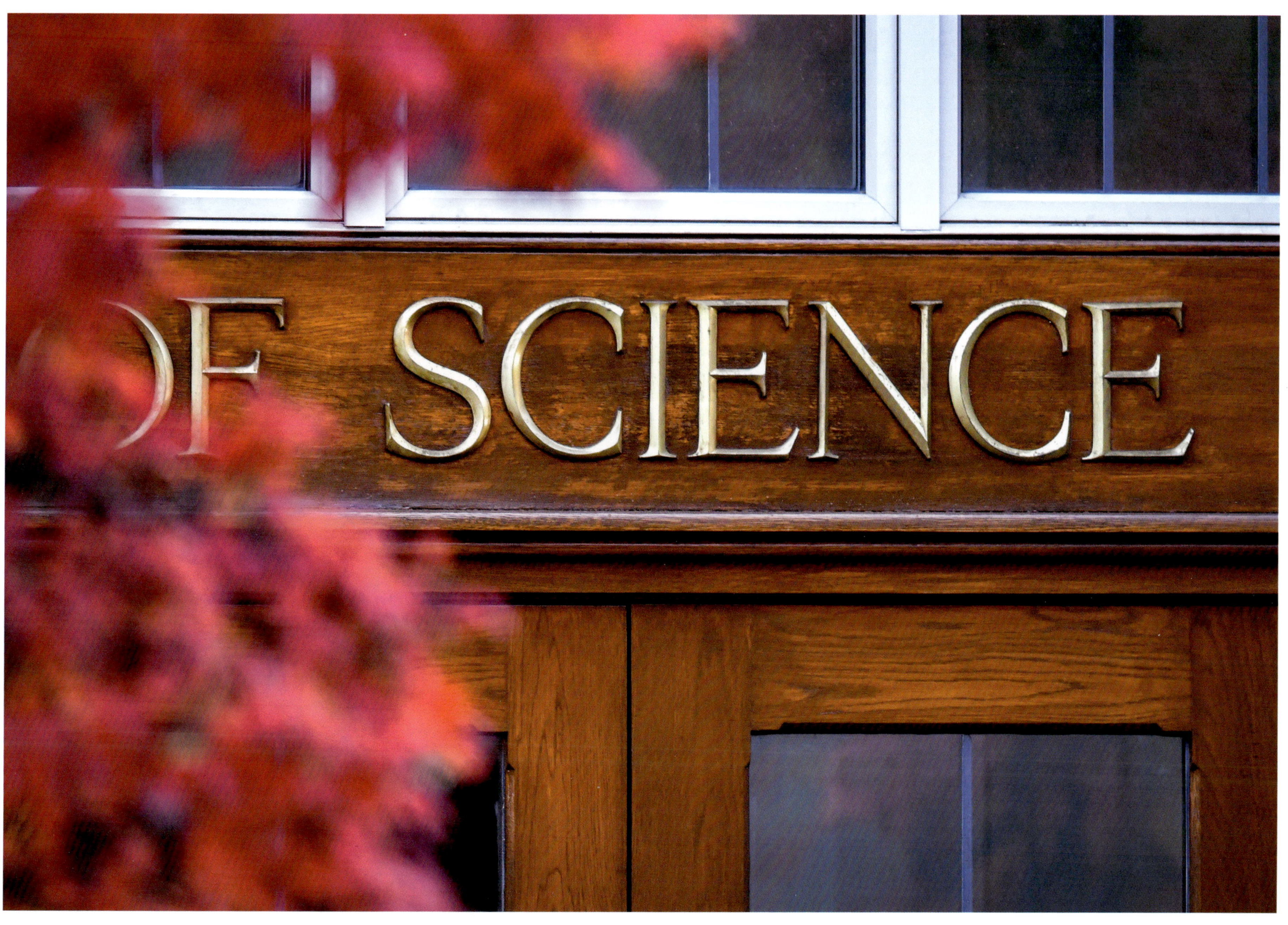

Main door of Jordan Hall of Science, Nikon D500, 400mm, 1/1000 f2.8, ISO1250

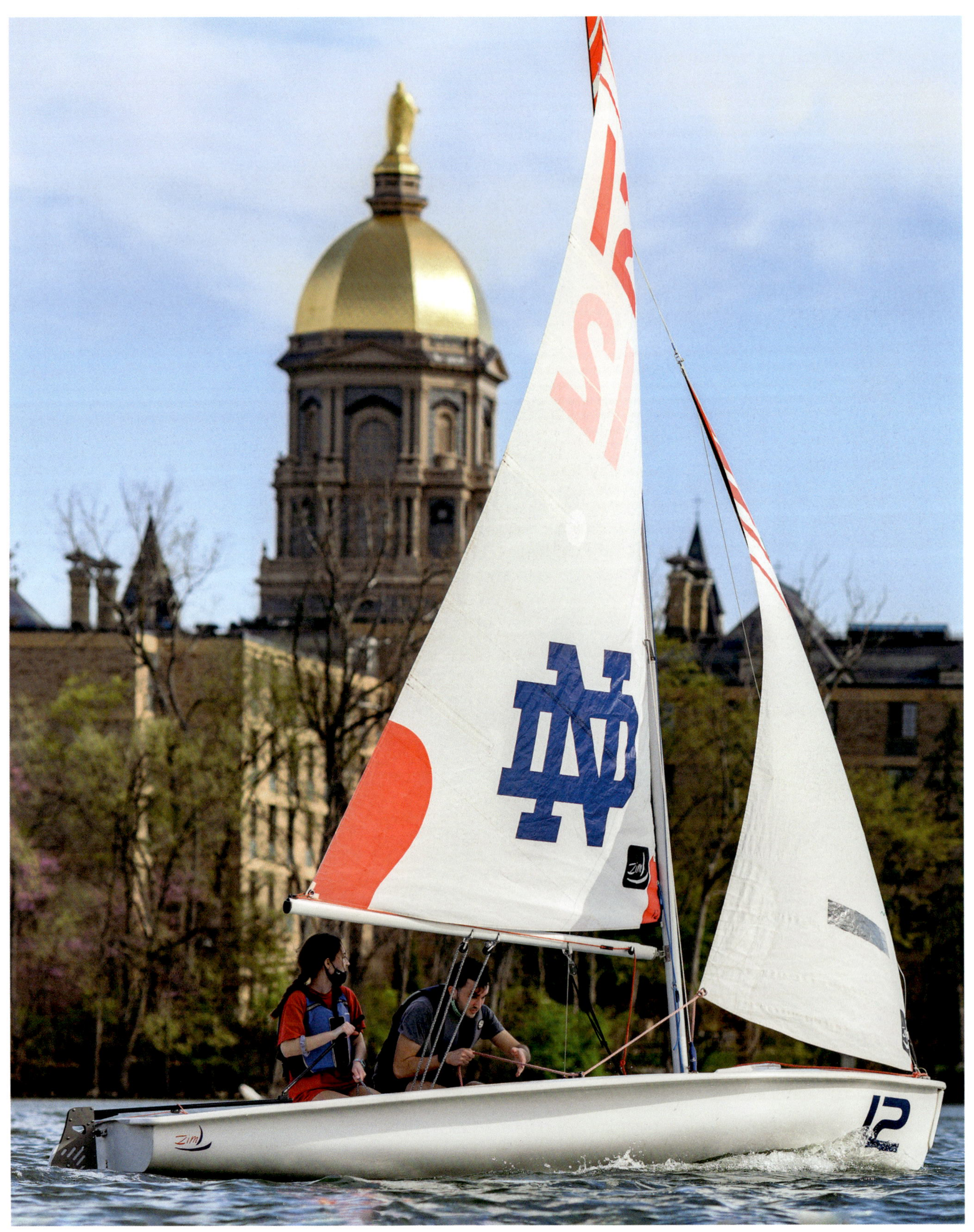

Sailboat on St. Joseph Lake,
Nikon Z7, 135mm, 1/800 f4, ISO64

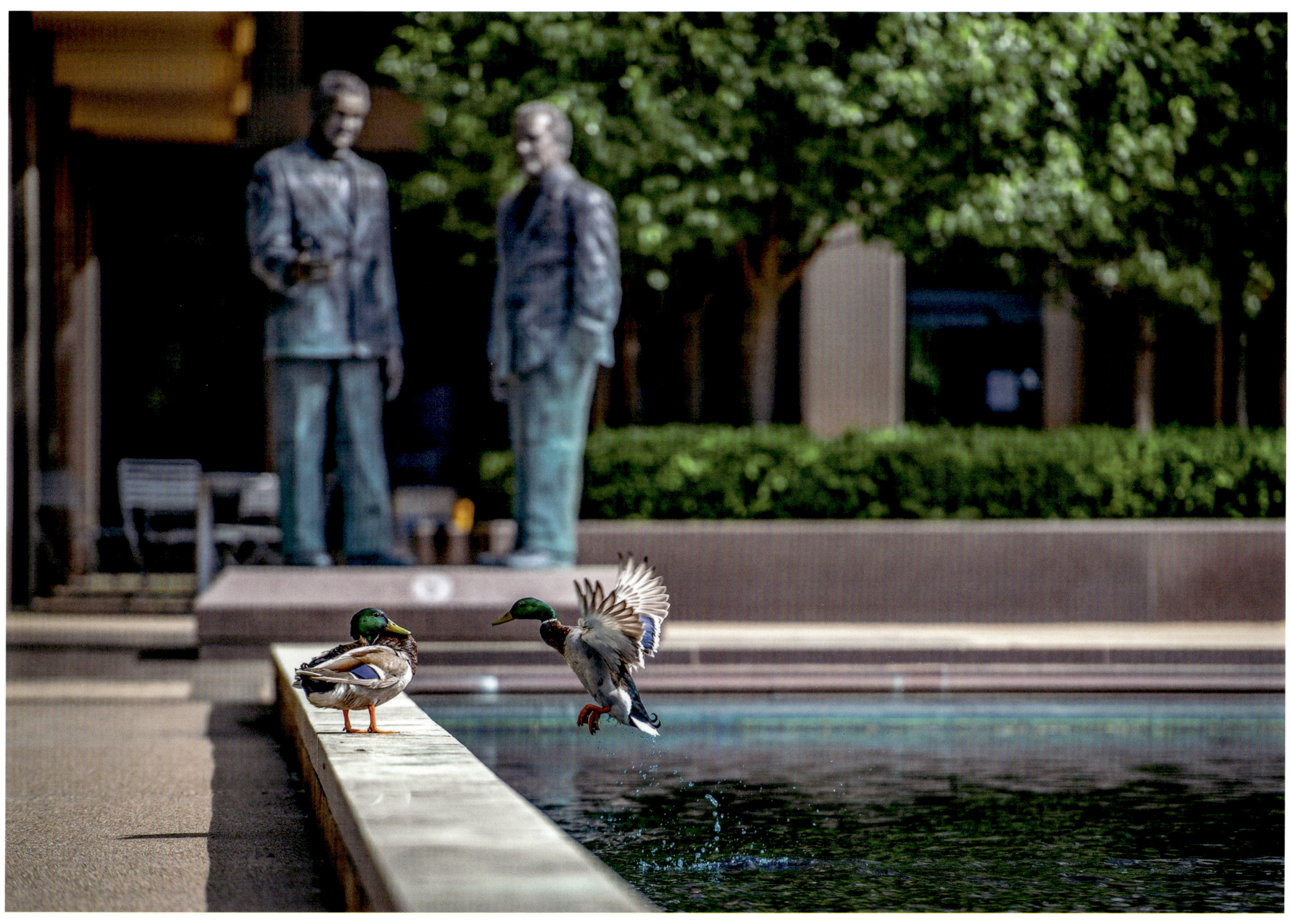

Ducks in Hesburgh Library reflecting pool, Nikon D5, 200mm, 1/1600 f3.5, ISO200

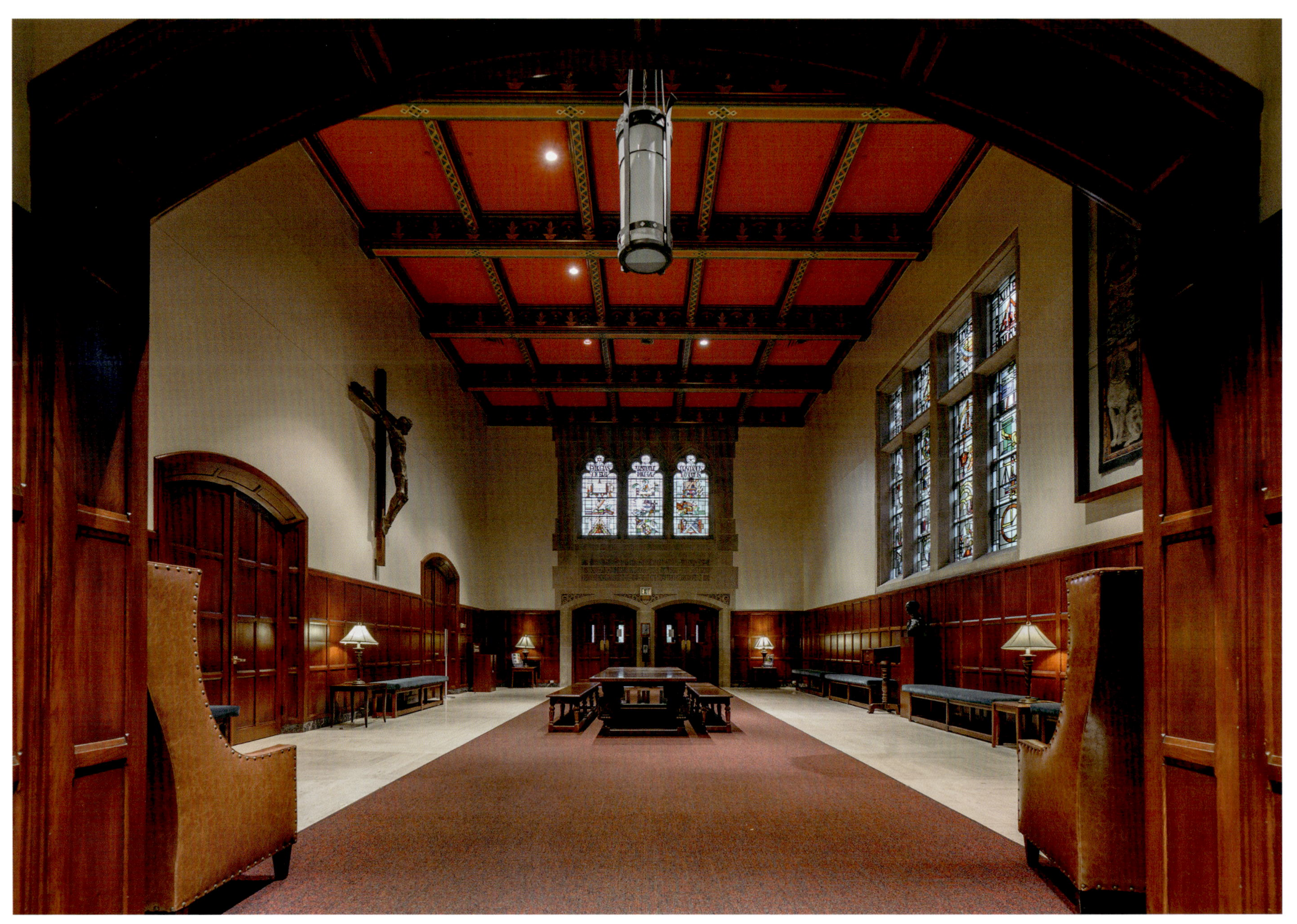

O'Shaughnessy Great Hall, Nikon Z7II, 17mm, 1/4 f7.1, ISO500

Notre Dame has over sixty chapels on campus and almost all have stained glass windows. The O'Shaughnessy Great Hall is one of the few non-chapel spaces with stained glass. When the sun is at the right angle, color expands beyond the window frames.

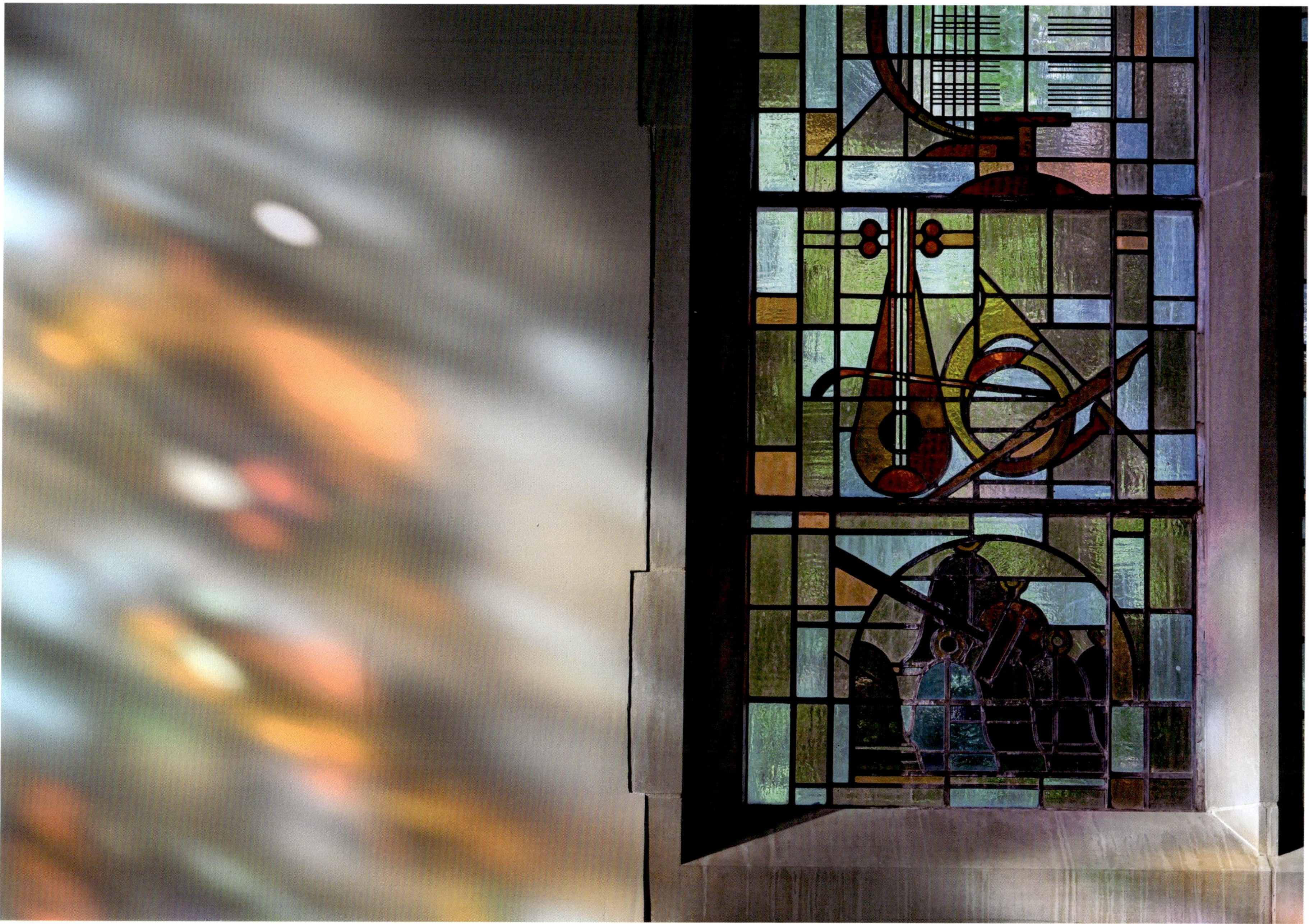

Stained glass in O'Shaughnessy Great Hall, Nikon Z9, 82mm, 1/160 f13, ISO1250

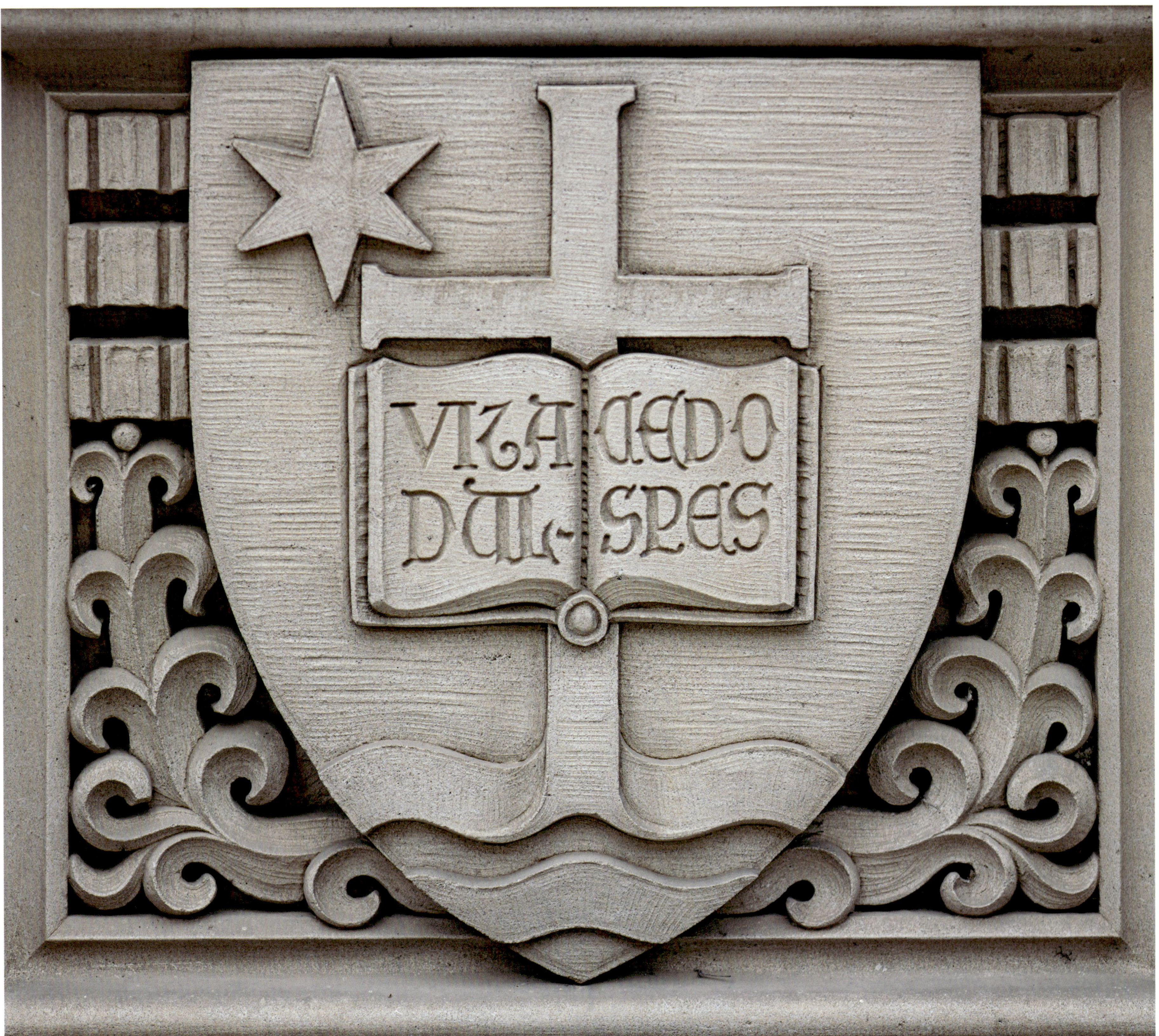

University seal relief over a door to O'Shaughnessy Hall, Nikon Z7, 135mm, 1/250 f2, ISO100

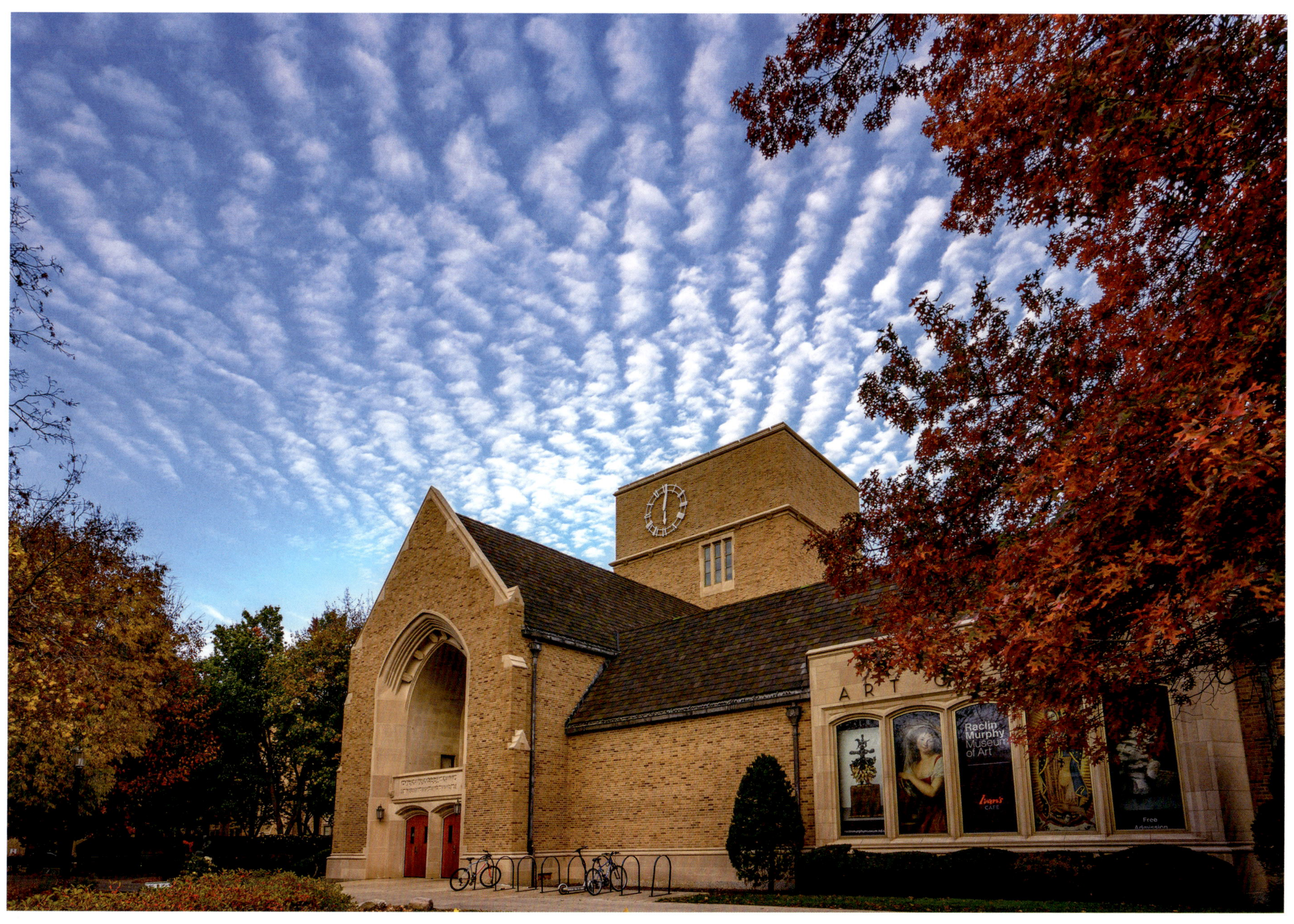

O'Shaughnessy Hall, Nikon Z7II, 17mm, 1/50 f7.1, ISO64

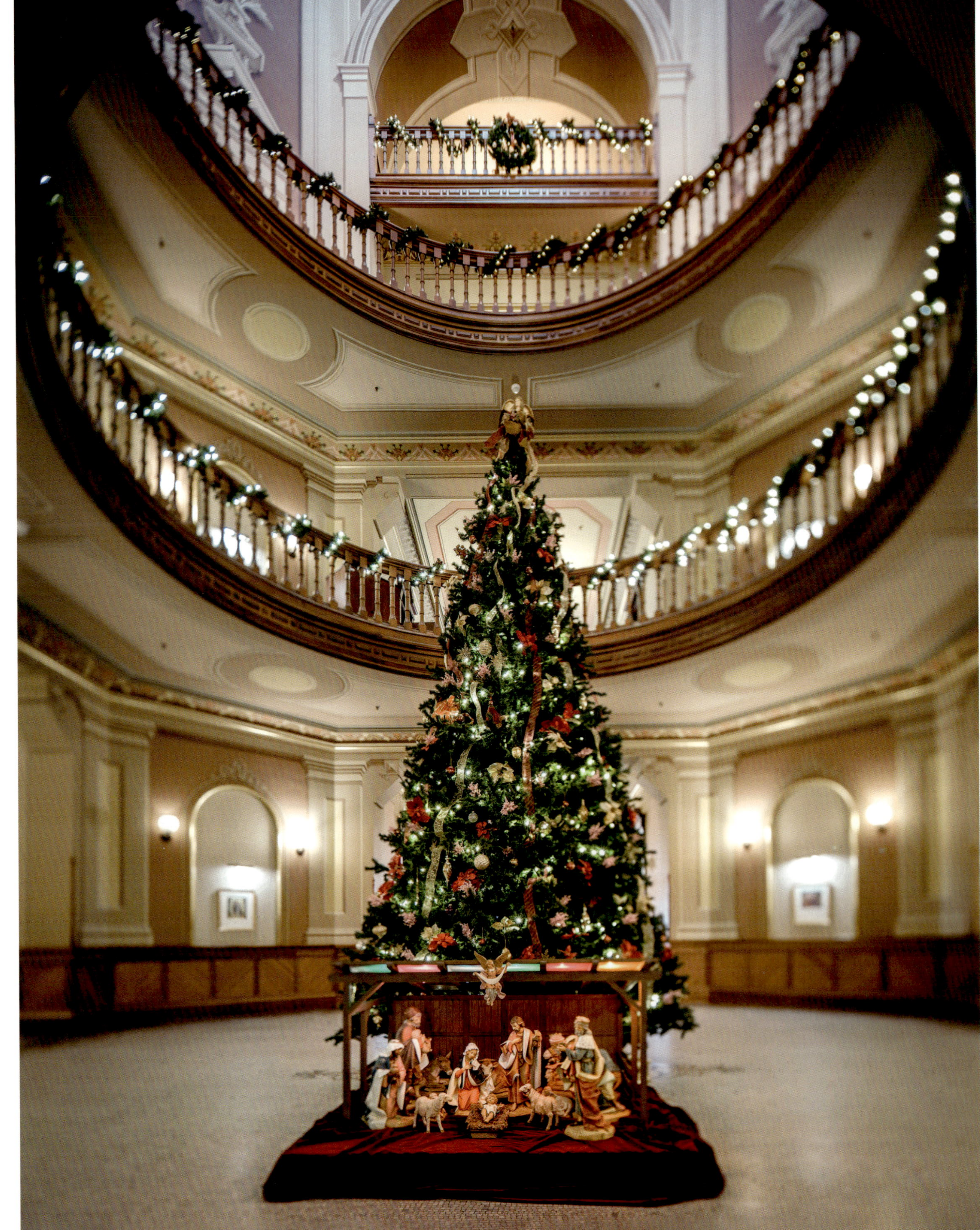

Main Building
rotunda Christmas tree,
Fuji GFX100s, 17mm,
1/3 f4.5, ISO100

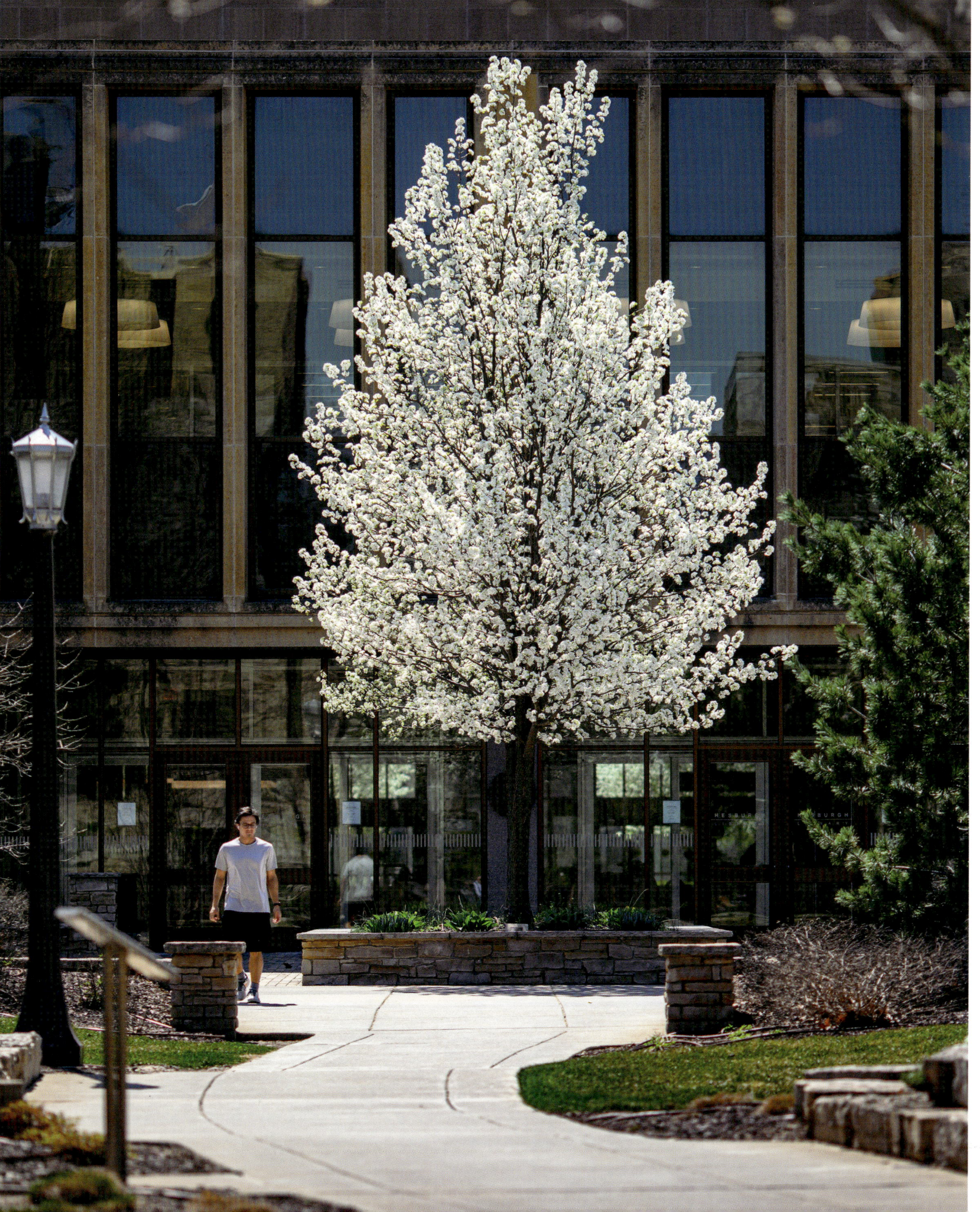

Hesburgh Library
north entrance, Nikon Z6II,
135mm, 1/2500 f2, ISO100

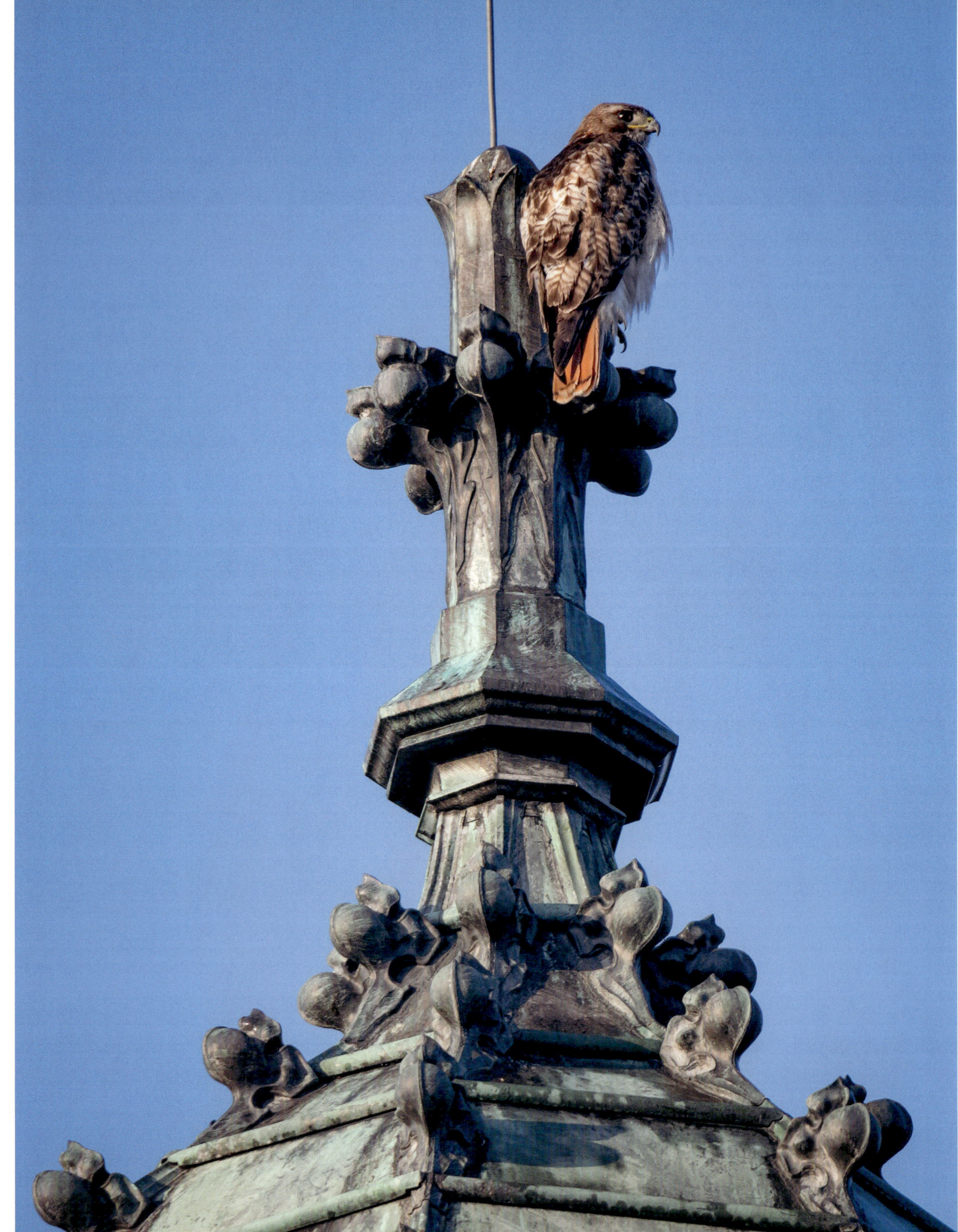

South Dining Hall spire,
Nikon D850, 500mm,
1/400 f7.1, ISO200

There's plenty of winter in northern Indiana, so you'd be surprised how tricky it is to make a nice winter photo. The best snow photos happen while it's fresh and unplowed. The trouble is Notre Dame grounds crews are very good at their jobs so there's not much time. Living year-round in South Bend means I can come to campus on weekends and during campus breaks when I might get a few more minutes of winter wonderland before it's swept and pushed into piles.

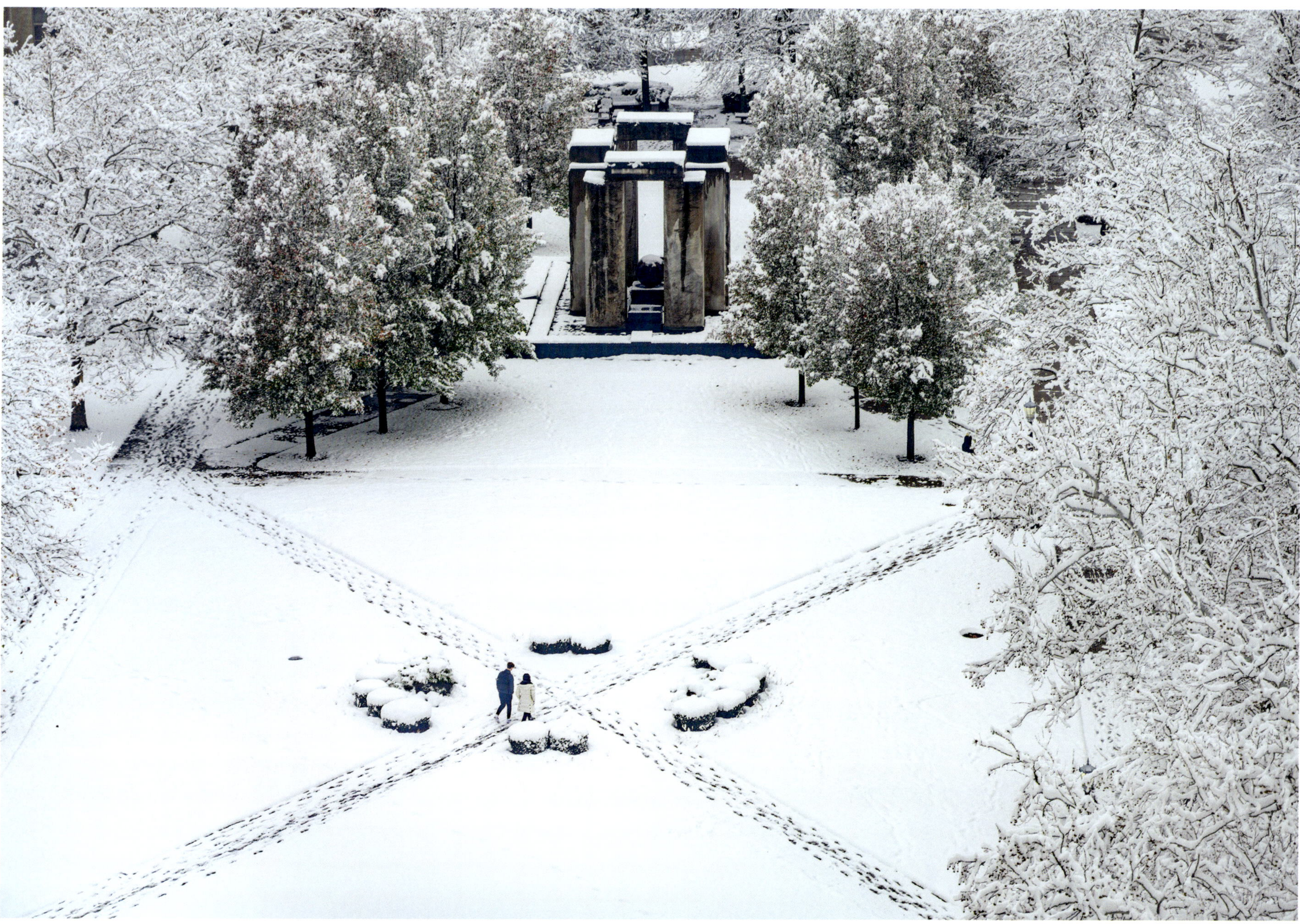

Fieldhouse Mall and Stonehenge from Hesburgh Library, Nikon Z7II, 120mm, 1/80 f4, ISO64

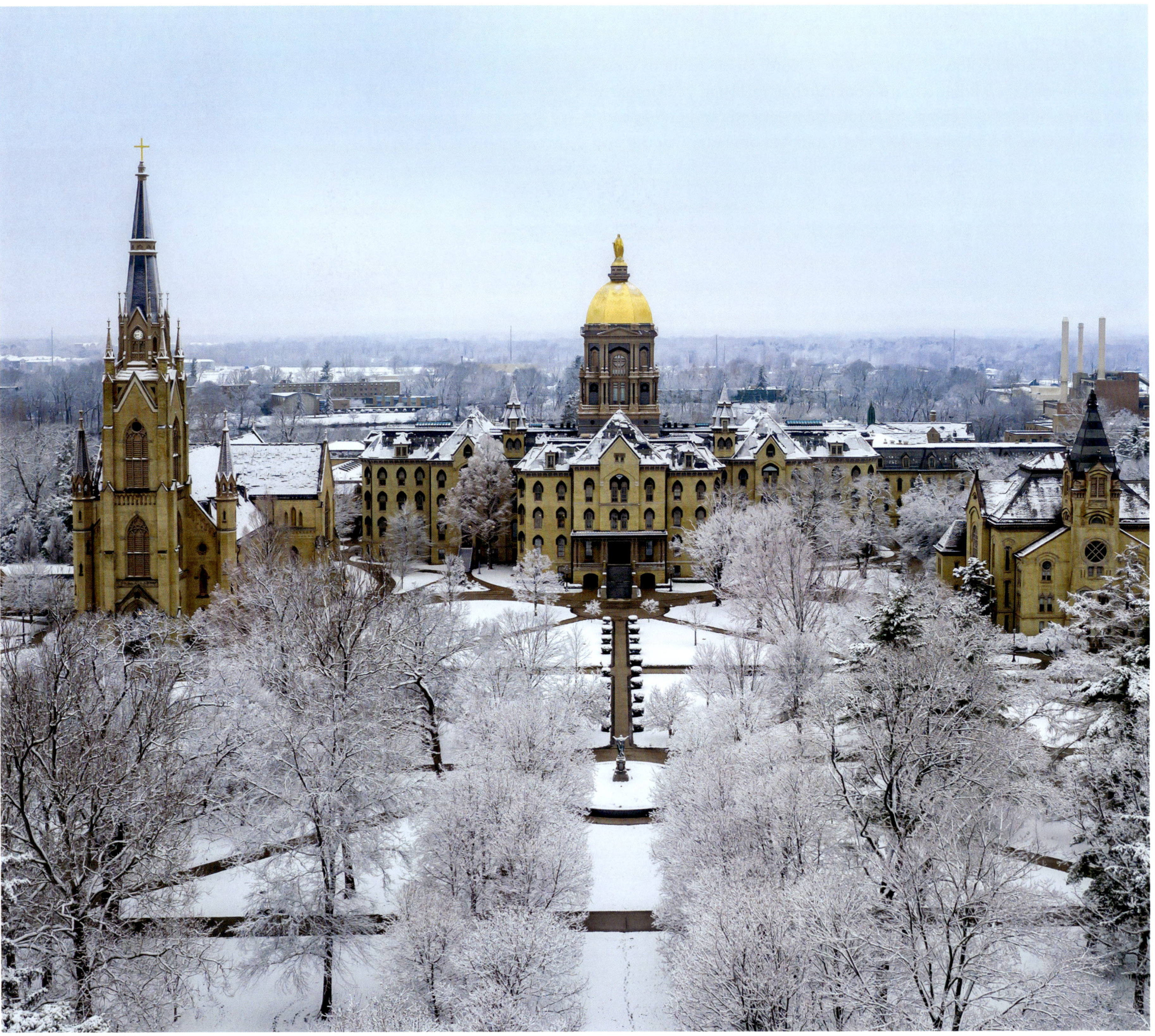

Aerial of Main Quad, Mavic 2 Pro drone, 24mm equivalent, 1/160 f4.5, ISO100

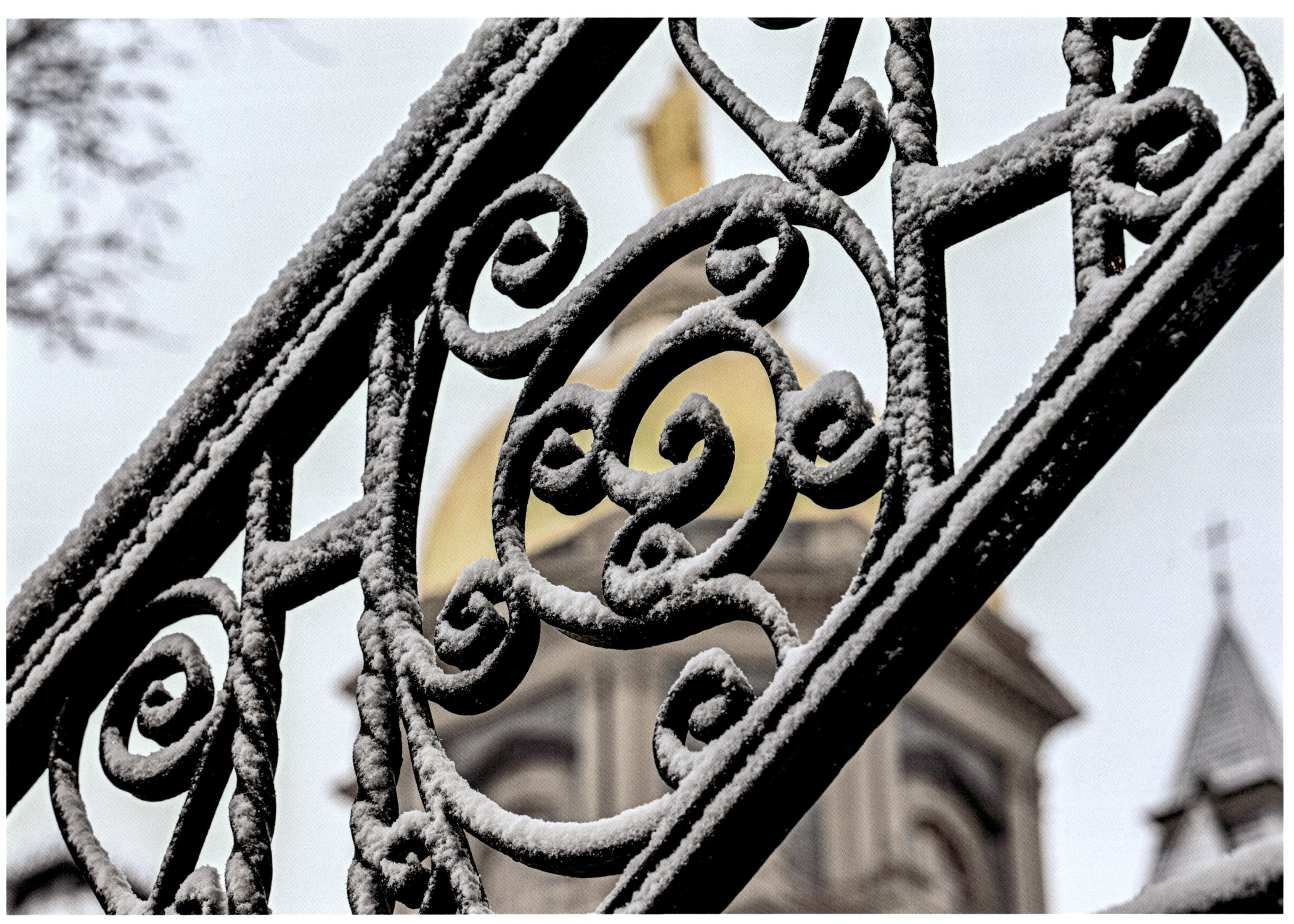

Railing on Washington Hall, Nikon Z9, 104mm, 1/25 f8, ISO400

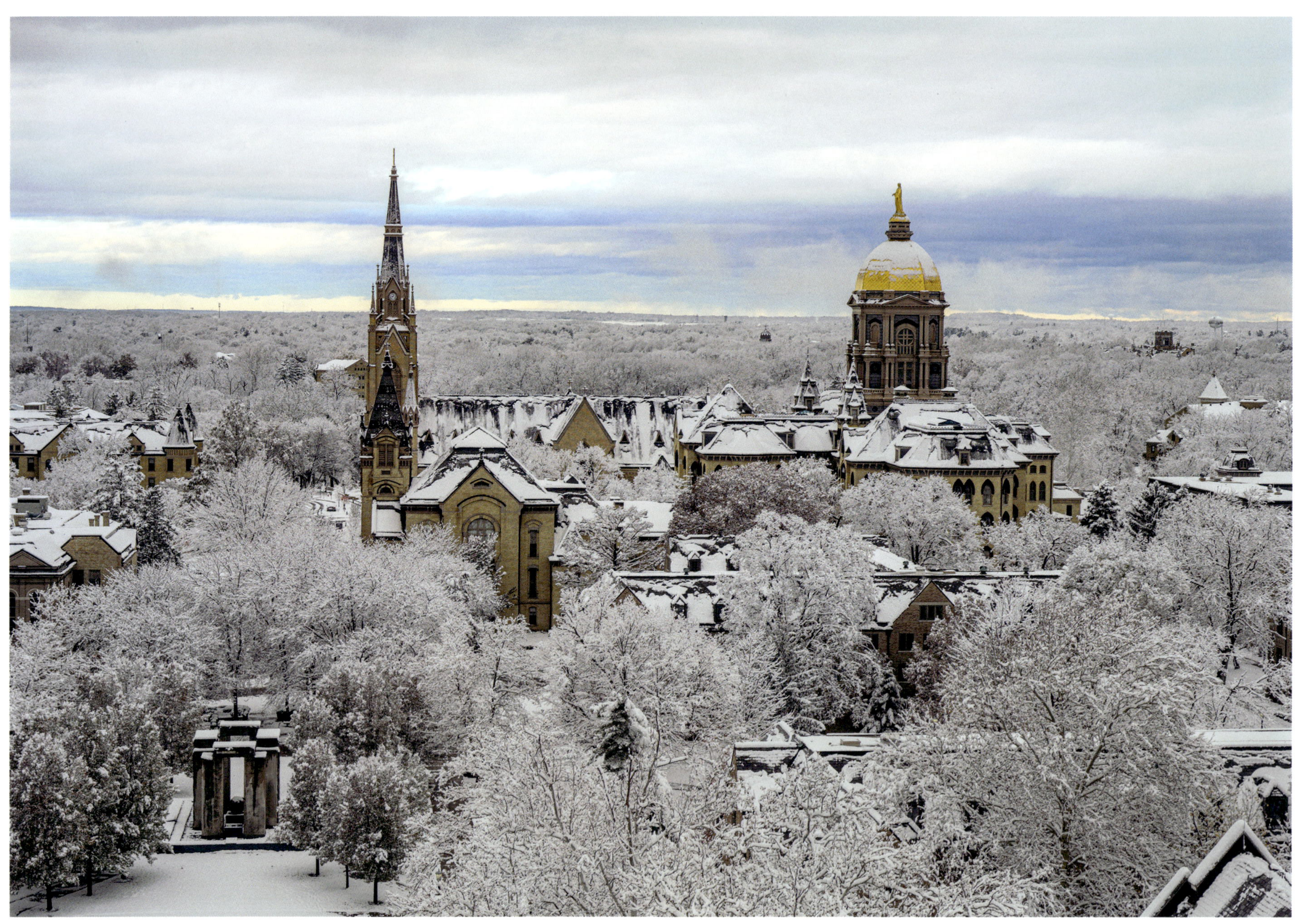

Campus skyline from Hesburgh Library, Nikon Z7II, 57mm, 1/80 f4, ISO64

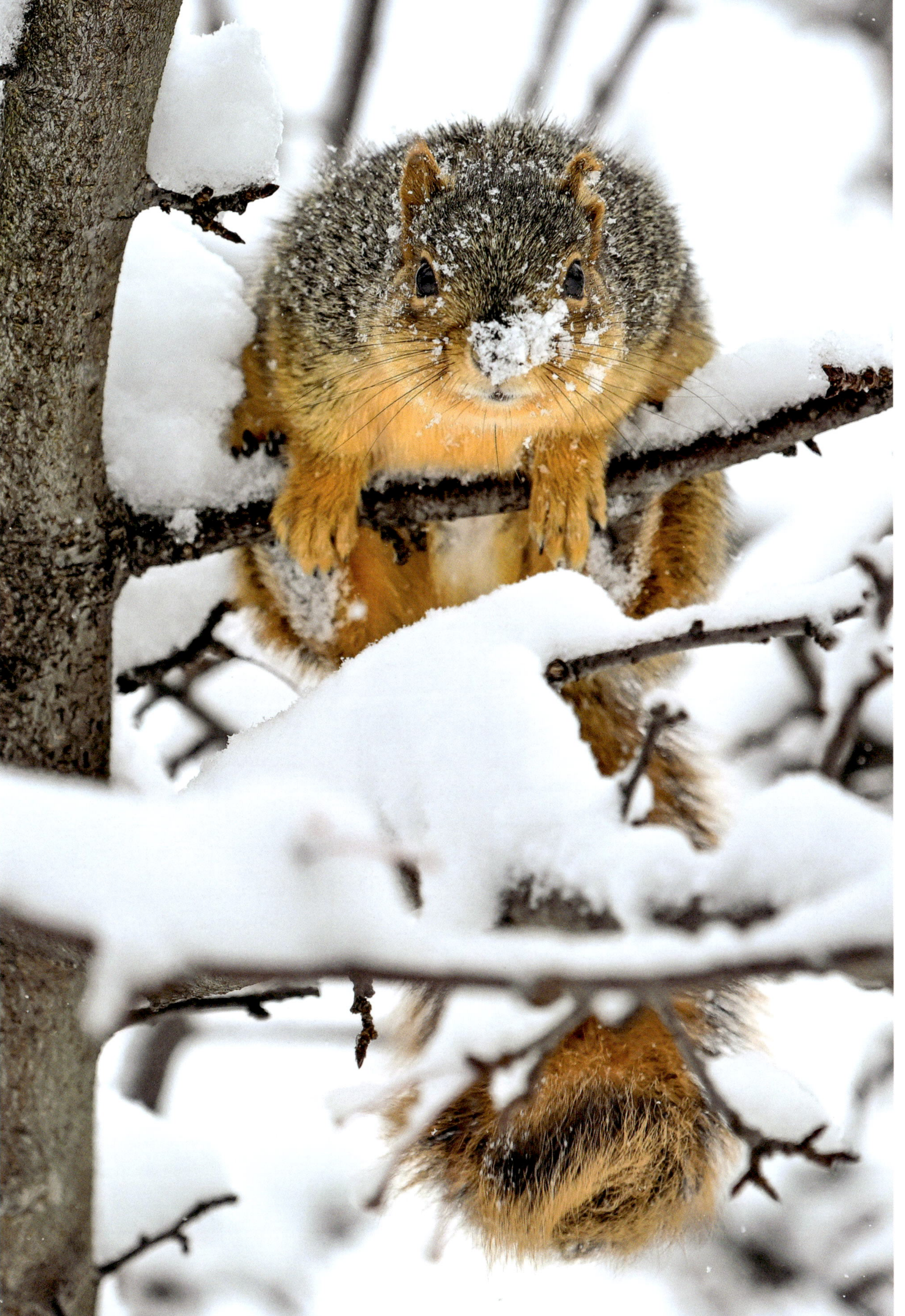

When I was a student, there was a note taped somewhere in the student newspaper darkroom that if you turned in a squirrel photo . . . you failed. The idea being, “Try harder than that.” What can I say? Notre Dame has photogenic squirrels.

Squirrel near Log Chapel, Nikon Z9, 120mm, 1/2500 f4, ISO800

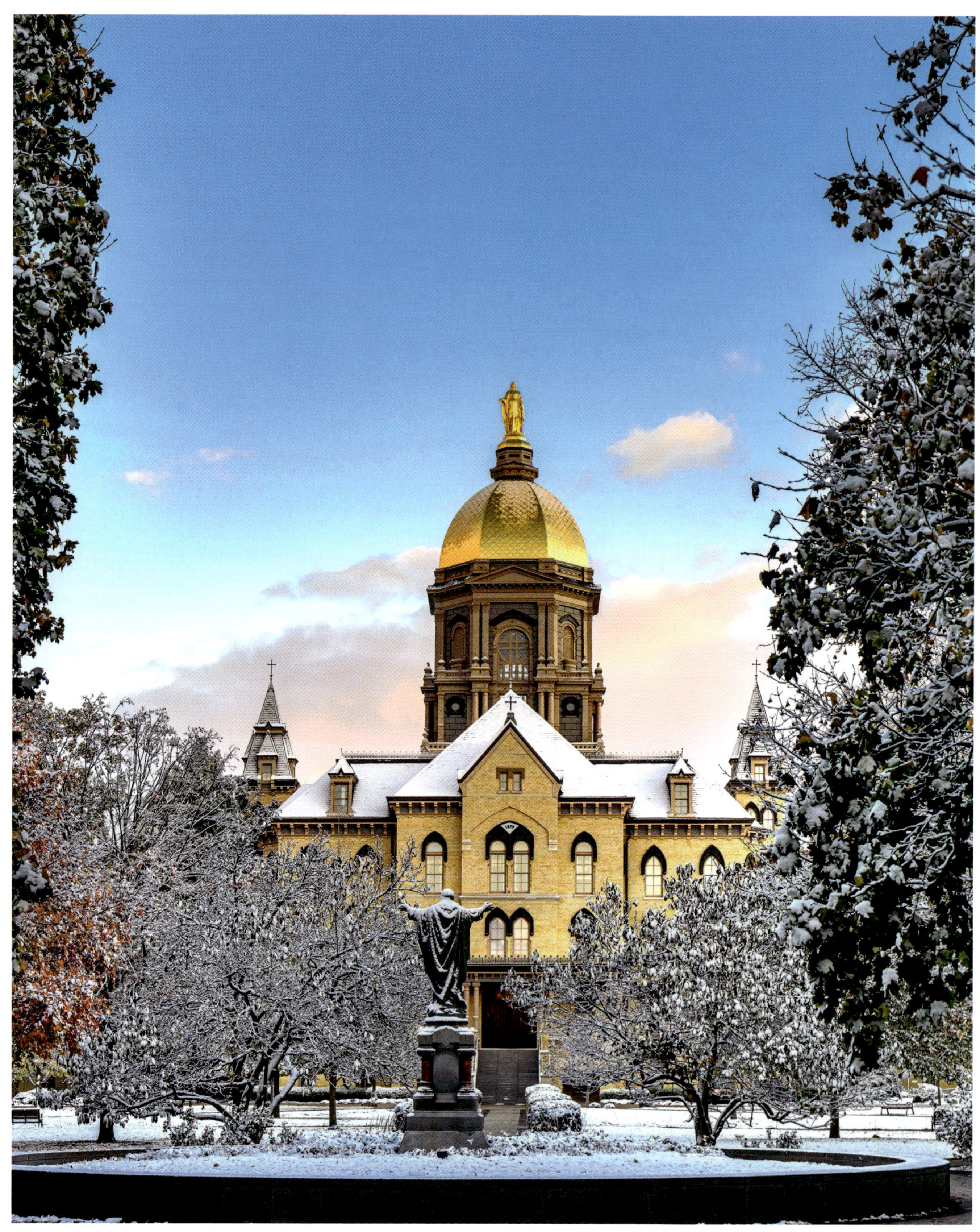

Snowy Main Building in the morning,
Nikon Z6II, 70mm, 1/125 f7.1, ISO400

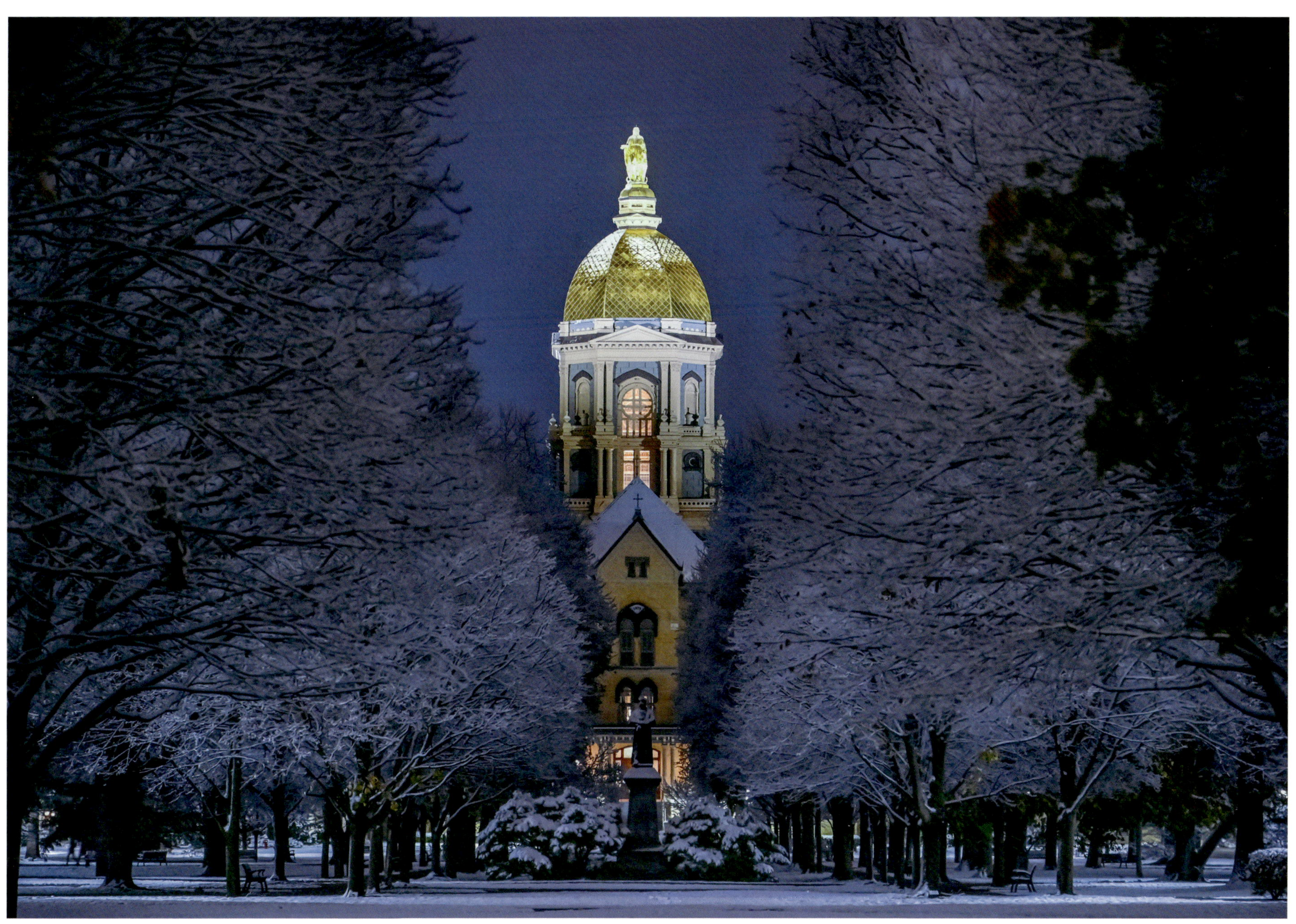

Snowy Main Building in the evening, Nikon Z6II, 120mm, 1/13 f4, ISO1600

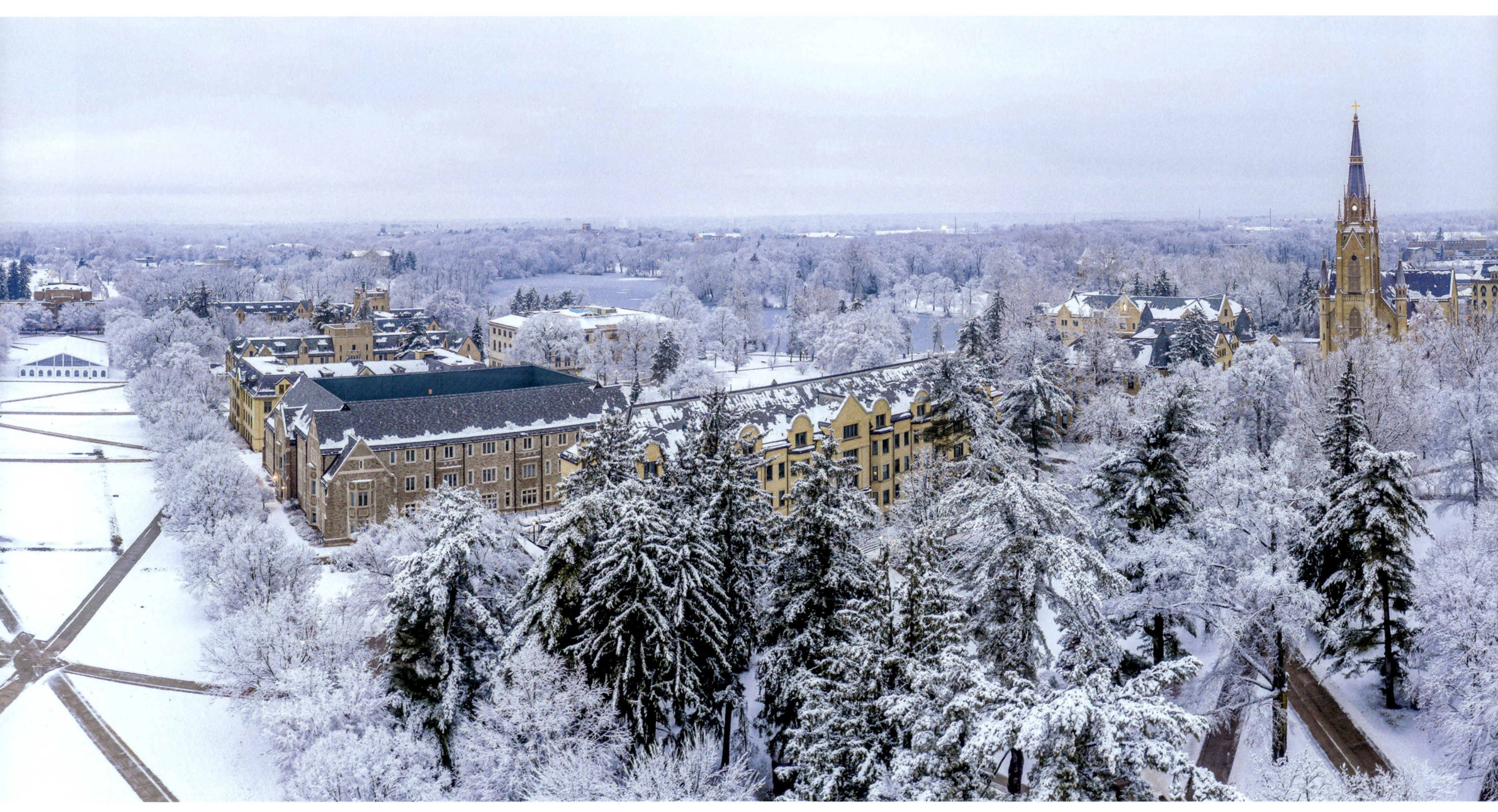

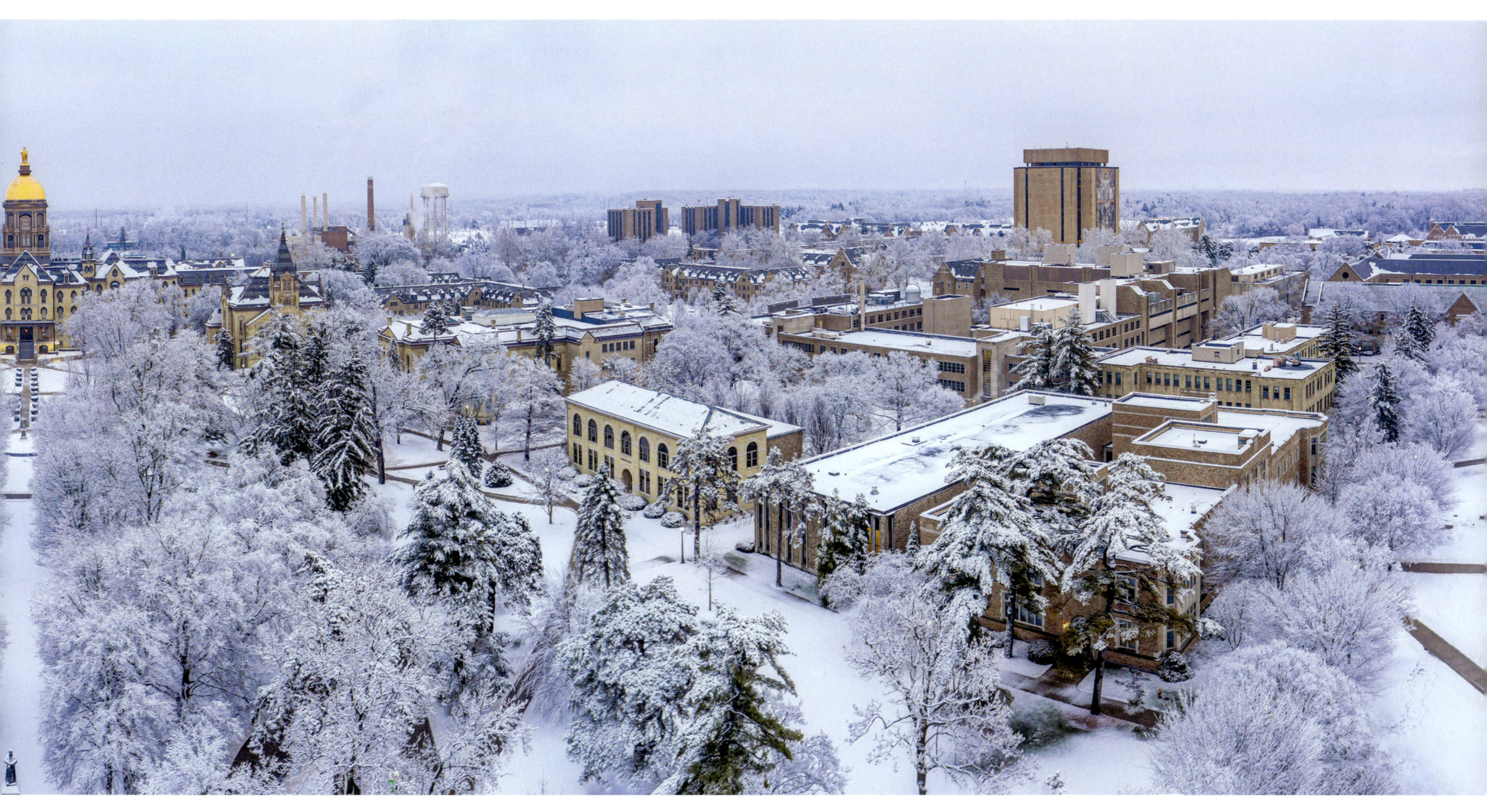

Aerial panorama, Mavic 2 Pro drone, 24mm equivalent, 1/10 f3.5, ISO100 stitched panorama

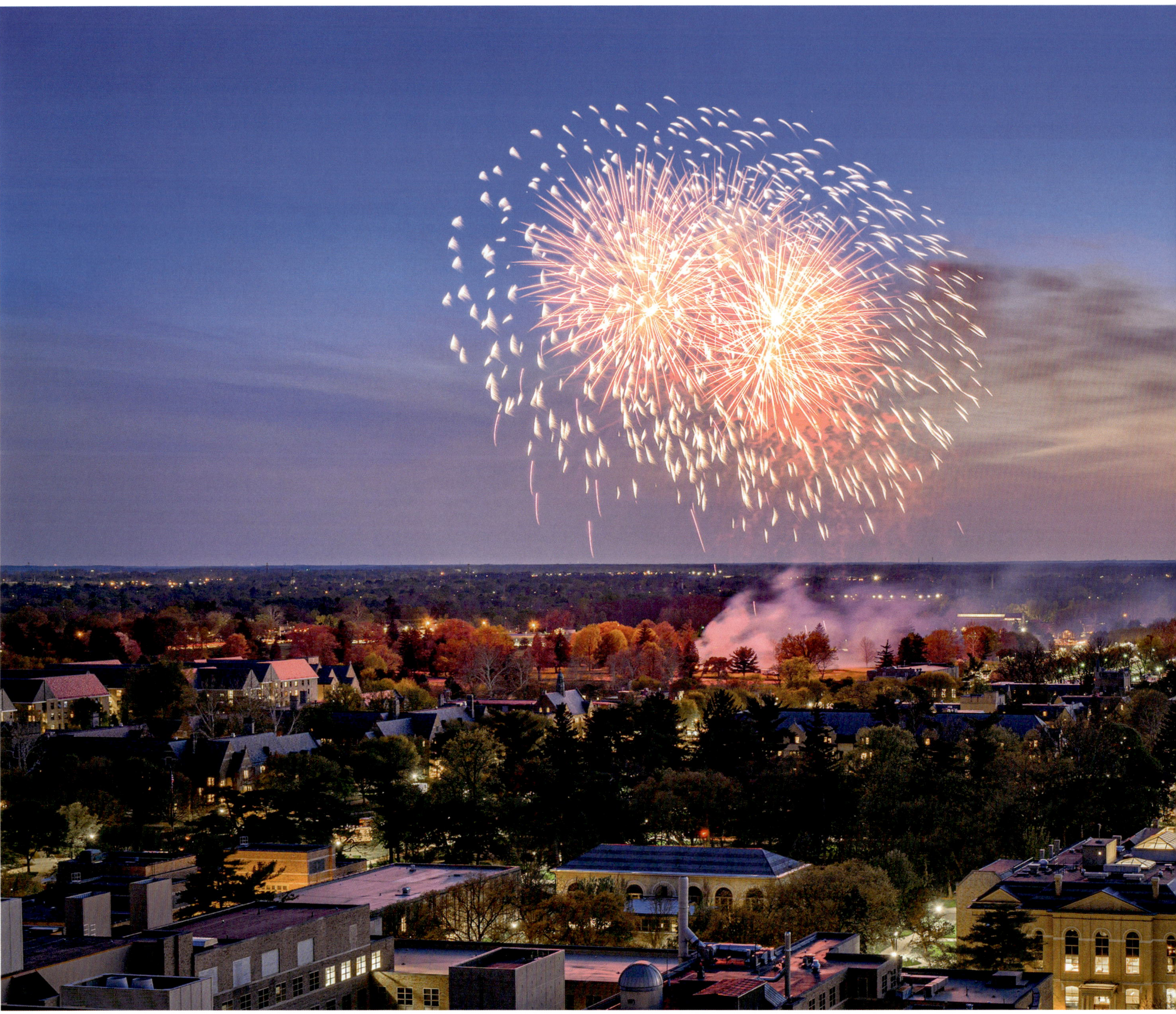

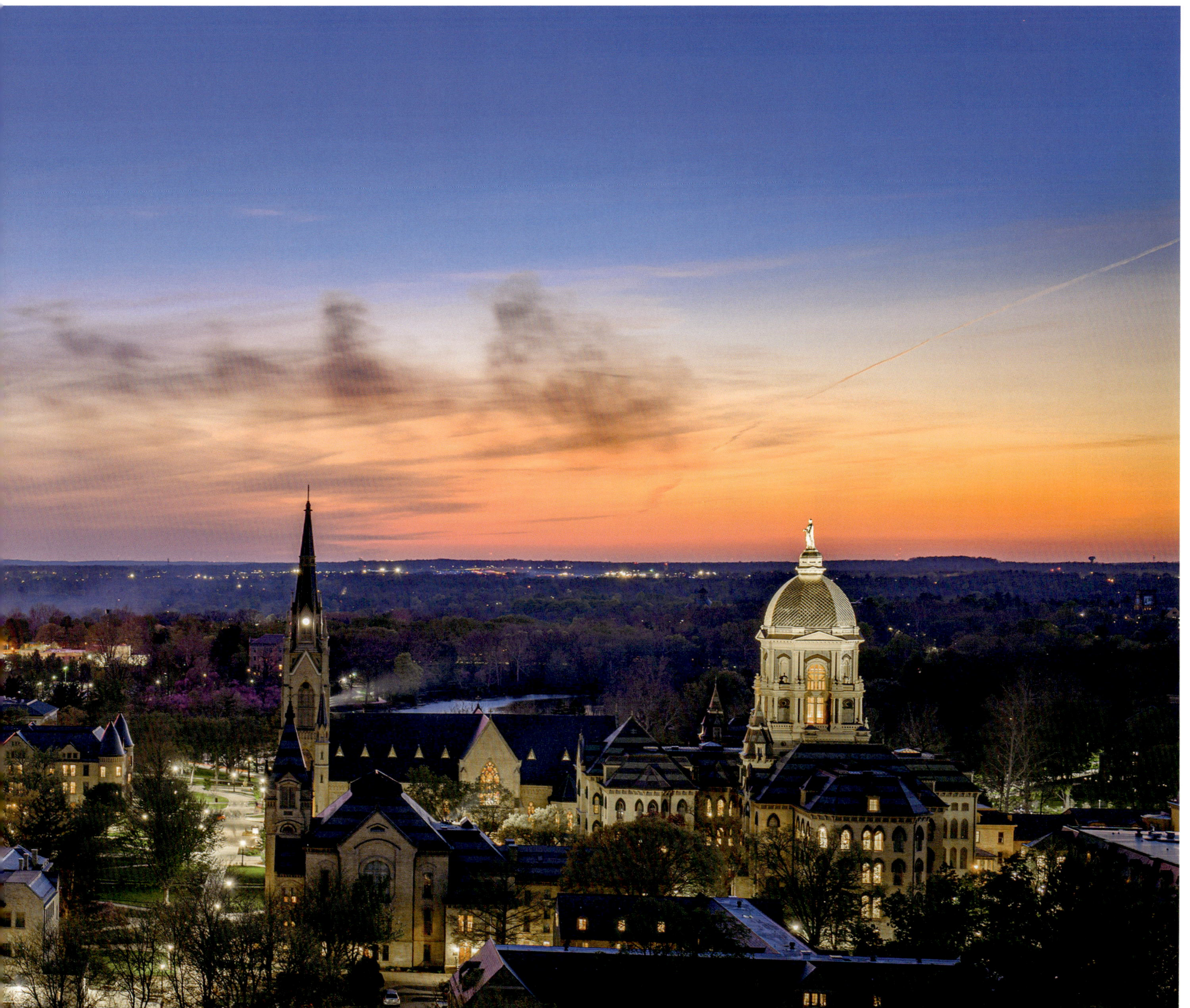

Fireworks over South Quad, taken from the Hesburgh Library penthouse balcony, Nikon Z9, 29mm, 6sec. f5.6, ISO64

I think I'm safe in saying all photographers like photographing reflections. We're drawn to them as if by gravity. My best guess is that if you've got all the elements of a good photo going—good light, good background, and good composition—a reflection makes it twice as nice. The opportunities for a good reflection photo are almost as fleeting as good snow photos. The lake isn't always calm enough and puddles drain or dry up quickly.

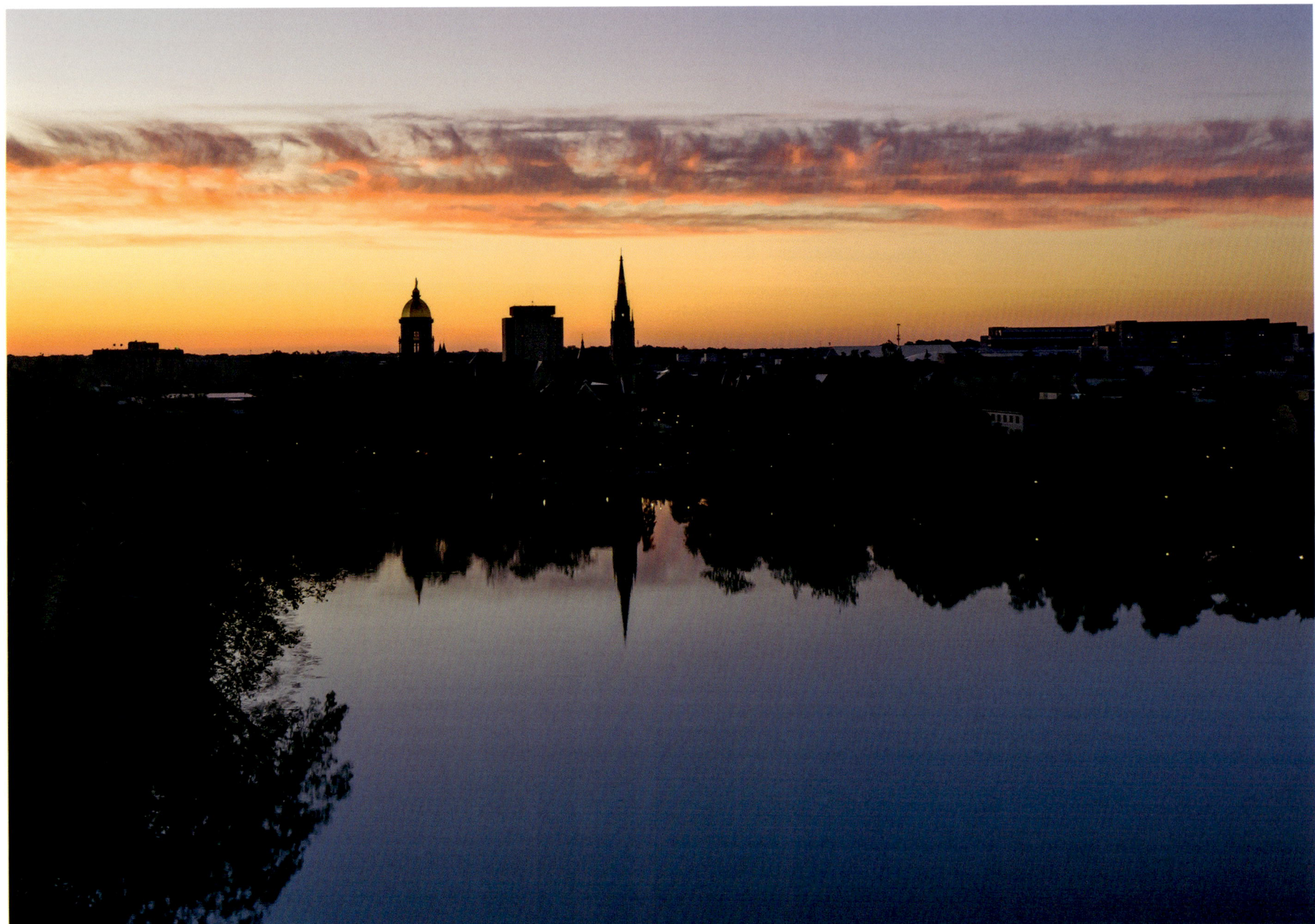

Aerial of Saint Mary's Lake, Mavic 2 Pro drone, 24mm equivalent, 1/50 f5, ISO100

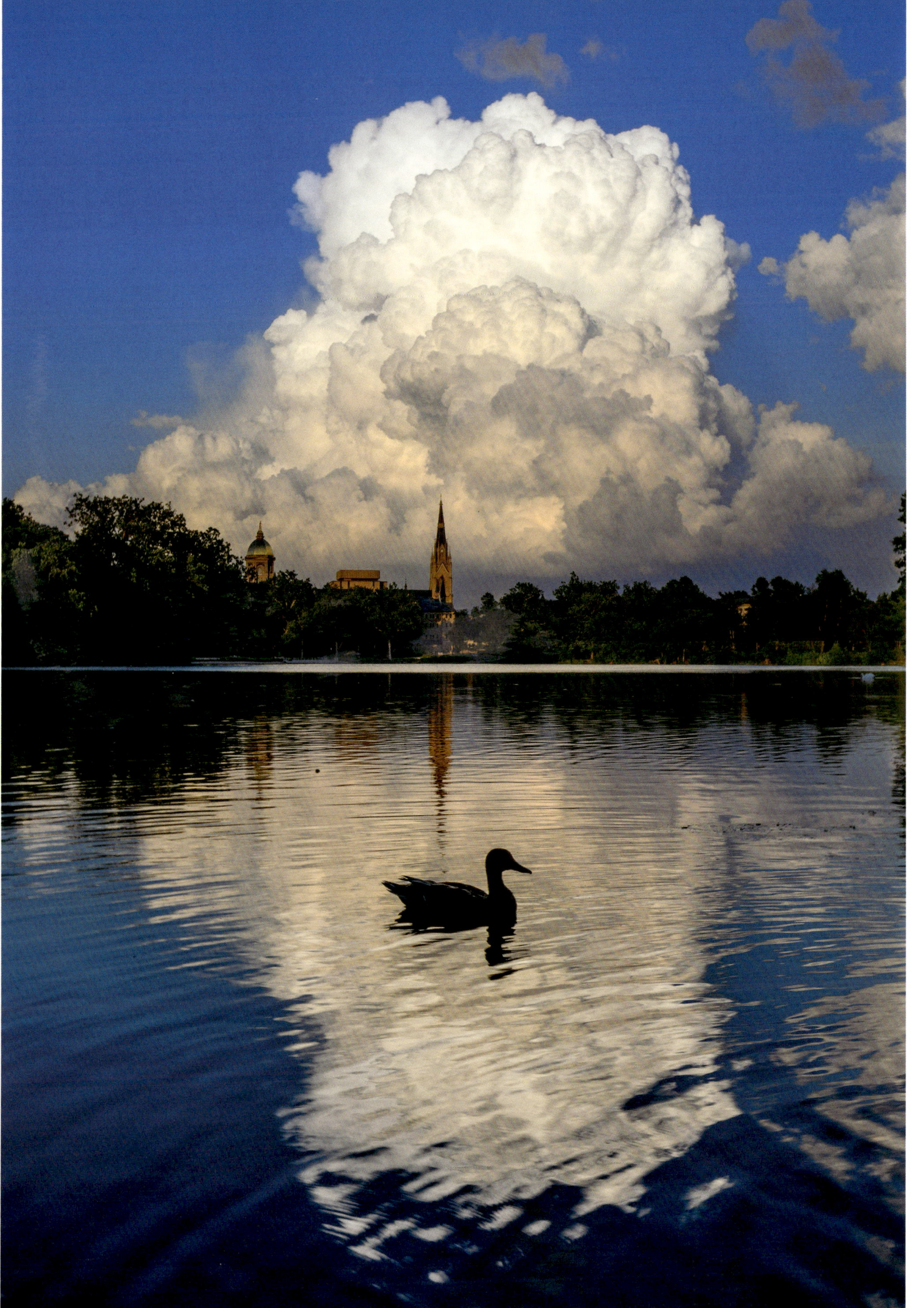

Storm clouds over Saint Mary's Lake,
Nikon Z8, 30mm, 1/30 f20, ISO64

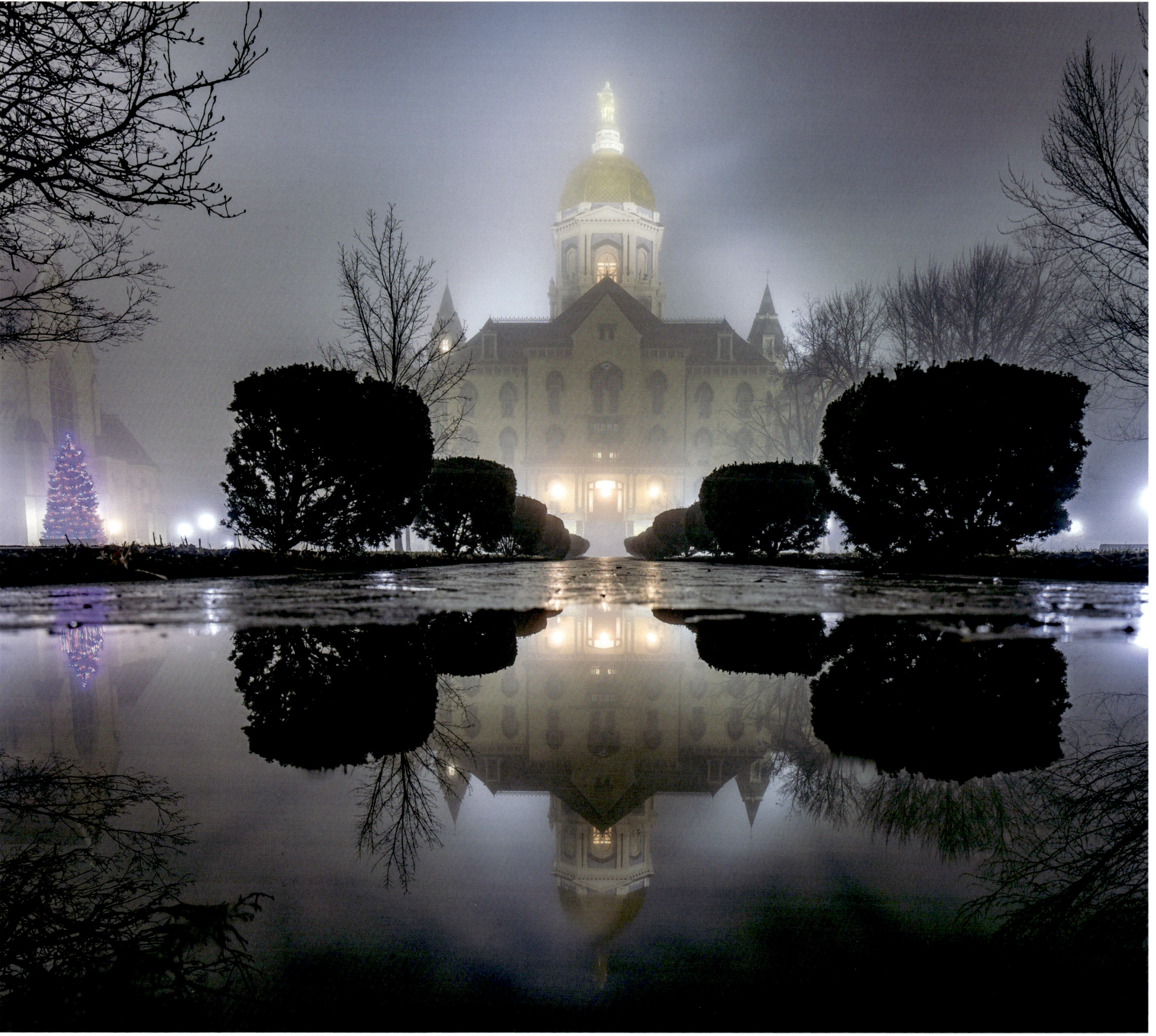

Main Building on a foggy fall evening, Nikon Z7, 24mm, 1/13 f5, ISO64

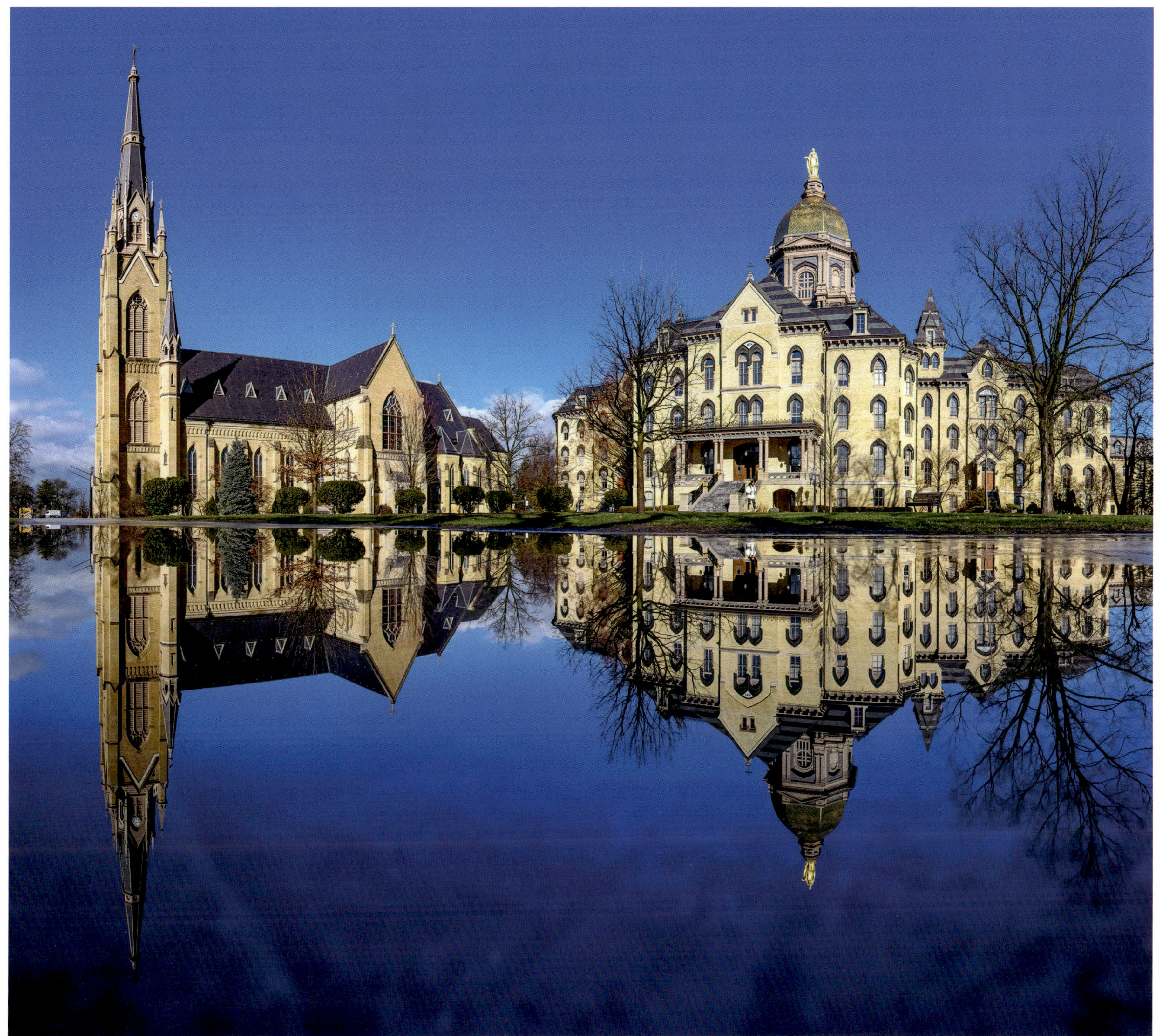

Main Quad after a sudden rain, Nikon Z7II, 14mm, 1/320 f6.3, ISO64

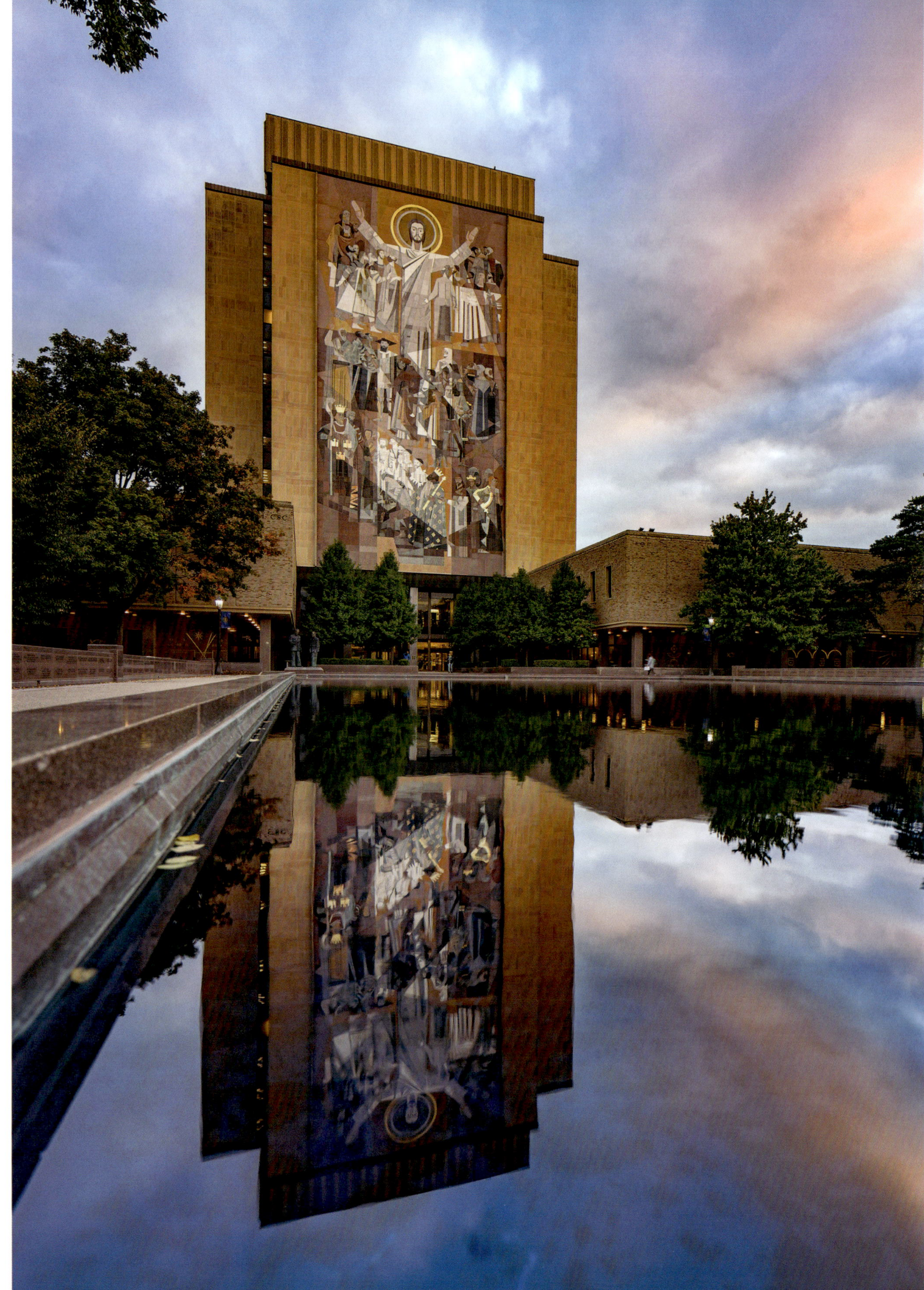

Hesburgh Library reflecting pool,
Nikon D850, 14mm, 1/30 f4.5, ISO64

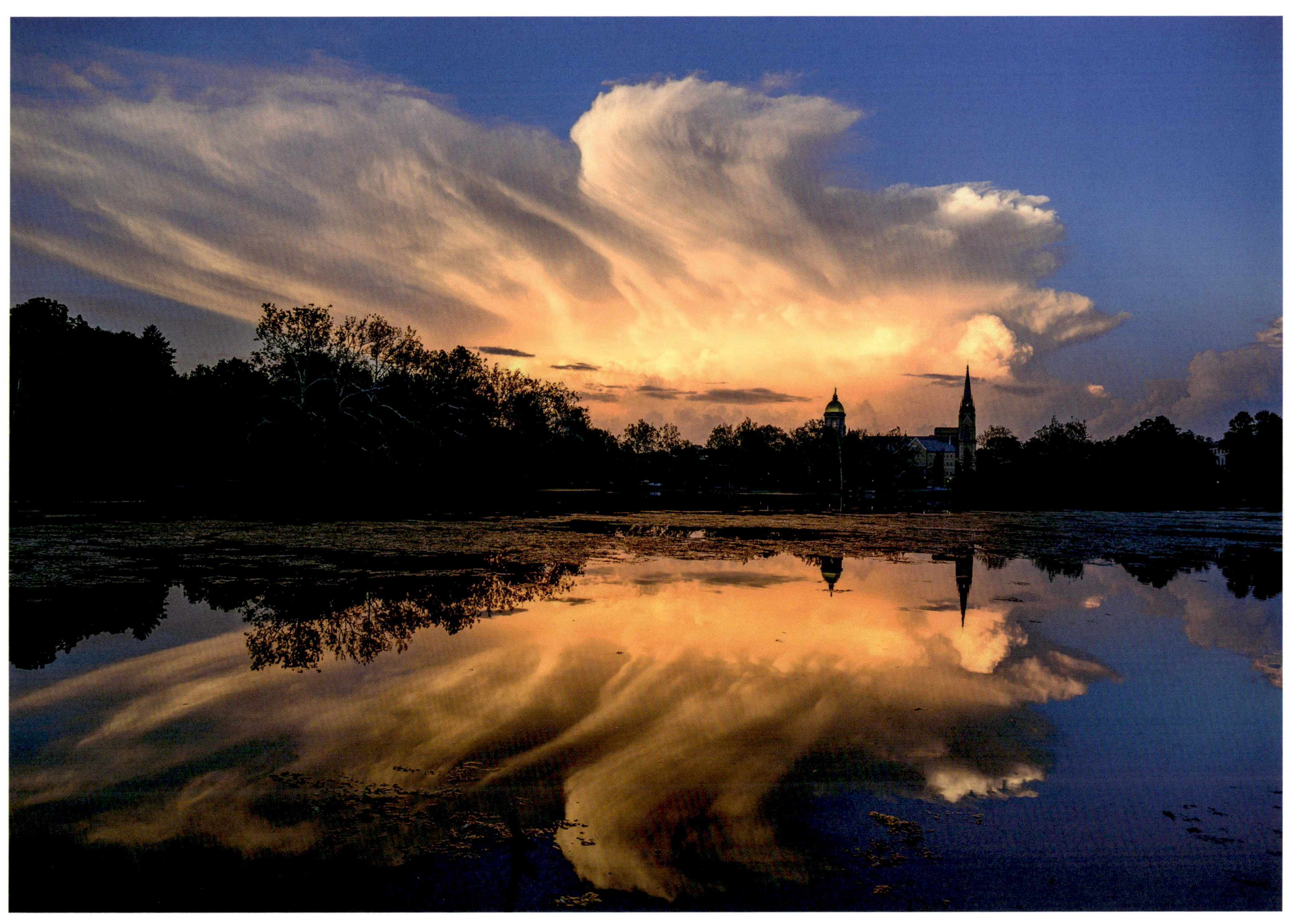

Saint Mary's Lake, Nikon Z6, 24mm, 1/160 f5.6, ISO100

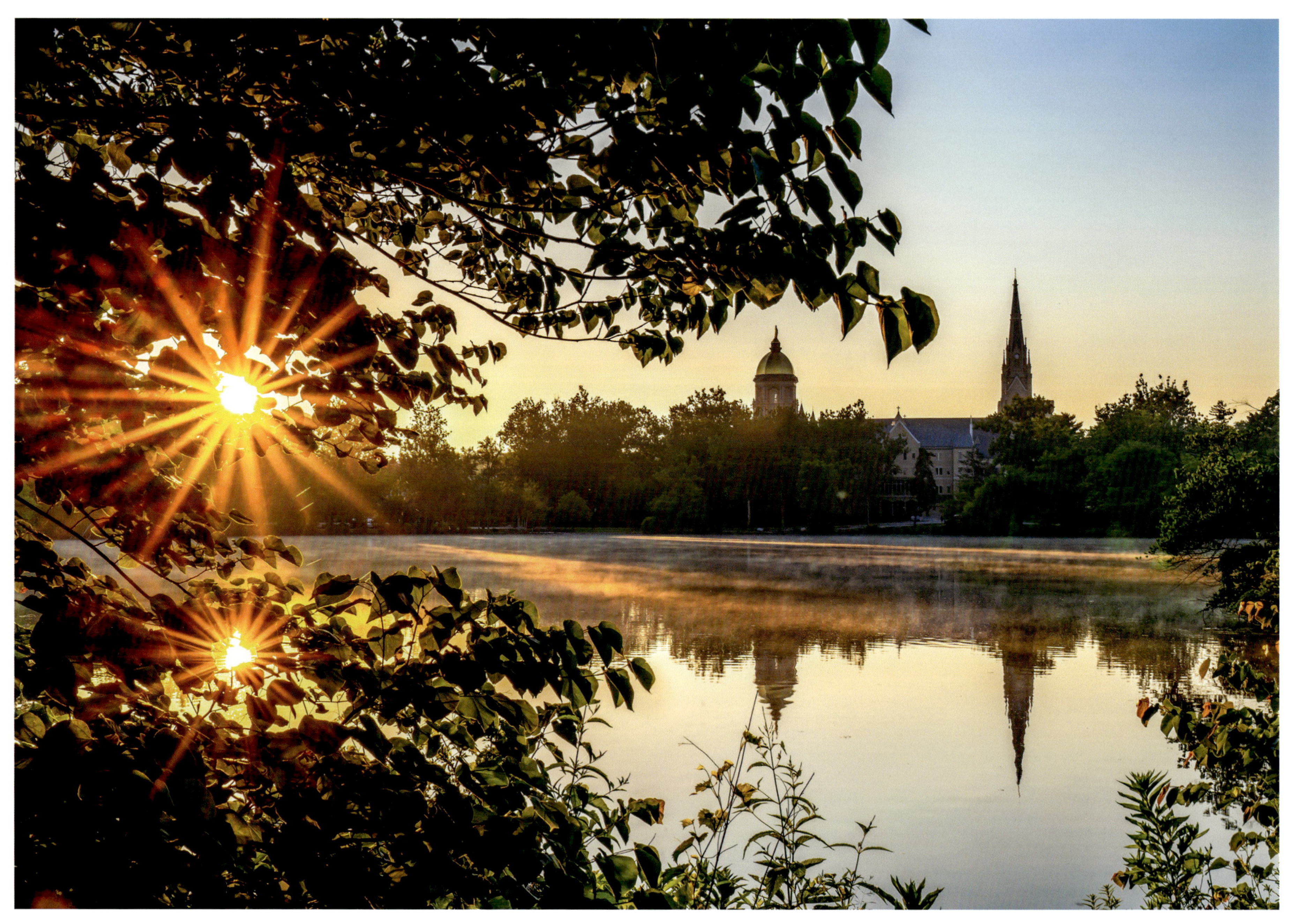

Saint Mary's Lake near Carroll Hall, Nikon Z6, 45mm, 1/30 f22, ISO100

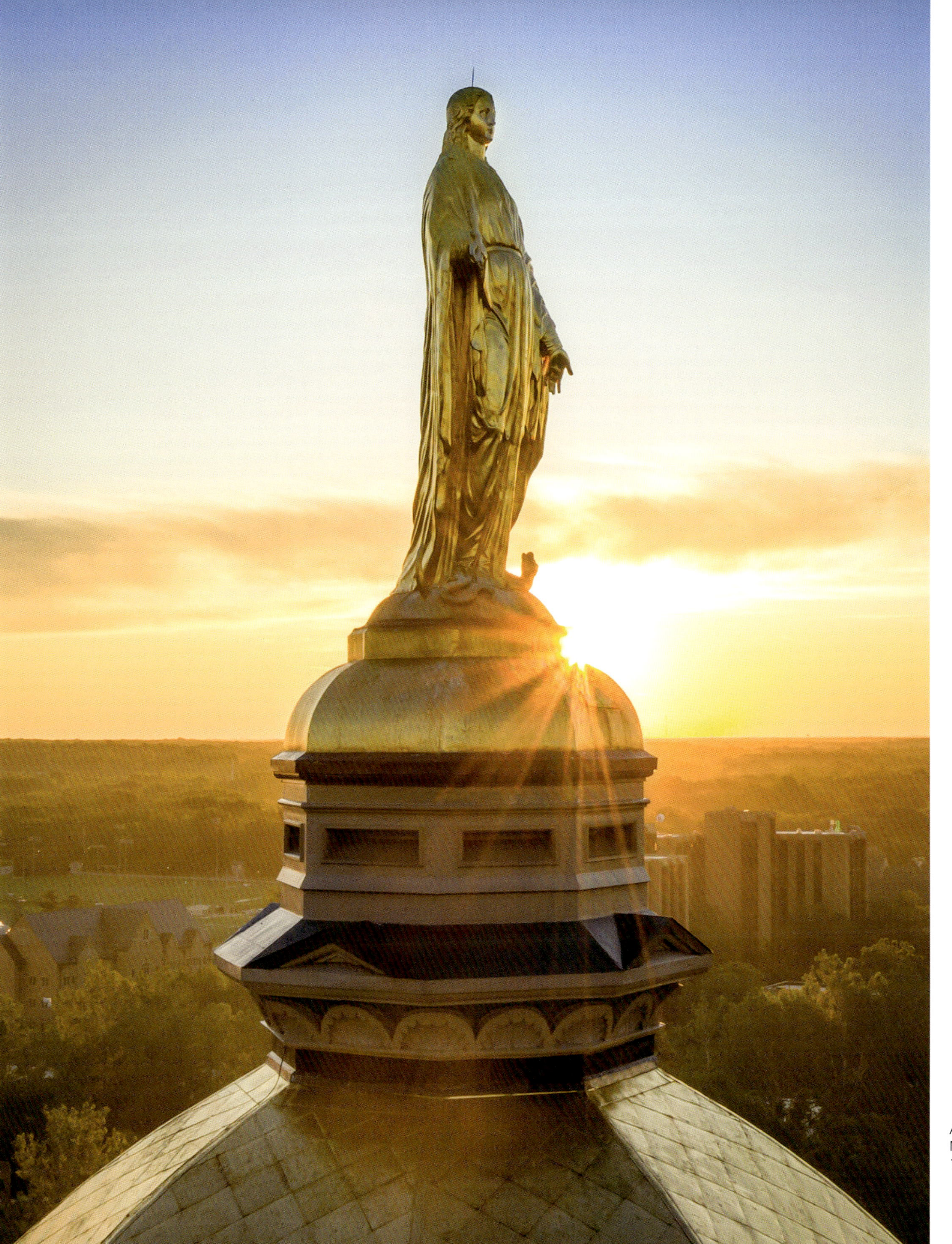

Aerial of Mary statue at sunrise,
Mavic 2 Pro drone, 24mm equivalent,
1/50 f11, ISO 100

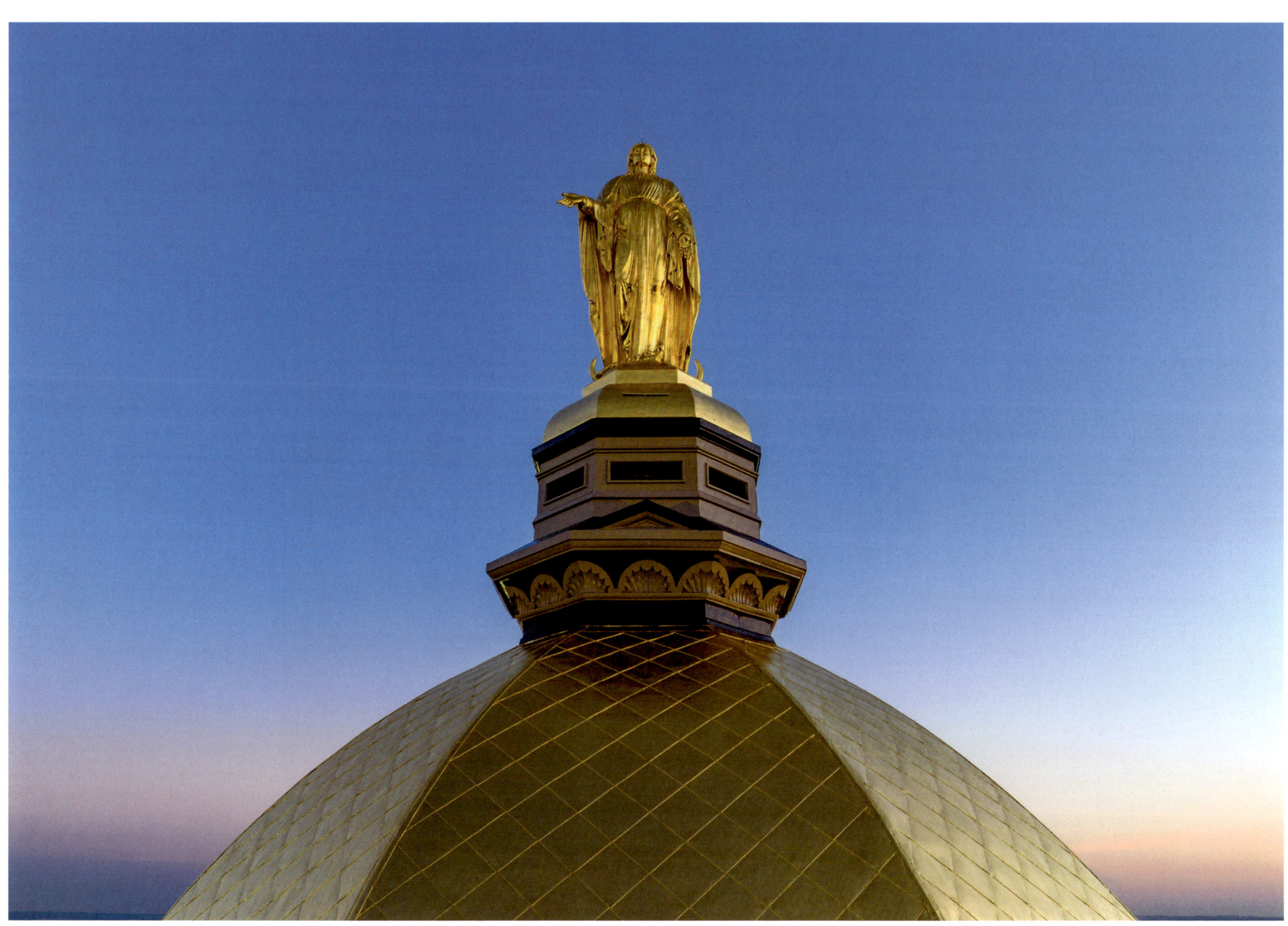

Aerial of Mary statue just after completion of 2023 regilding, Mavic 3 Pro drone, 24mm equivalent, 1/30 f4.5, ISO 100

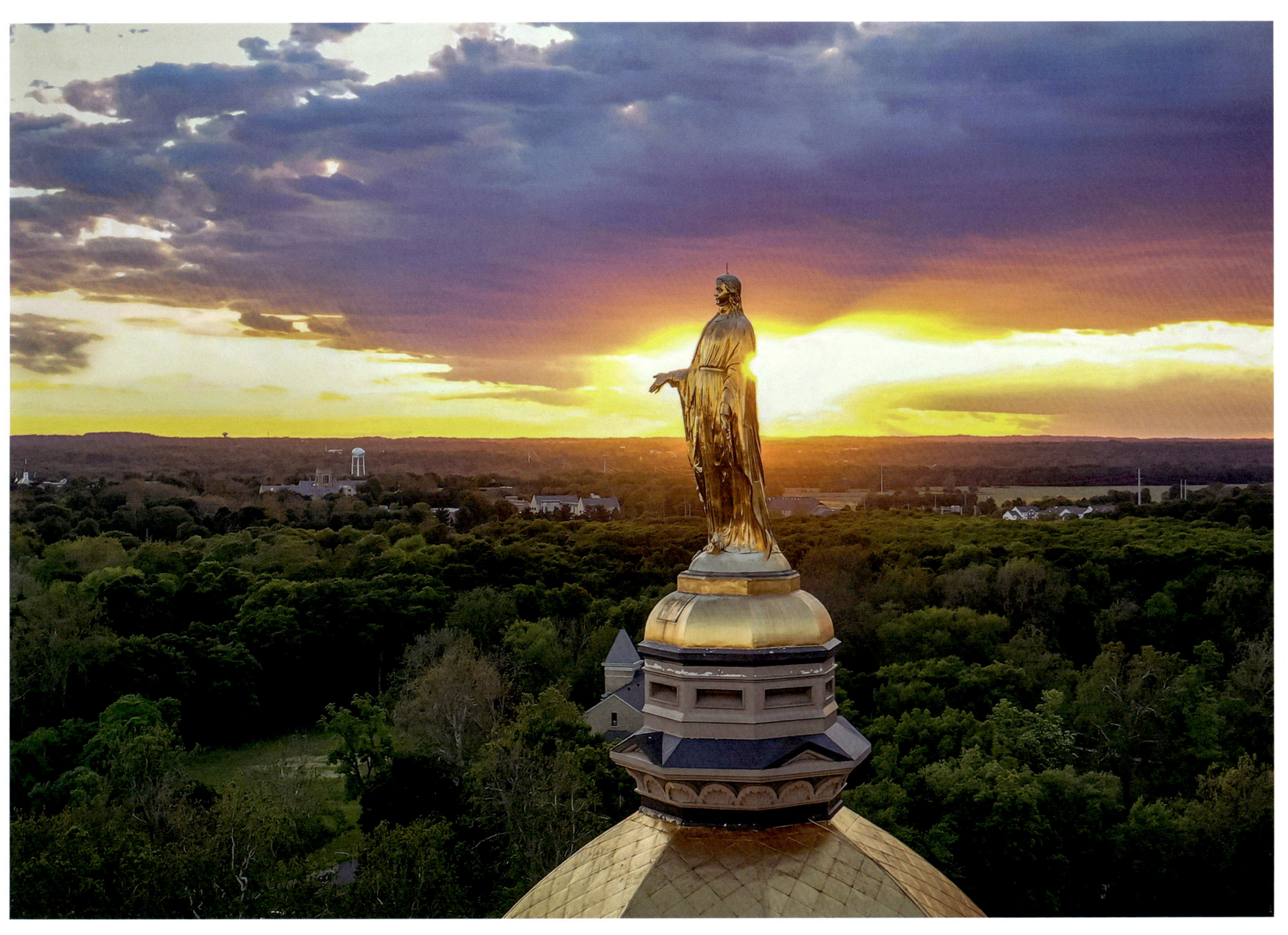

Sunset behind the Golden Dome, Mavic 2 Pro drone, 24mm equivalent, 1/60 f5.6, ISO100

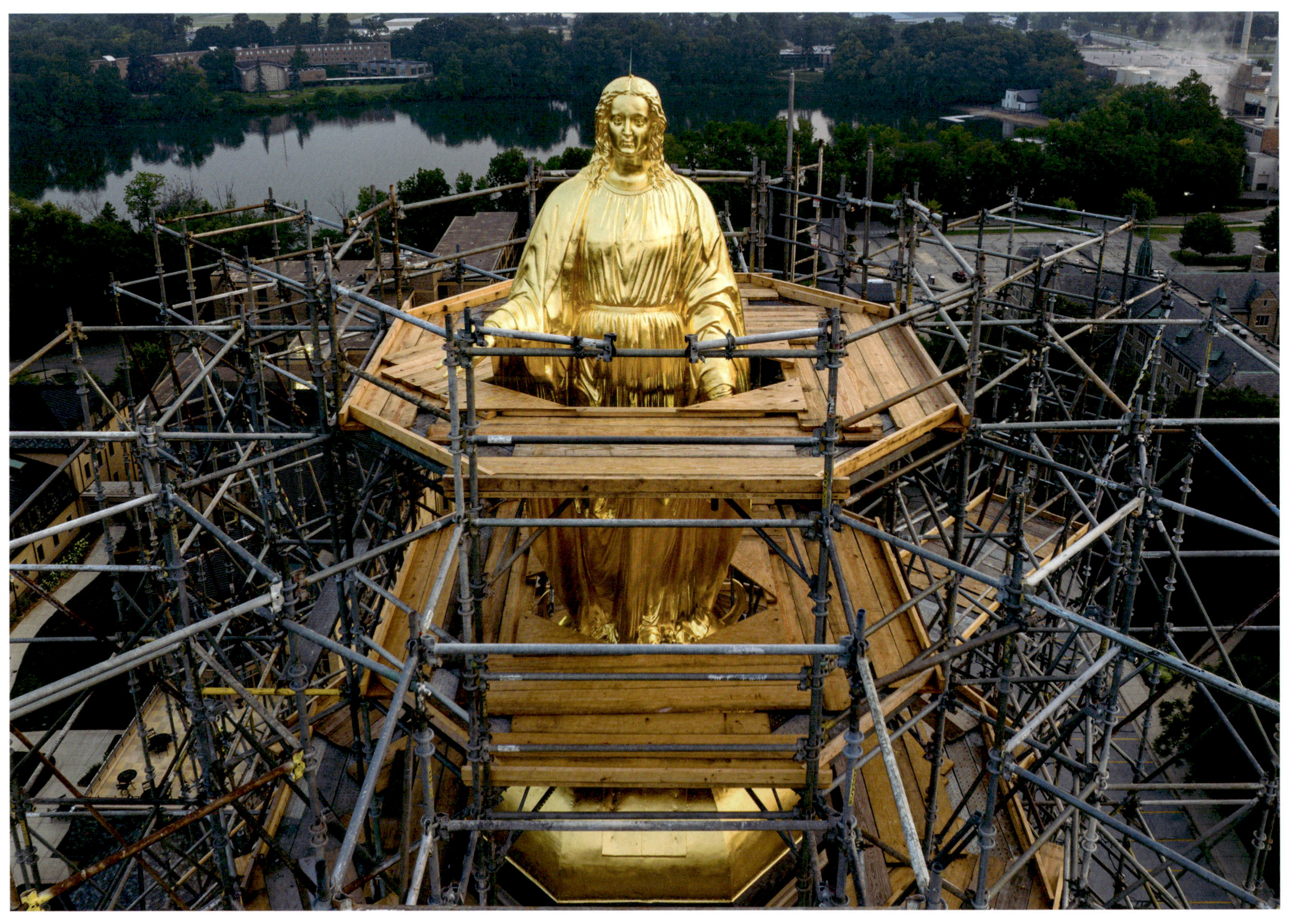

Mary statue surrounded by regilding scaffolding, Mavic 3 Pro drone, 24mm equivalent, 1/60 f5.6, ISO 100

The 2023 regilding was my second chance at seeing this process, so I had a good idea of what to expect. I thought the scaffolding was an engineering work of art—it securely surrounded but never touched the Dome, and I enjoyed finding unique views that showed it off. In 2023 I had a new tool that I didn't have in 2005—a drone. More on that later.

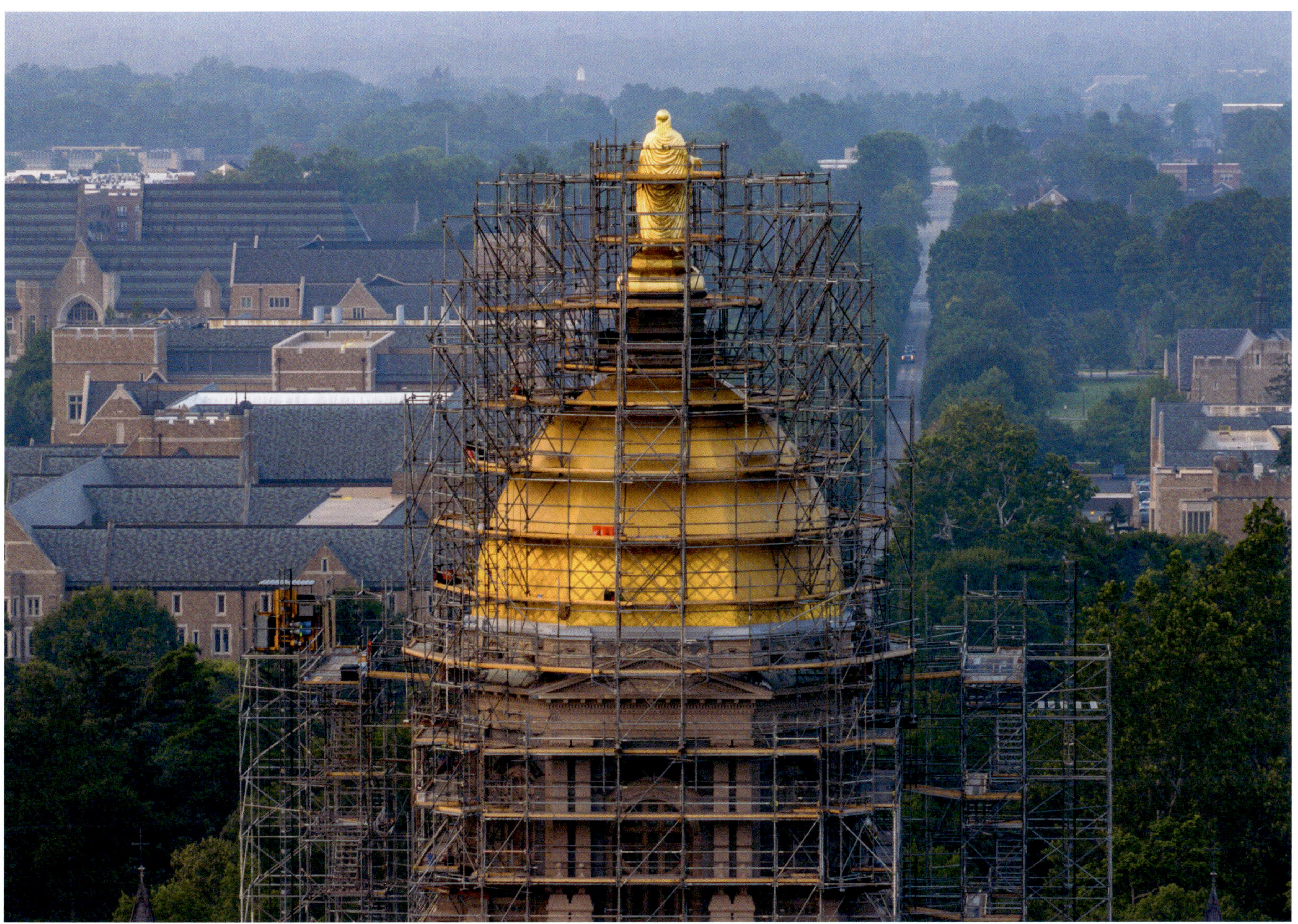

Aerial of regilding scaffolding looking south down Notre Dame Avenue, Mavic 3 Pro drone, 70mm equivalent, 1/100 f3.4, ISO 100

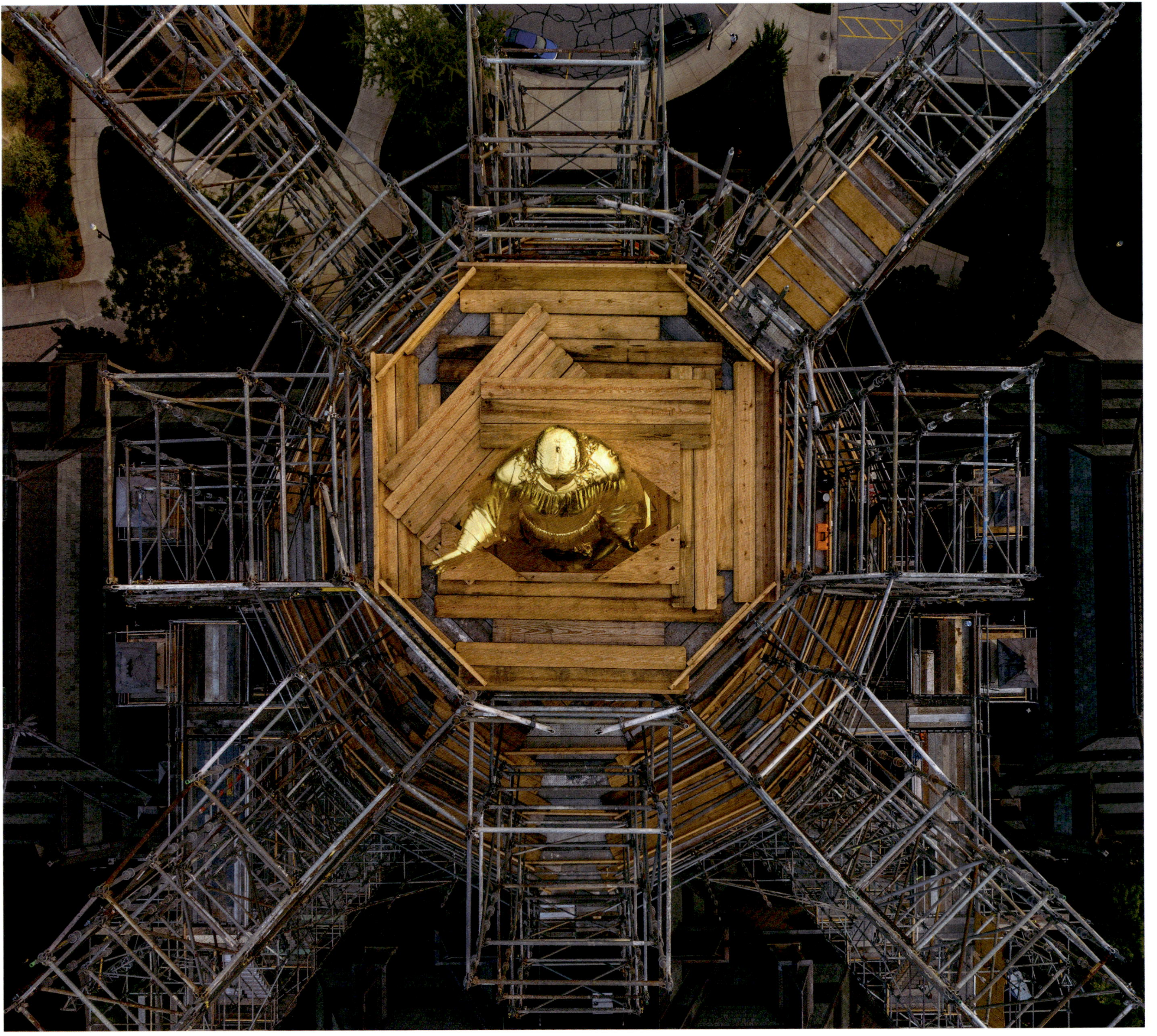

Top-down view of regilding, Mavic 3 Pro drone, 24mm equivalent, 1/100 f5.6, ISO 100

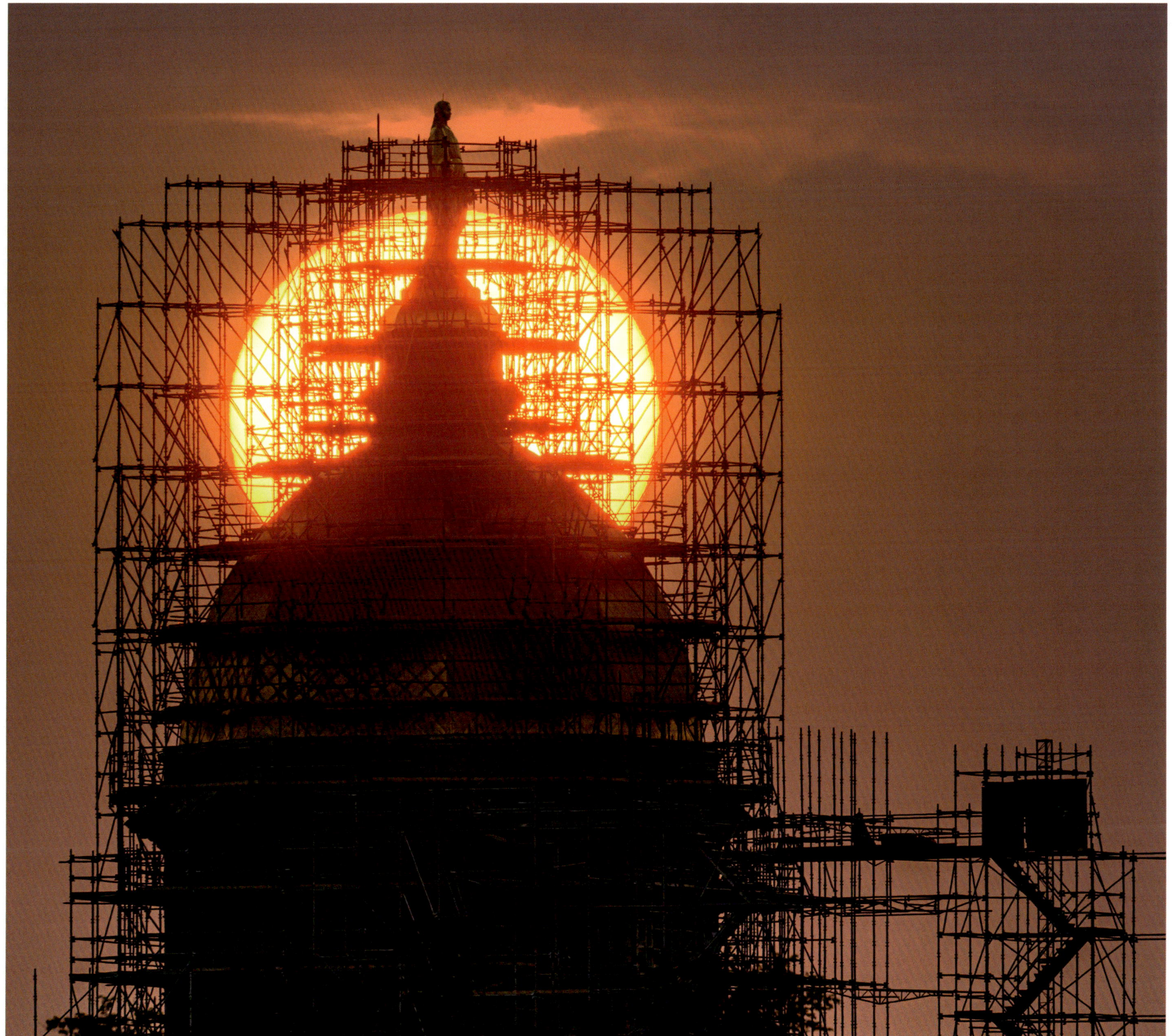
Main Building scaffolding seen from Holy Cross College, Nikon Z9, 850mm, 1/80 f16, ISO250

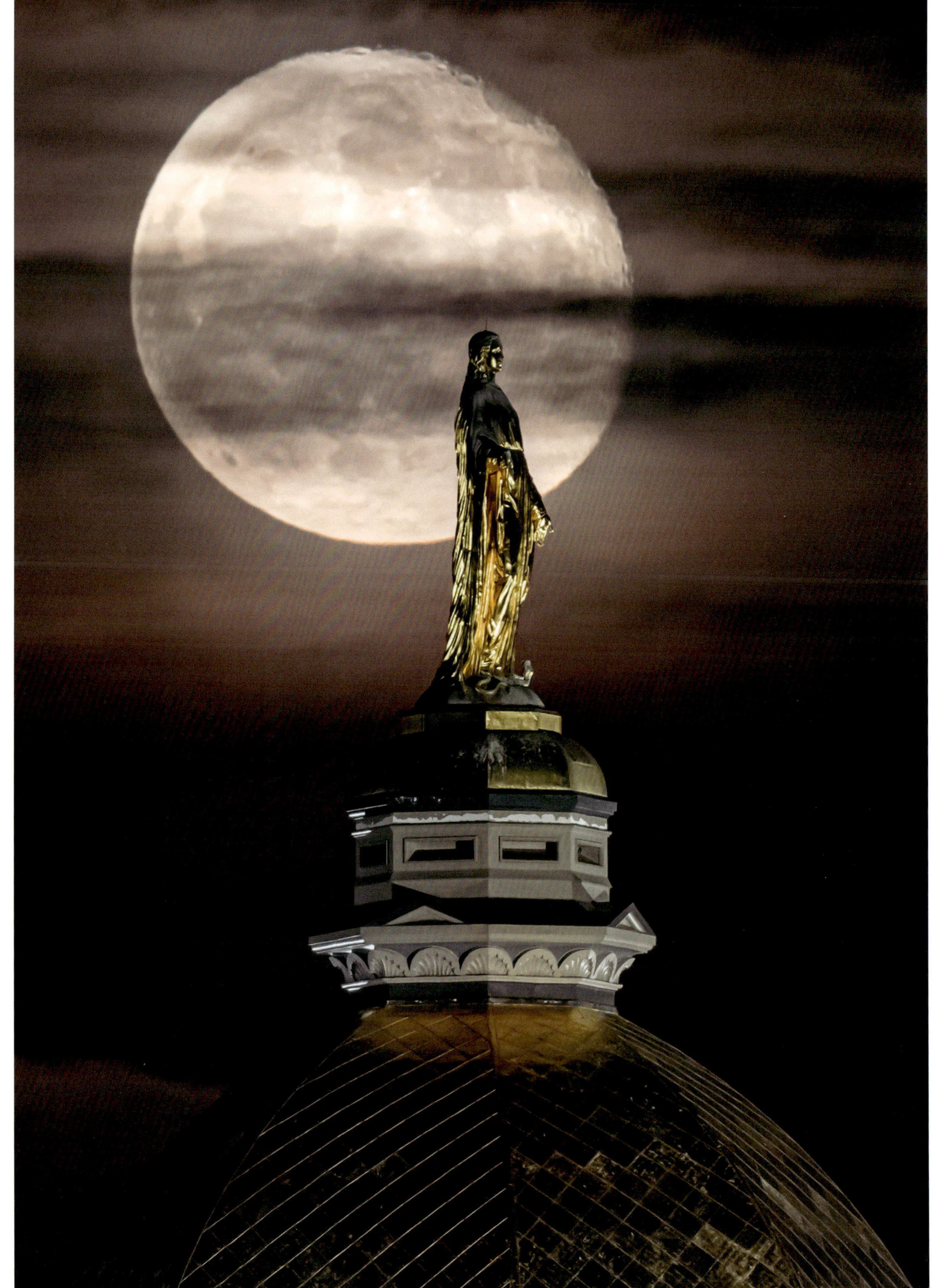

Moonrise from Dorr Road,
Nikon Z7, 600mm, 1/3 f16, ISO250

There are any number of smartphone apps that will give you the exact location of the moon at any given time. But that doesn't always mean "The Magic" will be there. Most people don't realize how bright the moon is. It reflects the sun, after all! And like the sun, the moon is best when it's rising and setting. An eclipse every now and then helps, too!

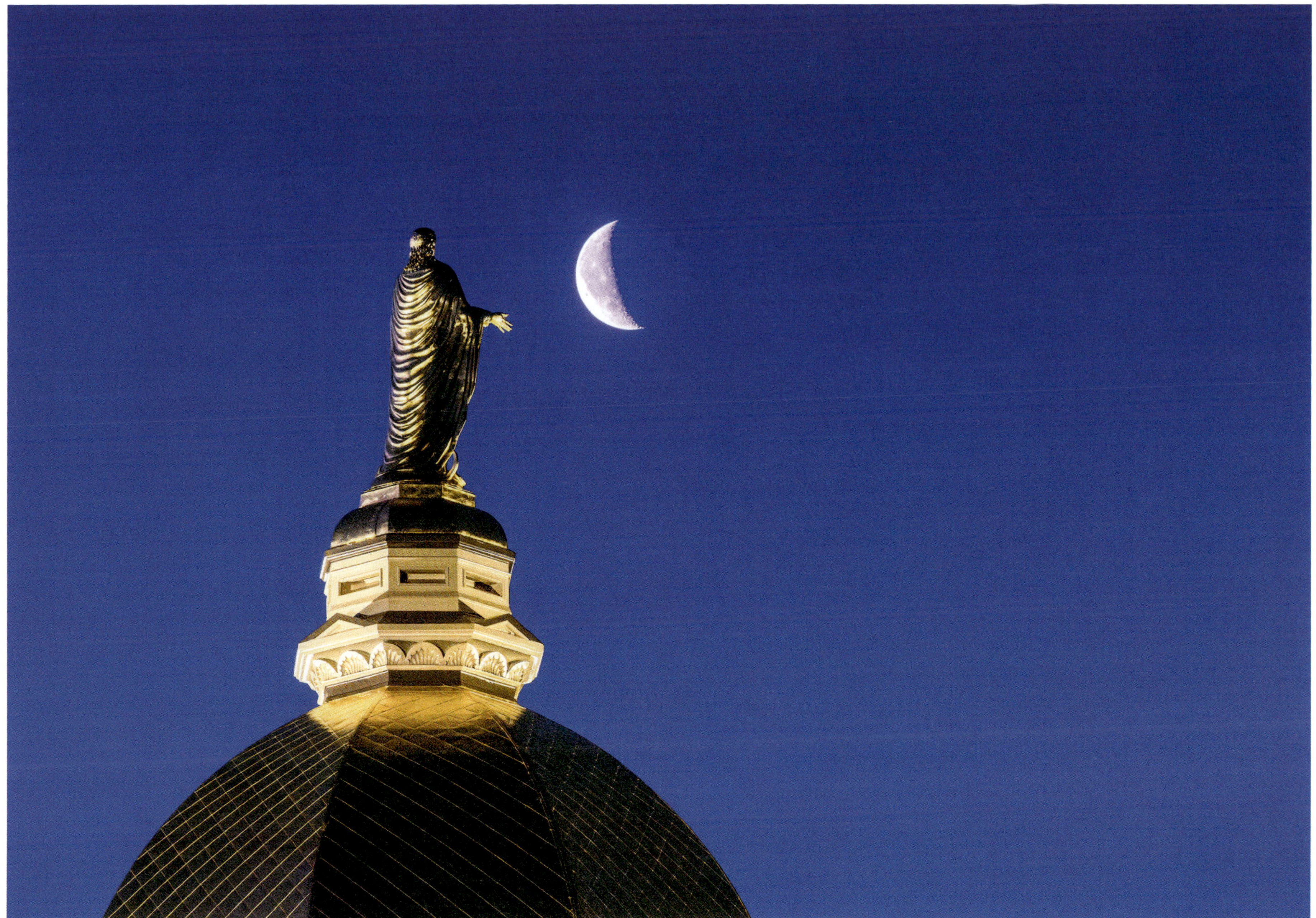

Moon over the Dome, Nikon Z9, 200mm, 1/25 f10, ISO250

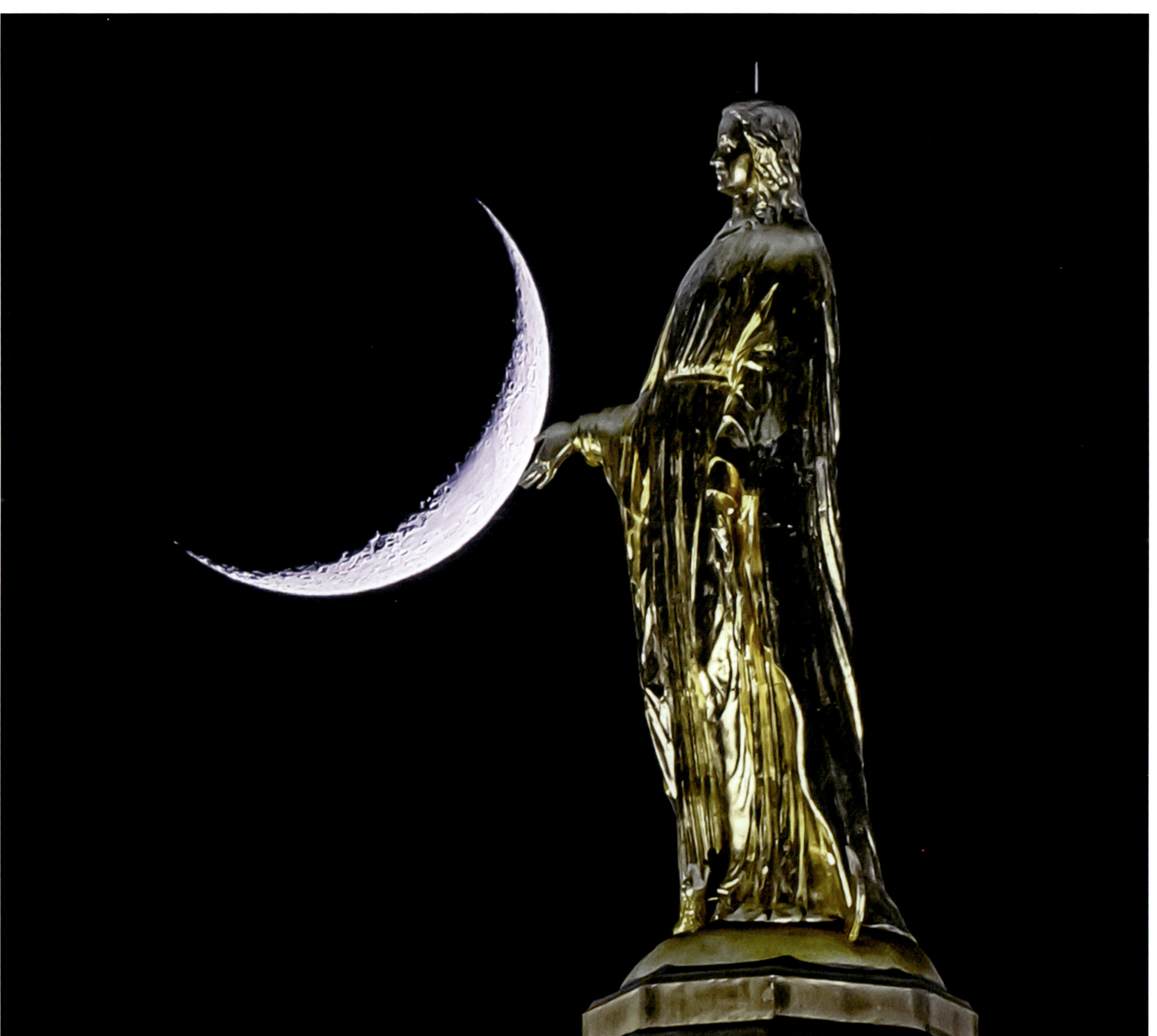

Dome and crescent moon from North Quad, Nikon Z7, 300mm, 1/20 f10, ISO400

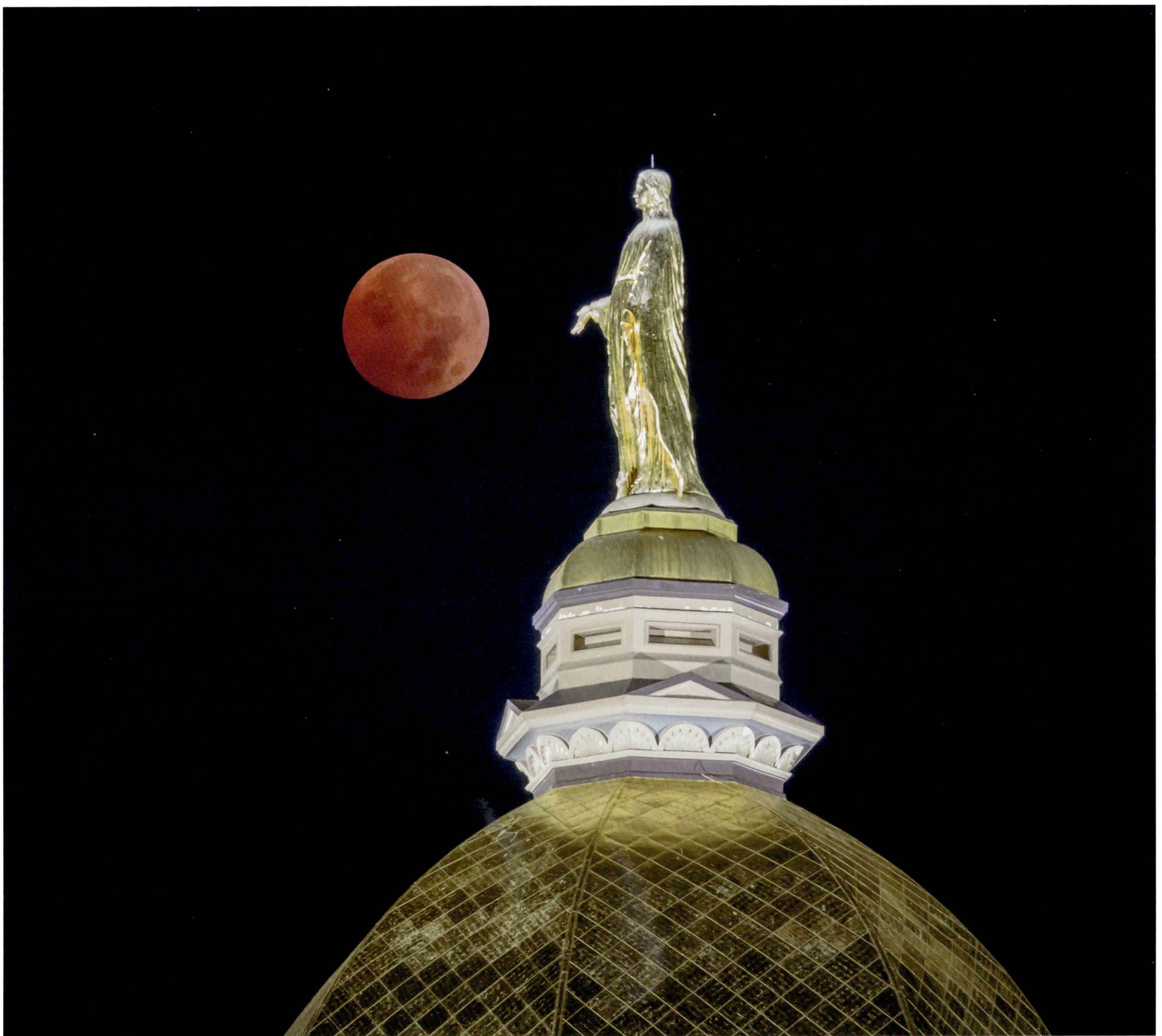

"Blood Moon" lunar eclipse, Nikon Z7II, 300mm, 1/4 f8, ISO3200

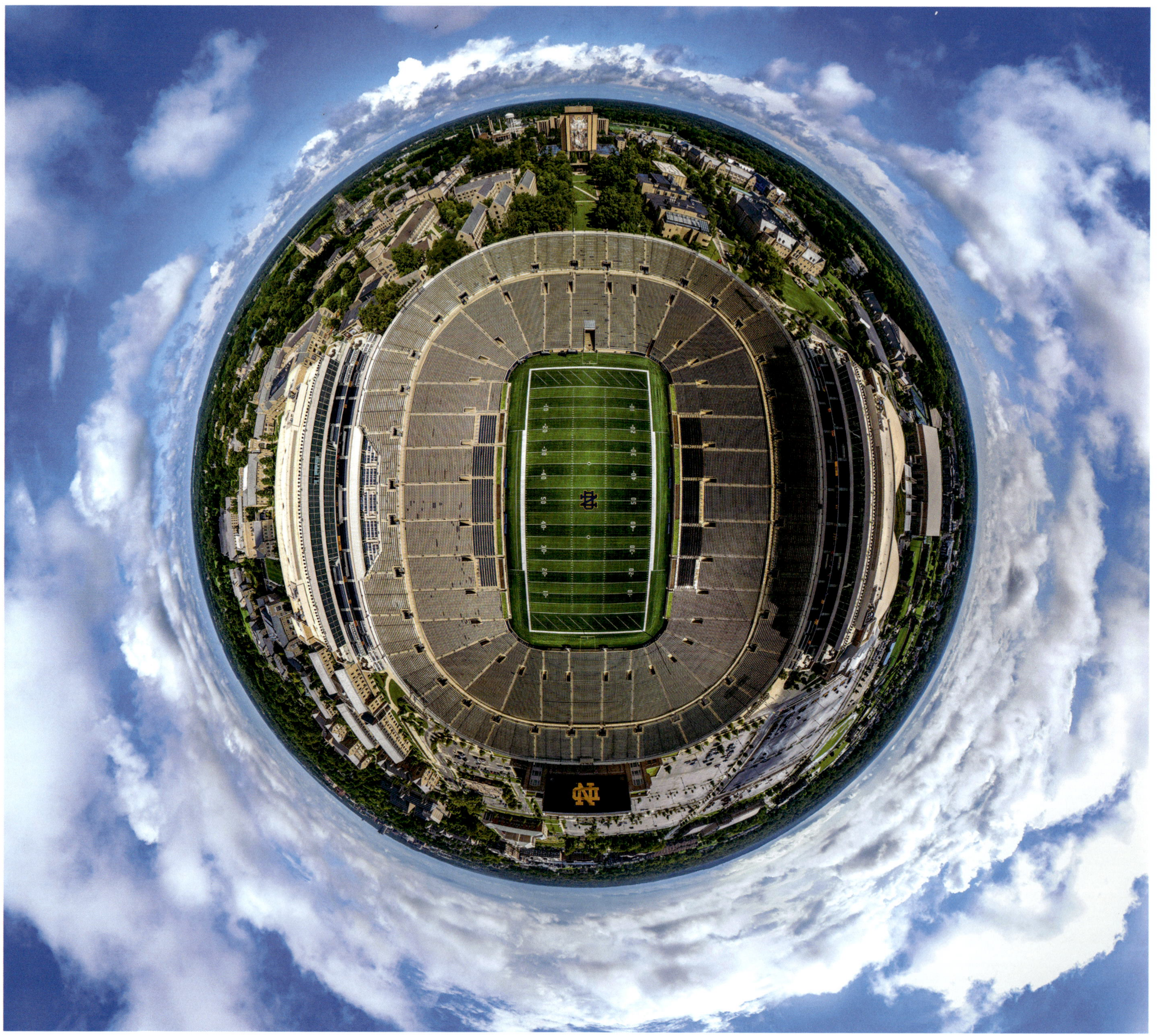

"Tiny planet" style image over Notre Dame Stadium, Mavic 3 Pro drone, 24mm equivalent, multiple image stitch

The aerial photos on this page and the previous page are stitched panoramas made with a drone. They are a style commonly referred to as a "tiny planet" fisheye. A lot of Notre Dame Football fans feel like the world metaphorically revolves around Notre Dame Stadium so why not make that a photo? If you look closely at the stadium image you can see the Dome covered in scaffolding for its regilding. When the stadium image worked so well I instantly knew I wanted to make a similar photo of the main building with a fresh application of gold leaf. The image on the next page is made with a circular fisheye lens and the camera pointed straight up. The lens has just over a 180-degree field of view, meaning it sees behind itself just a little bit. The trickiest part of that photo was making sure I didn't get myself in the frame. And on one dewy morning, nature provided a fisheye lens!

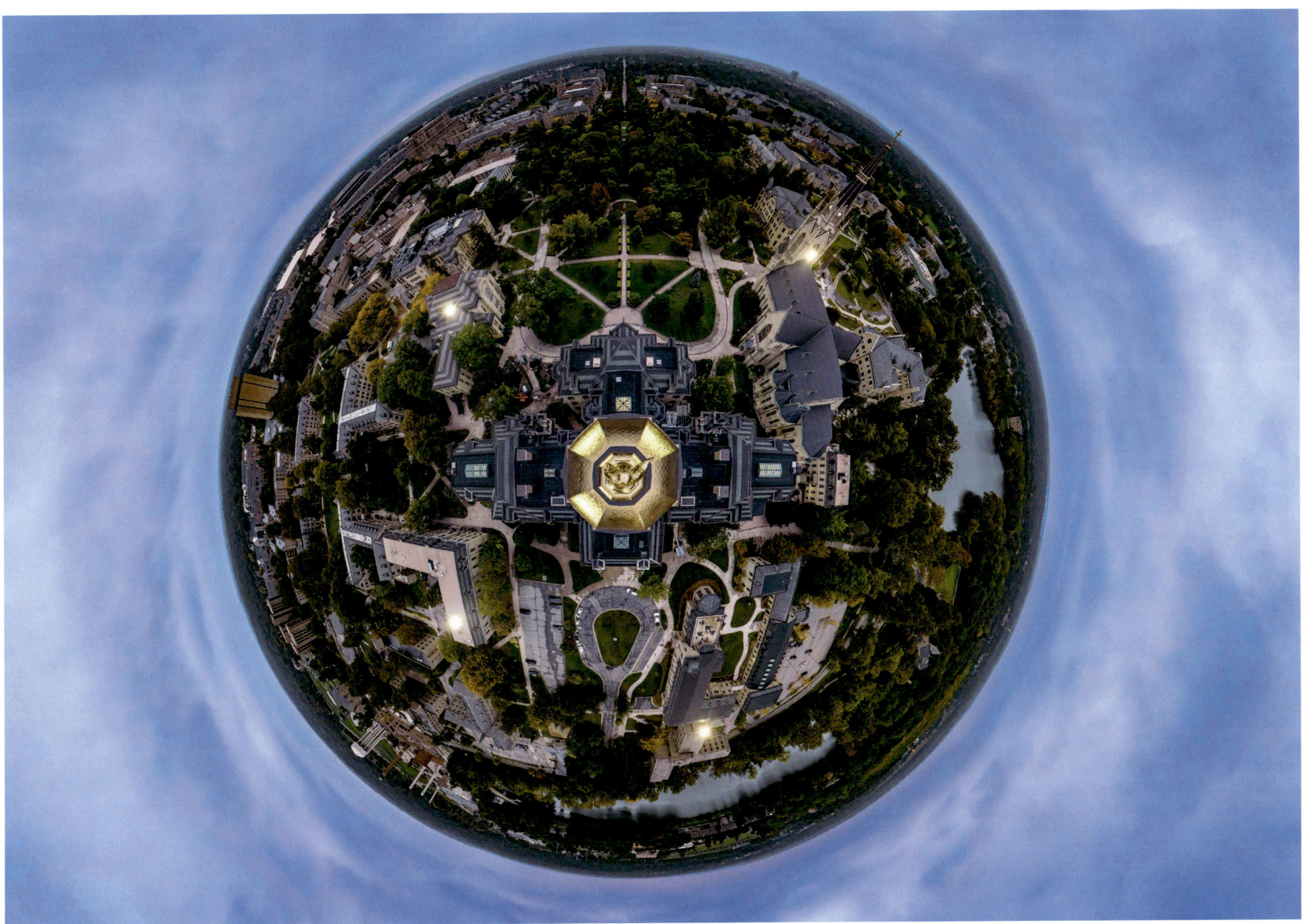

"Tiny planet" style image over Main Building, Mavic 3 Pro drone, 24mm equivalent, multiple image stitch

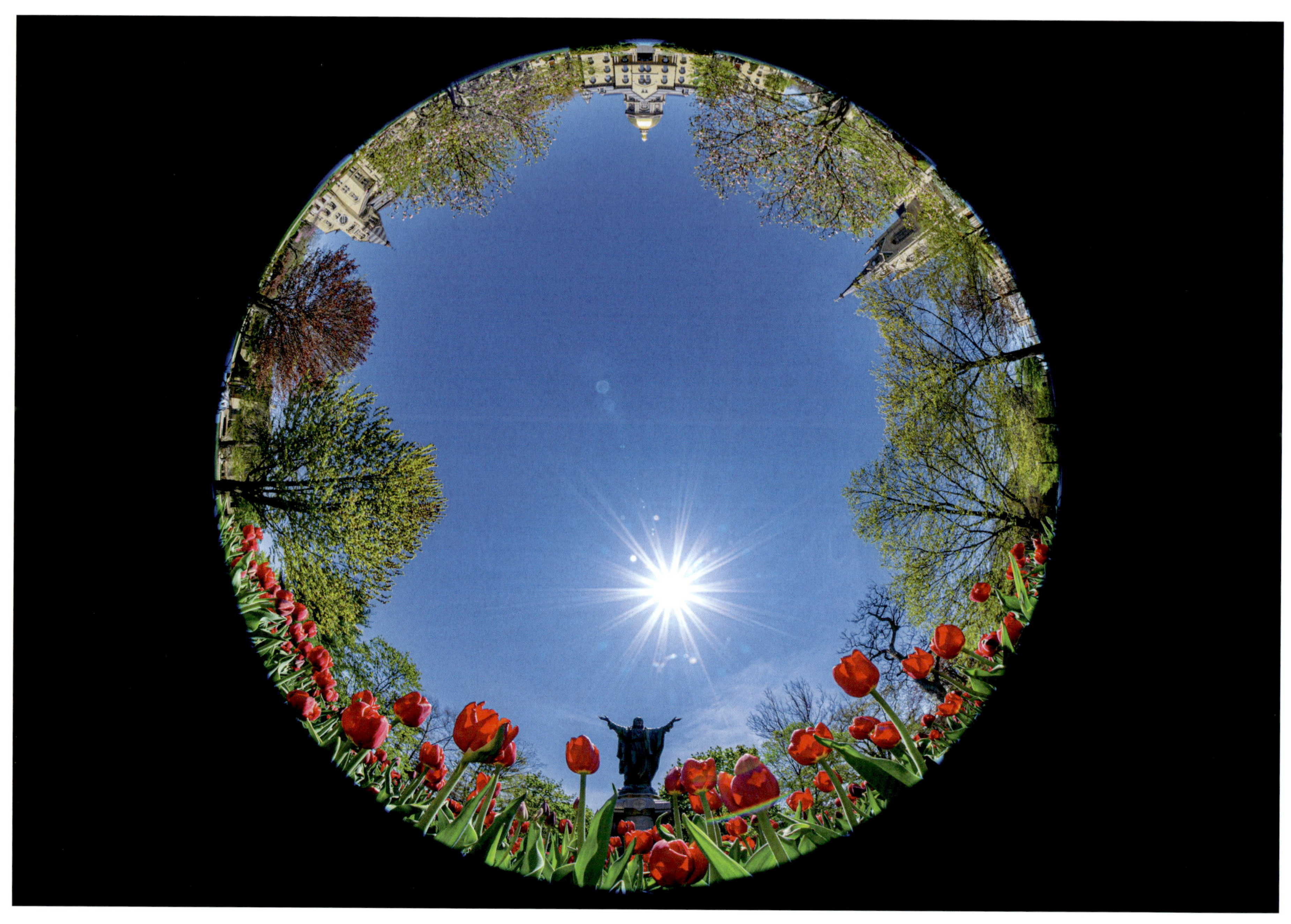

Looking up from the flowers around the Main Quad Jesus statue, Nikon Z7, 8mm circular fisheye, 1/50 f20, ISO100

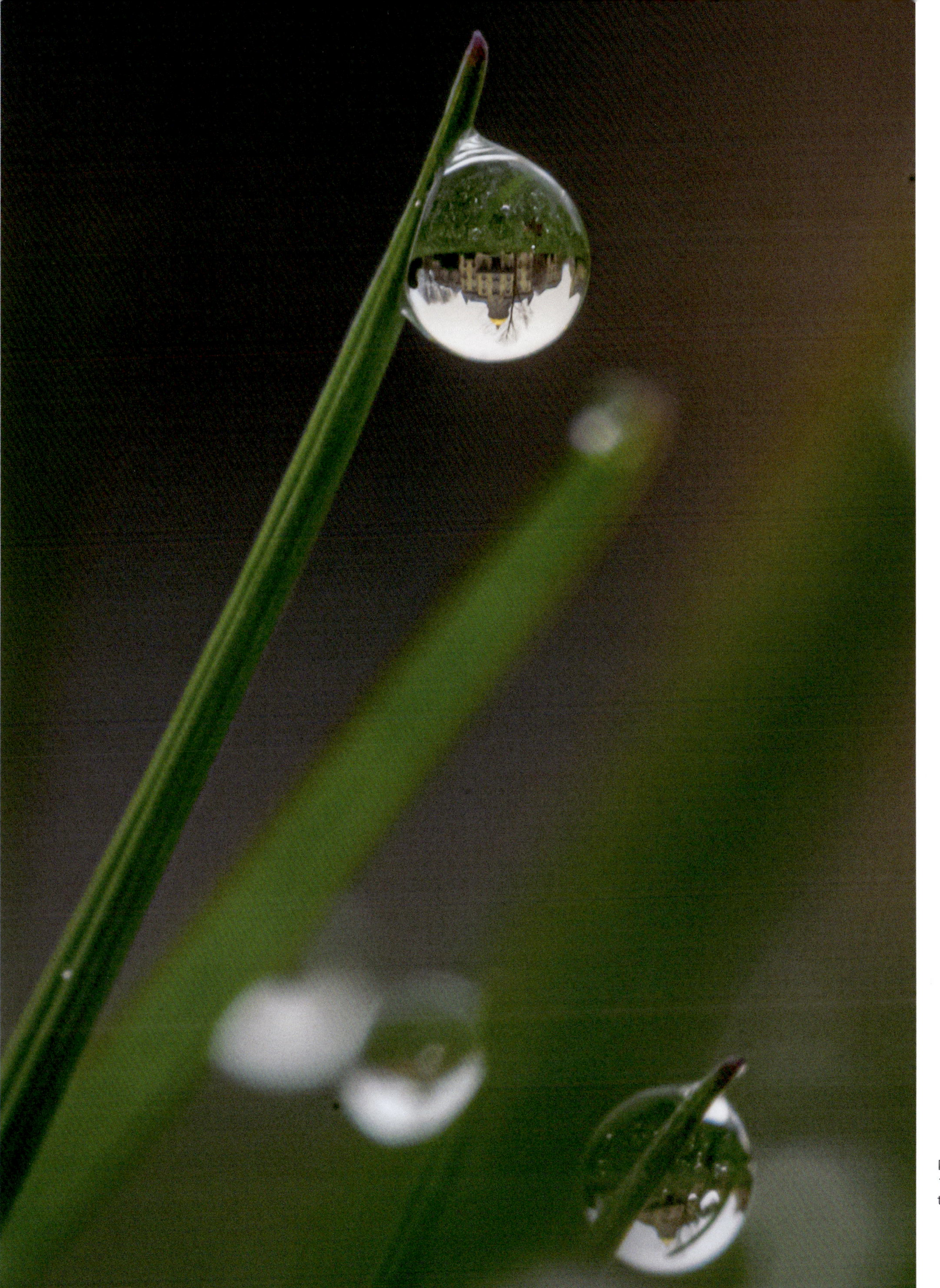

Dewy grass on Main Quad, Nikon Z7,
105mm macro with extension
tube, 1/160 f22, ISO1600

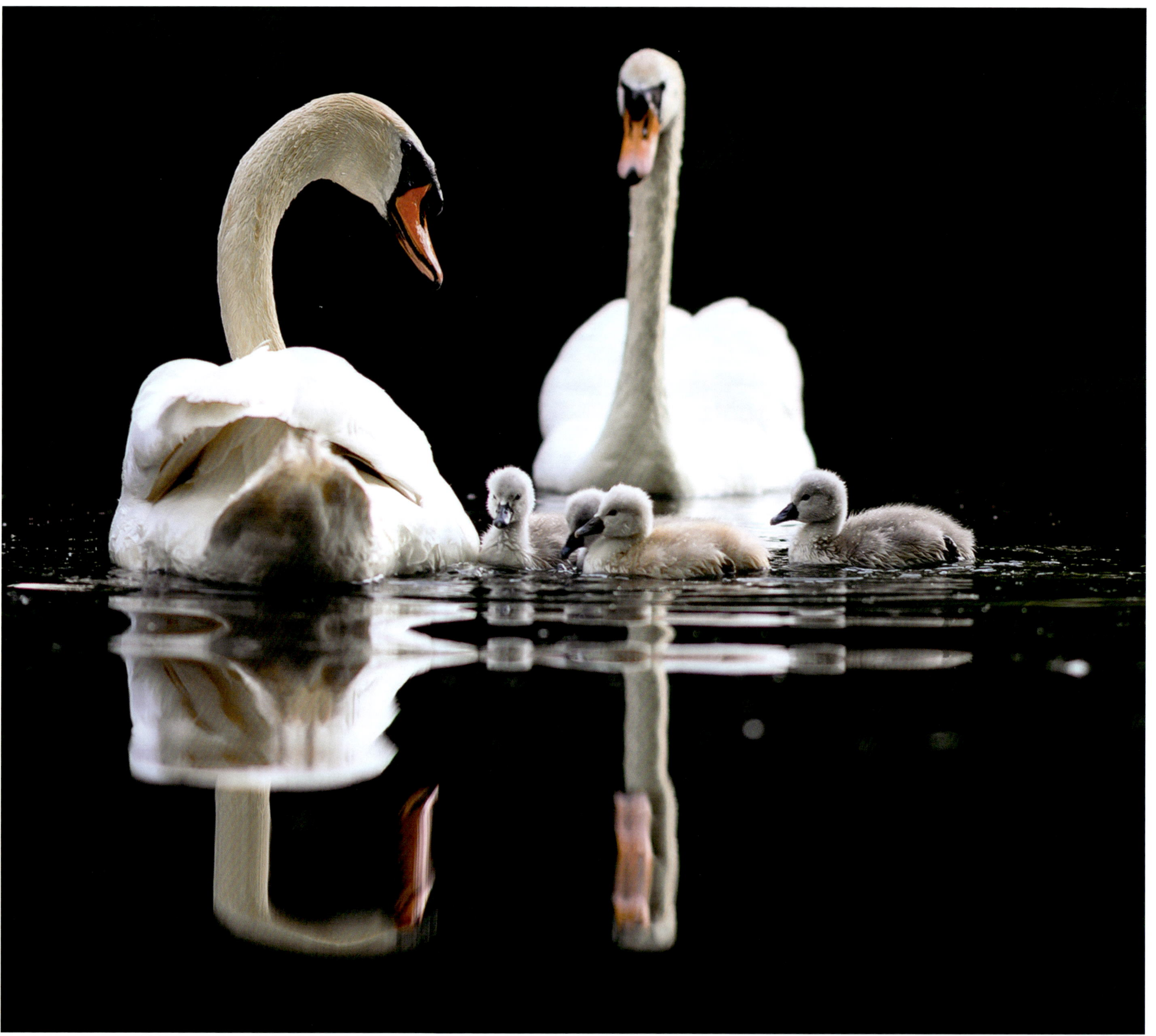

Swans on Saint Mary's Lake, Nikon D850, 300mm, 1/400 f4, ISO125

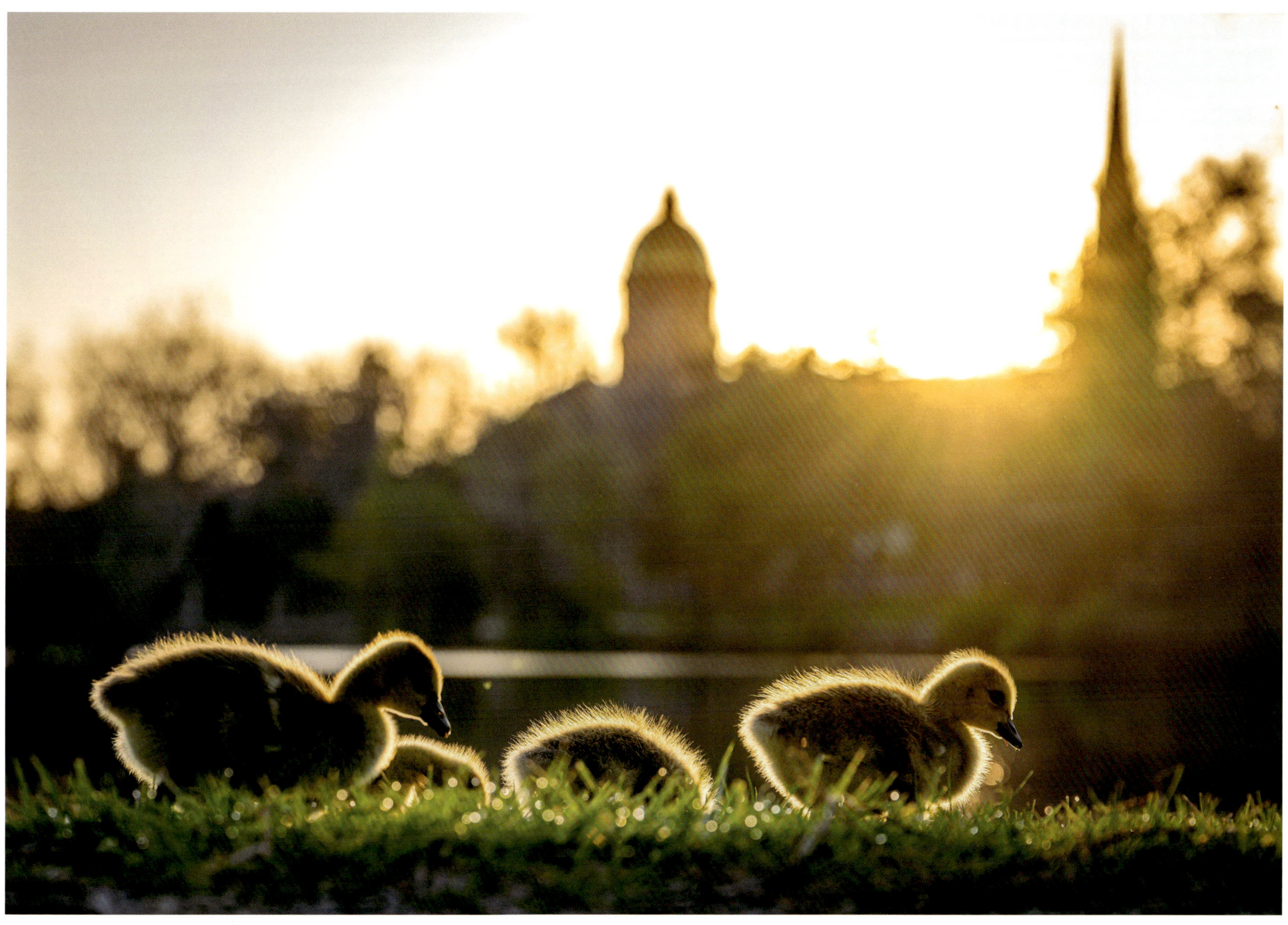

Goslings near Saint Mary's Lake, Nikon Z7, 70mm, 1/250 f4, ISO64

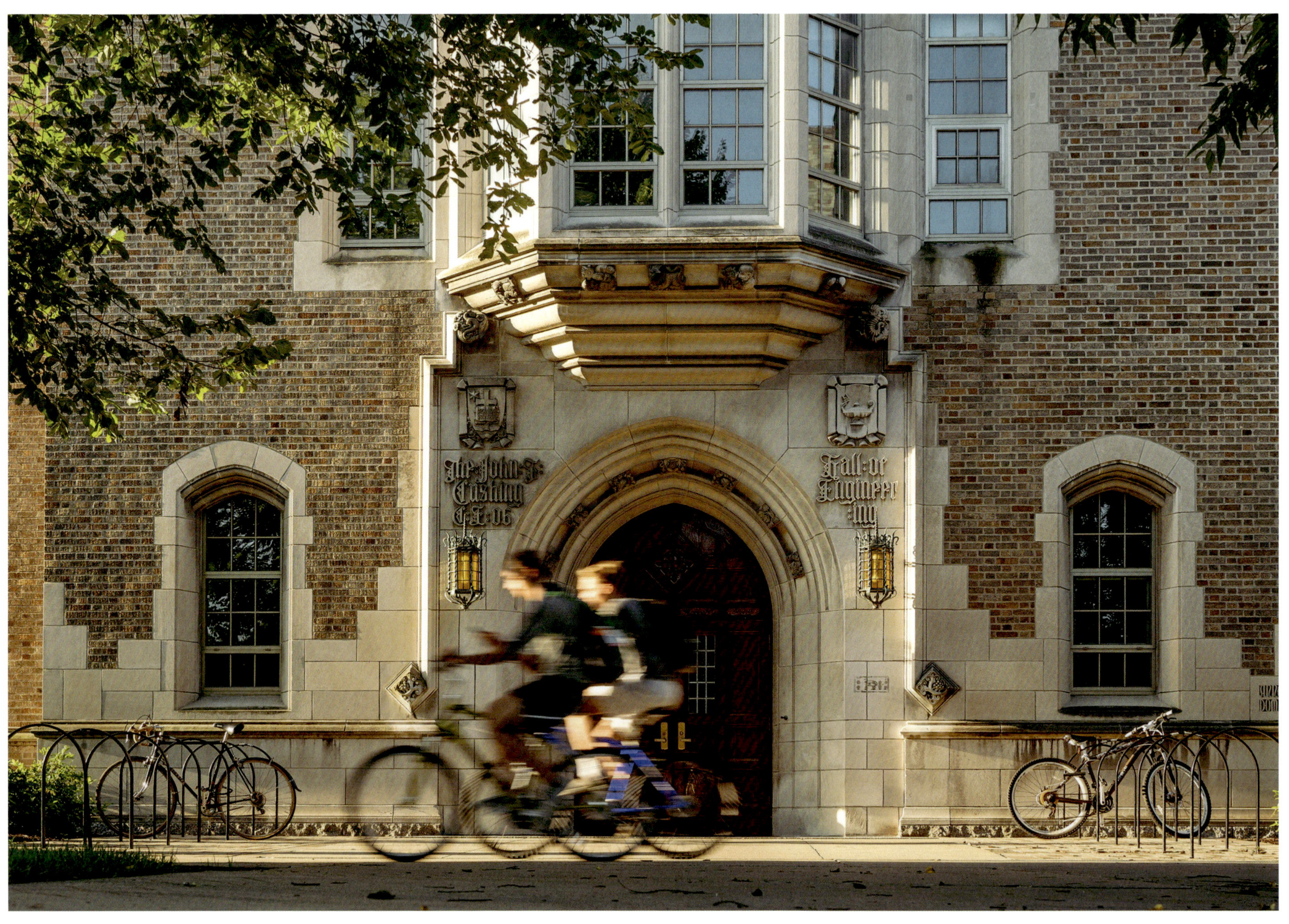

Cushing Hall, Nikon D5, 45mm, 1/40 f7.1, ISO100

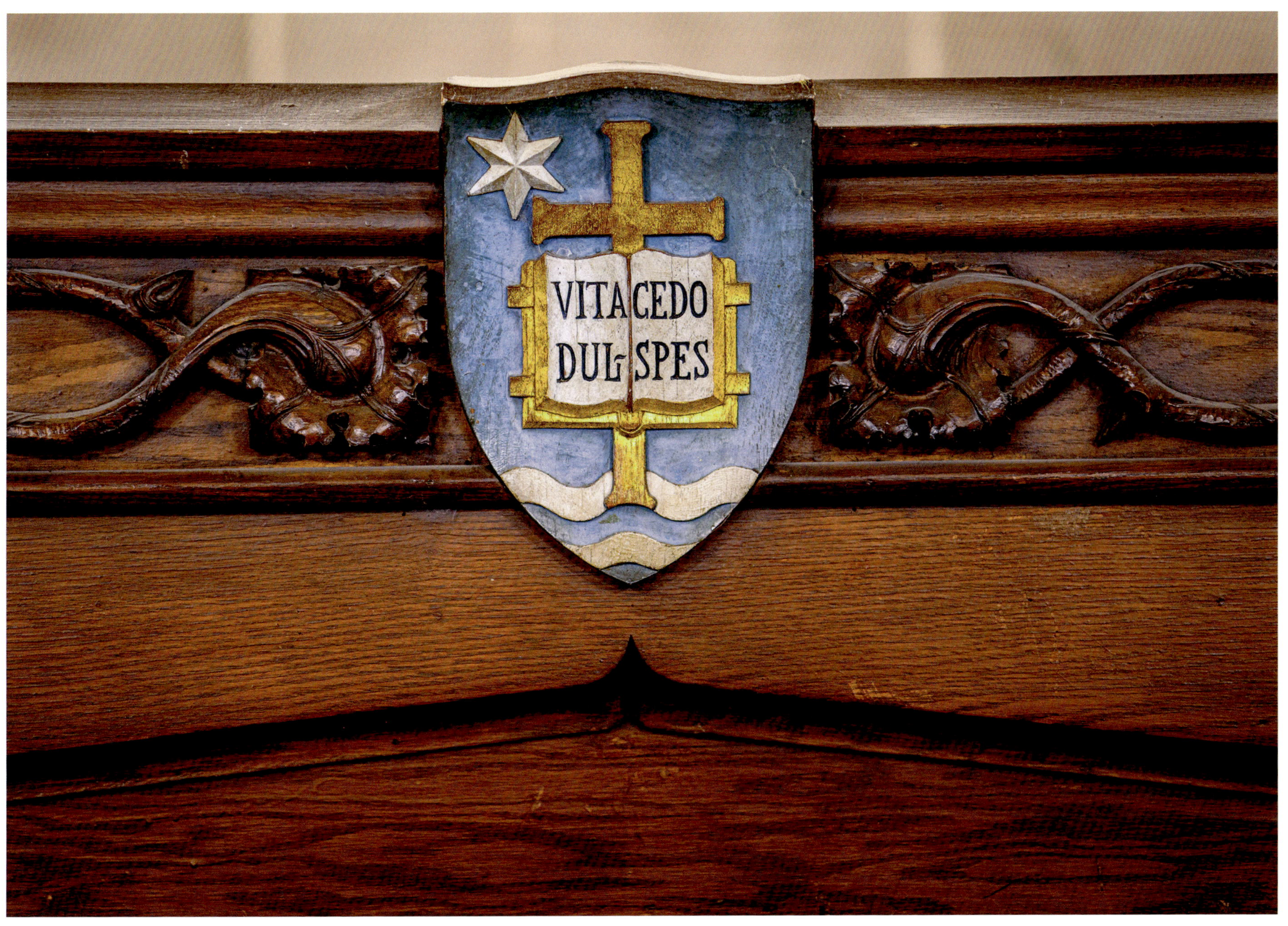

University seal just inside Cushing Hall, Nikon Z8, 135mm, 1/40 f2, ISO1000

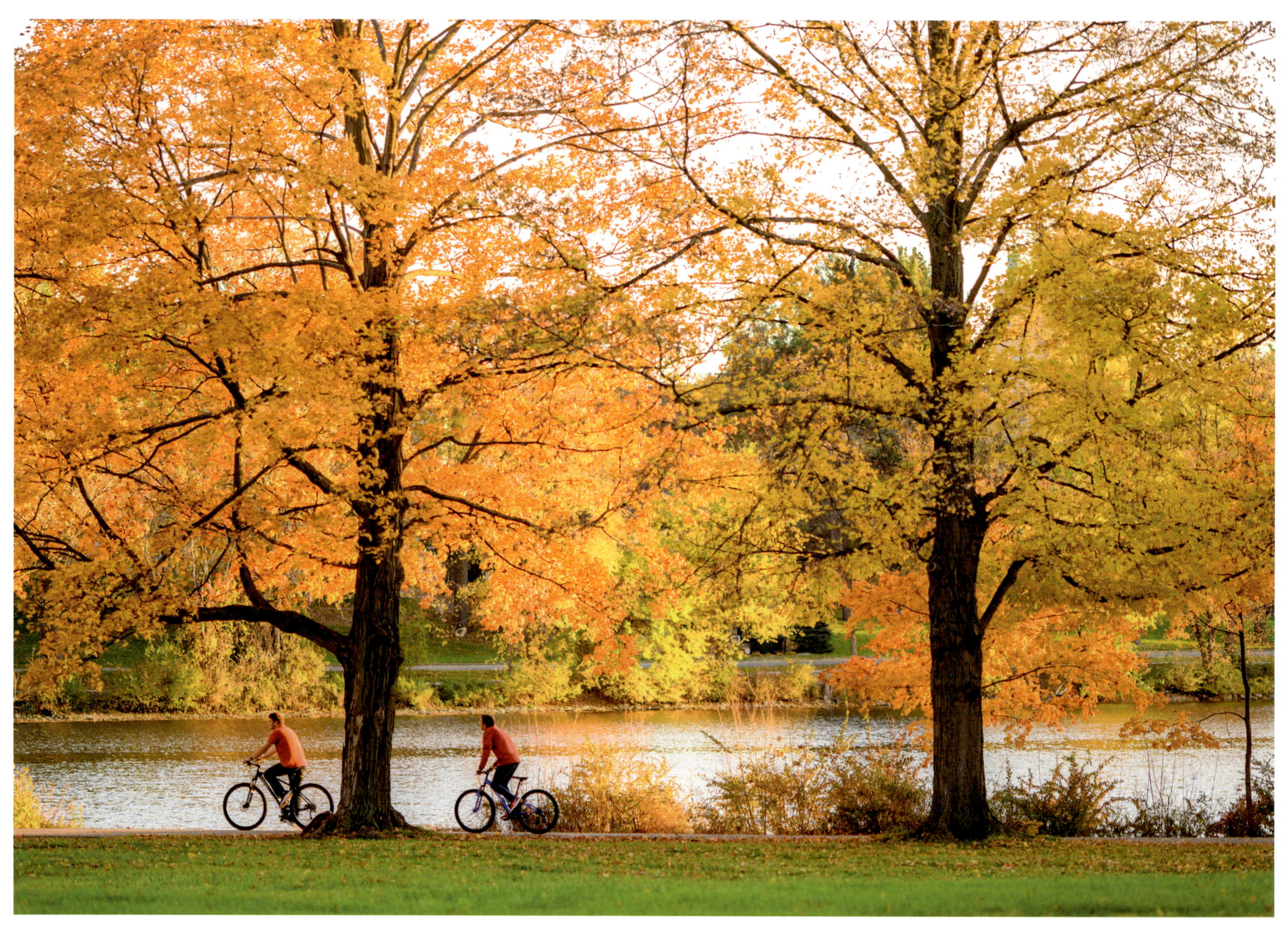

Saint Mary's Lake, Nikon Z6, 135mm, 1/320 f2, ISO200

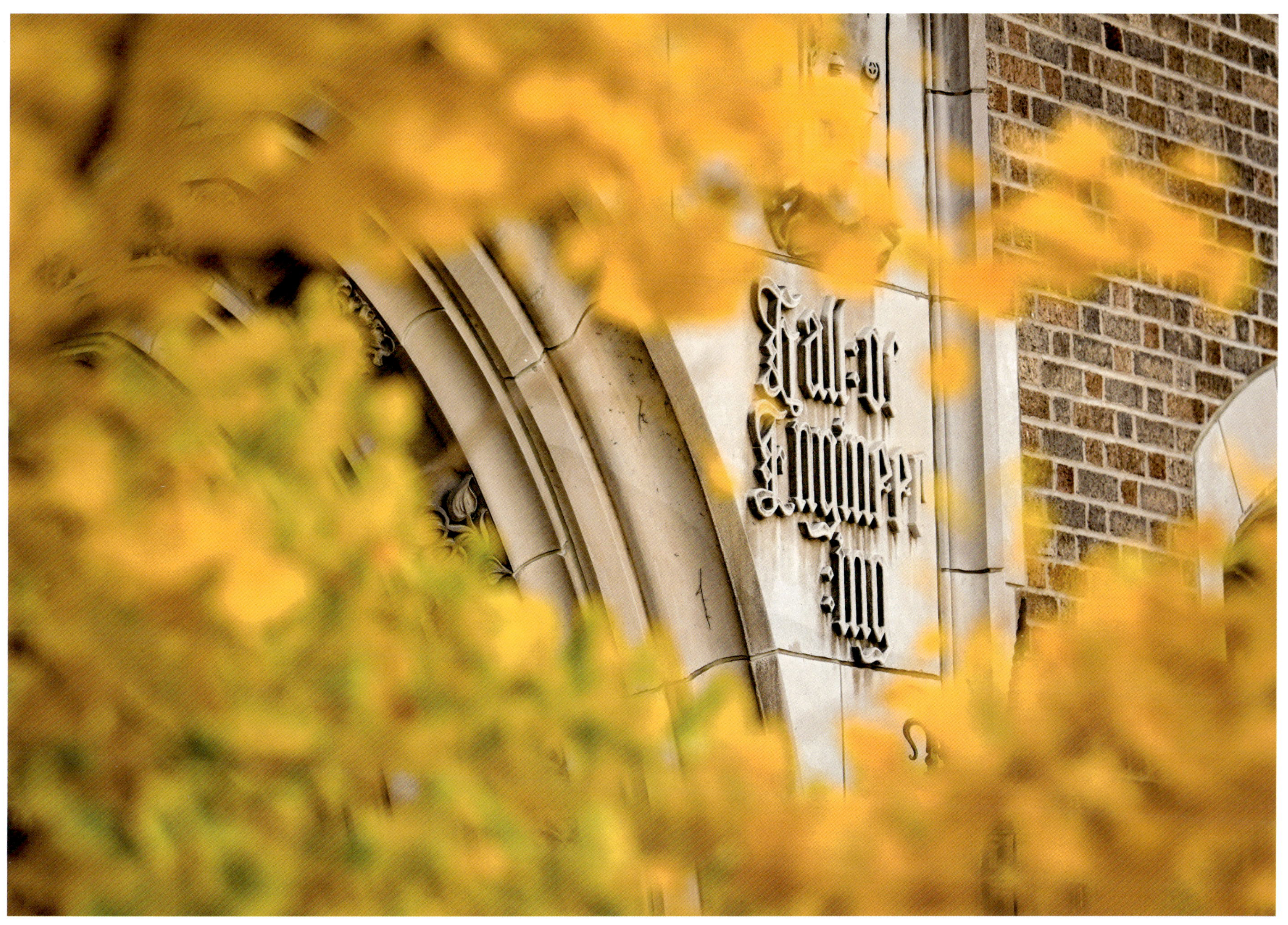

Cushing Hall entrance relief, Nikon Z9, 130mm, 1/1250 f3.2, ISO500

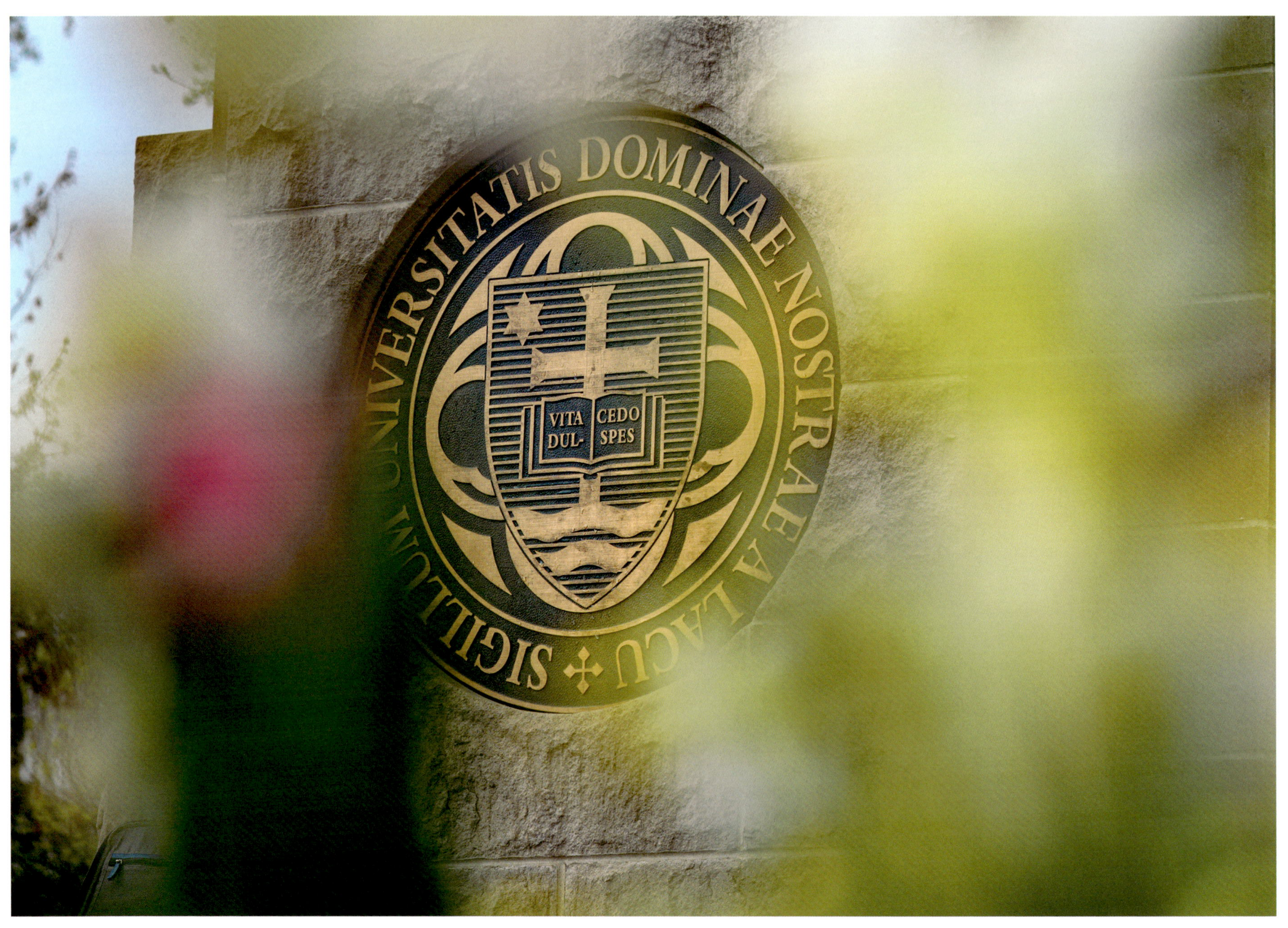

Pillars at Notre Dame Avenue entrance, Nikon Z7, 135mm, 1/200 f5.6, ISO64

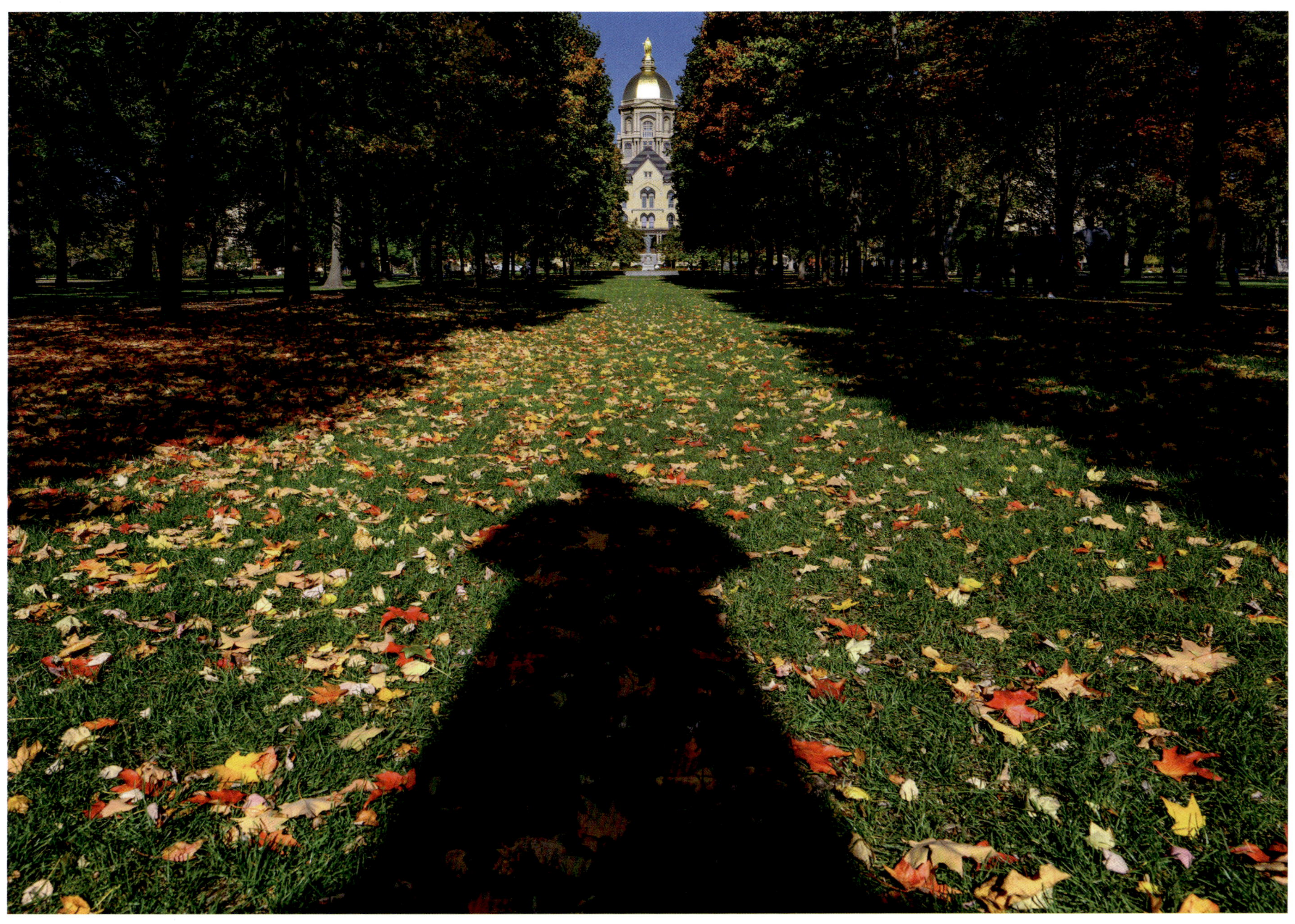

Shadow of Fr. Sorin Statue on Main Quad, Nikon Z7II, 24mm, 1/500 f8, ISO125

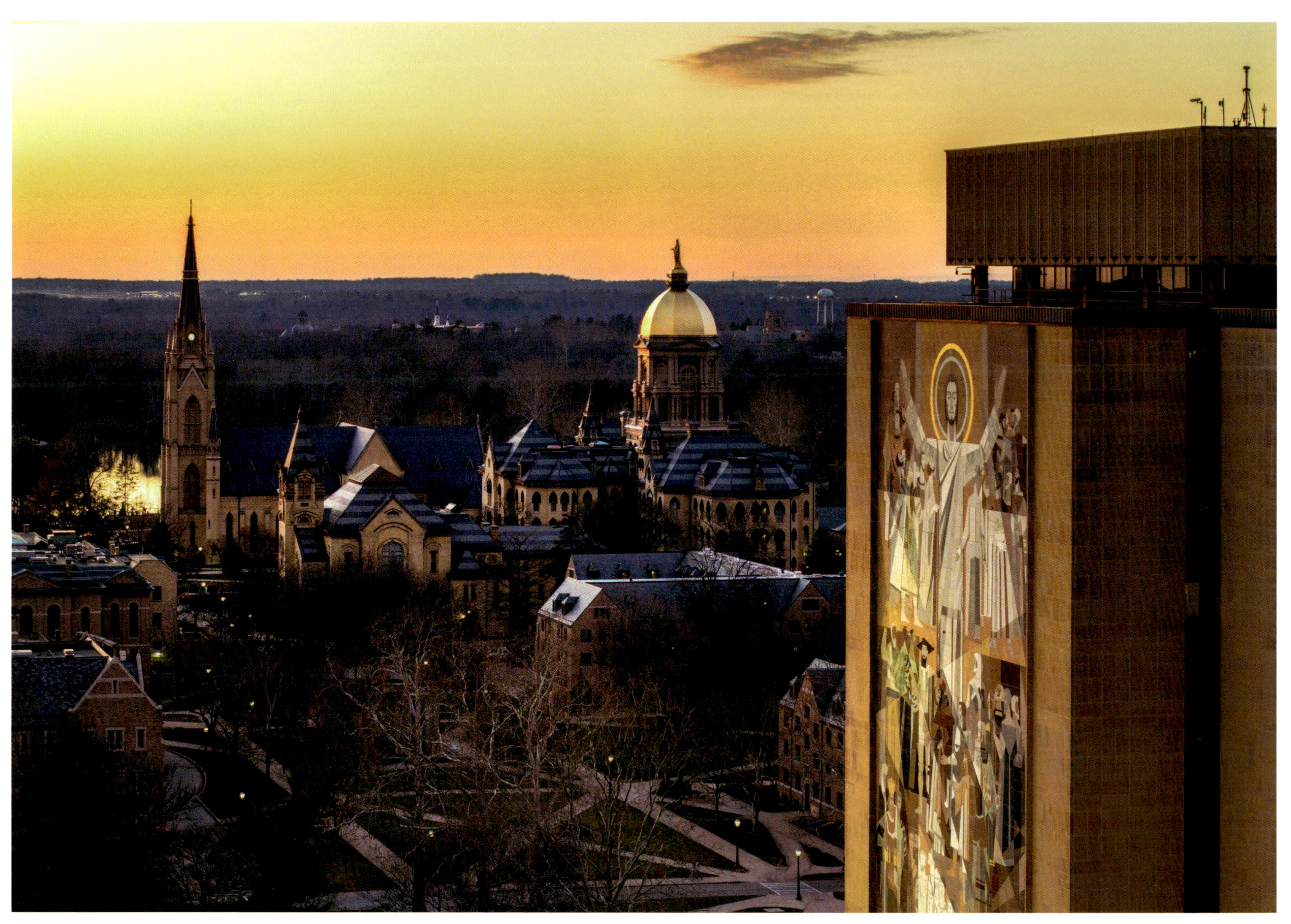

Aerial of Basilica, Dome, and Touchdown Jesus, Mavic 3 Pro drone, 70mm equivalent, 1/60 f2.8, ISO100

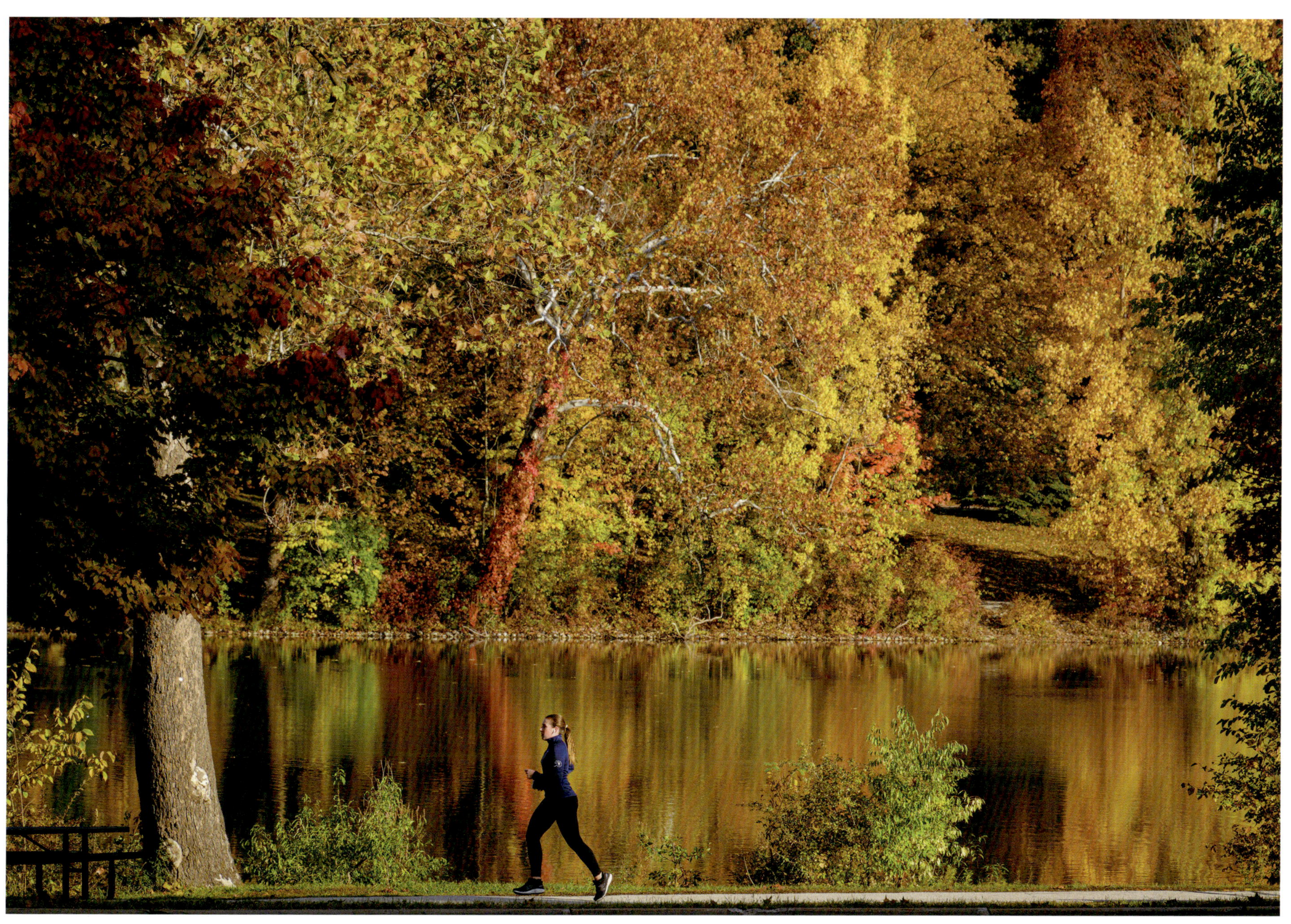

Saint Mary's Lake, Fuji GFX100s, 200mm, 1/800 f10, ISO800

Some were concerned that when an upper deck was added to Notre Dame Stadium in the mid 1990s, Touchdown Jesus lost his view of the game. Not to worry!

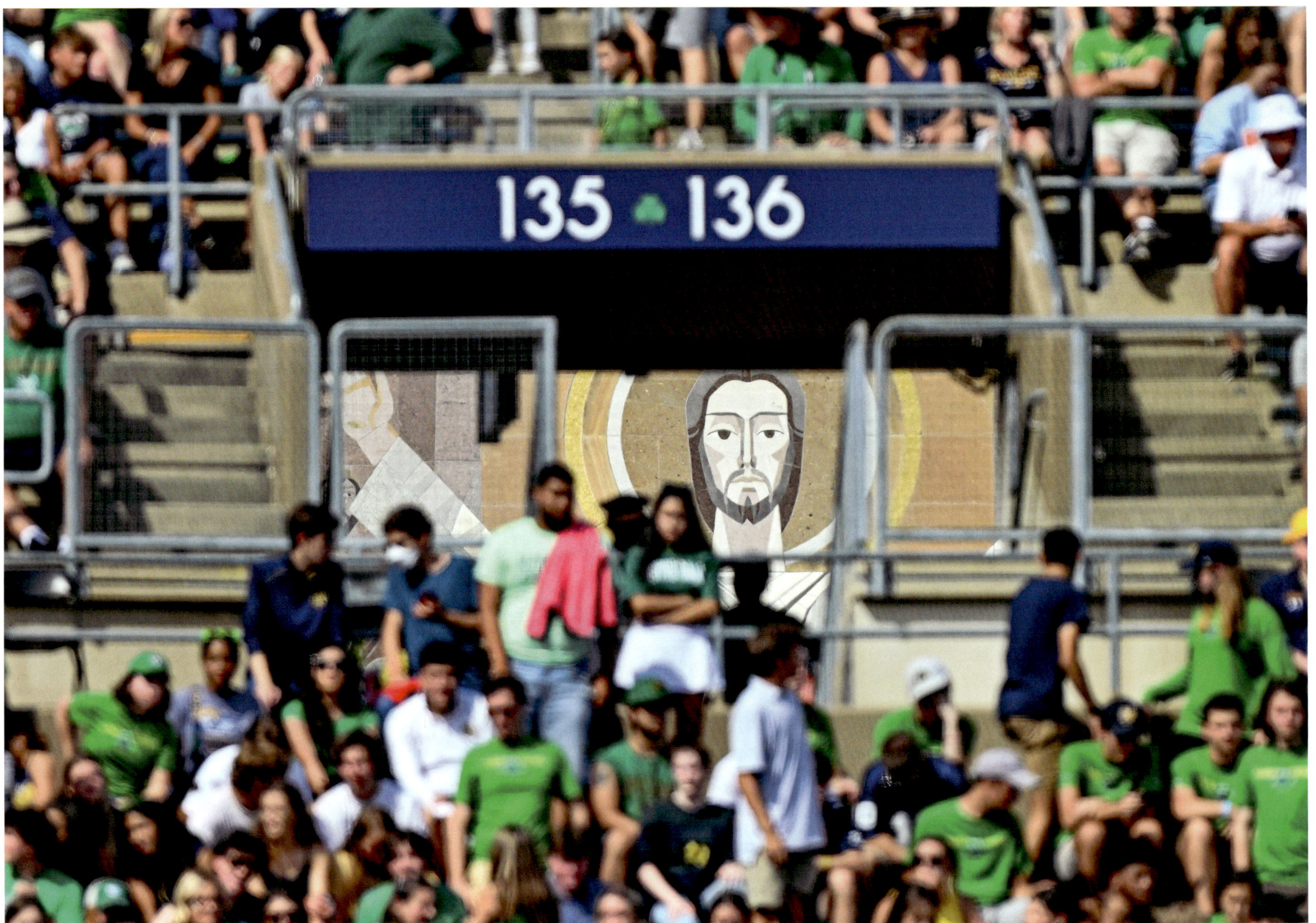

The face of Touchdown Jesus through an upper deck entrance to Notre Dame Stadium, Nikon Z6II, 490mm, 1/5000 f6.3, ISO800

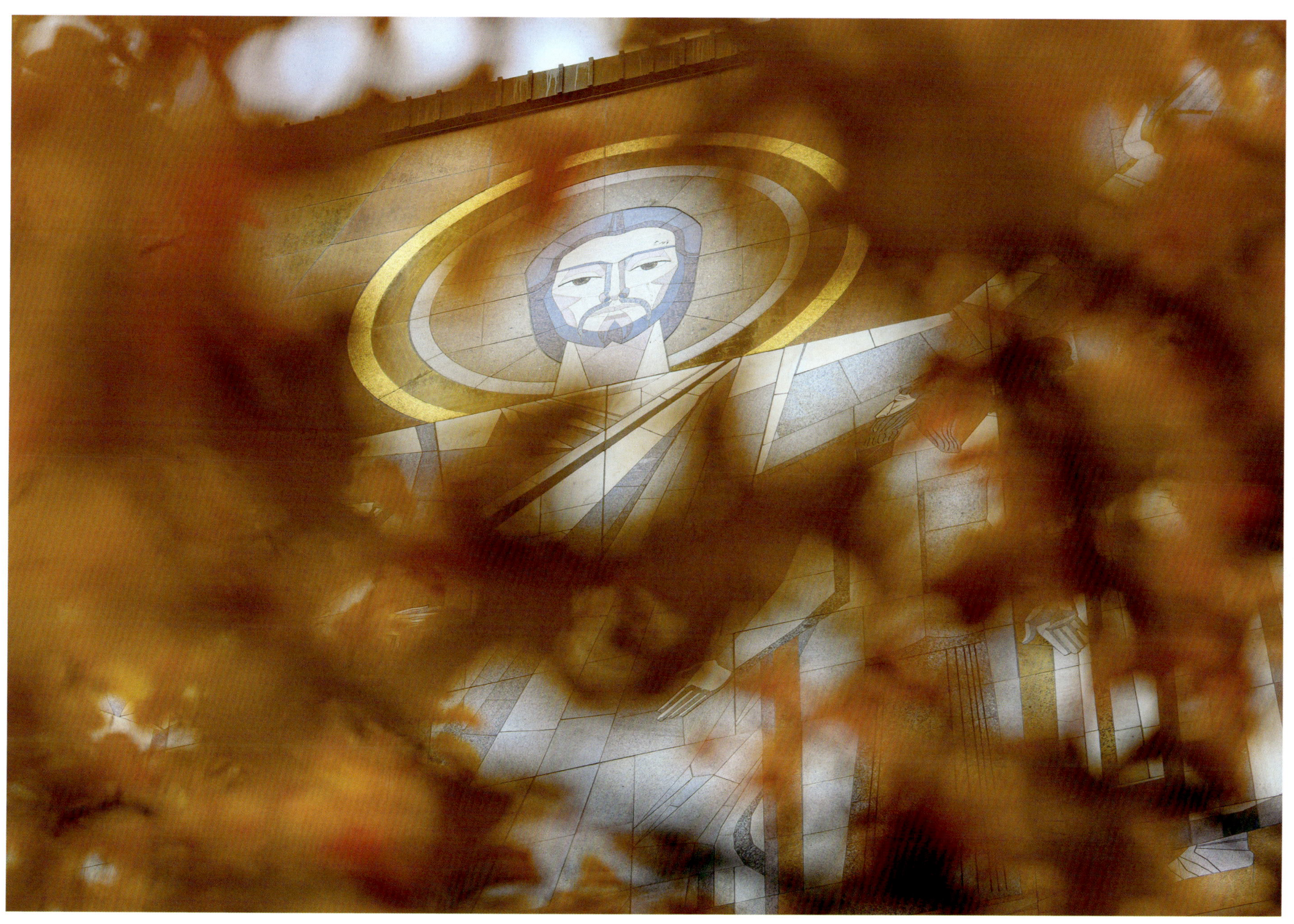

The Word of Life mural, commonly known as "Touchdown Jesus," Nikon Z7II, 135mm, 1/50 f4.5, ISO250

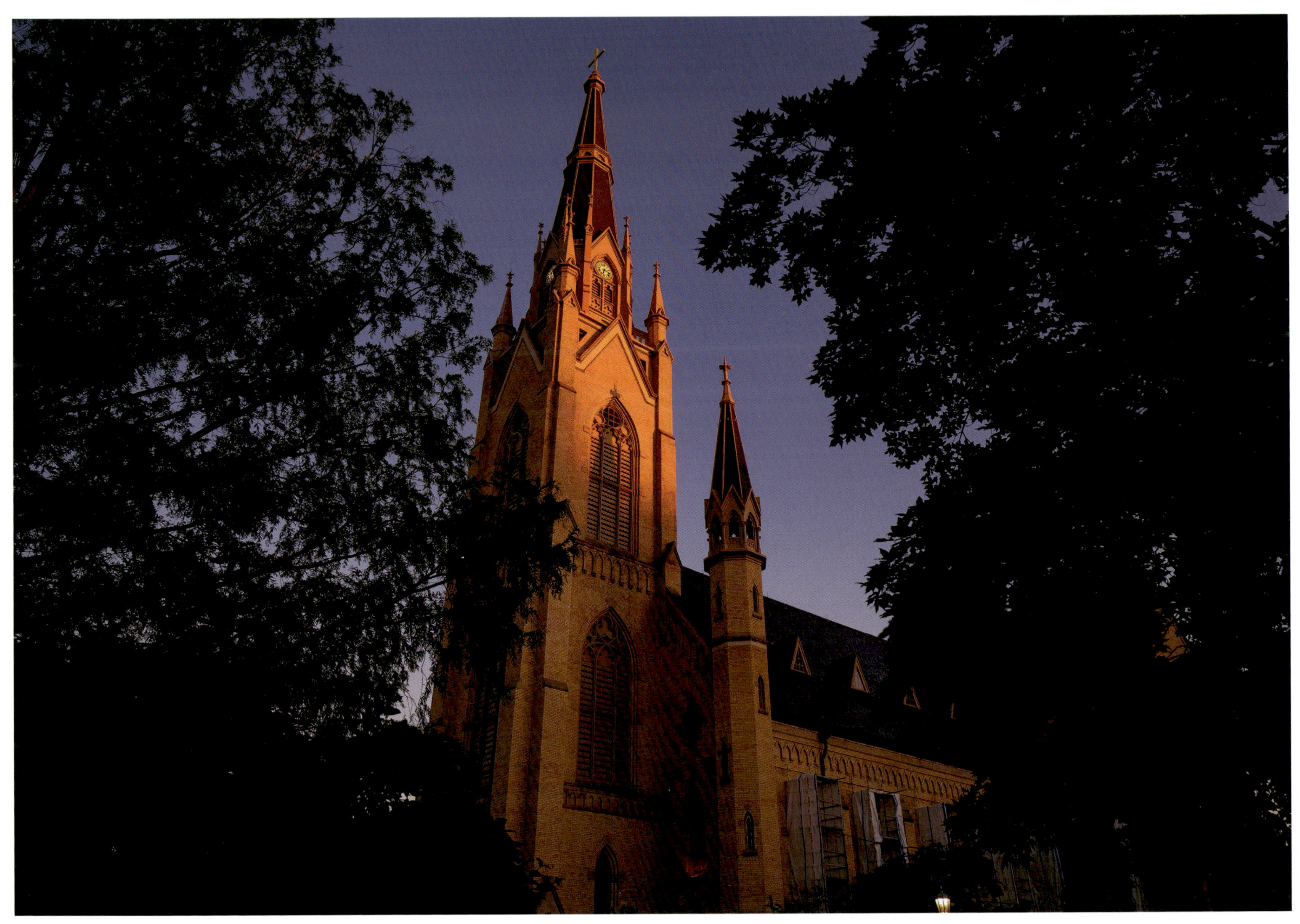

Sunrise on the Basilica steeple, Nikon Z6, 24mm, 1/160 f4, ISO100

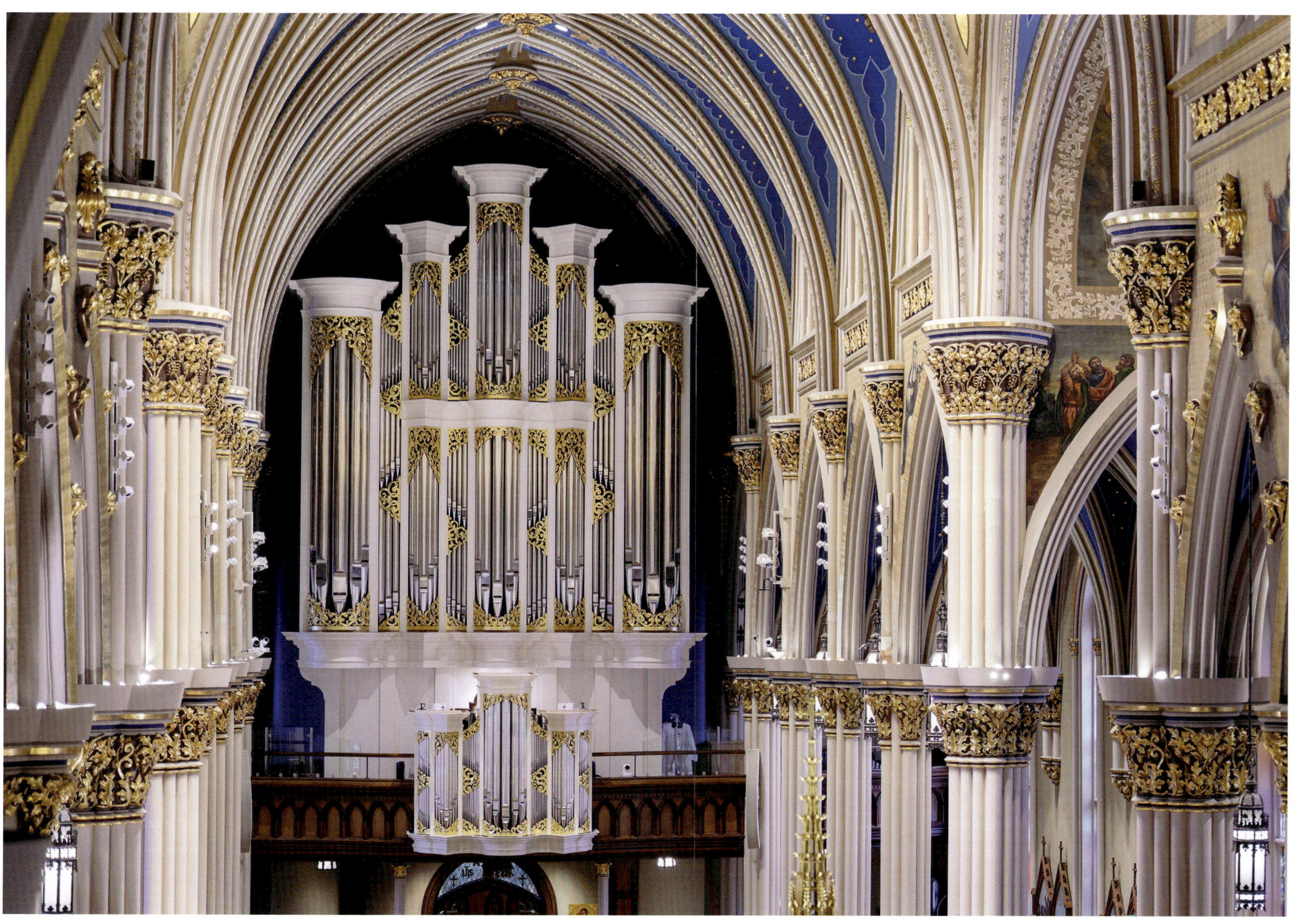

The Murdy Family Organ in the Basilica of the Sacred Heart, Nikon Z6II, 62mm, 1/40 f2.8, ISO800

The Basilica of the Sacred Heart is a visual treat both inside and out. There's color and detail in every corner. Easter is a particularly bright and vibrant time.

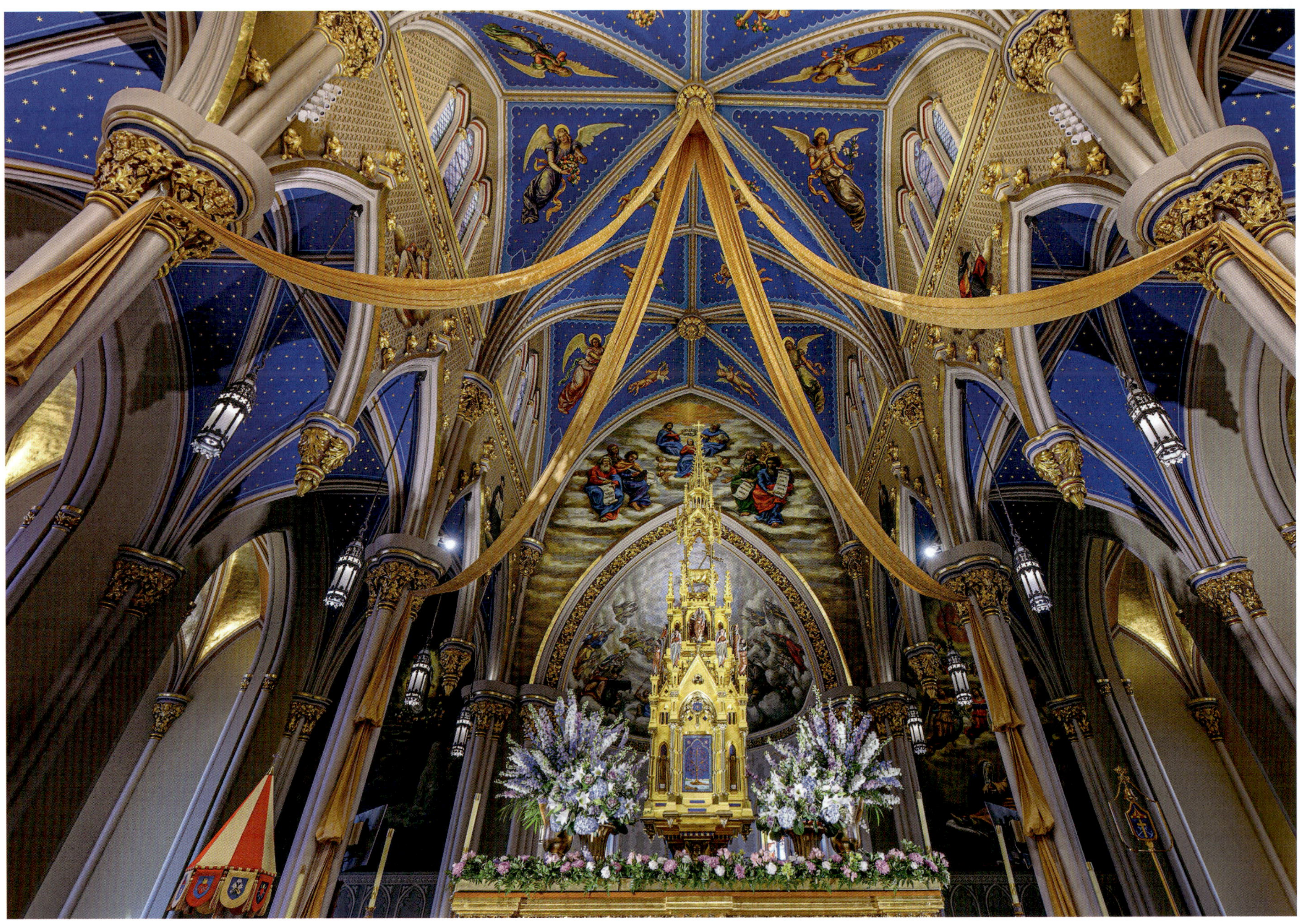

The Basilica of the Sacred Heart during Easter season, Nikon Z6II, 17mm, 1/8 f4.5, ISO100

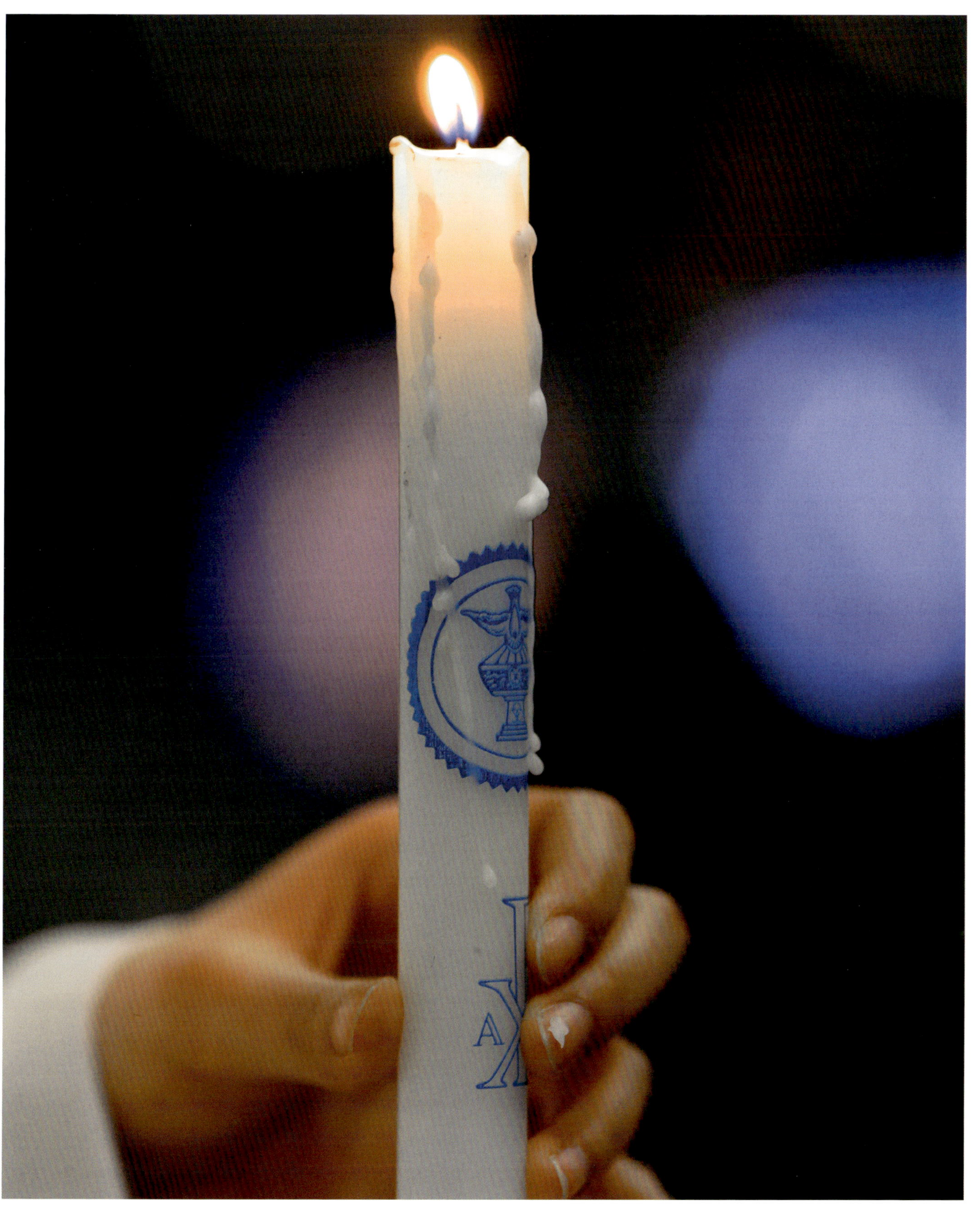

Baptismal candle during Easter Vigil Mass,
Nikon Z7, 135mm, 1/100 f2.5, ISO1600

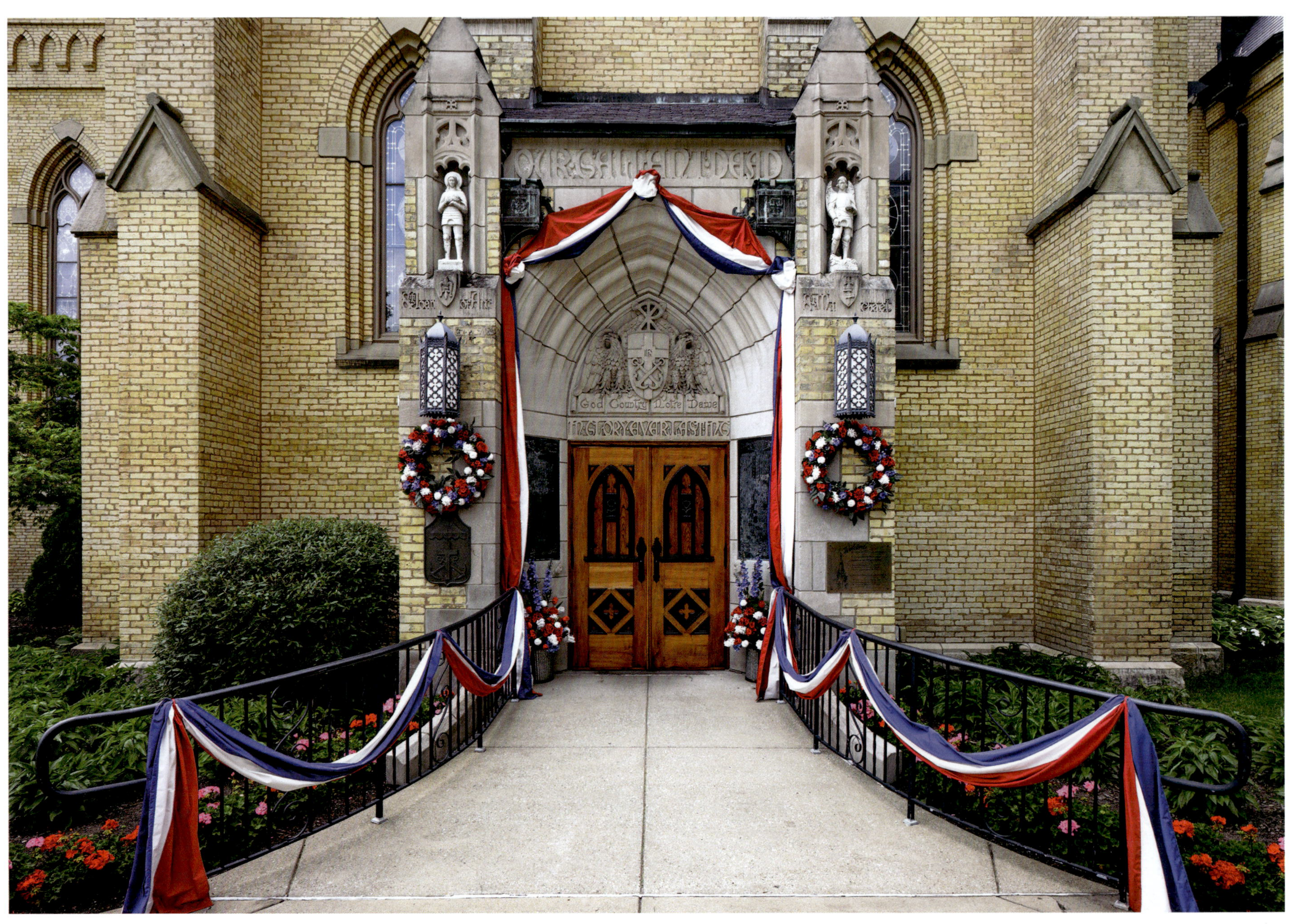

Basilica east door decorated for Memorial Day, Nikon Z8, 20mm, 1/160 f5.6, ISO64

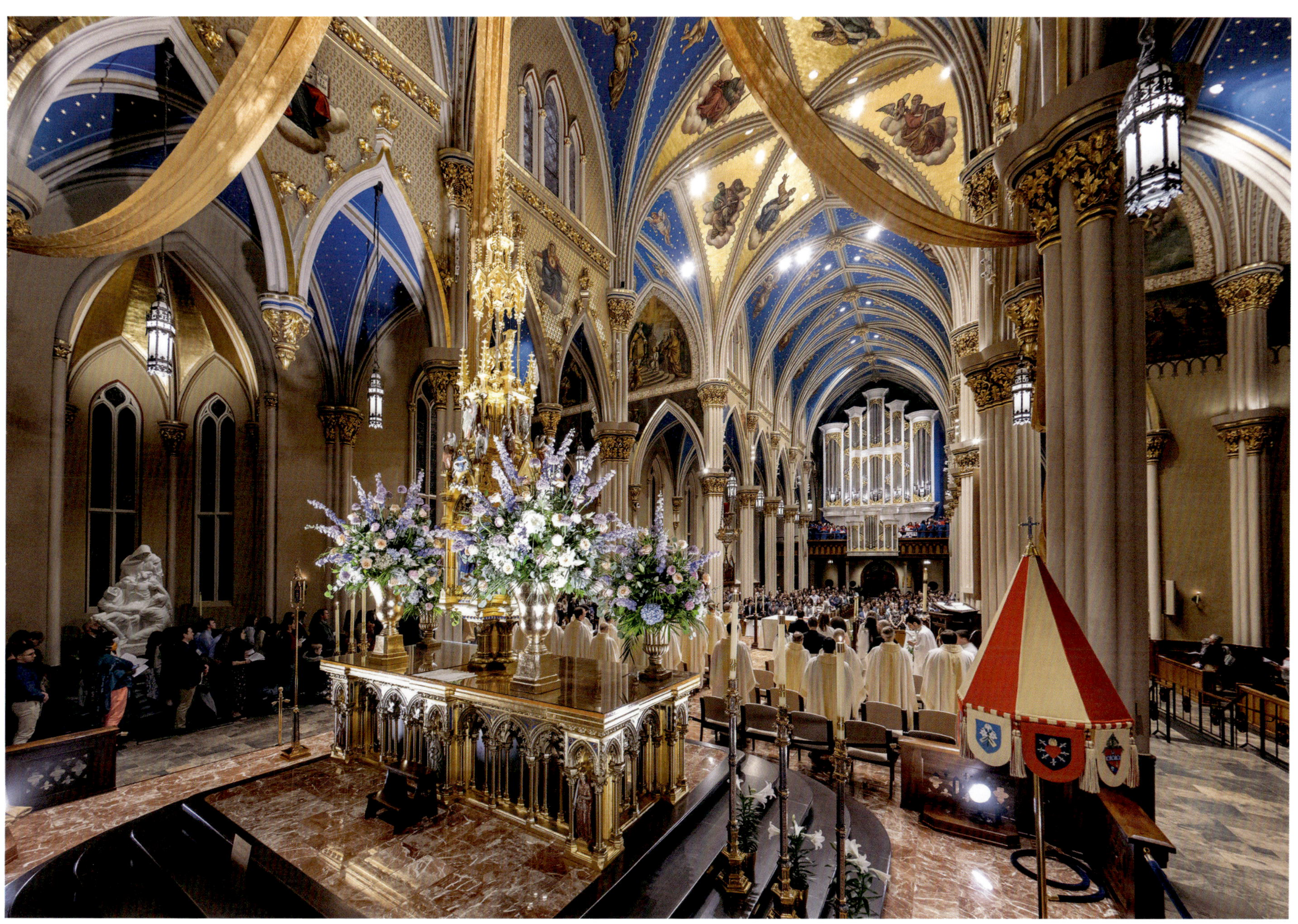

Easter Vigil Mass in the Basilica, Nikon Z7II, 14mm, 1/20 f4.5, ISO640

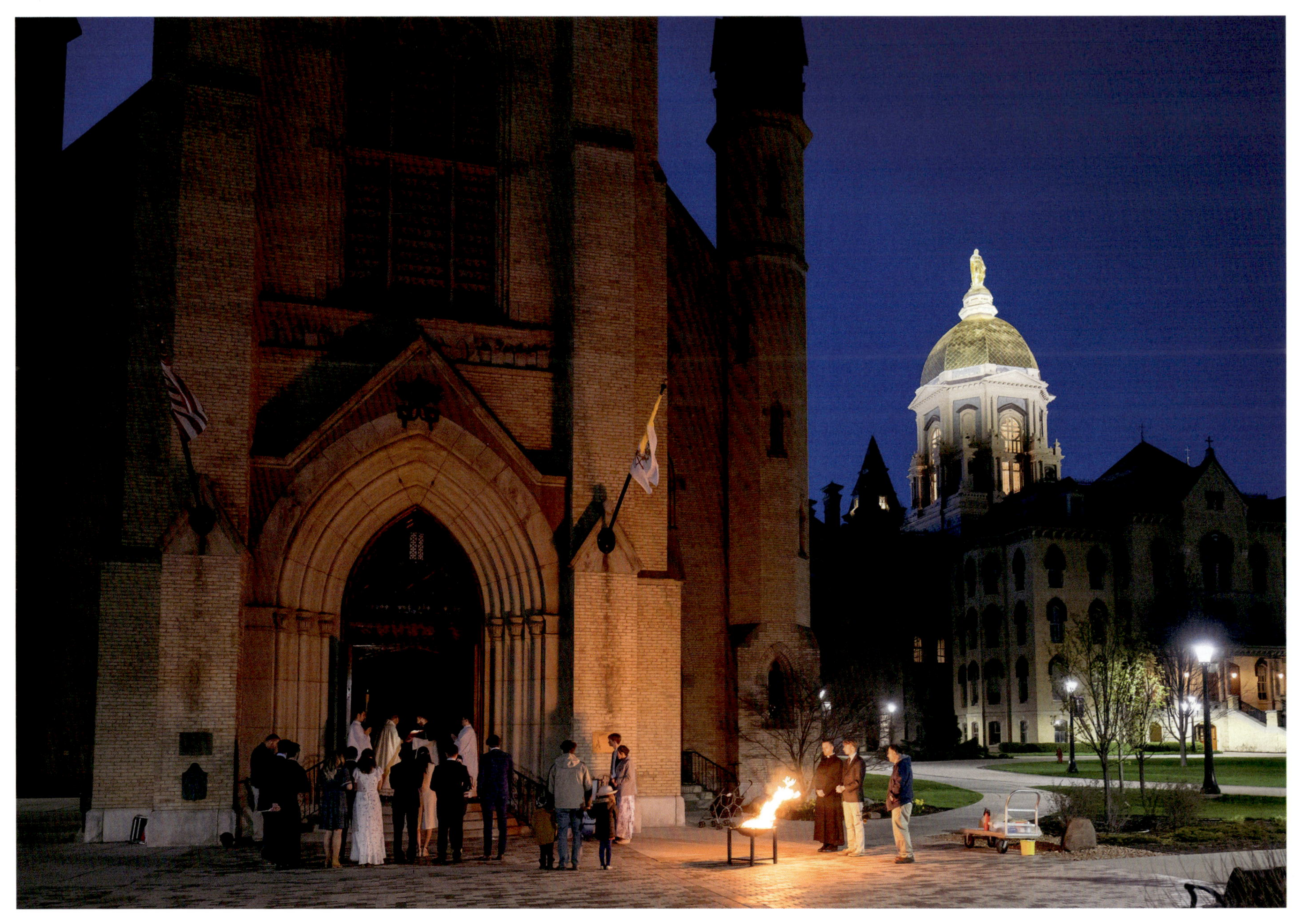

Paschal fire outside the Basilica at Easter Vigil Mass, Nikon Z6II, 24mm, 1/50 f2.8, ISO3200

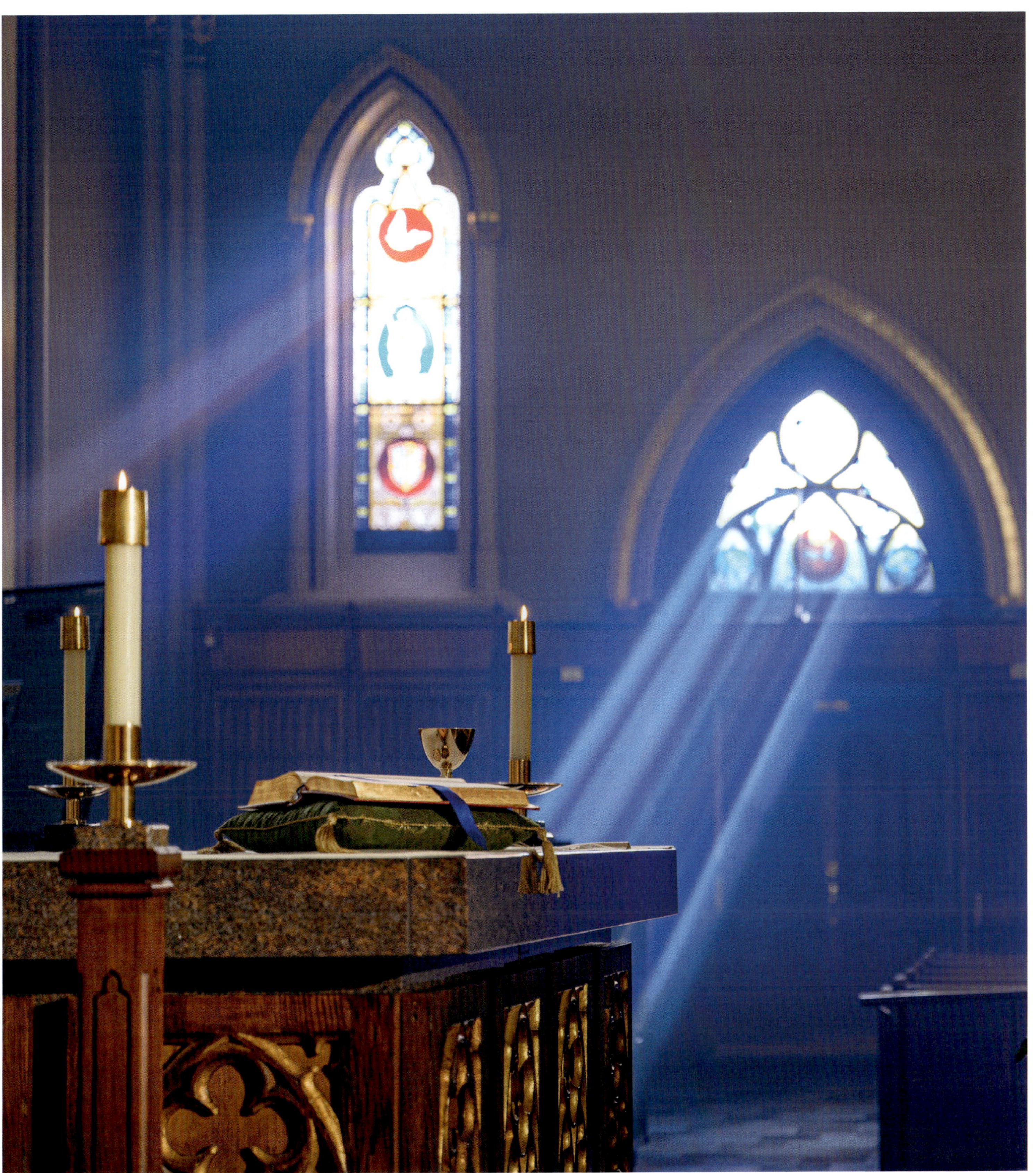

The Basilica full of incense smoke, Nikon Z7II, 70mm, 1/40 f2.8, ISO250

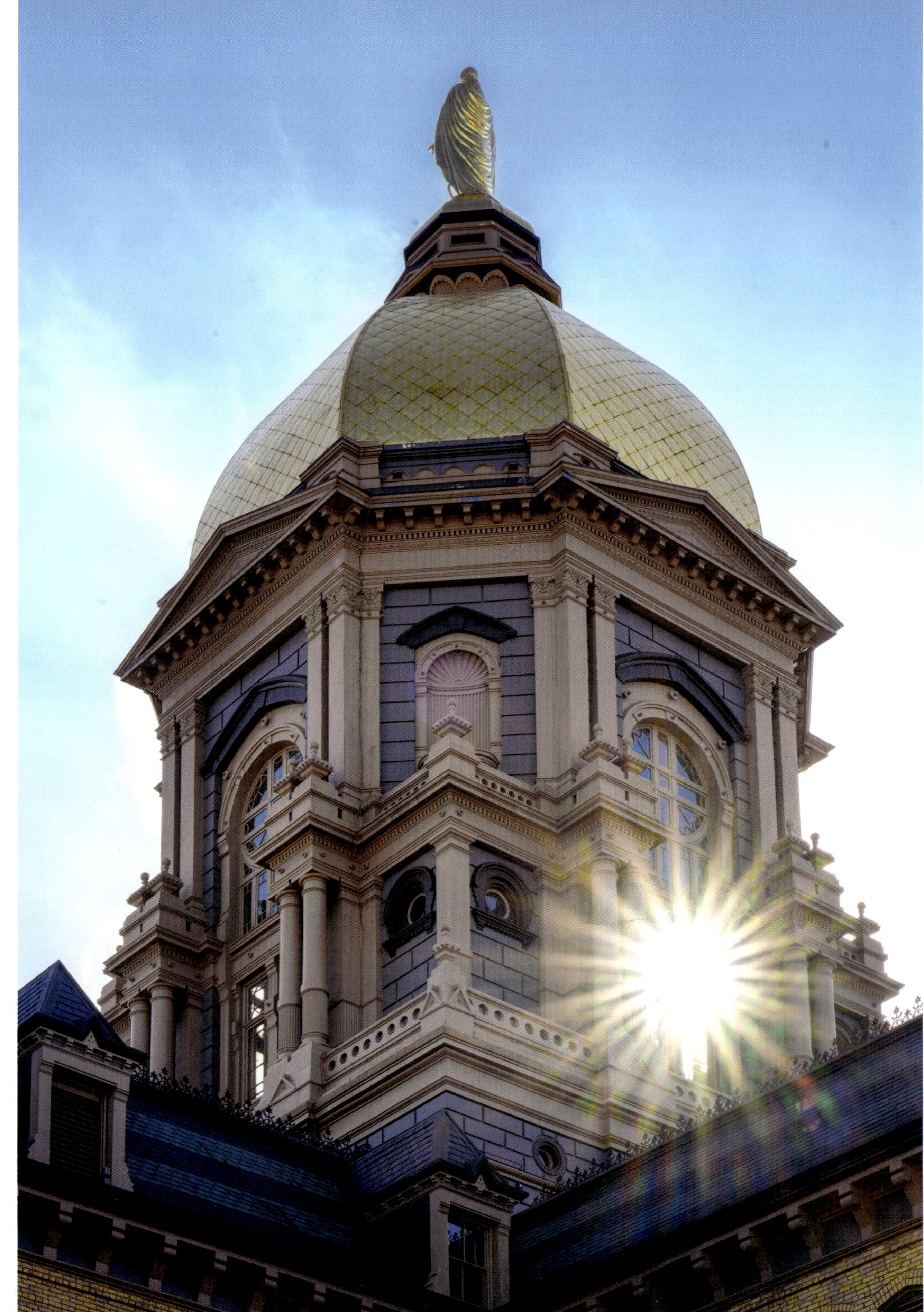

The Dome photographed from St. Edward's Hall,
Nikon Z9, 70mm, 1/20 f20, ISO64

If I have a photographic "signature" so to speak, it's probably sunstars. On most lenses, closing the aperture to near the smallest opening (which is counterintuitively the biggest number, like f16 or f22) makes bright, pinpoint light sources like the sun flare in a way that makes them appear as multipointed stars. It's like a photographic exclamation point.

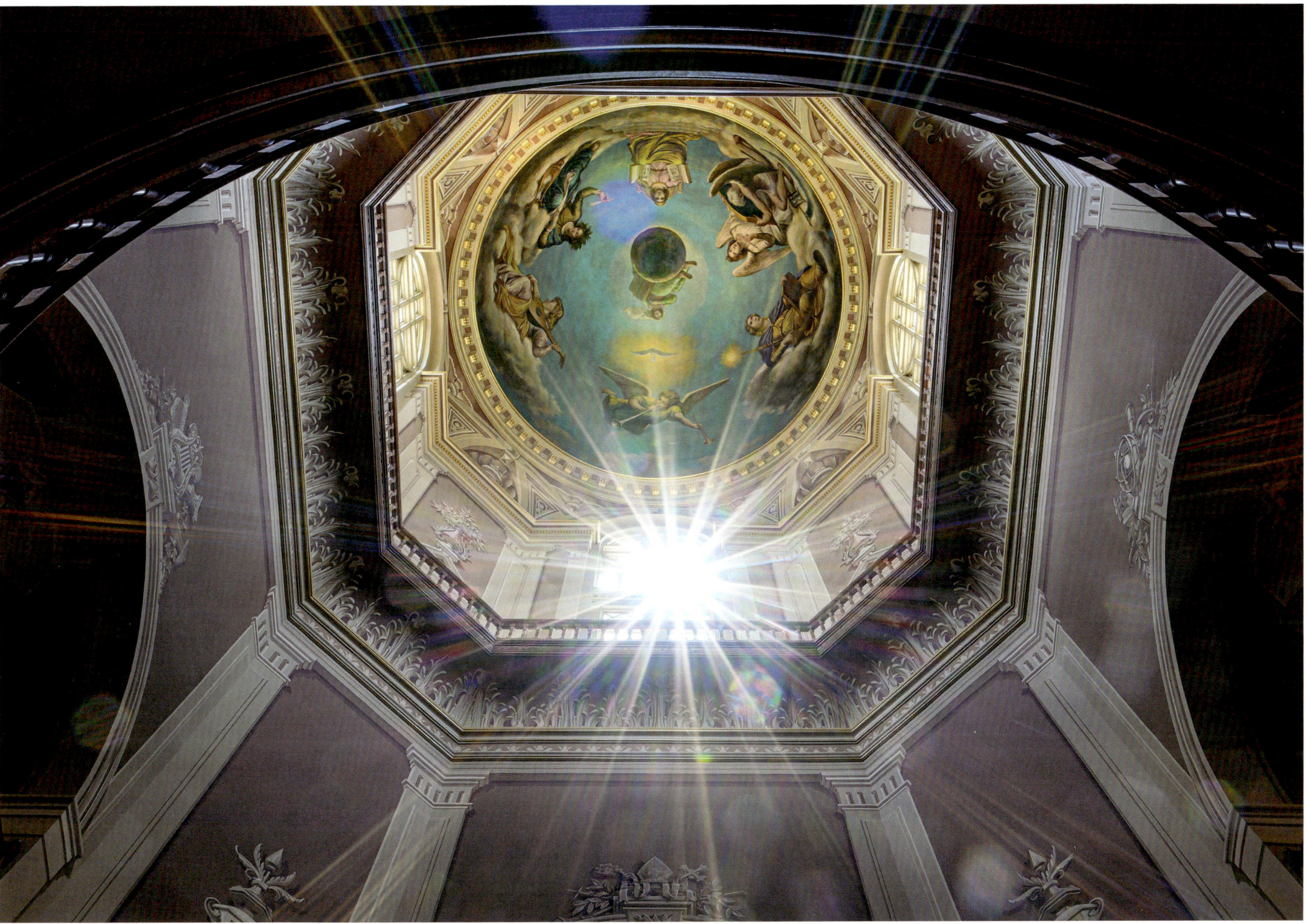

Main Building rotunda from fourth floor, Nikon Z6, 30mm, 1/6 f18, ISO500

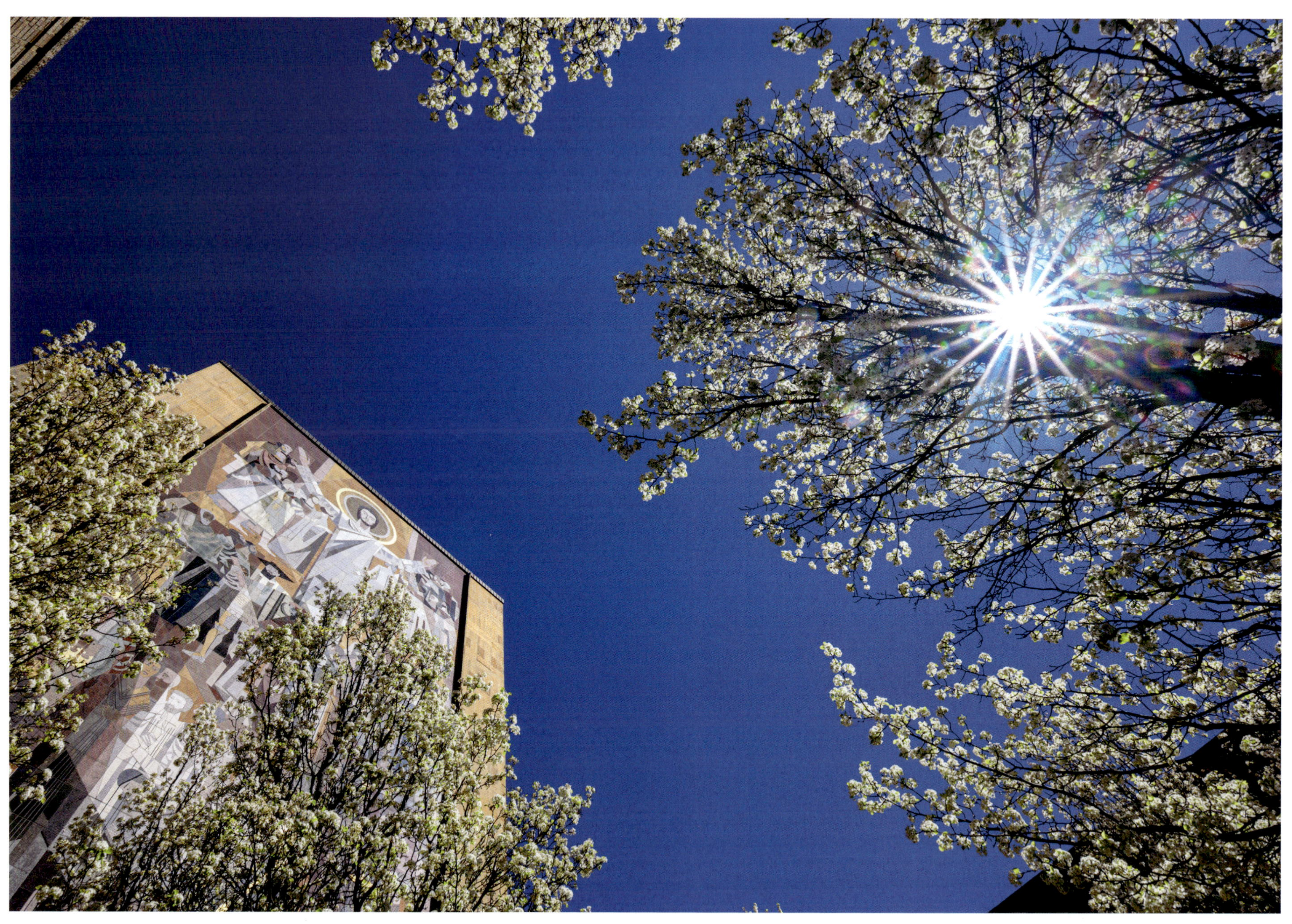

Hesburgh Library courtyard, Nikon Z8, 17mm, 1/60 f22, ISO64

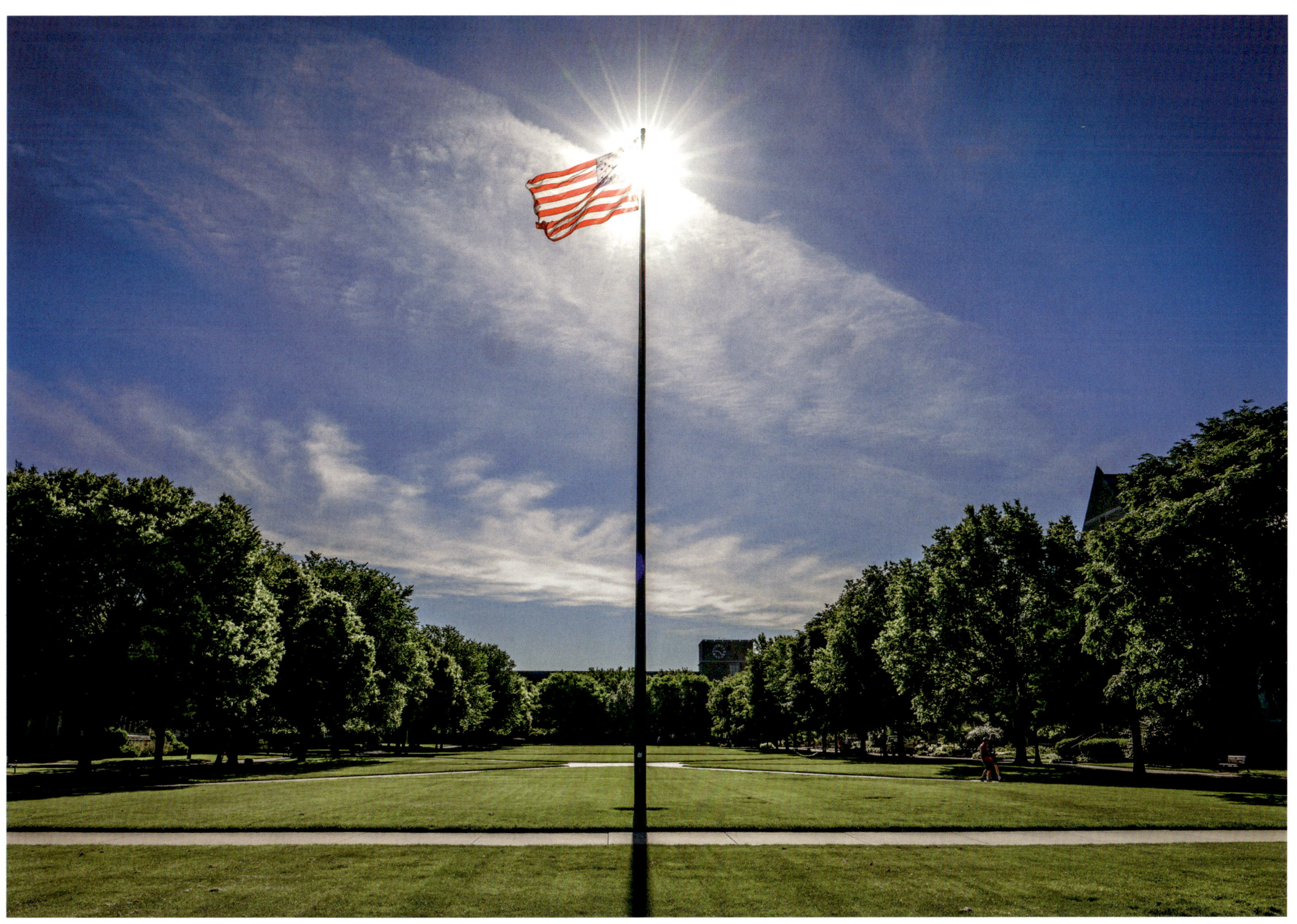

South Quad flag, Nikon Z8, 24mm, 1/250 f20, ISO64

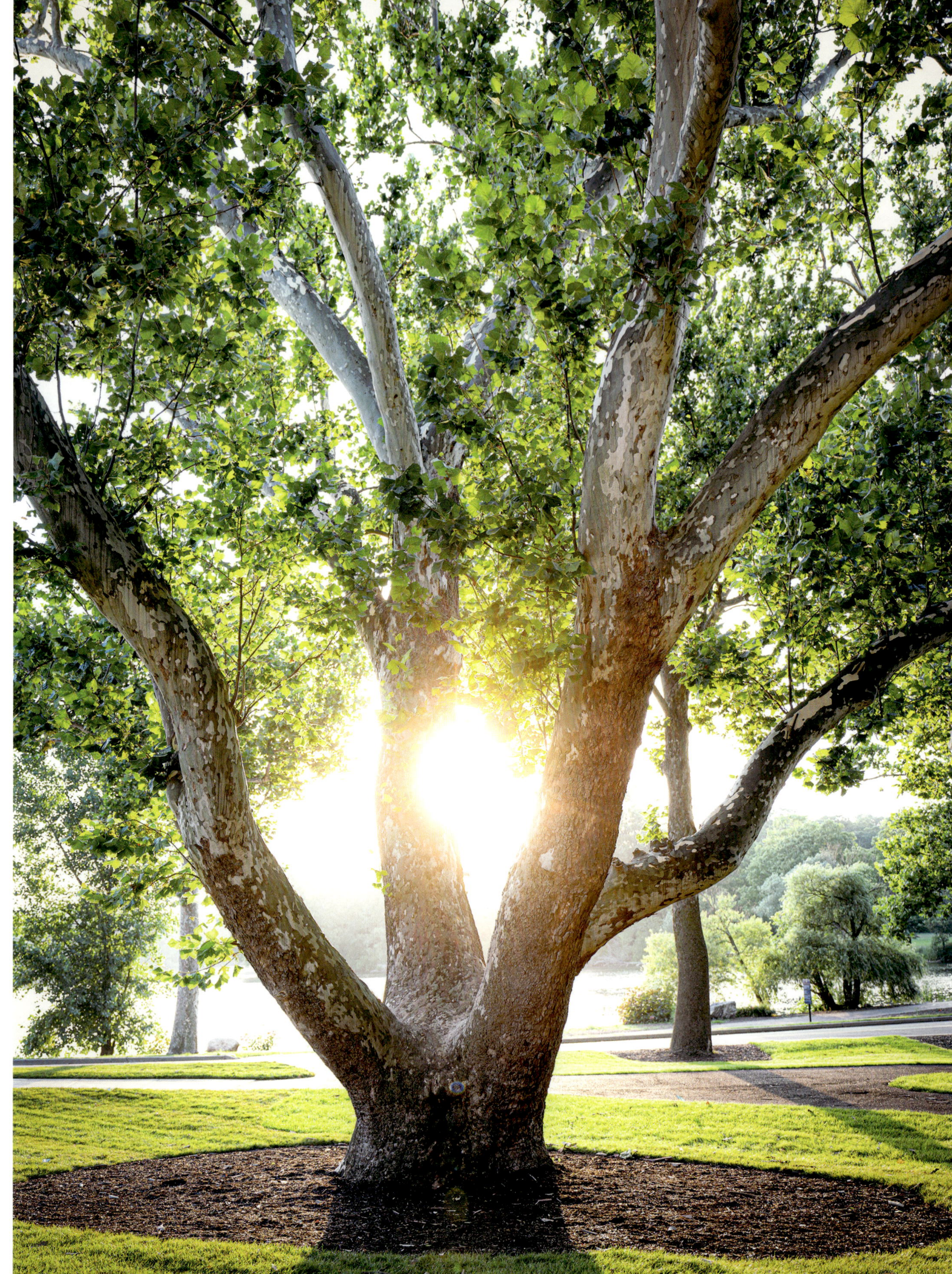

Sycamore near the Grotto,
Nikon Z6, 41mm, 1/50 f2.8, ISO100

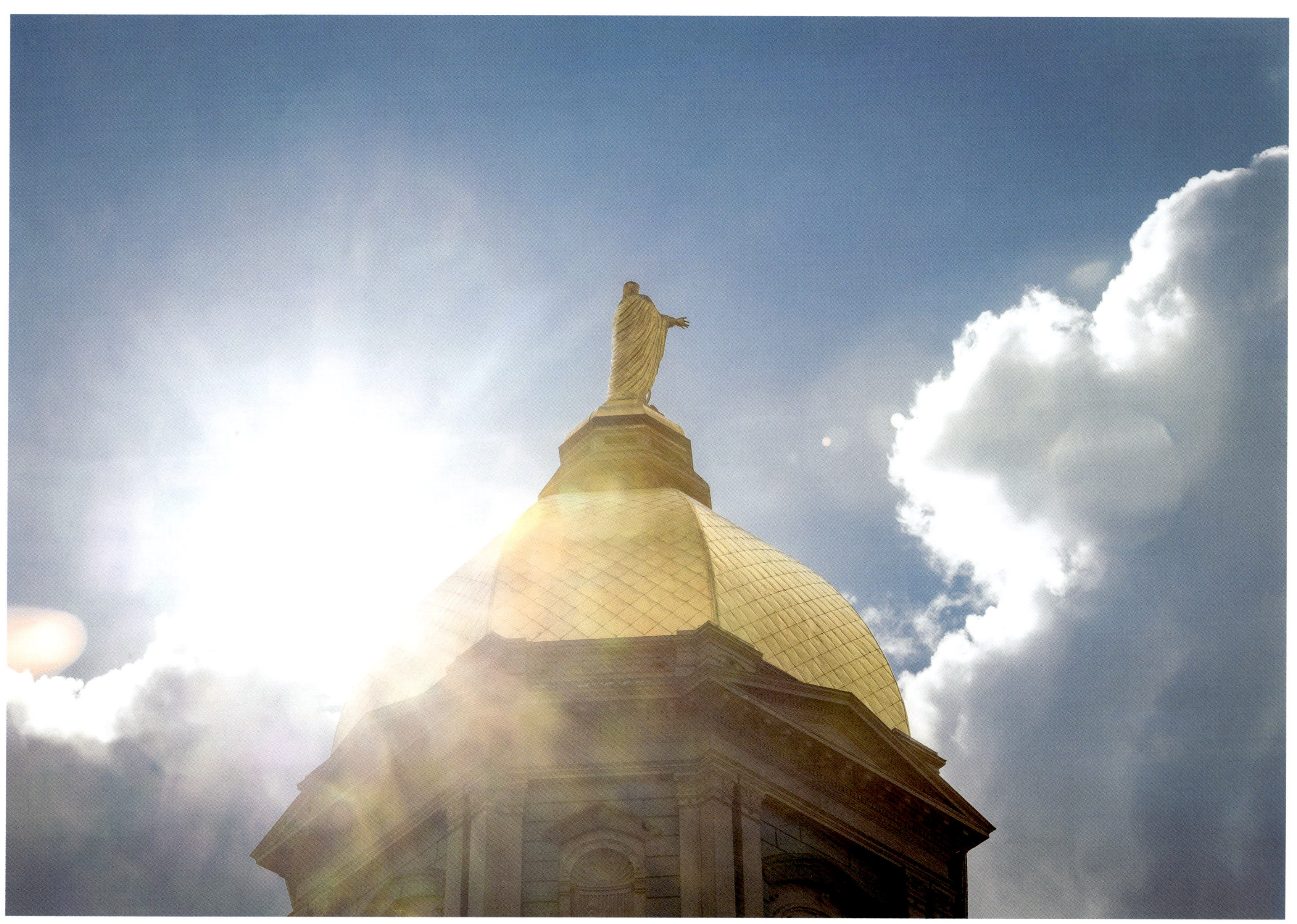

Main Building from the northwest side, Nikon D5, 80mm, 1/320 f22, ISO100

"Golden hour" is a term that refers to the time just after sunrise or before sunset when the sun is low on the horizon and the atmosphere softens and warms the light. Any kind of photo–landscapes, portraits . . . even sports–looks better in golden hour.

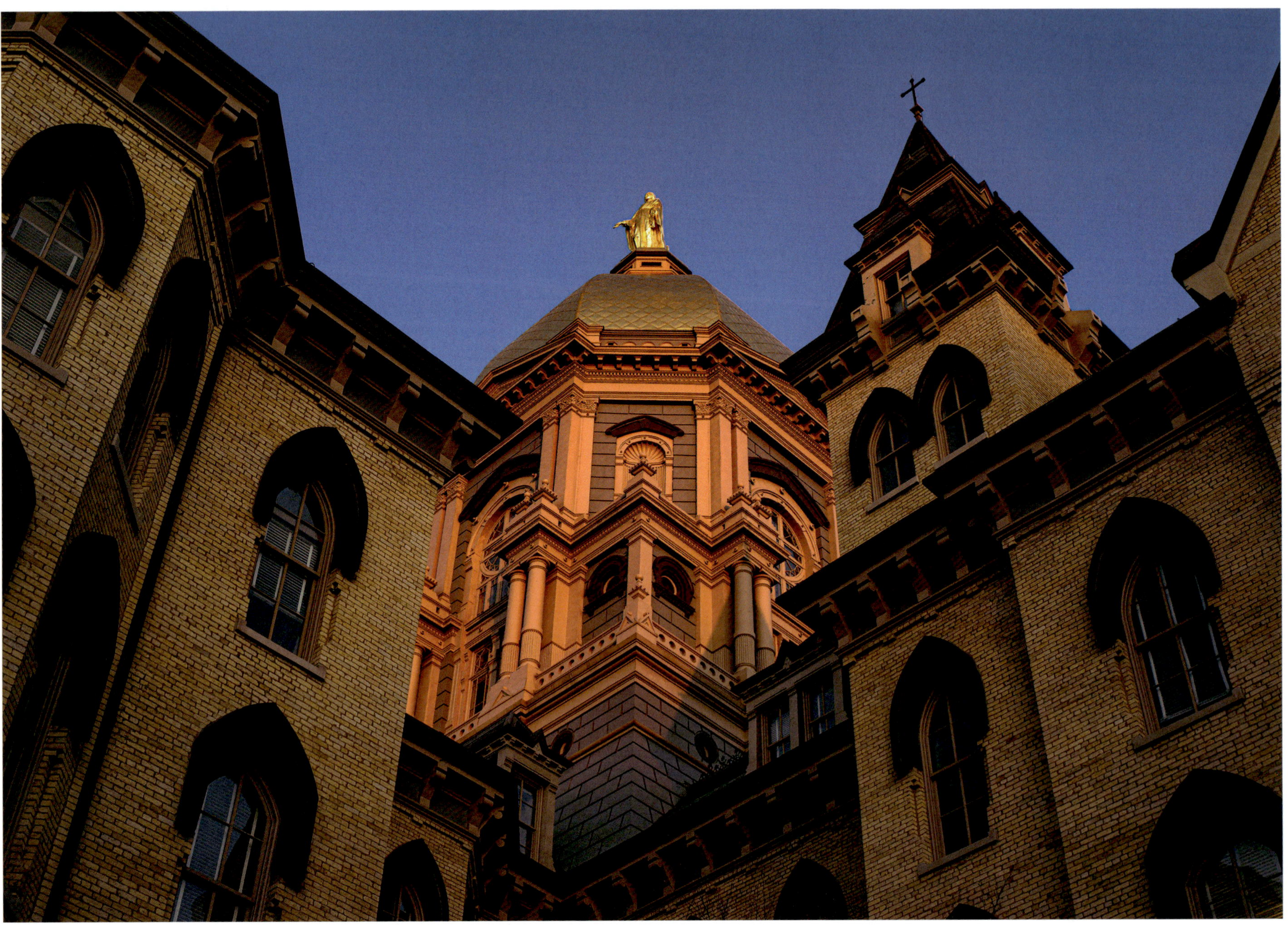

Main Building from the southeast side, Pentax 645Z, 55mm, 1/250 f5.6, ISO400

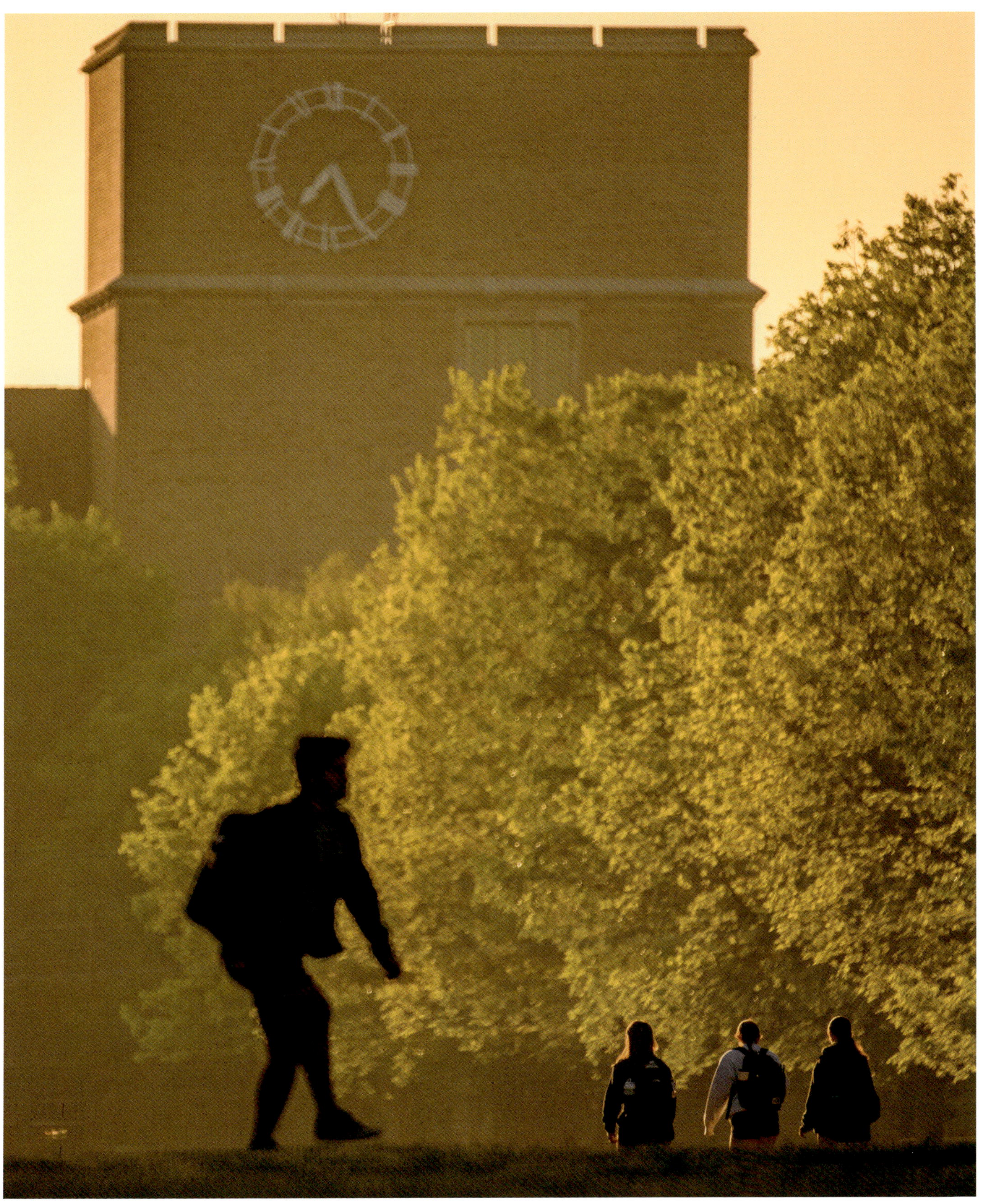

South Quad, Nikon D5, 500mm mirror lens,
1/2000 f8, ISO64

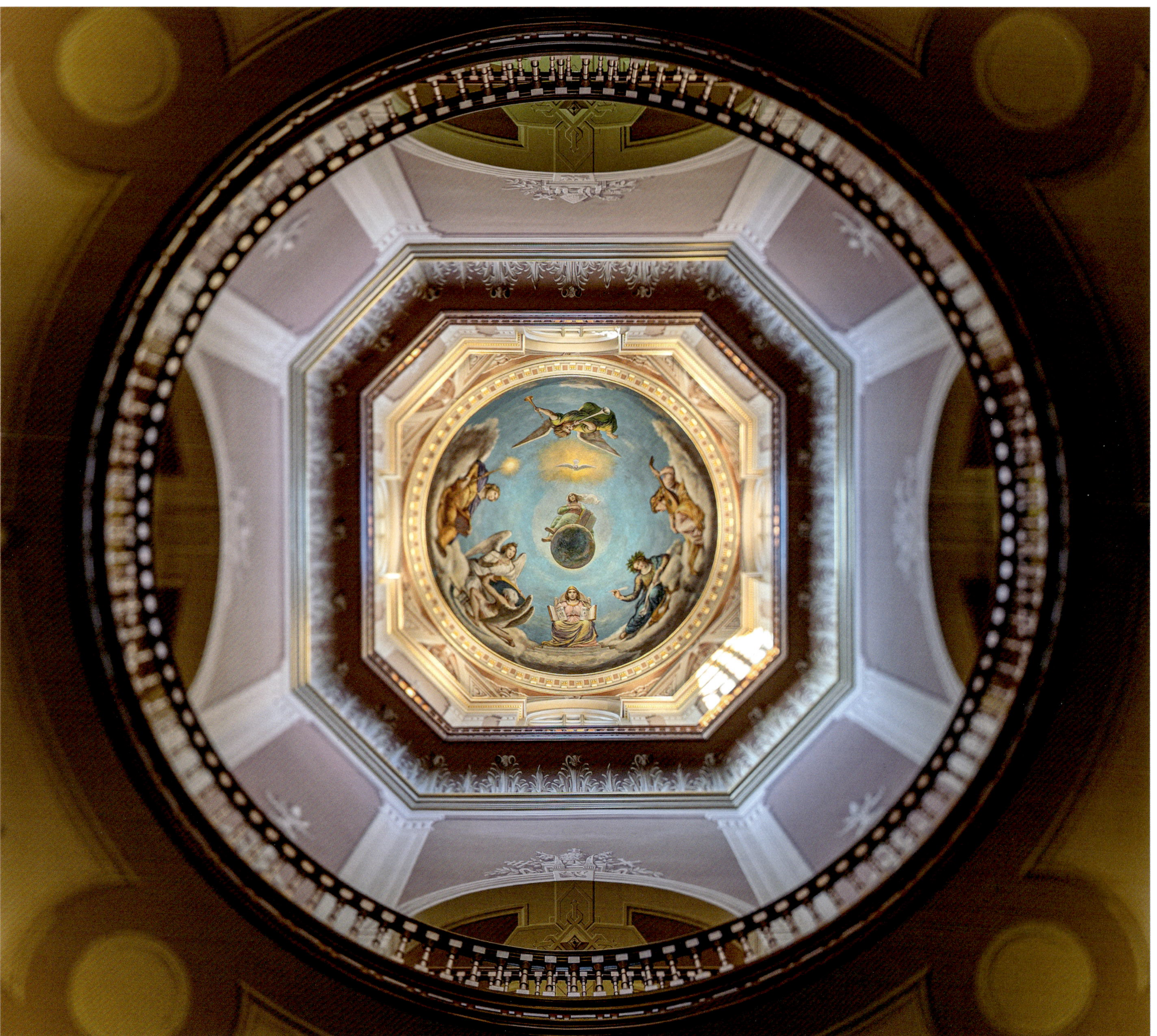

Main Building rotunda, Fuji GFX50R, 17mm Tilt/Shift lens, 1/6 f4, ISO100

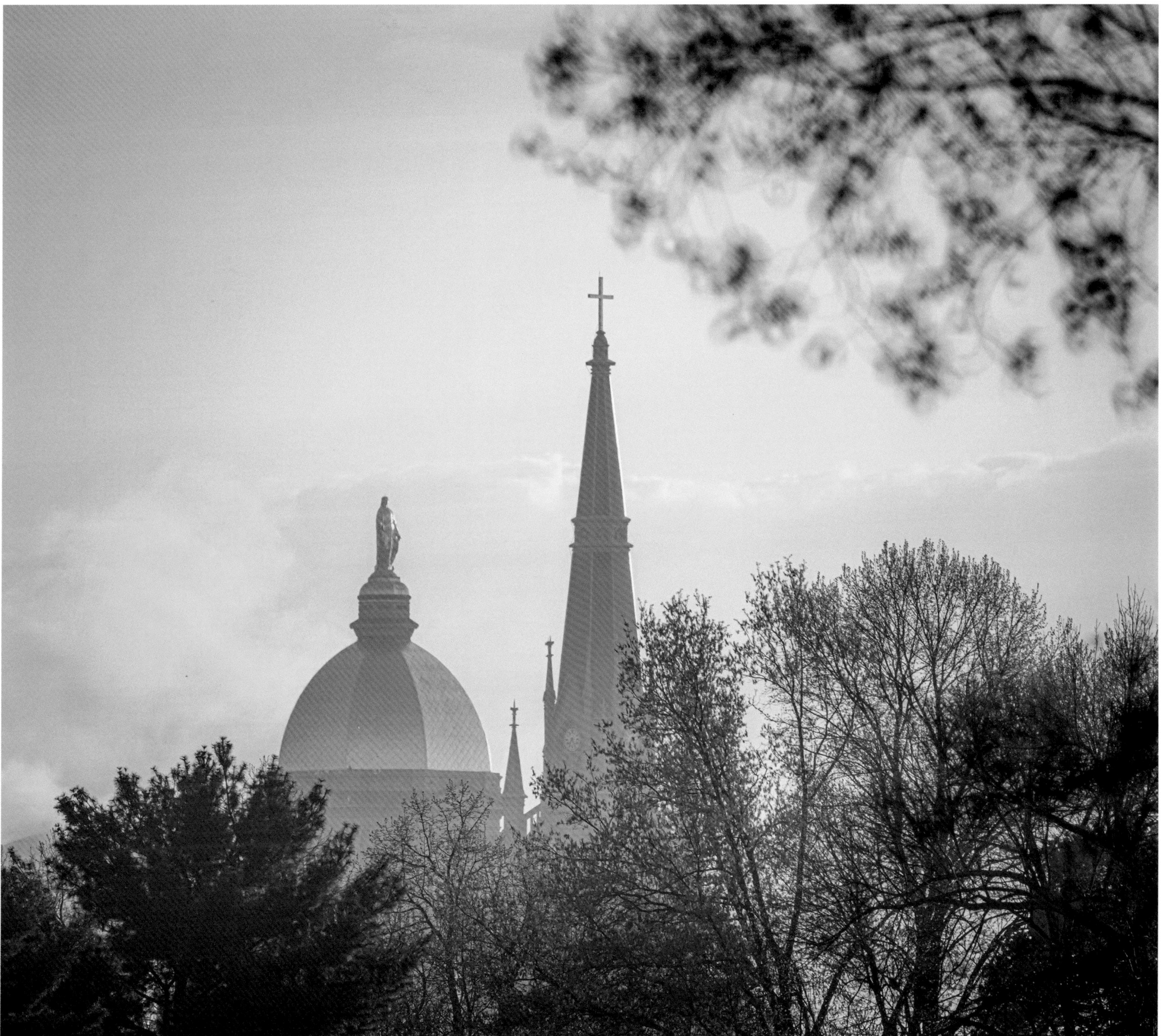

The Dome and Basilica from corner of Angela and SR933, Nikon D850, 500mm mirror lens, 1/400 f8, ISO125

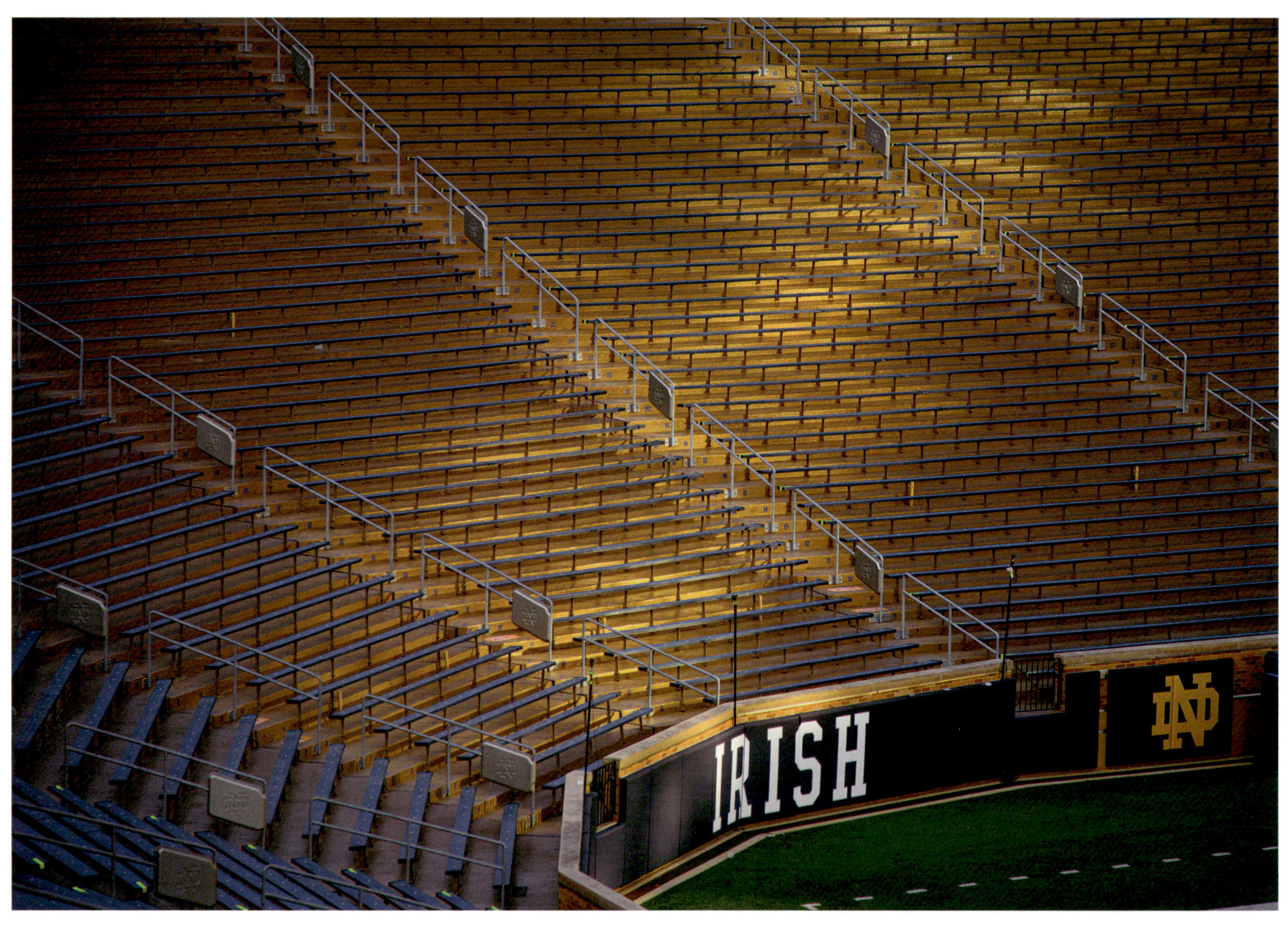

Empty Notre Dame Stadium, Nikon D850, 120mm, 1/1000 f4, ISO250

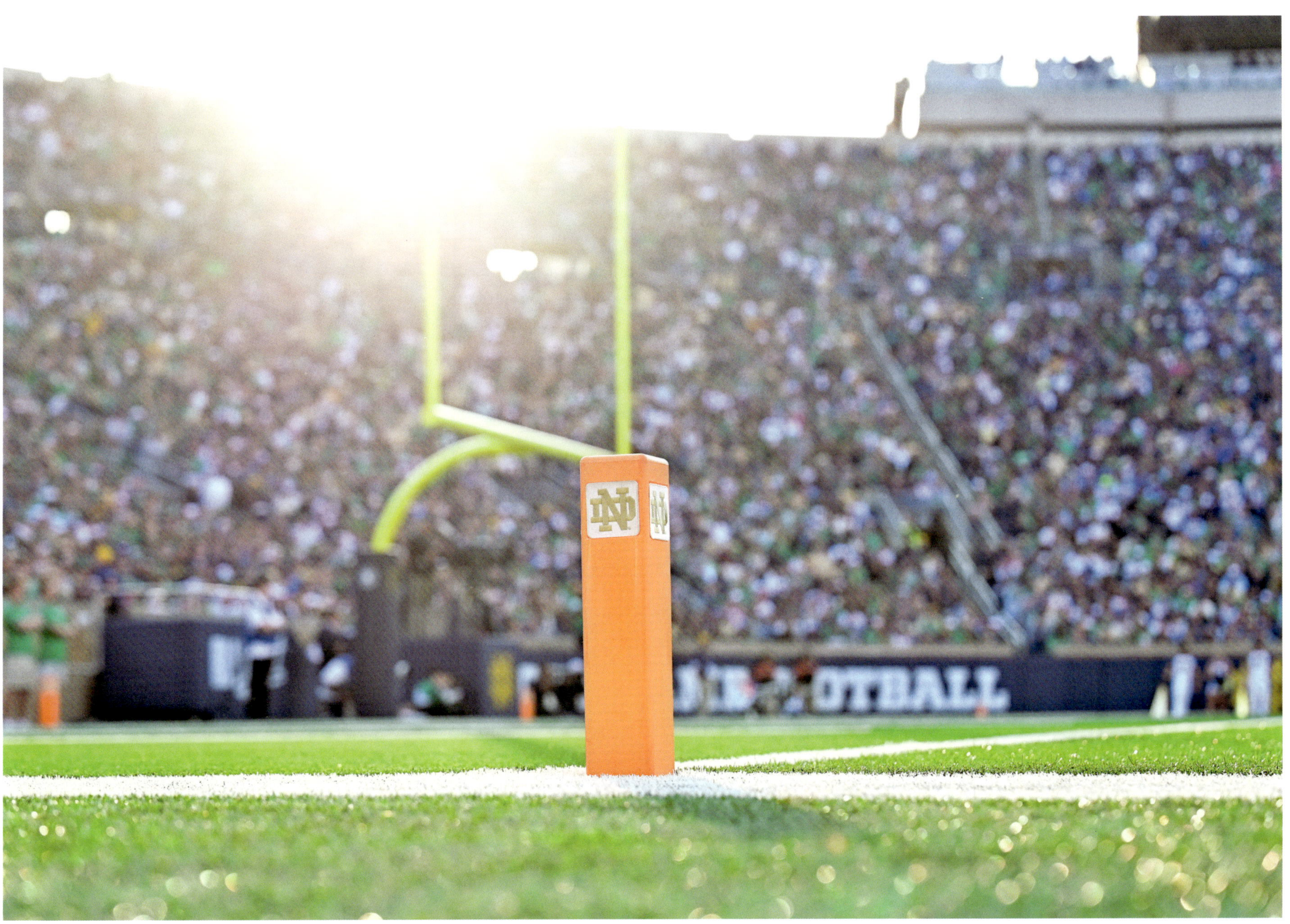

Game day, Nikon Z6, 70mm, 1/800 f3.5, ISO400

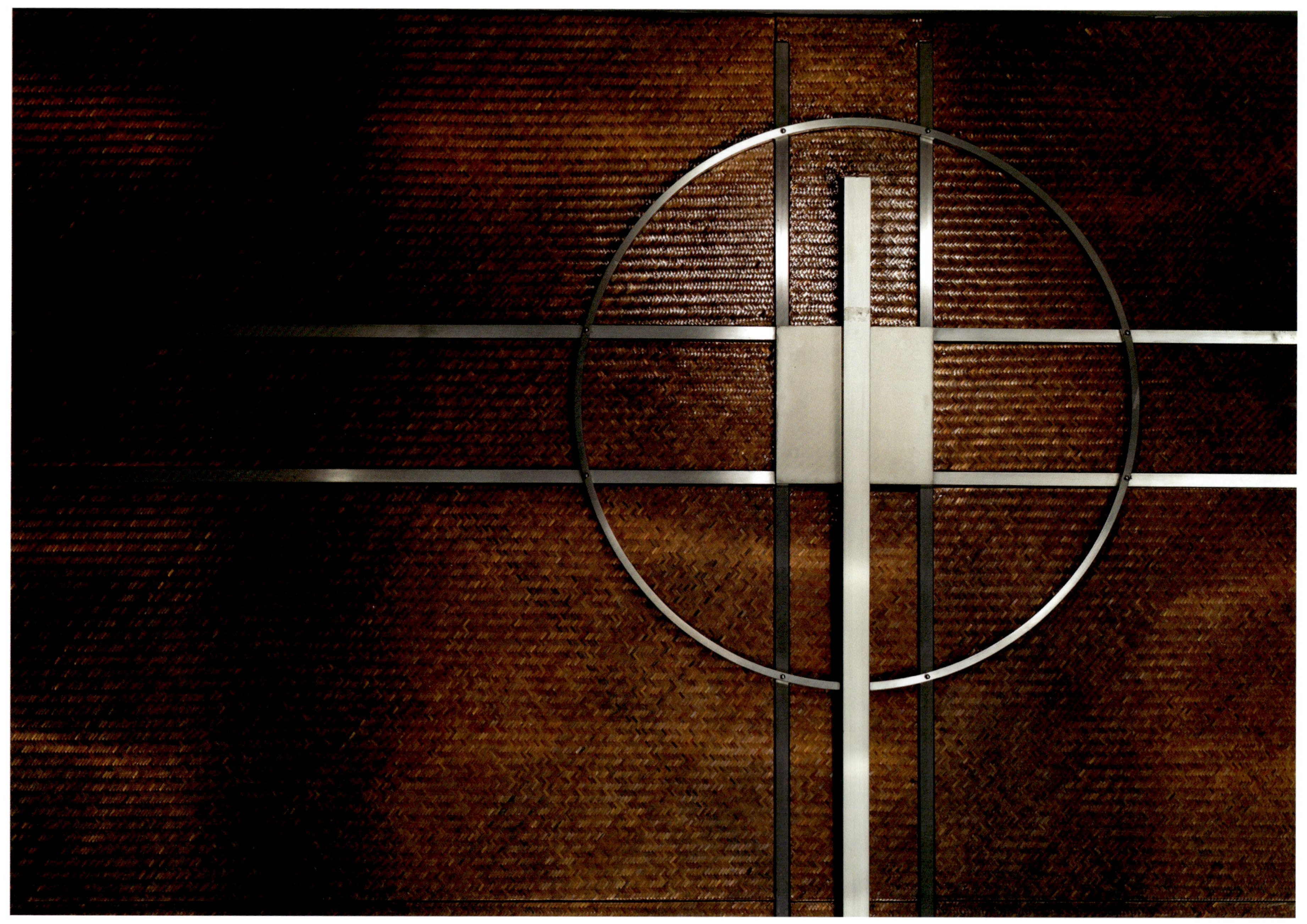

Jordan Auditorium, Mendoza College of Business, Nikon Z6, 135mm, 1/800 f4.5, ISO320

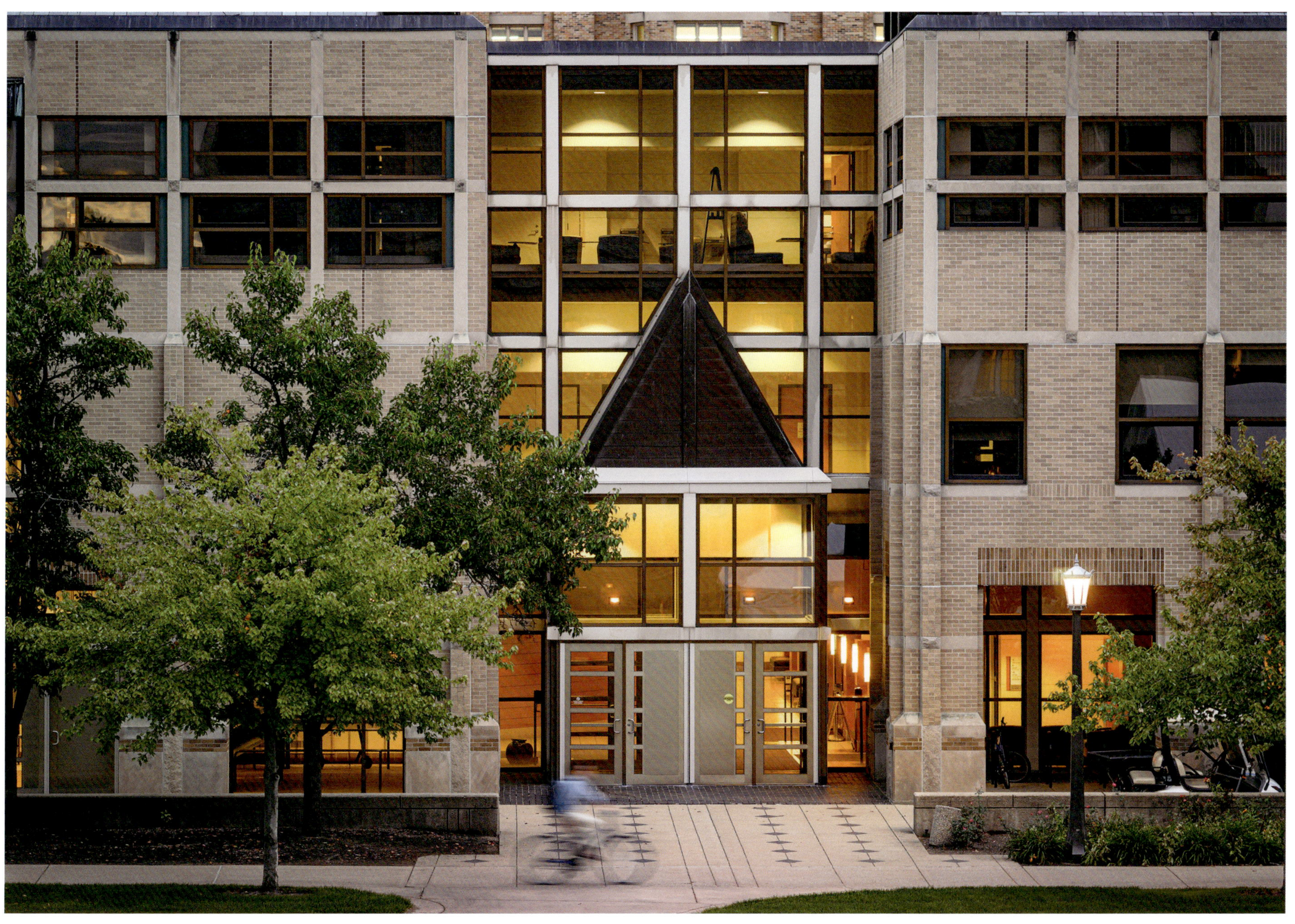

DeBartolo Hall, Nikon Z6, 135mm, 1/13 f2, ISO200

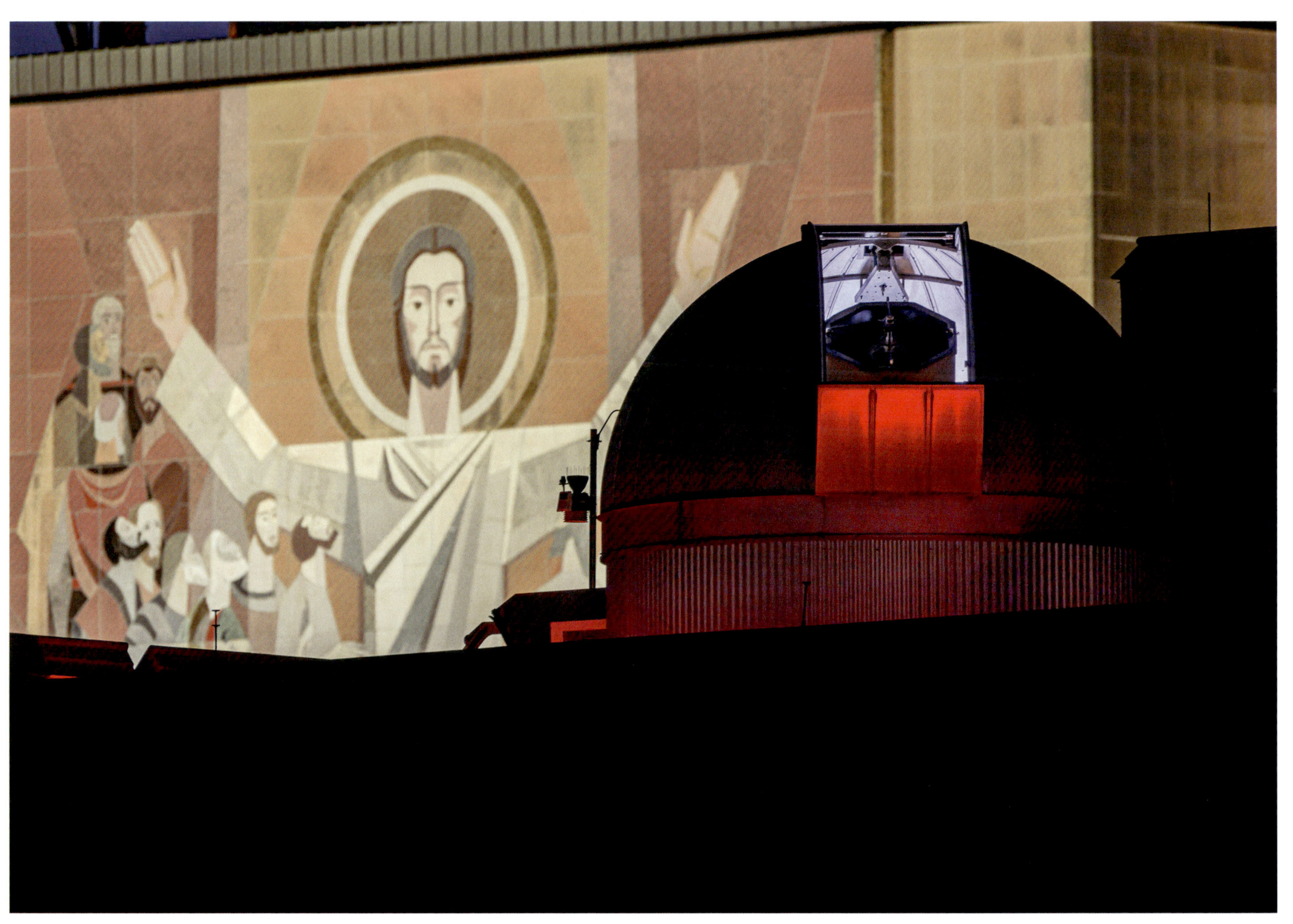

Jordan Hall of Science observatory, Nikon Z9, 850mm, 1/1.2 f8, ISO400

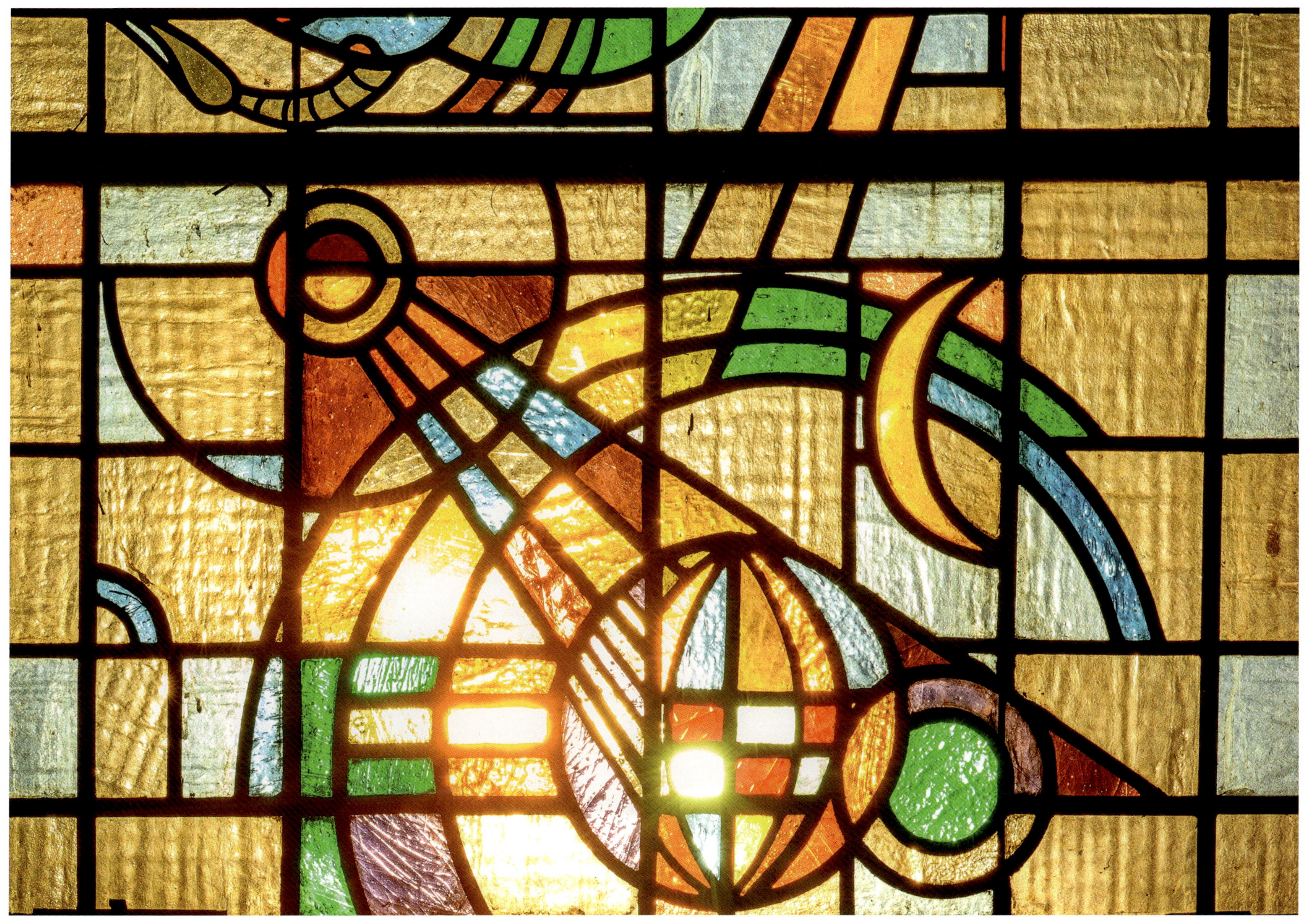

O’Shaughnessy Hall stained glass, Nikon Z6, 400mm, 1/320 f22, ISO100

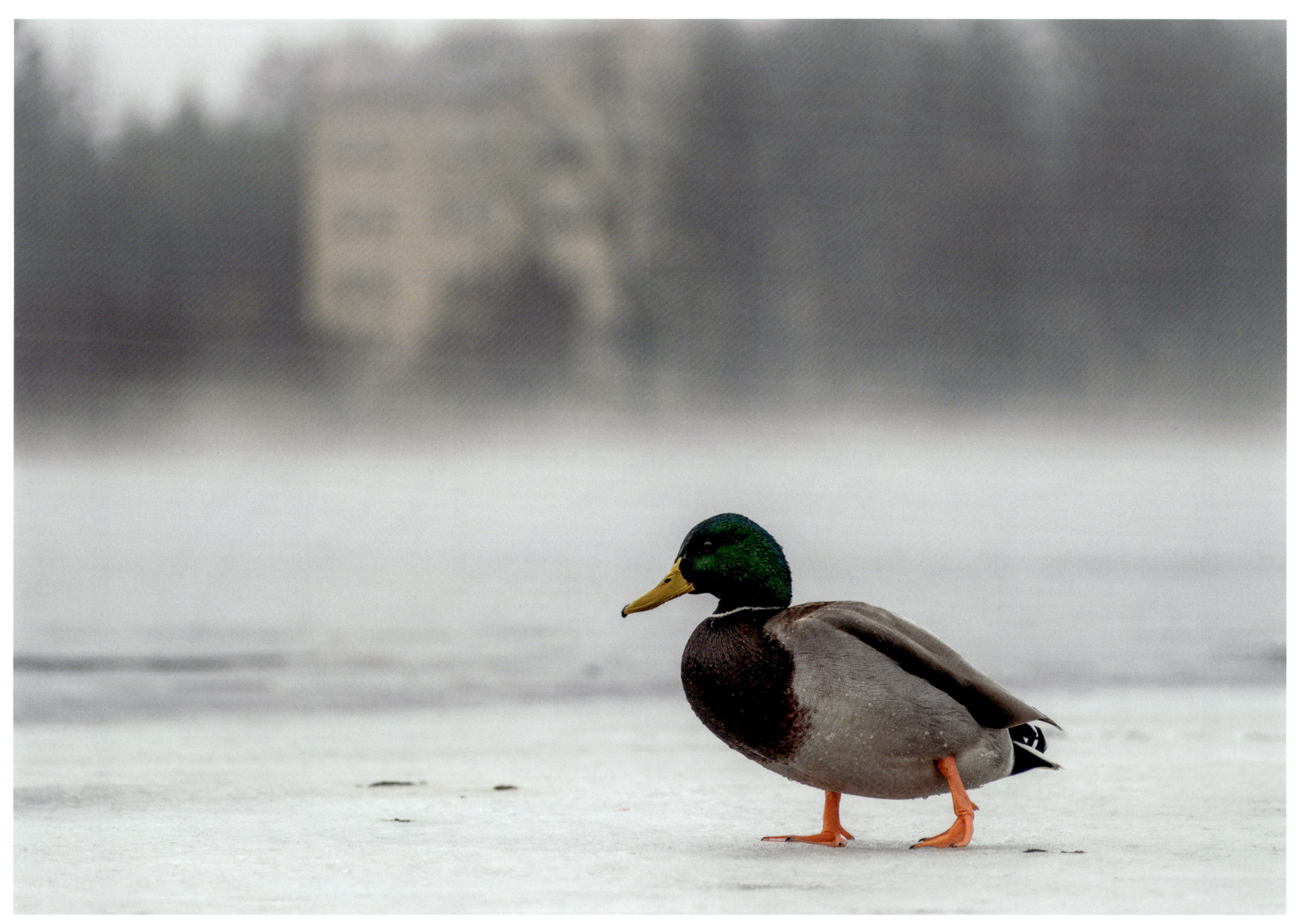

Duck on Saint Mary's Lake, Fuji GFX100s, 200mm, 1/320 f5.6, ISO200

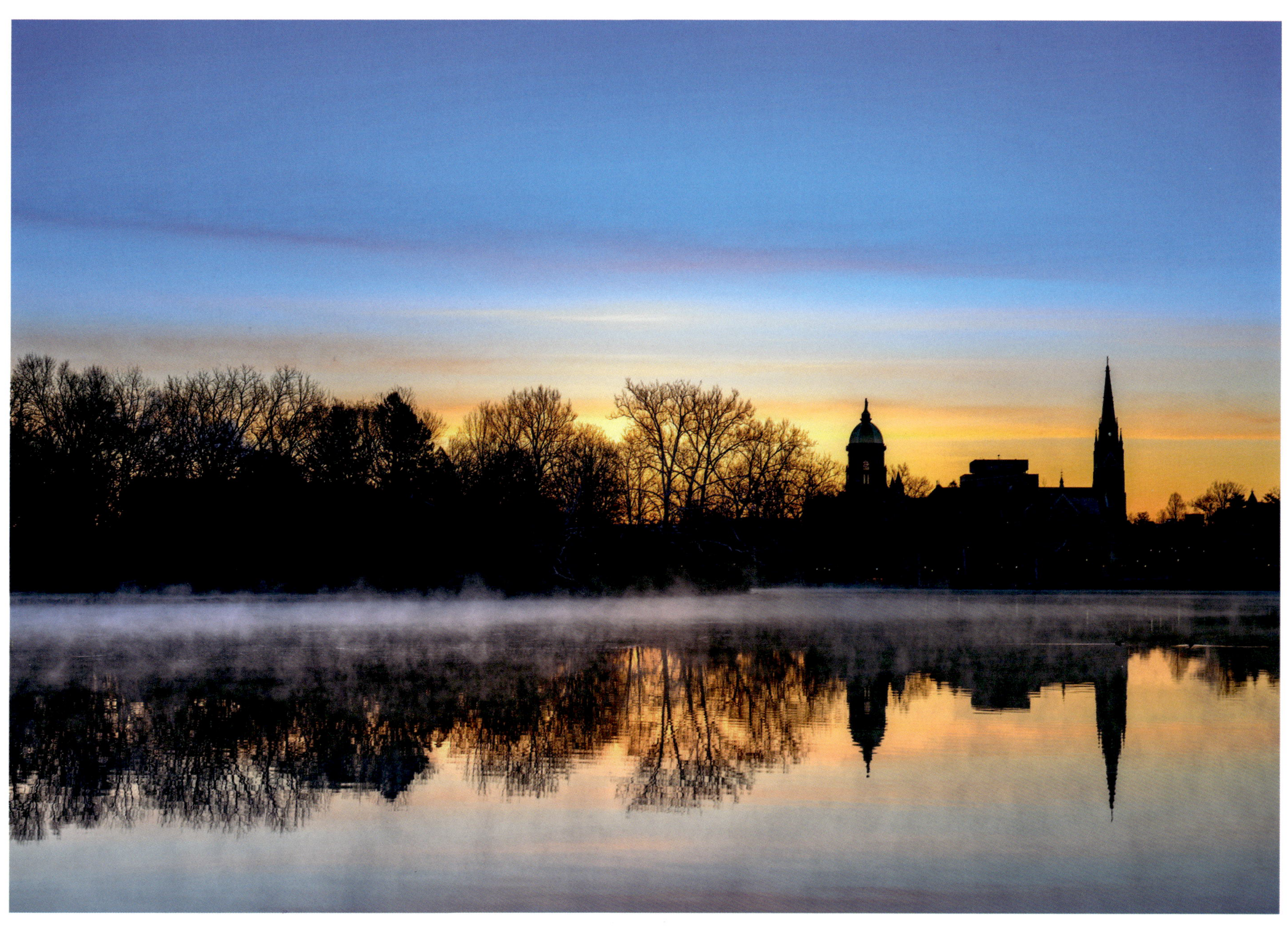

Saint Mary's Lake sunrise, Nikon Z7, 52mm, 1/10 f6.3, ISO64

The variety of weather means a variety of backdrops for campus landmarks as the clouds and sun do their thing.

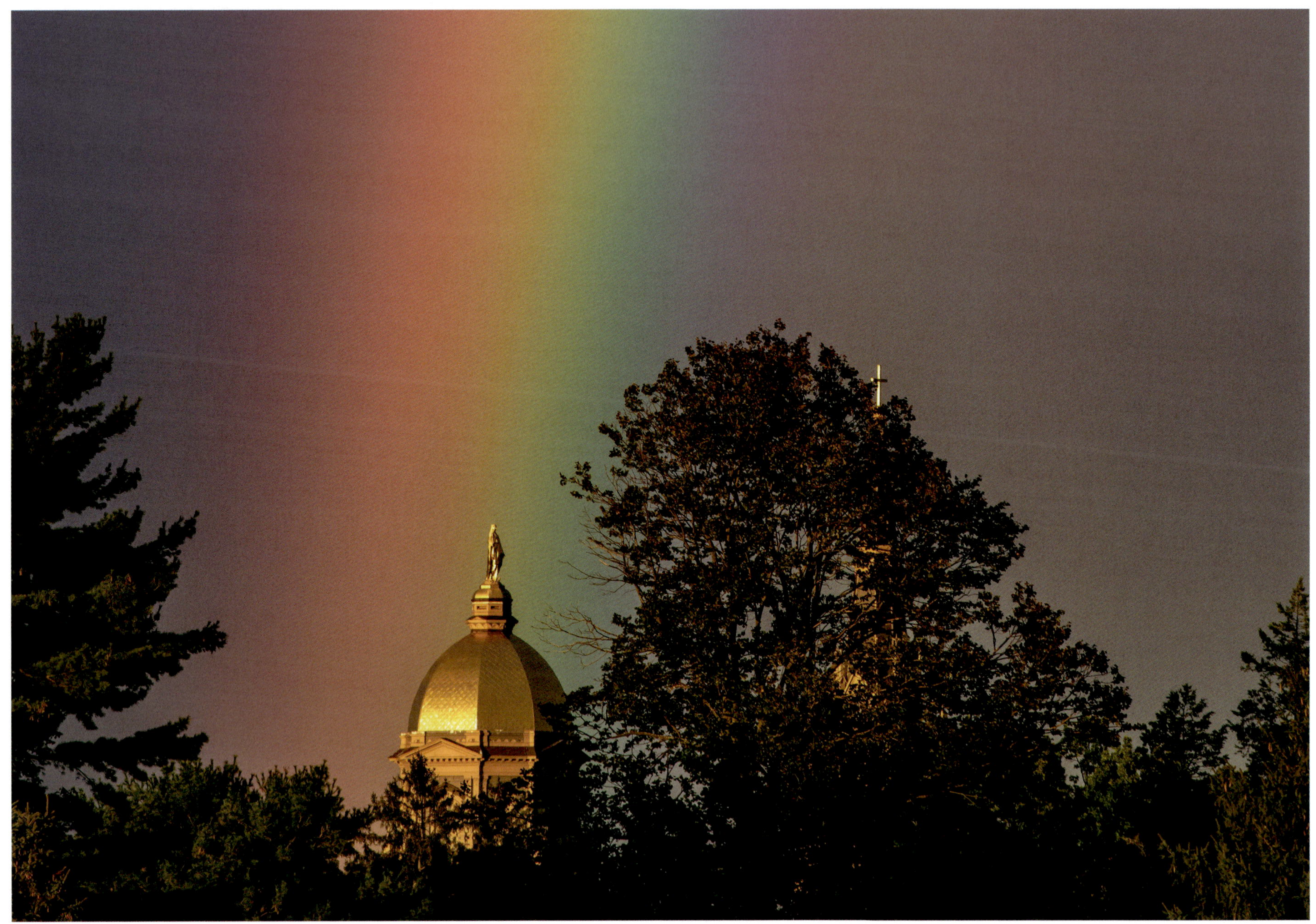

Rainbow over the Dome from Holy Cross College, Nikon D850, 300mm, 1/160 f9, ISO125

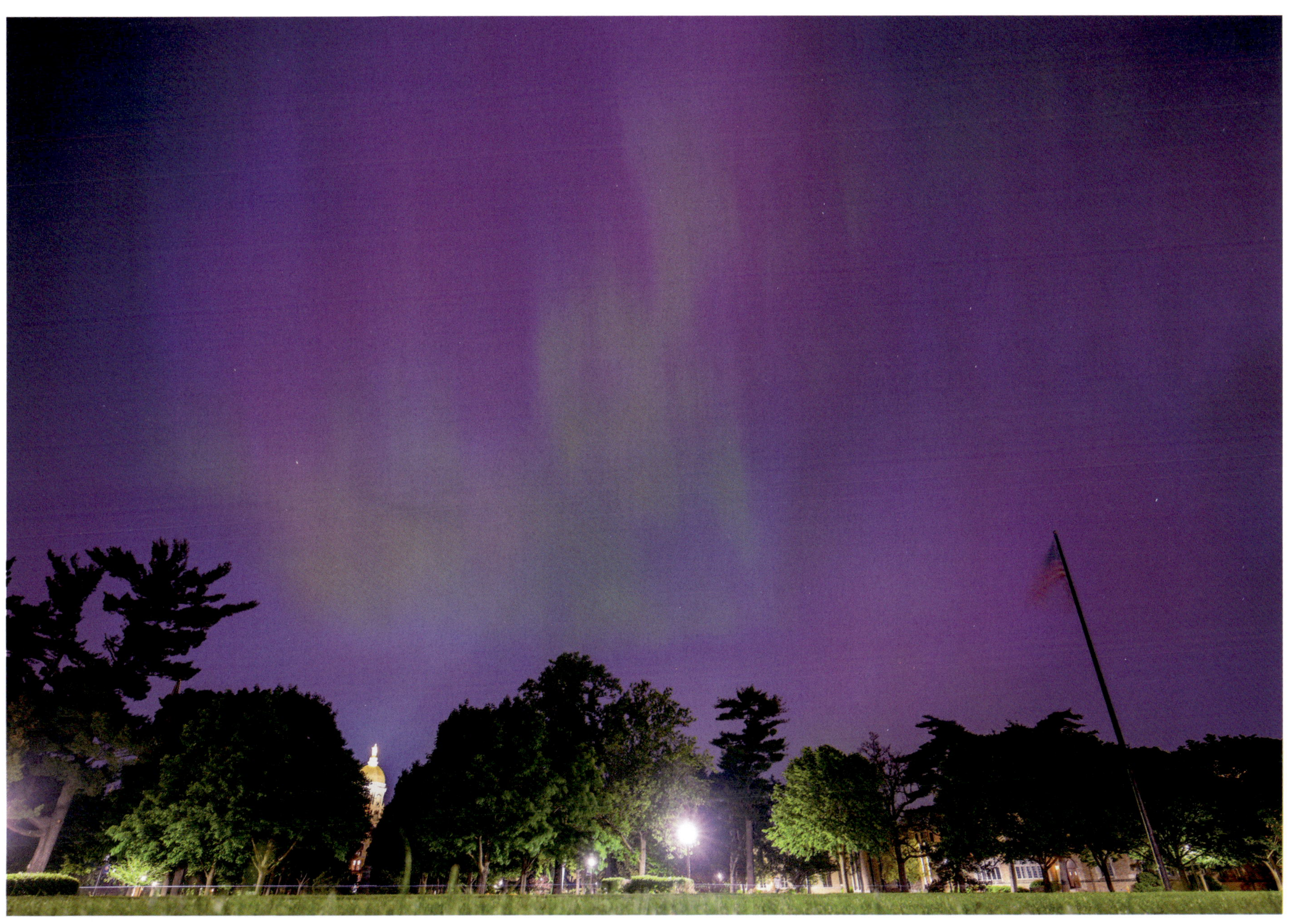

Aurora Borealis, Nikon Z8, 17mm, 30sec. f2.8, ISO64

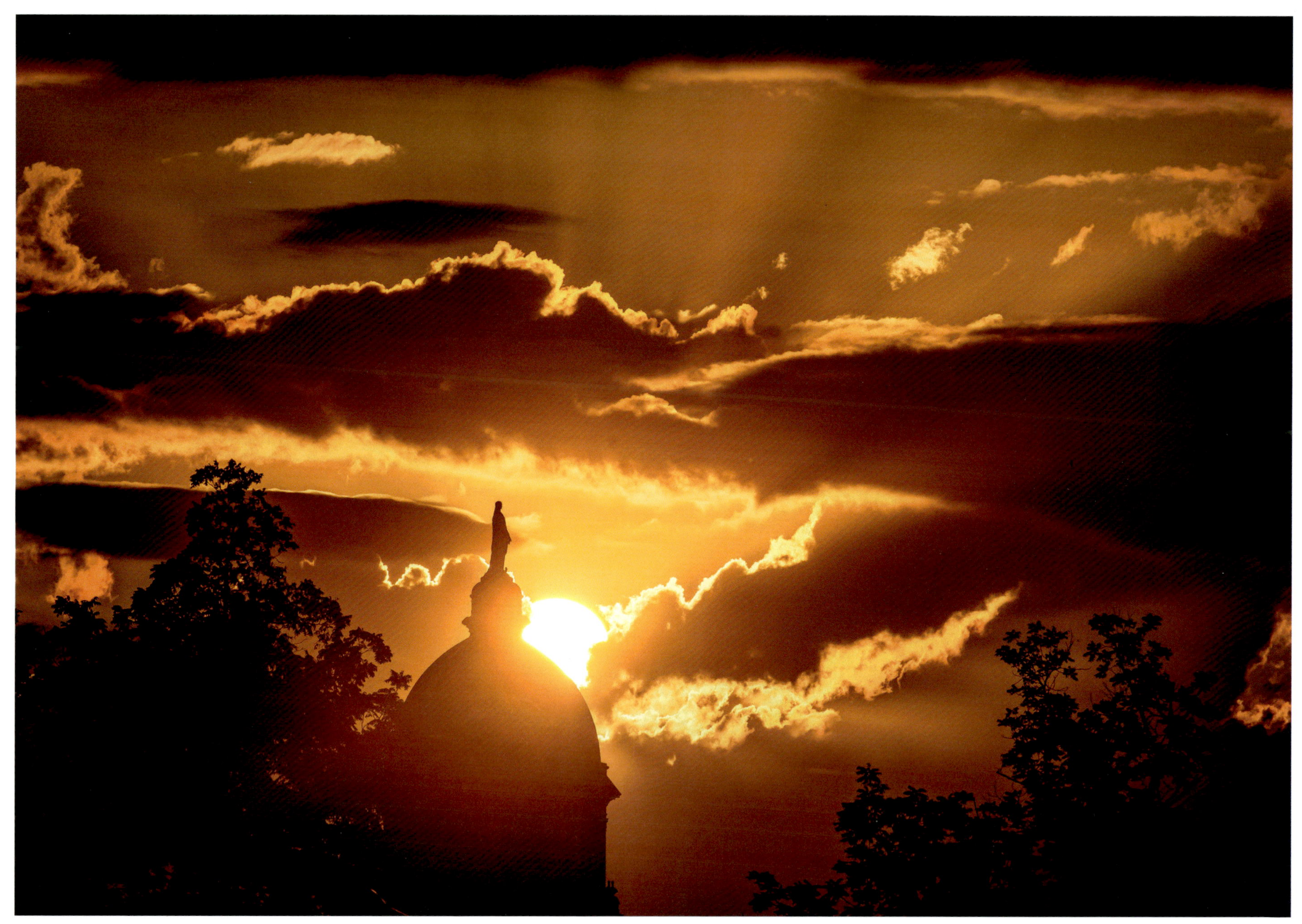

Summer sunrise, Nikon D850, 200mm, 1/1600 f20, ISO64

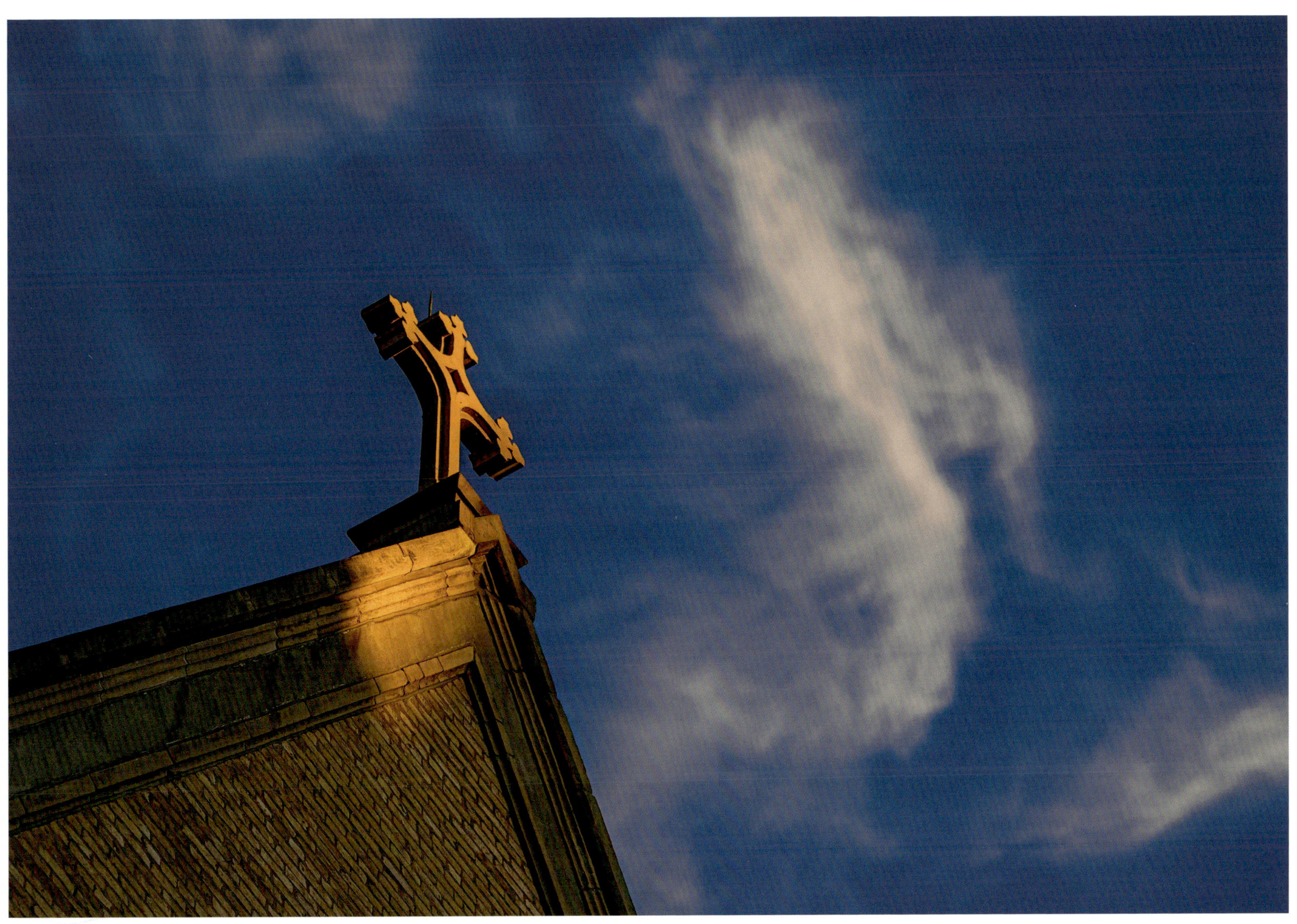

Cross on Basilica transept, Nikon Z6, 135mm, 1/800 f3.2, ISO100

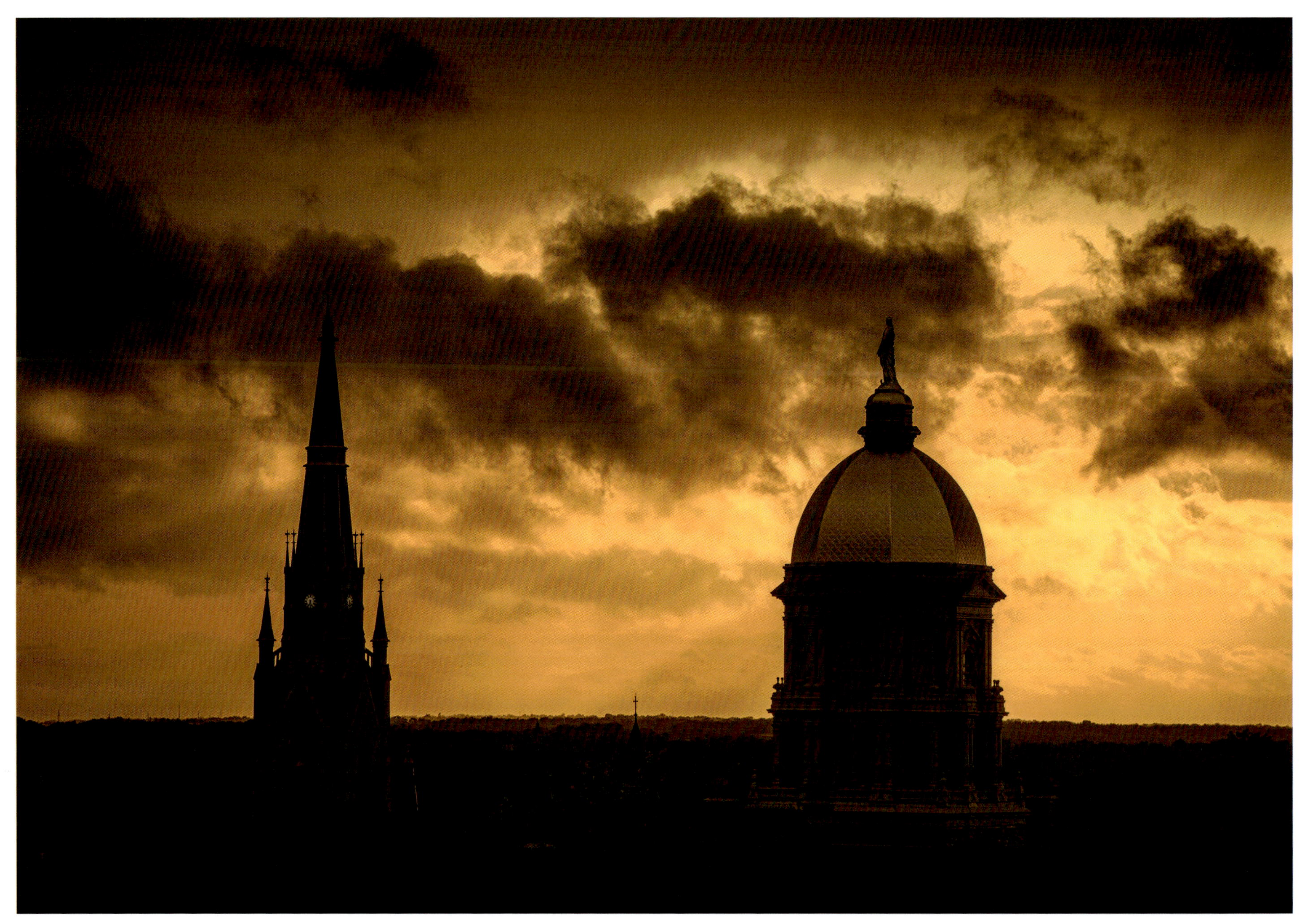

Basilica and the Dome from the top floor of Grace Hall, Nikon D850, 175mm, 1/800 f5.6, ISO125

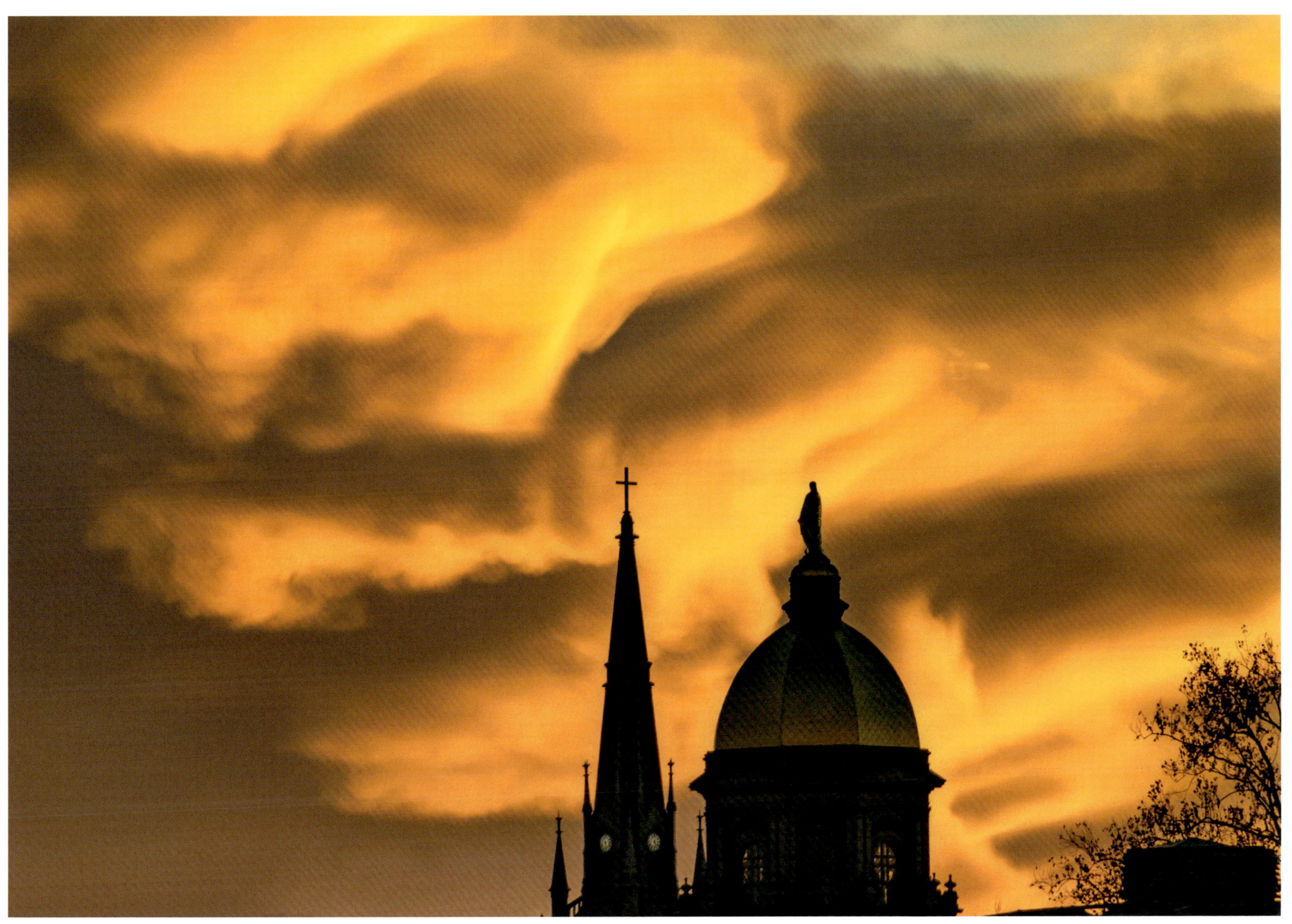

Lake-effect snow clouds, Nikon D5, 200mm, 1/1000 f2.8, ISO200

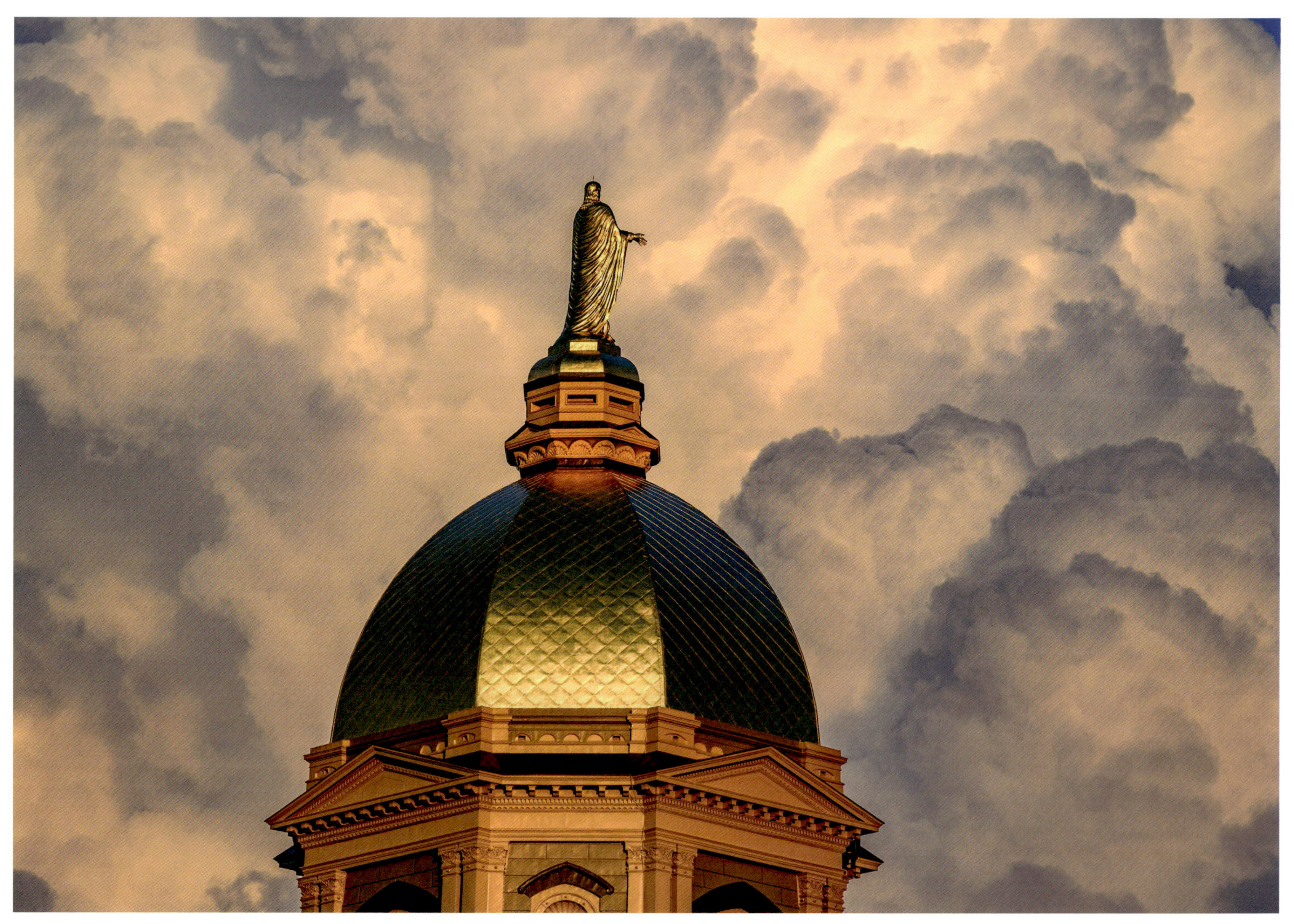

Summer storm clouds, Nikon Z8, 120mm, 1/400 f6.3, ISO64

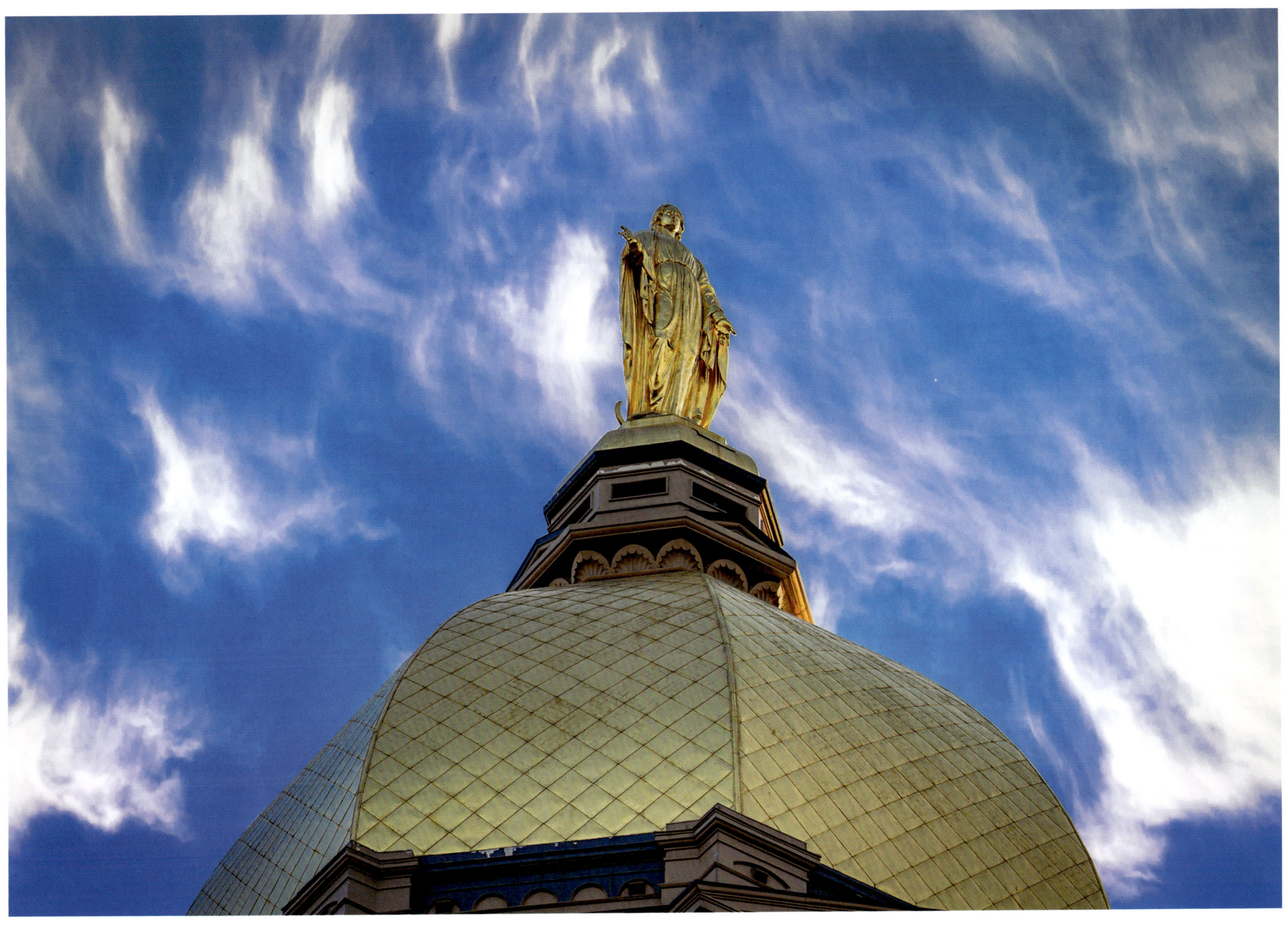

Wind-swept clouds over the Dome, Nikon Z6, 135mm, 1/320 f3.5, ISO100

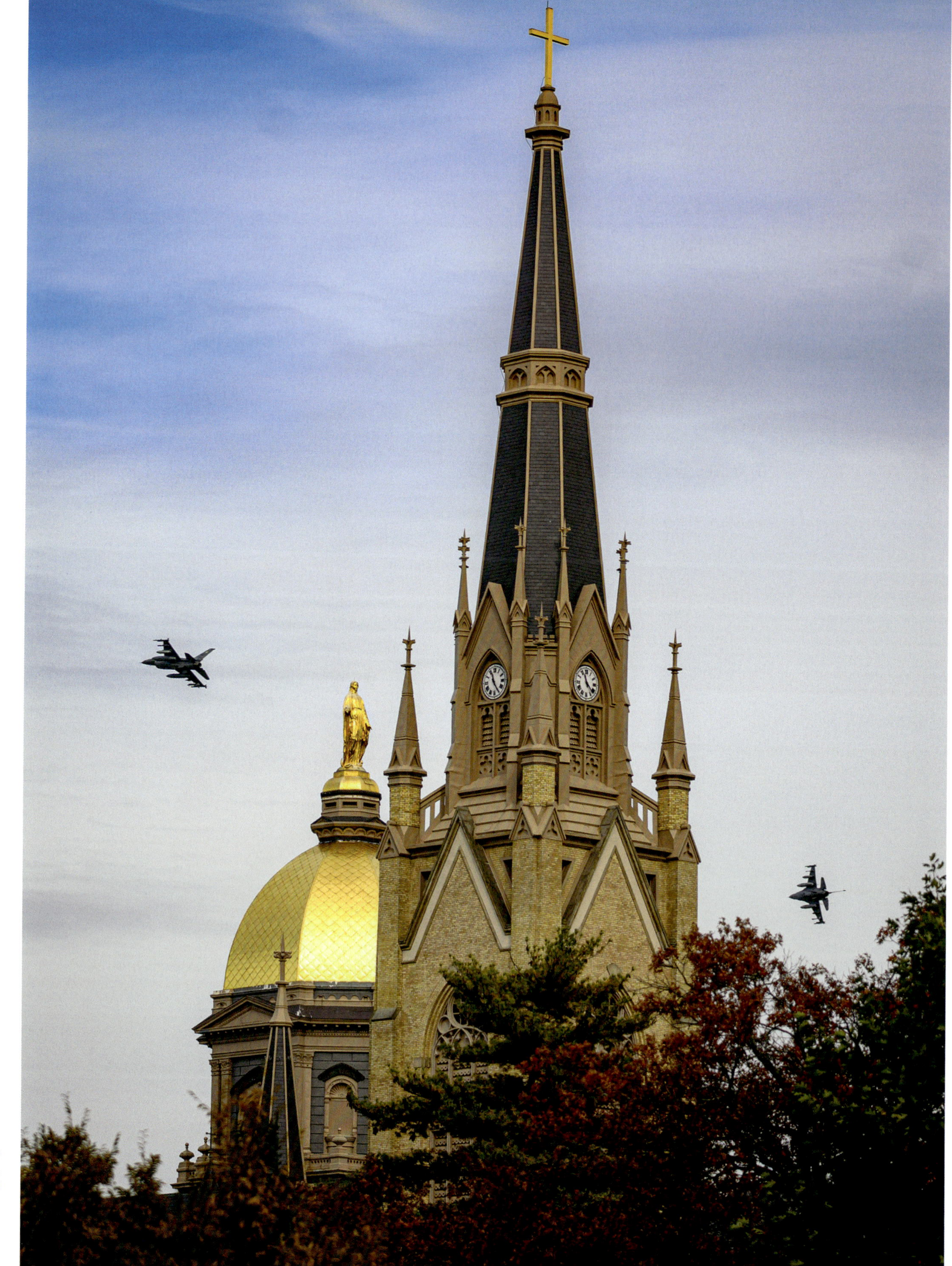

F-16s practice the day before a home football game, Nikon Z6, 112mm, 1/1000 f4, ISO100

I like airplanes. A lot! We're lucky to get a good frequency and variety of military aircraft to fly over Notre Dame football games. Football Fridays can also be an opportunity to see the airplanes doing their practice runs.

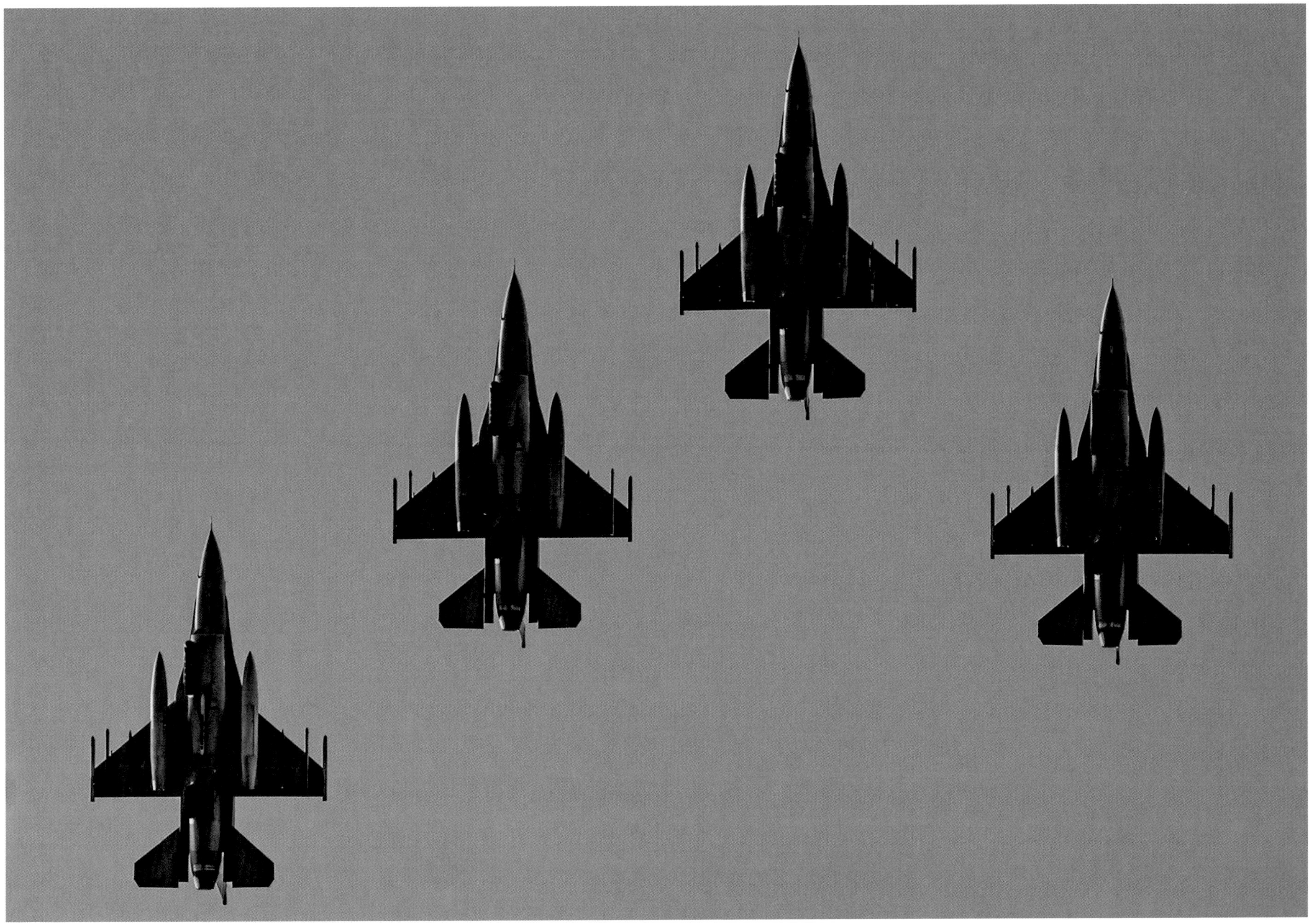

F-16s fly over Notre Dame Stadium, Nikon Z6II, 93mm, 1/2500 f6.3, ISO400

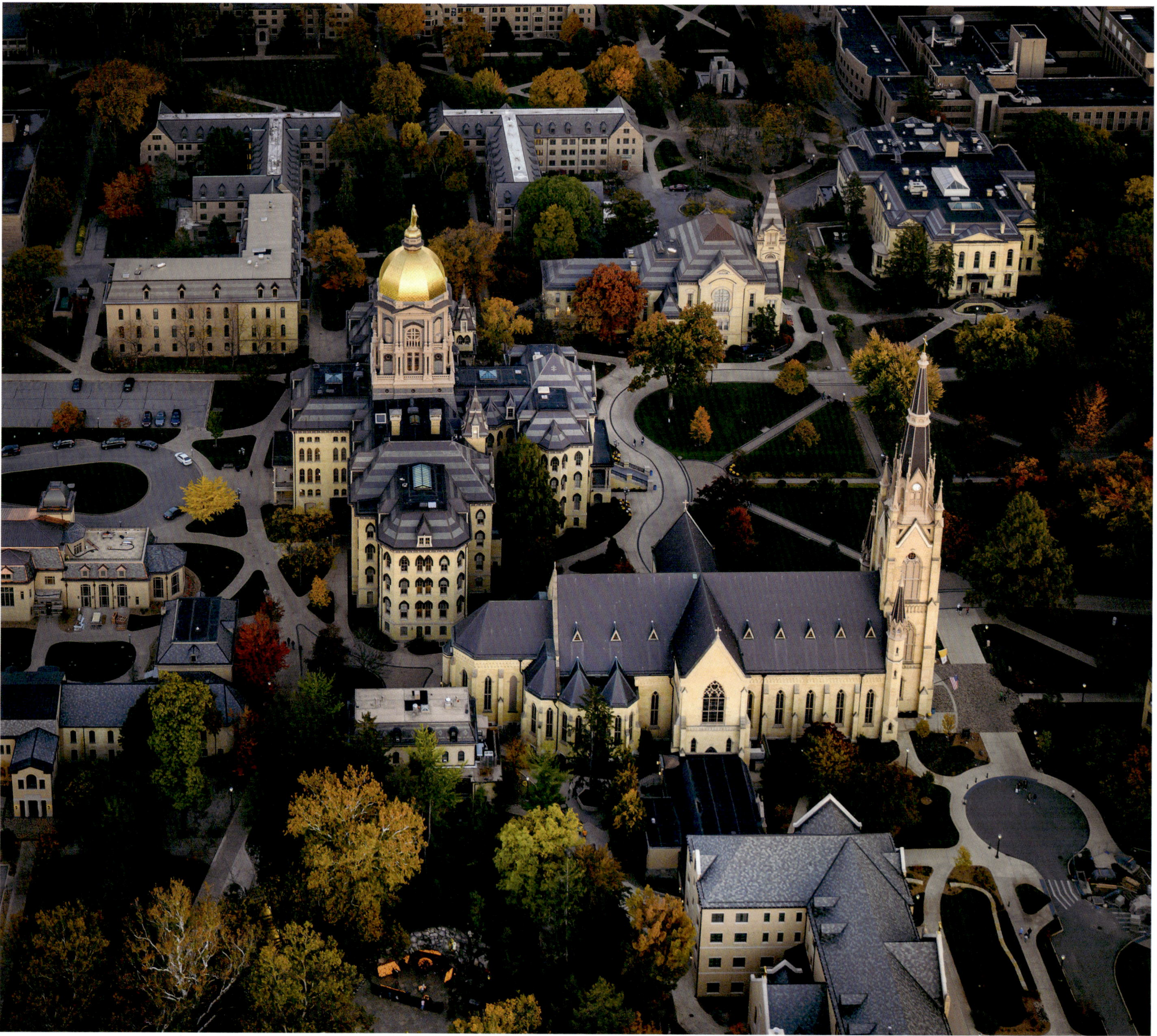

Aerial of the Dome, Basilica, and Grotto, Nikon Z7II, 51mm, 1/250 f3.2, ISO640

In the last ten years or so, drones have evolved from a toy to a serious photographic tool. I've taken FAA tests and I work with Notre Dame administrators and police to fly in a safe and responsible way. Drones can give a unique perspective that's taller than a rooftop but lower than a helicopter can comfortably fly.

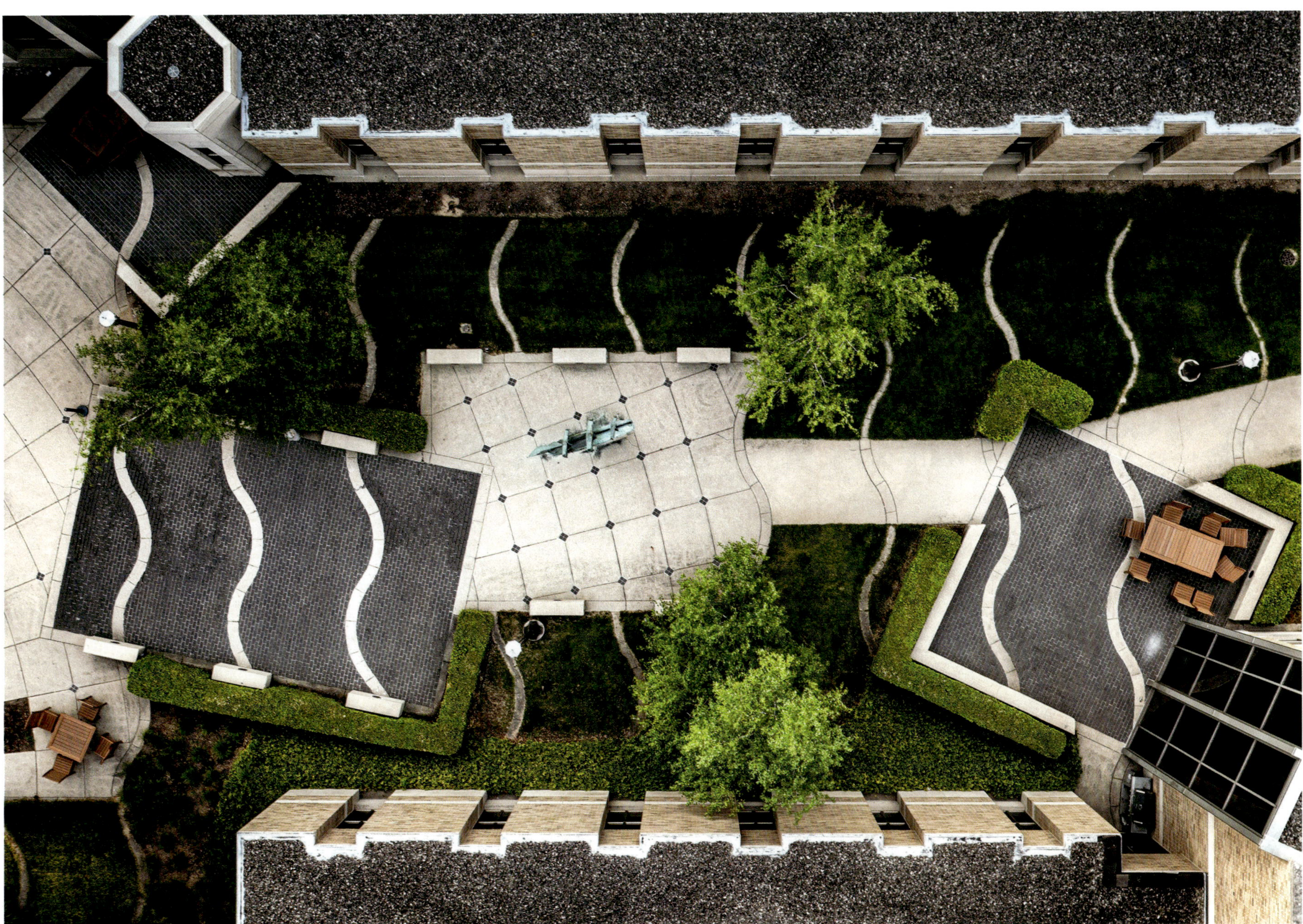

Aerial of Mendoza College of Business courtyard, DJI Mavic 2 Pro drone, 24mm equivalent, 1/40 f5.6, ISO100

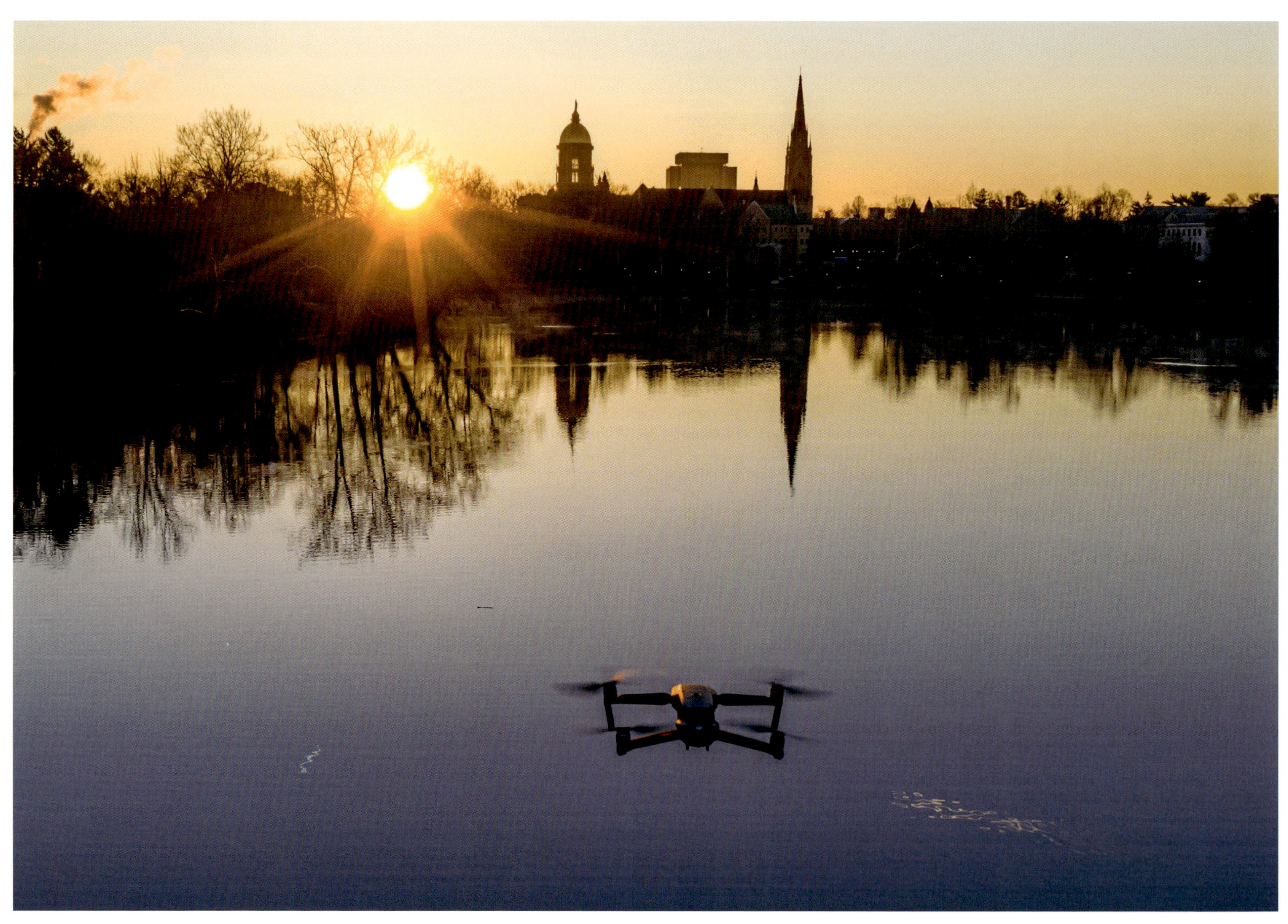

Drone air-to-air over Saint Mary's Lake, DJI Mavic 2 Pro, 24mm equivalent, 1/320 f5, ISO100

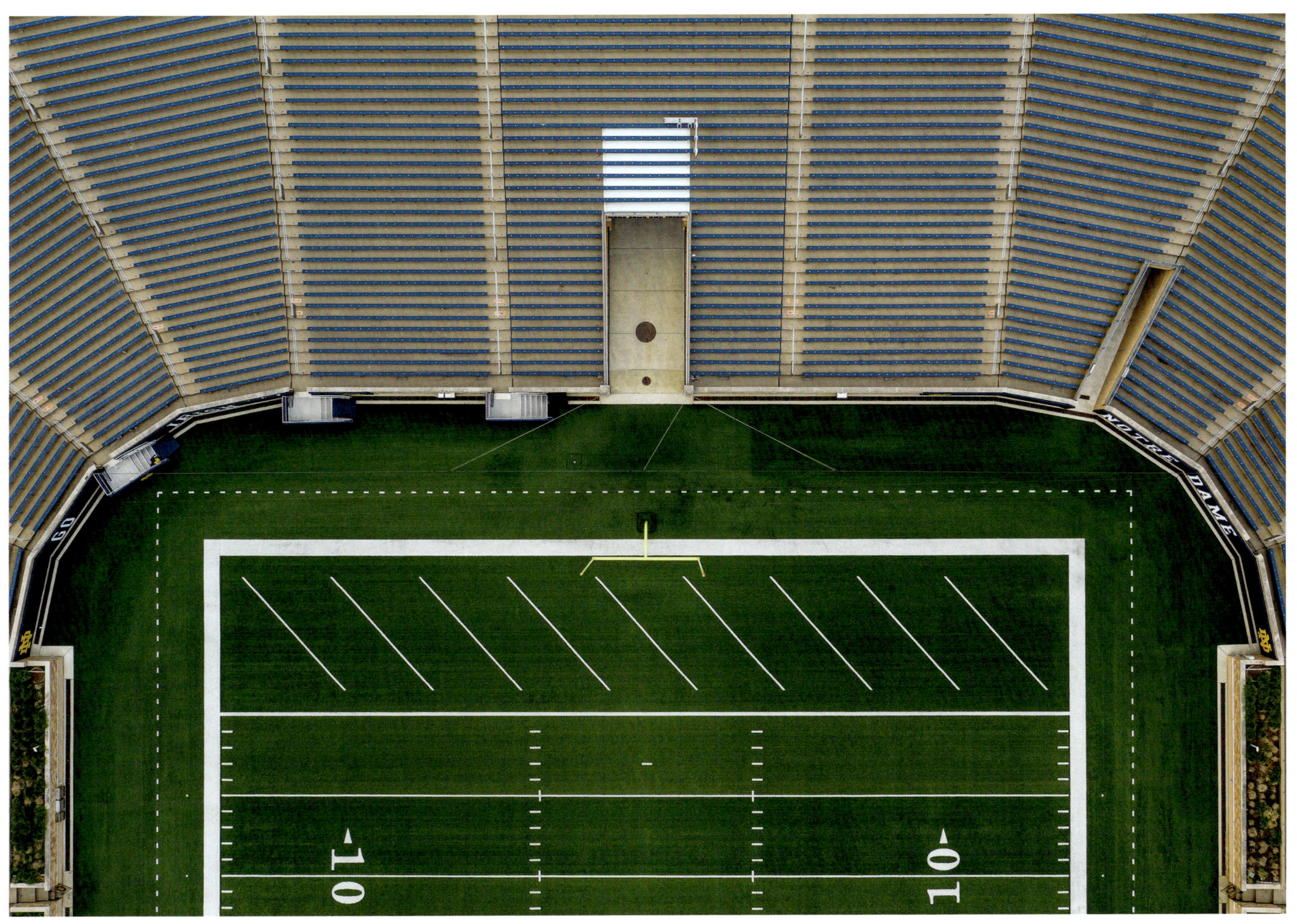

Aerial of north end zone of Notre Dame Stadium, DJI Mavic 2 Pro, 24mm equivalent, 1/30 f4, ISO100

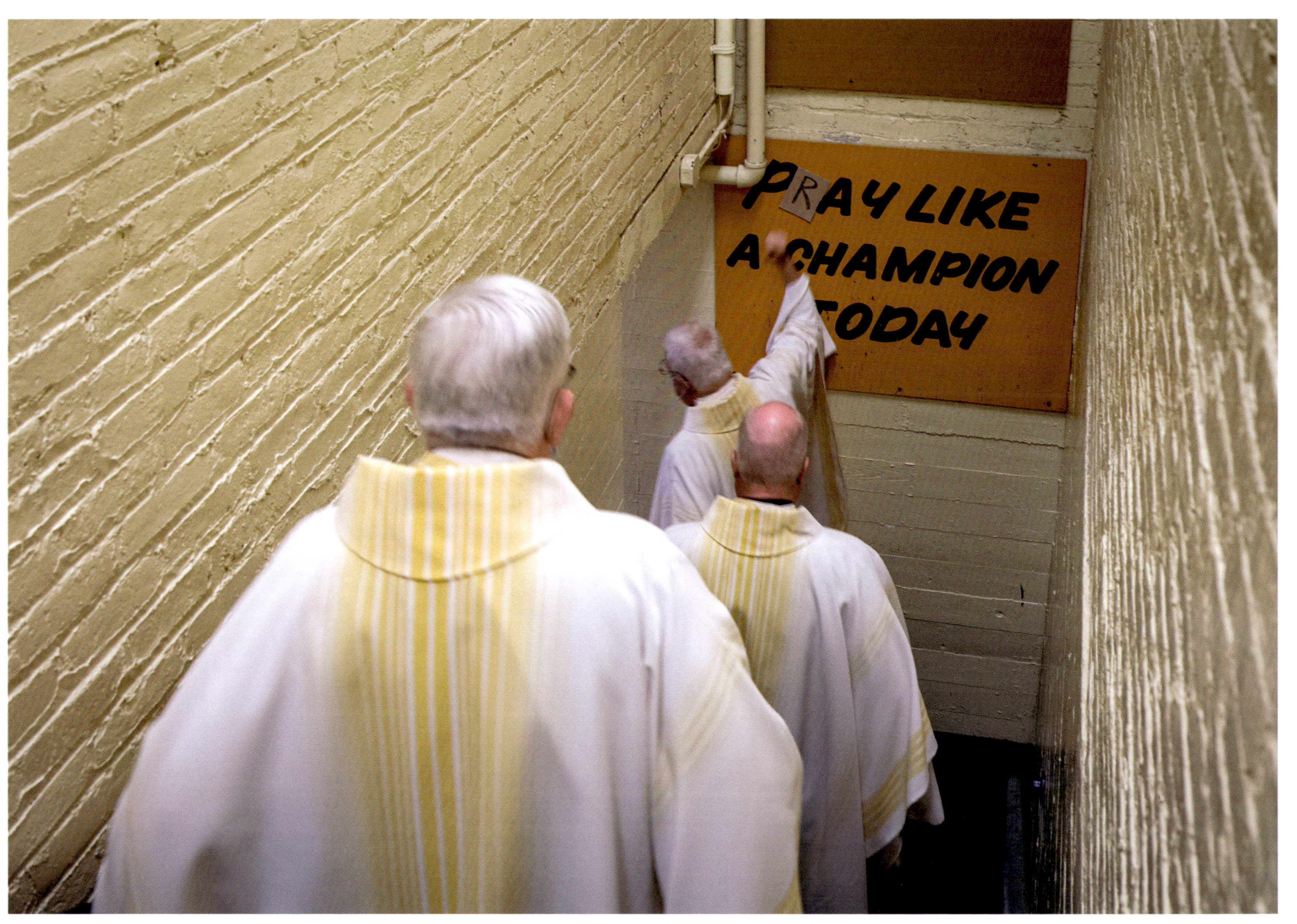

Notre Dame Stadium locker room used as a sacristy for Mass, Nikon Z7, 24mm, 1/50 f4.5, ISO640

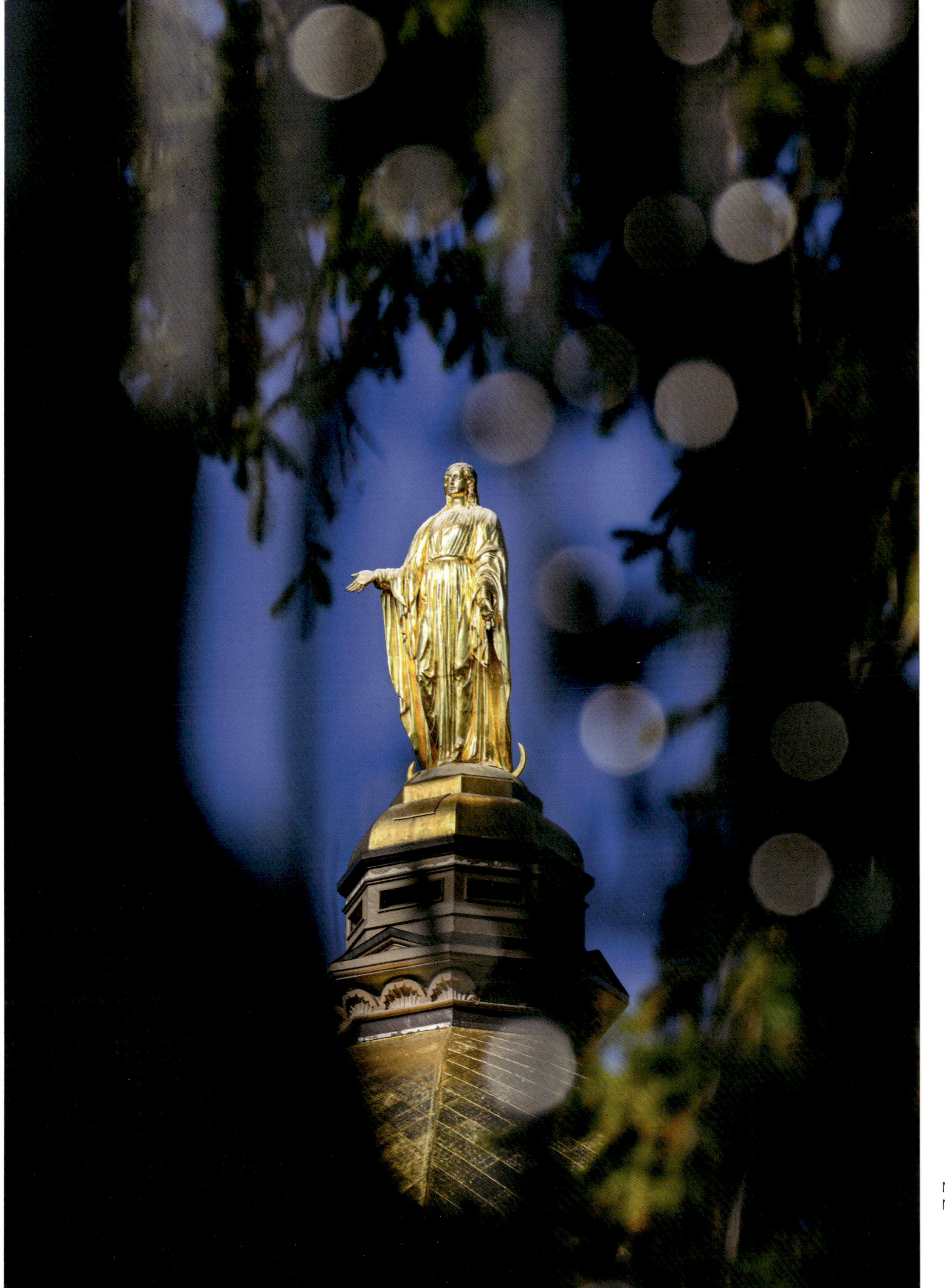

Main Building through a LaFortune railing,
Nikon Z9, 200mm, 1/400 f7.1, ISO64

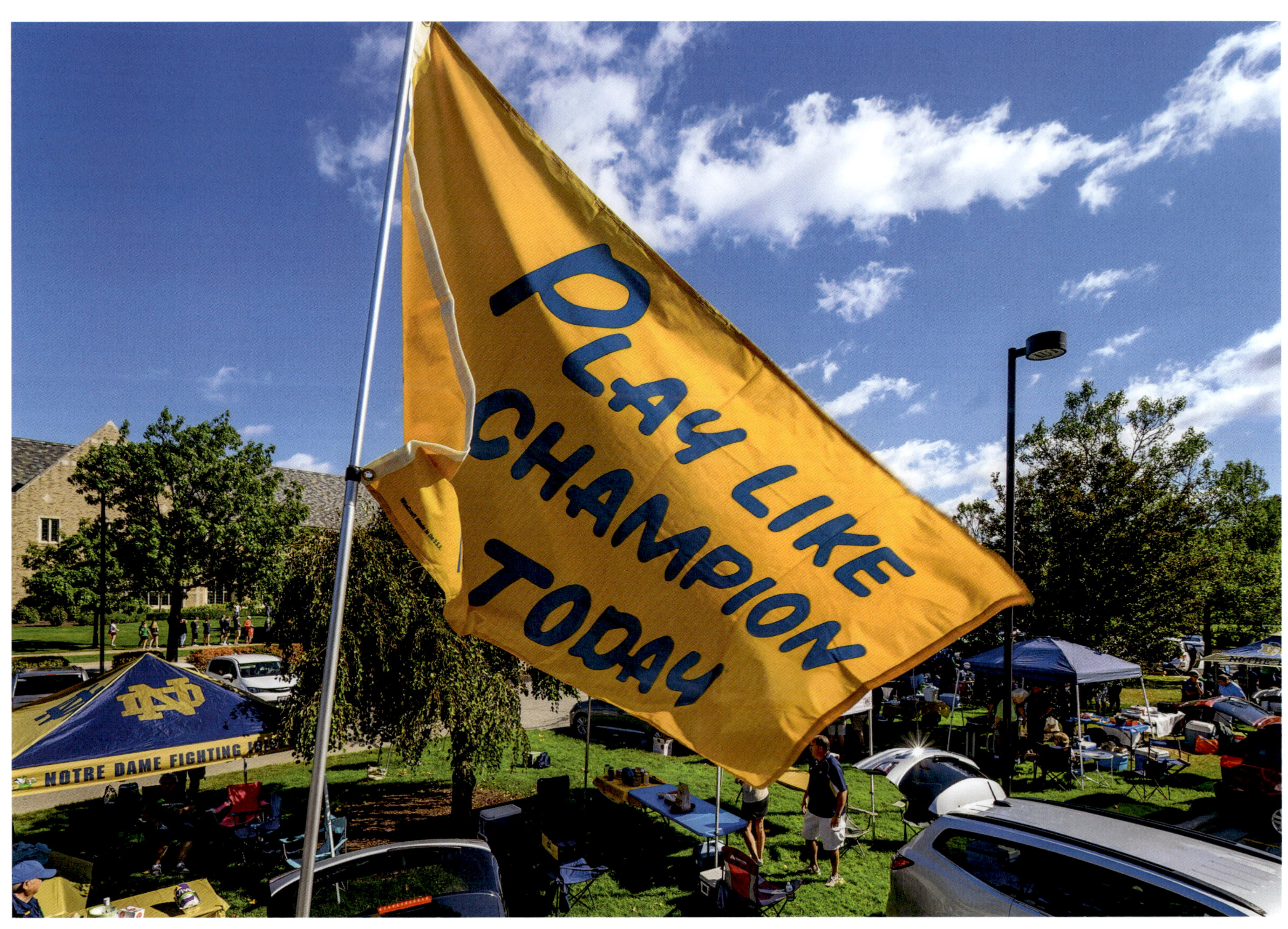

Tailgating near the bookstore, Nikon Z6, 14mm, 1/250 f9, ISO100

Notre Dame football is timeless. Notre Dame football players and coaches change. I look for football photos that speak to the tradition, pageantry, and spectacle of a game day.

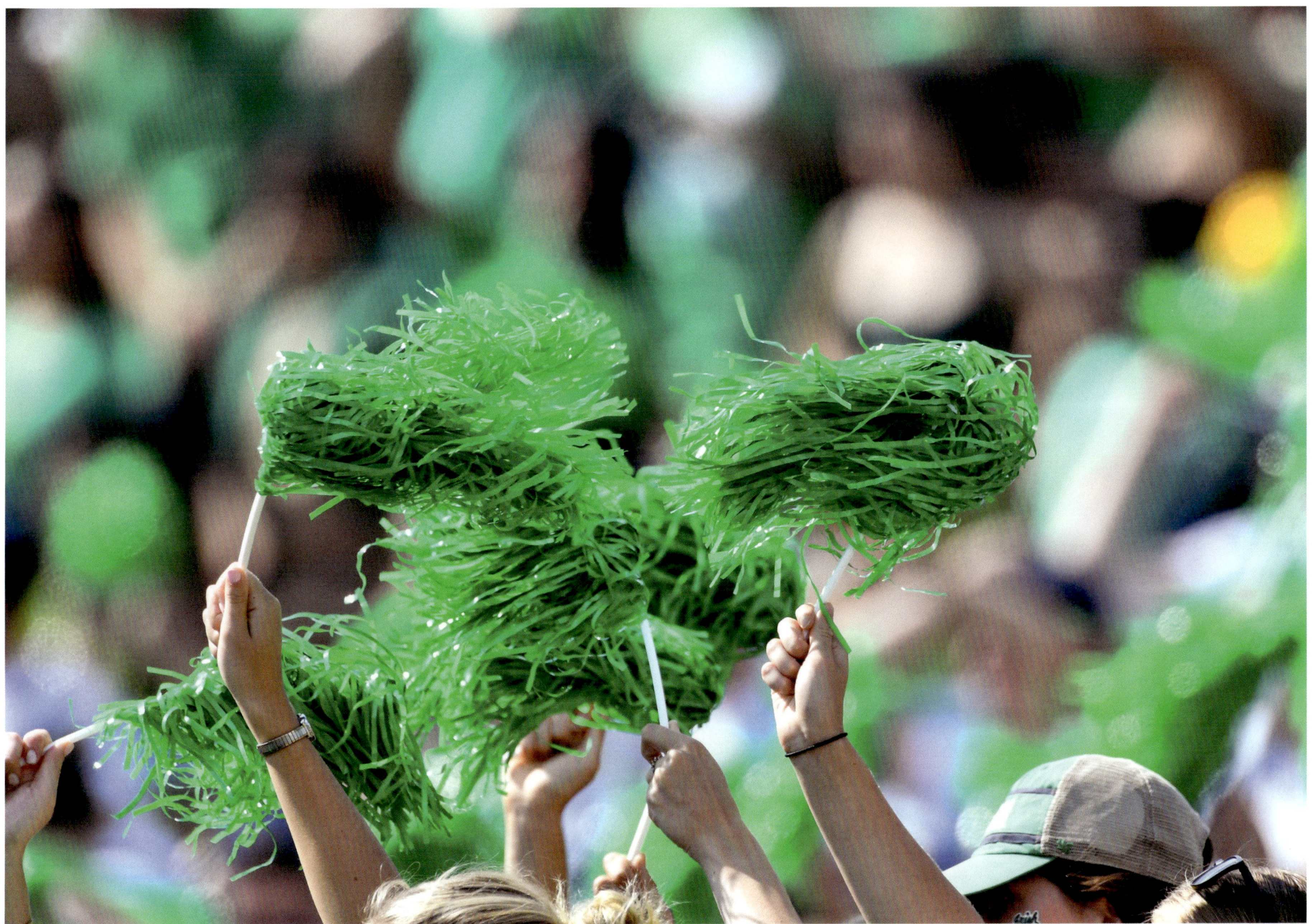

Notre Dame Stadium student section, Nikon D5, 850mm, 1/1600 f6.3, ISO500

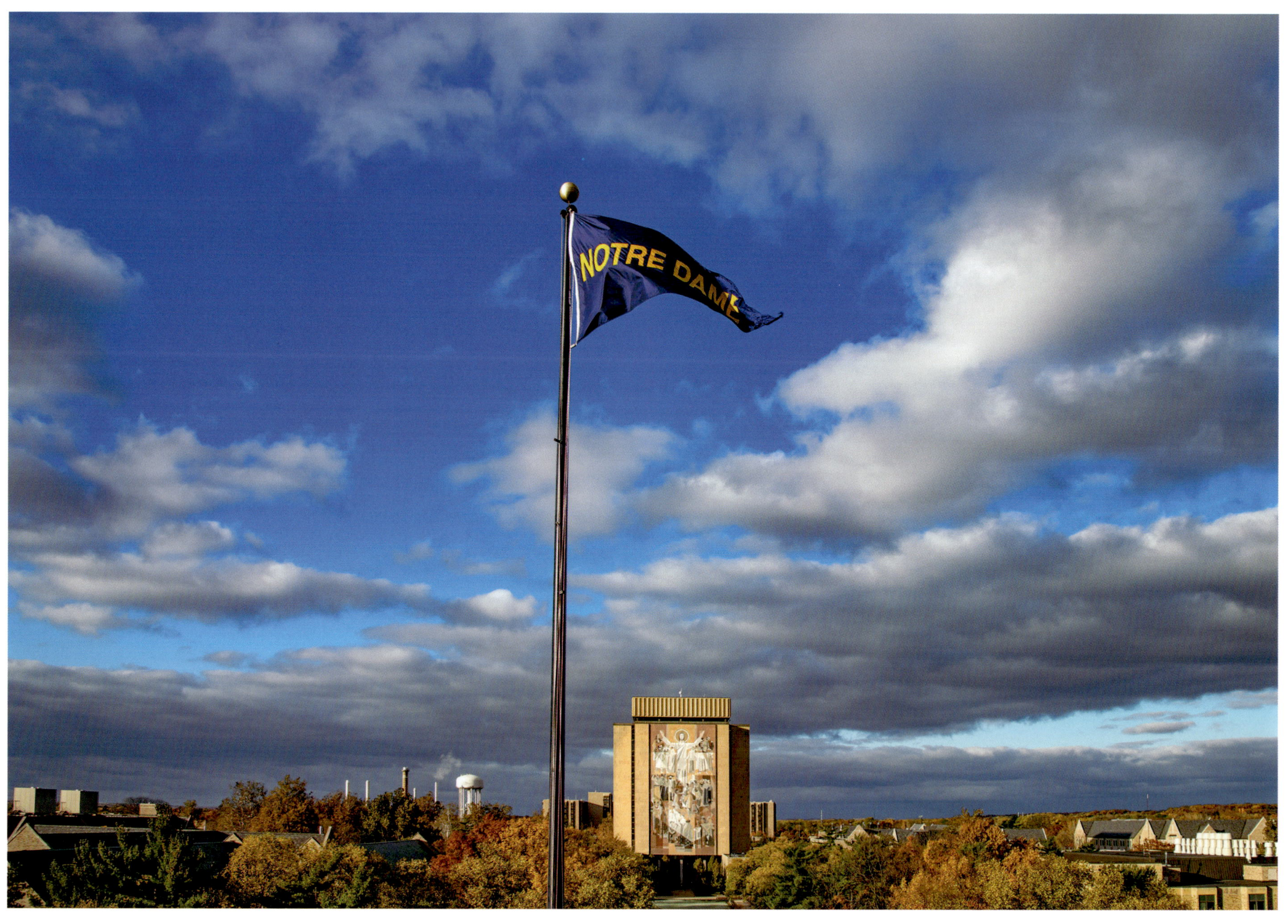

Notre Dame Stadium pennant from the top row, Nikon D850, 24mm, 1/400 f5.6, ISO64

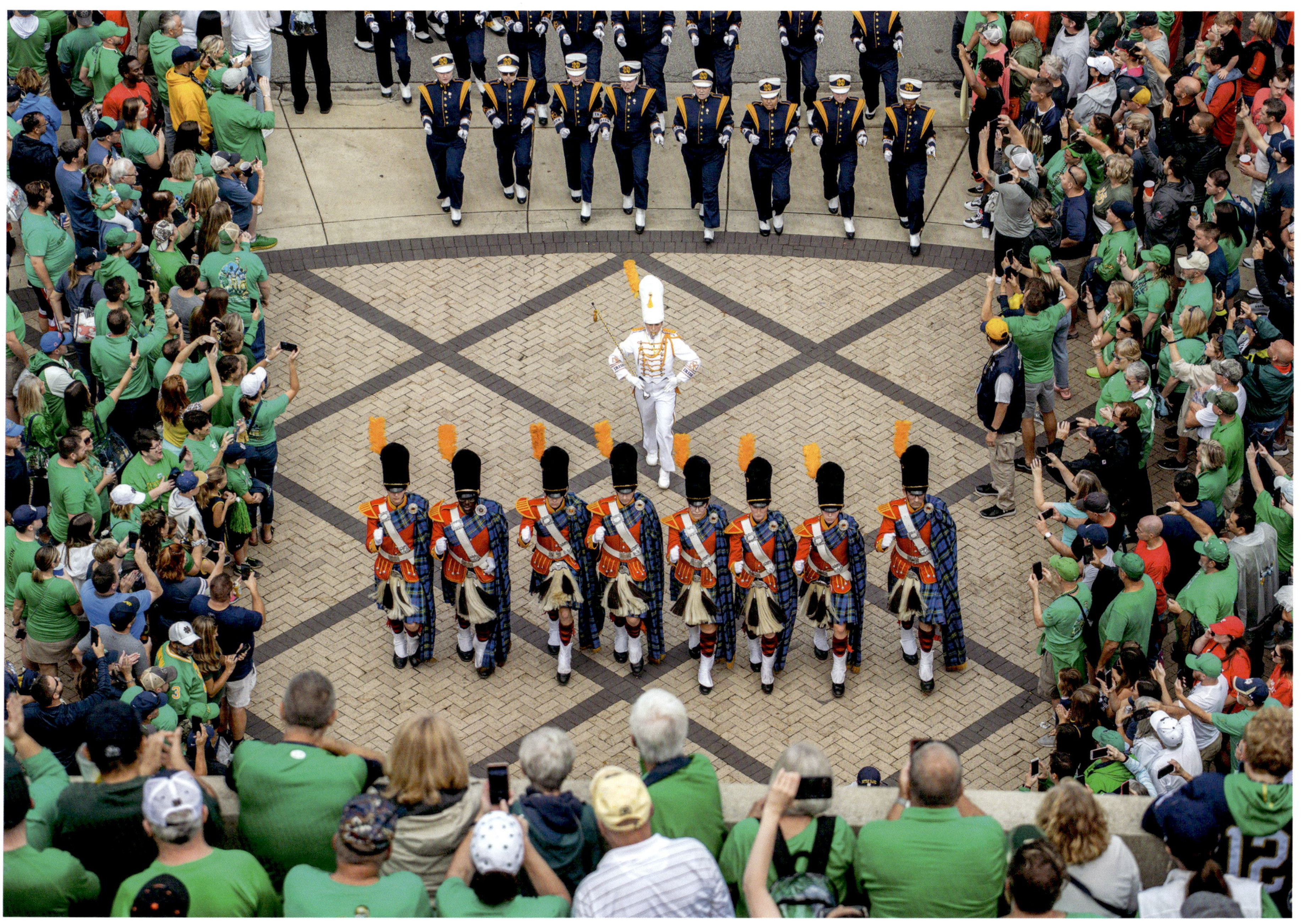

The Notre Dame Marching Band enters Notre Dame Stadium, Nikon D850, 120mm, 1/200 f5.6, ISO64

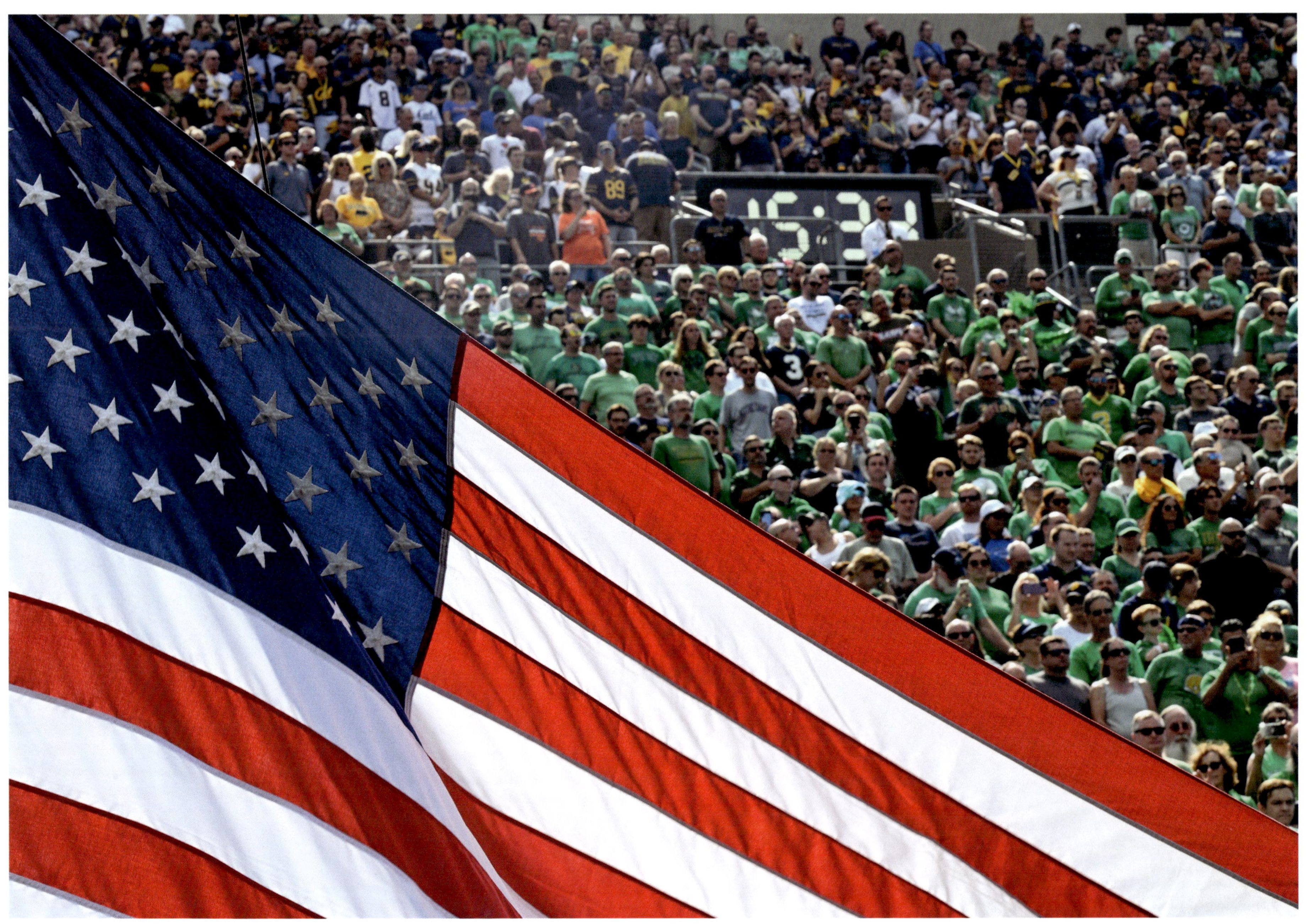

Flag-raising at a football game, Nikon Z6II, 140mm, 1/40 f18, ISO100

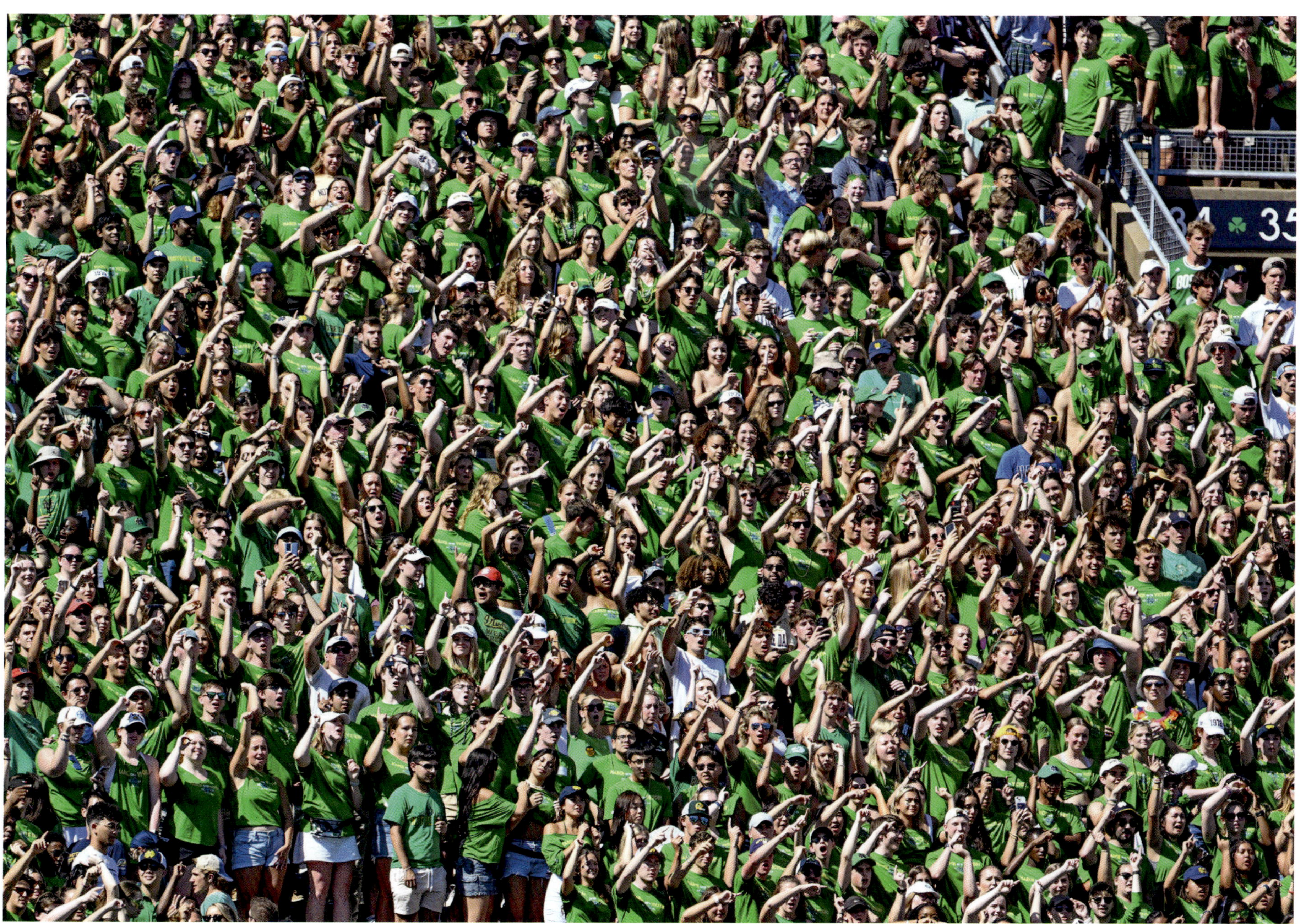

Football game student section, Nikon Z9, 500mm, 1/4000 f6.3, ISO800

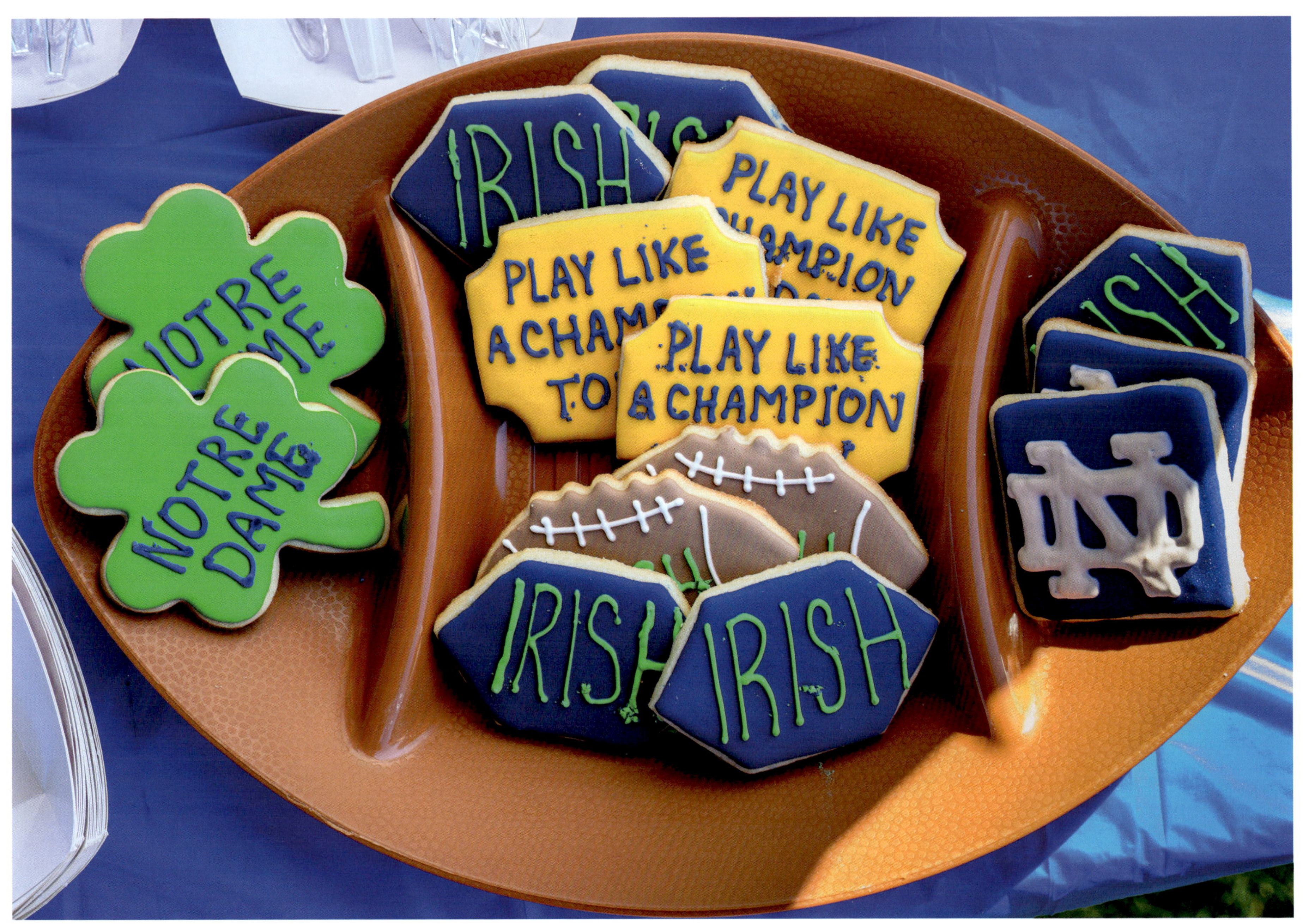

Football tailgater, Nikon Z7II, 74mm, 1/160 f13, ISO250

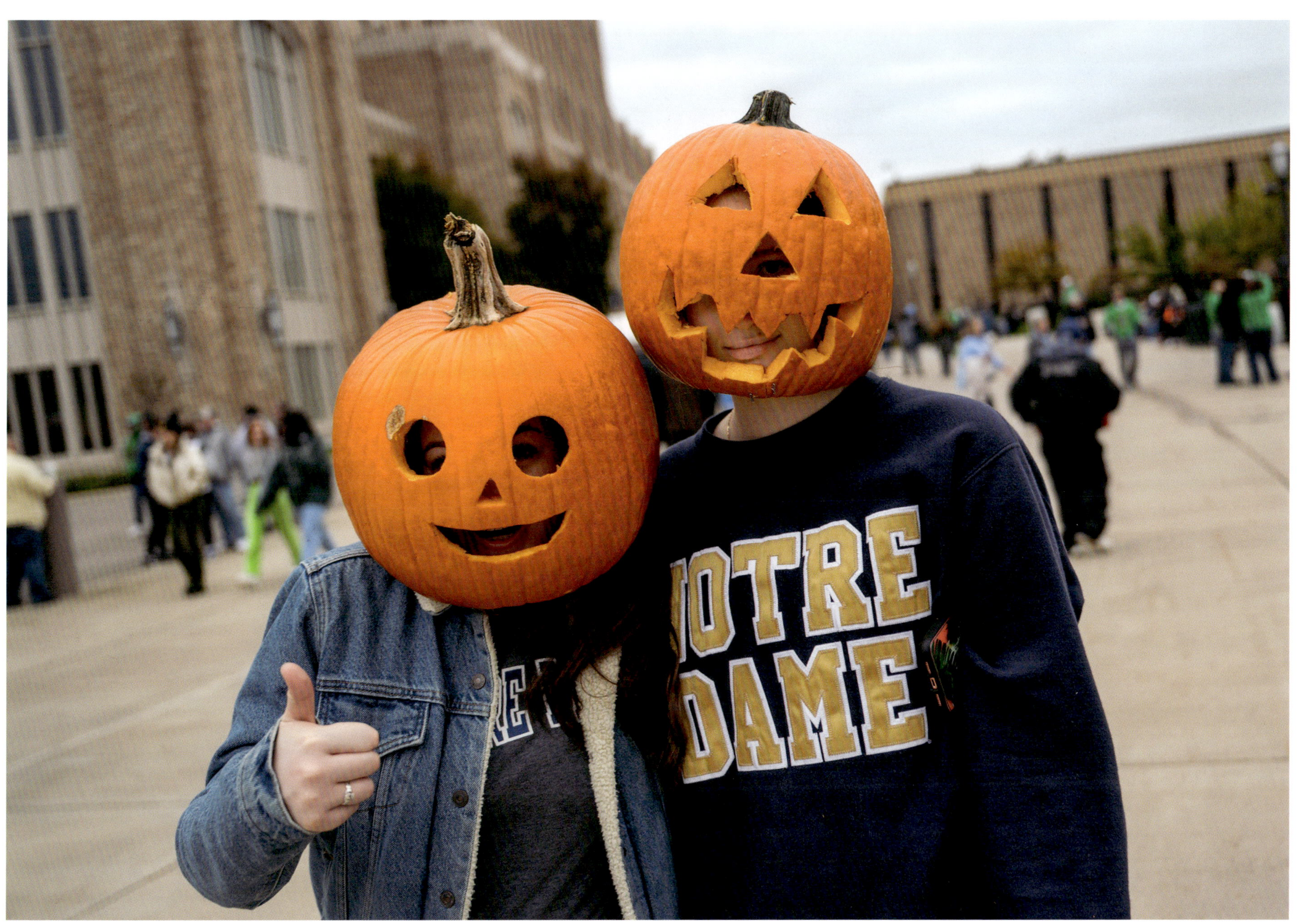

A football game the day before Halloween, Nikon Z6, 32mm, 1/100 f2.8, ISO100

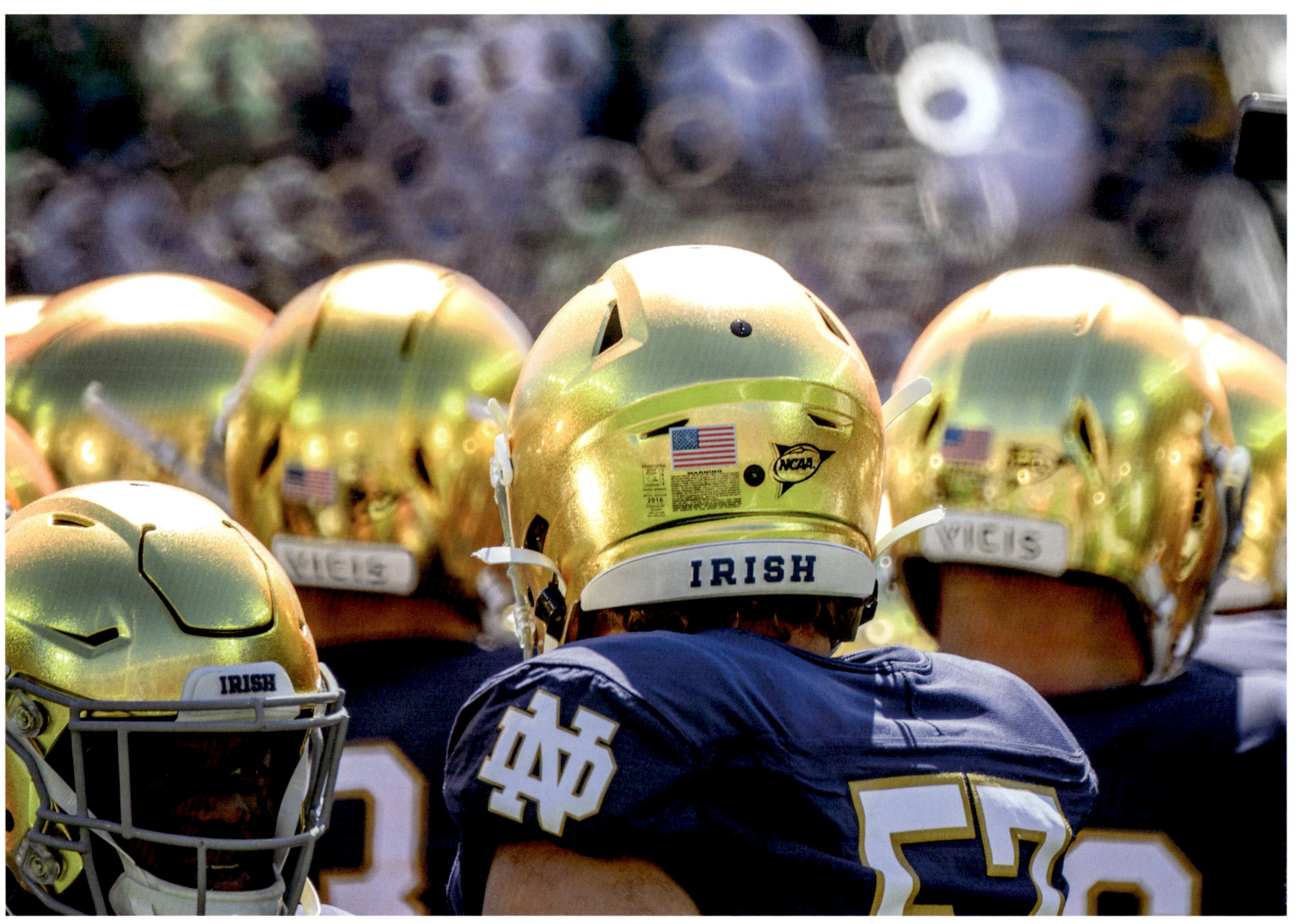

Football game warmups, Nikon D5, 500mm mirror lens, 1/800 f8, ISO1000

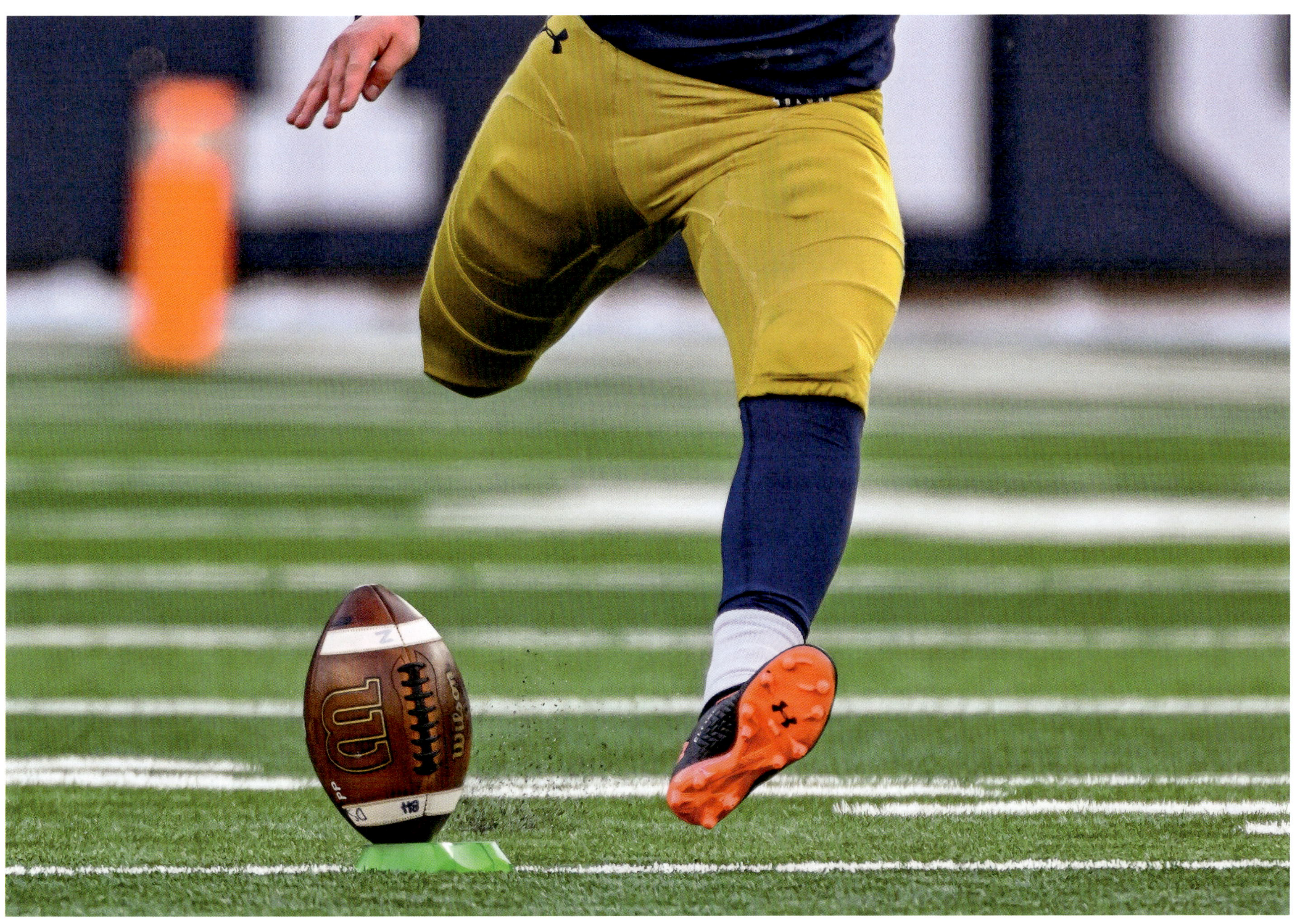

Kickoff, Nikon Z9, 1120mm, 1/1600 f8, ISO3200

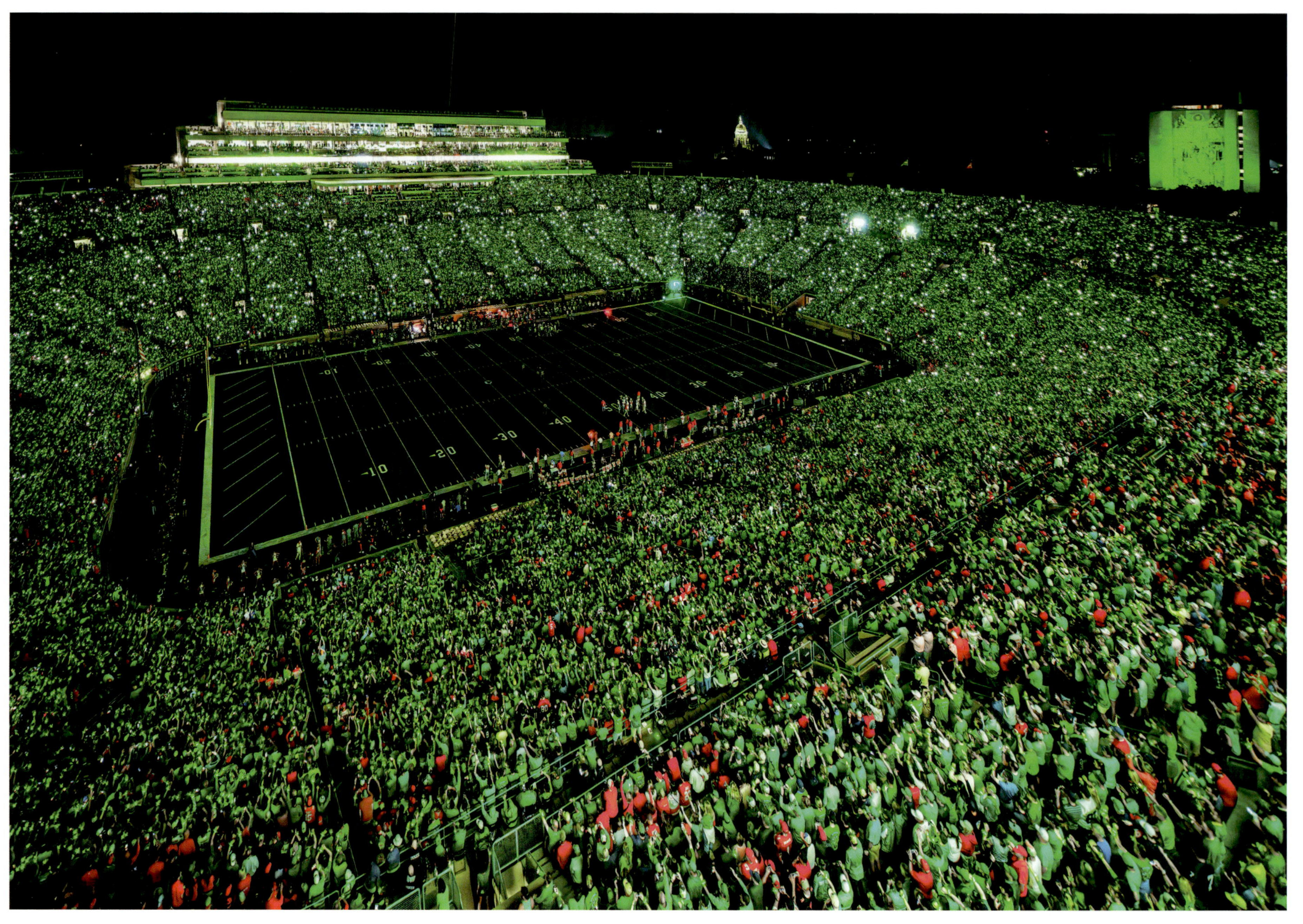

Notre Dame Stadium lit with green wristbands, Fuji GFX100s, 17mm, 1/50 f5, ISO1600

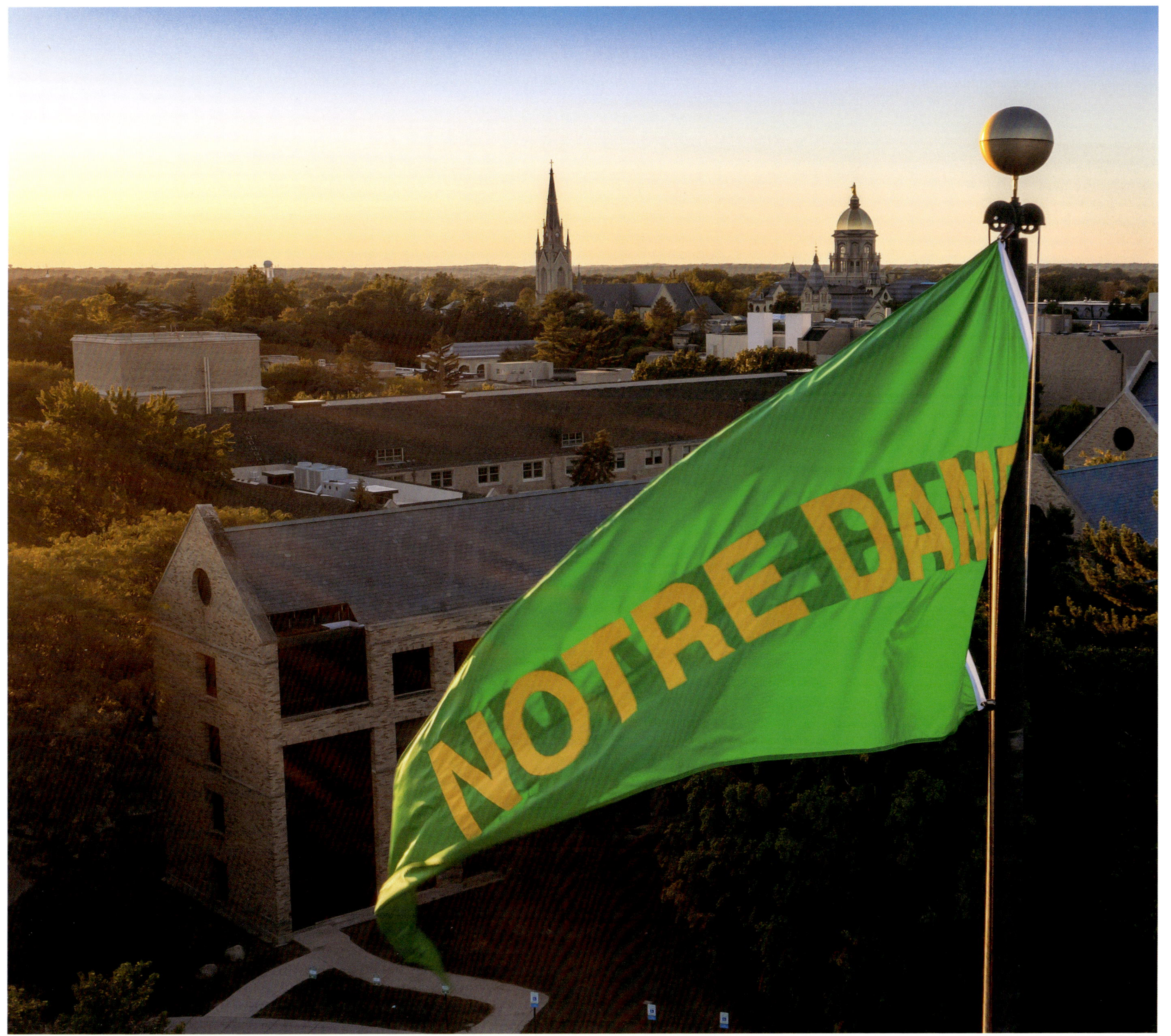

Green pennant over Notre Dame Stadium, Mavic 2 Pro drone, 24mm equivalent, 1/160 f5.6, ISO100

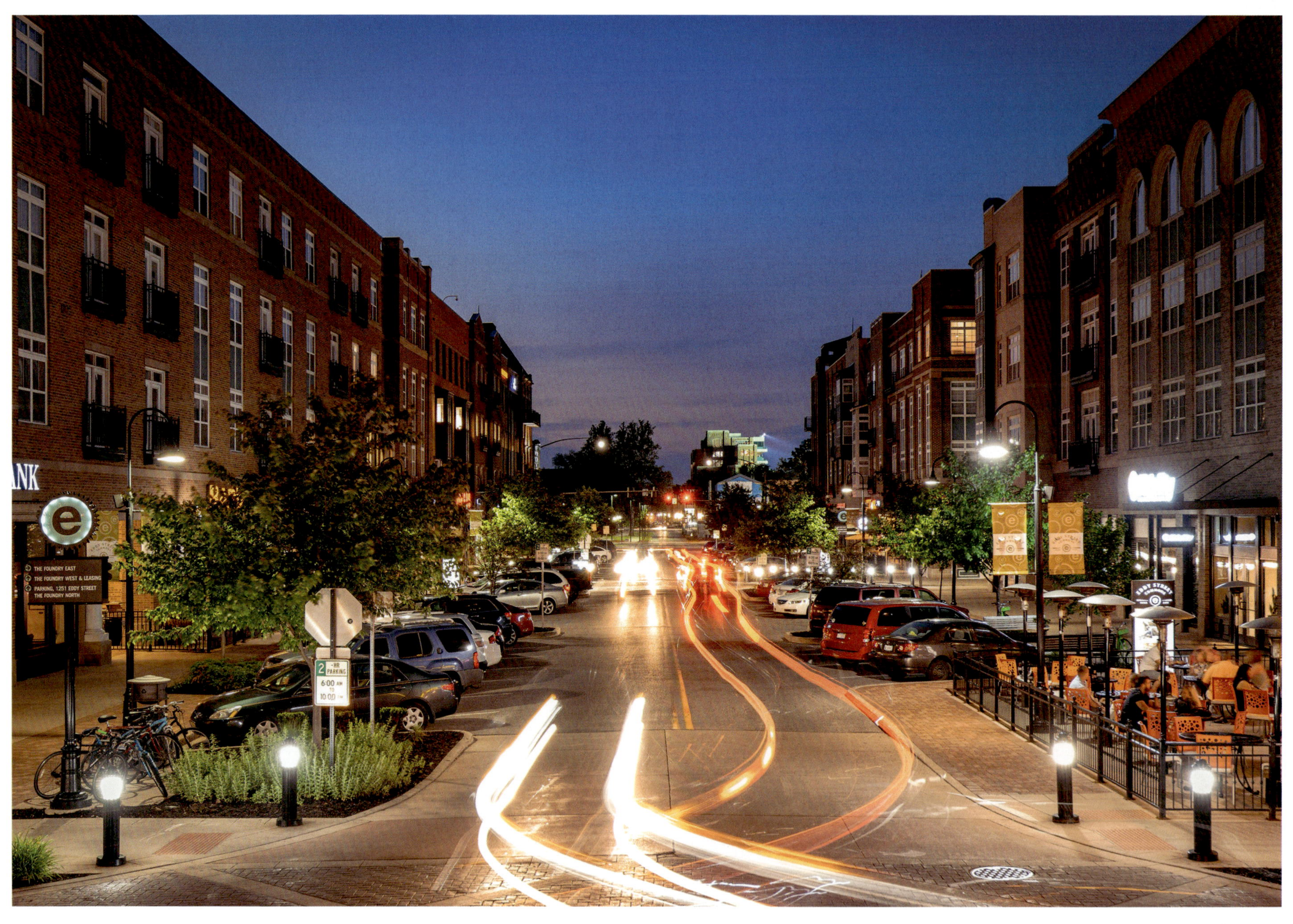

Eddy Street Commons, Nikon D850, 35mm, 30sec. f8, ISO32

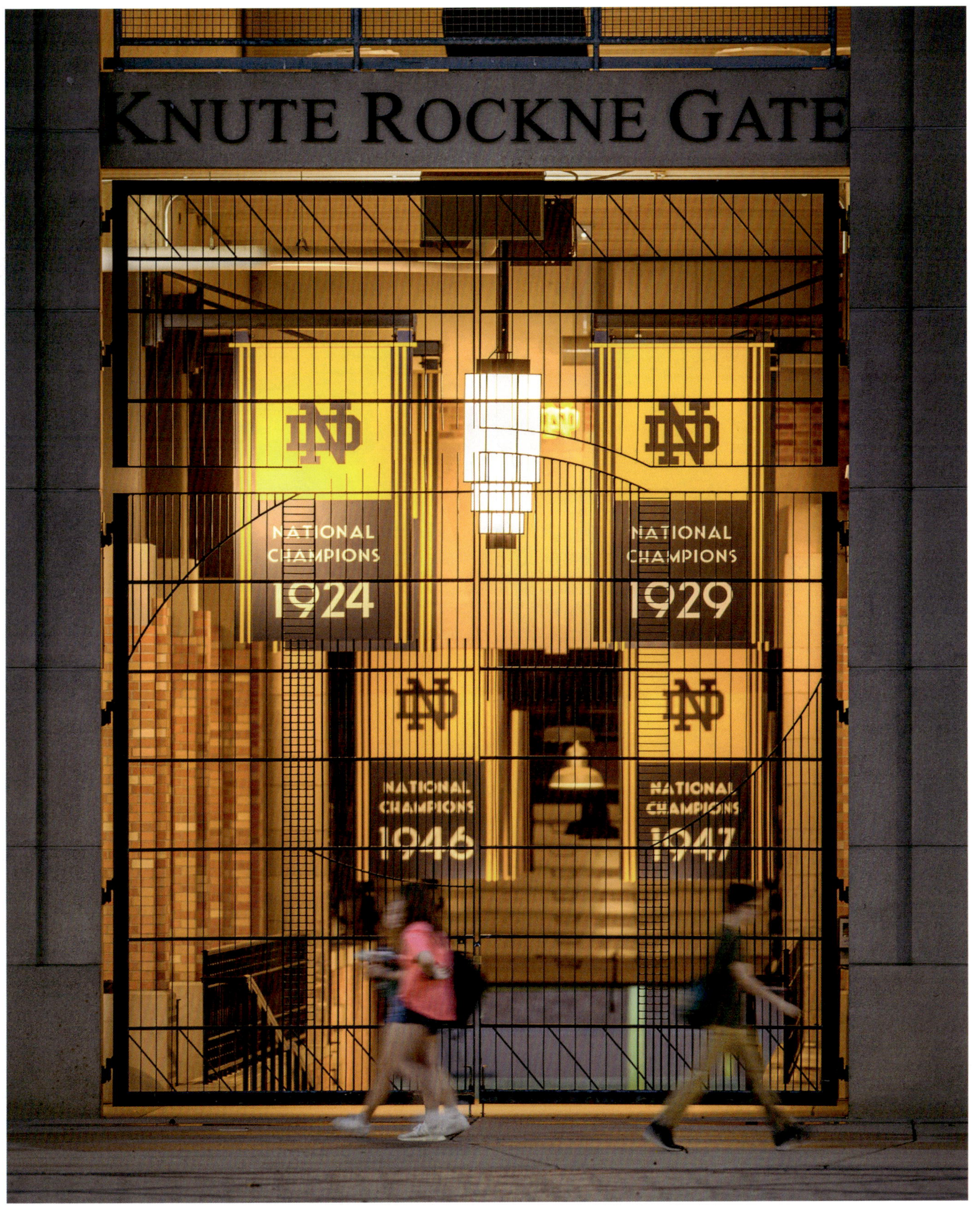

Notre Dame Stadium tunnel, Nikon D5, 400mm, 1/15 f2.8, ISO250

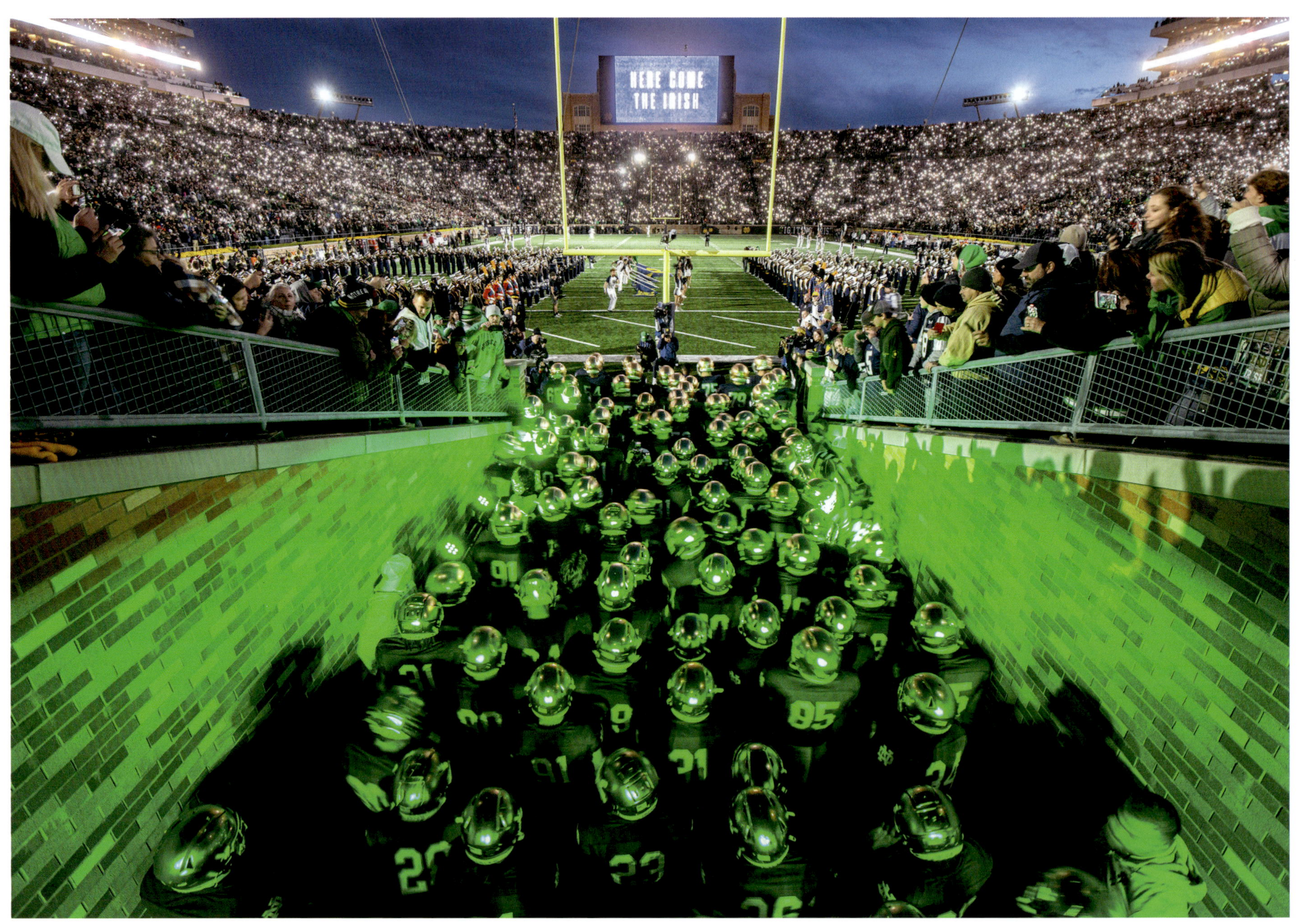

Football team in the tunnel, Nikon D850, 16mm, 1/5 f6.3, ISO800

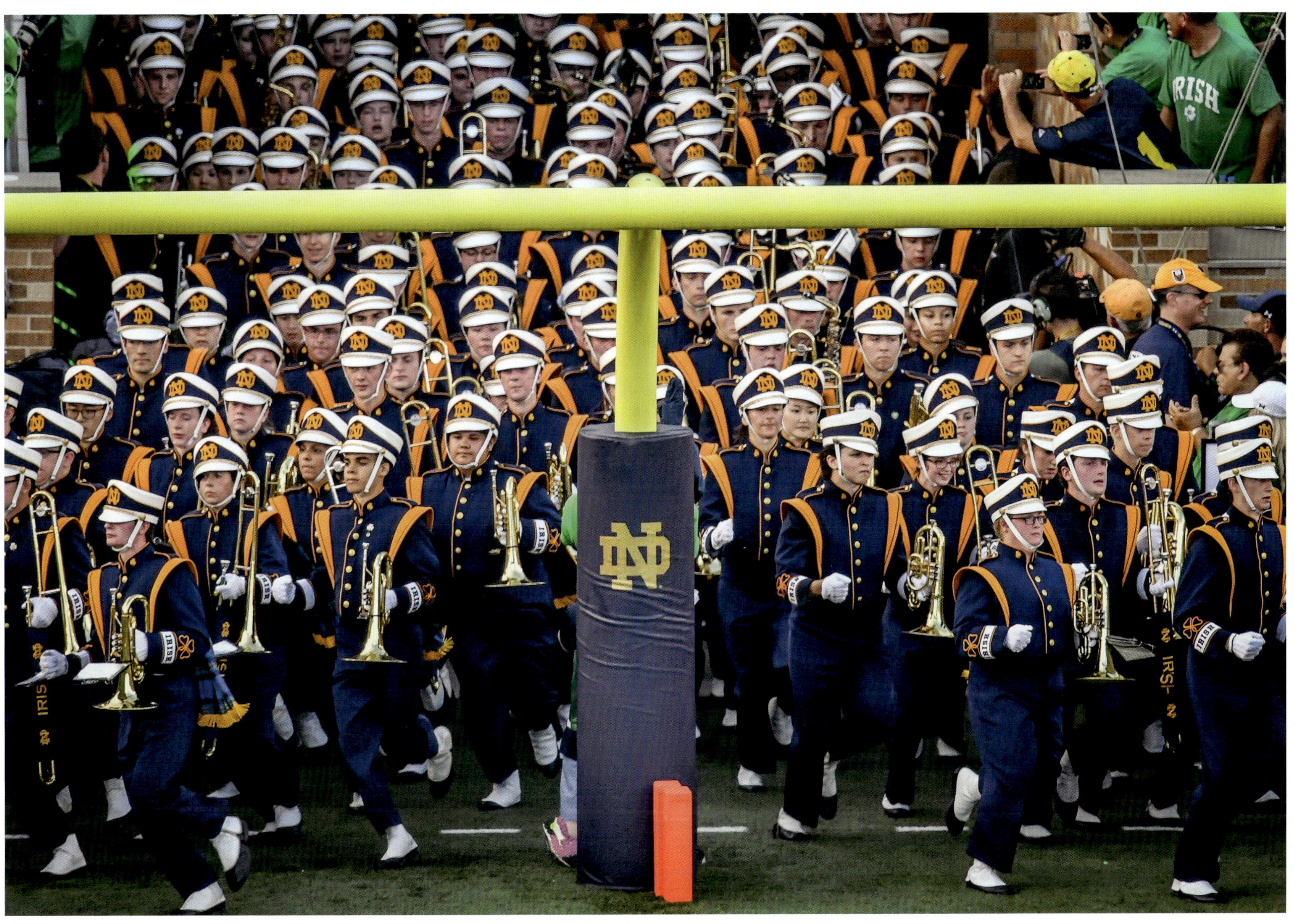

The Band of the Fighting Irish, Nikon D500, 560mm, 1/1250 f5, ISO1250

No two football games look the same. There are night games, day games, and, in the past few years, light shows and fireworks have added to the visuals. And with the season lasting from late summer to almost the first day of winter, weather can—to use a football metaphor—call an audible as well!

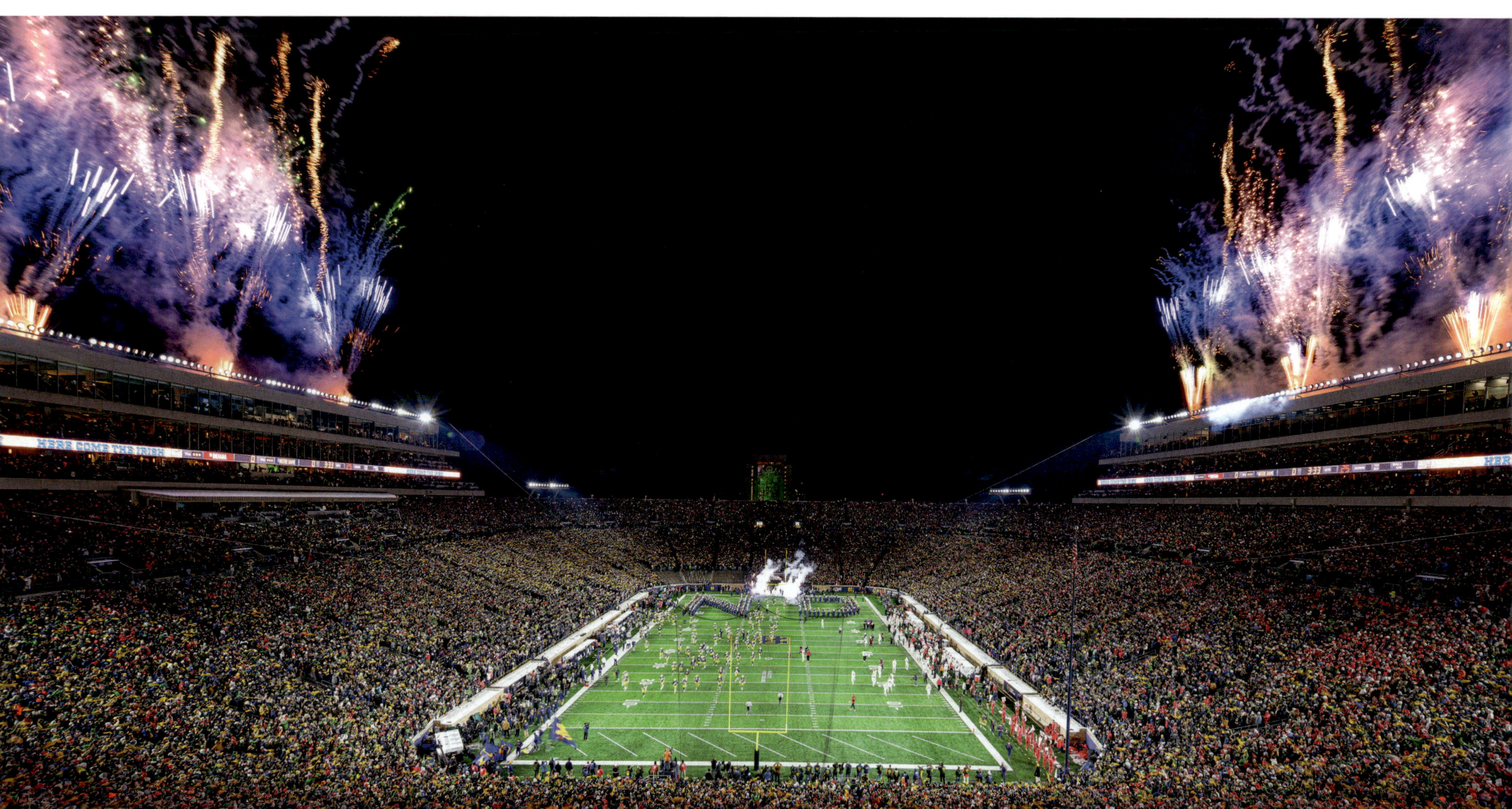

The football team takes the field, Fuji GFX100s, 17mm, 1/7 f9, ISO200

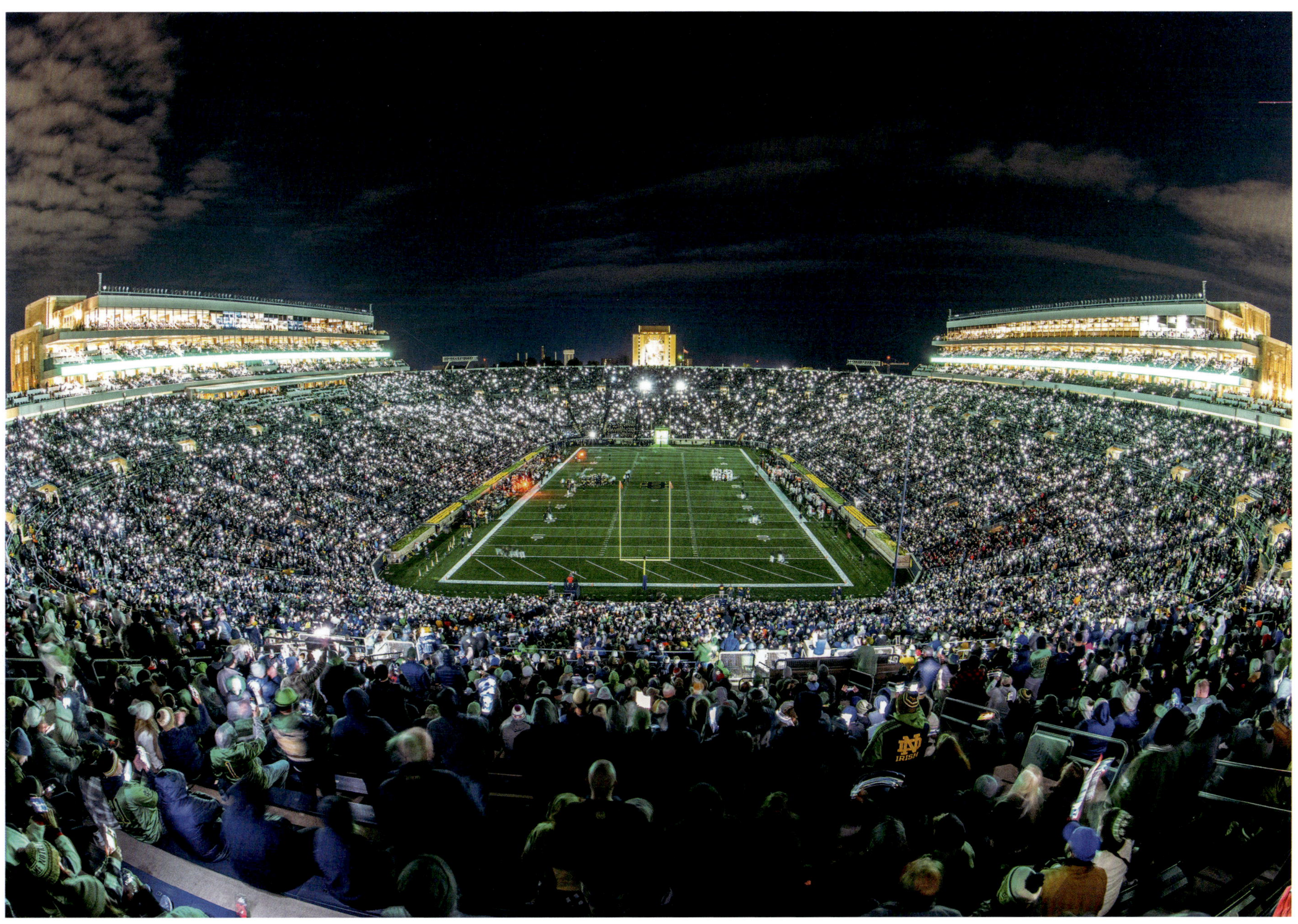

"Lights Out" at a night game, Nikon Z7II, 14mm, 1/4 f7.1, ISO500

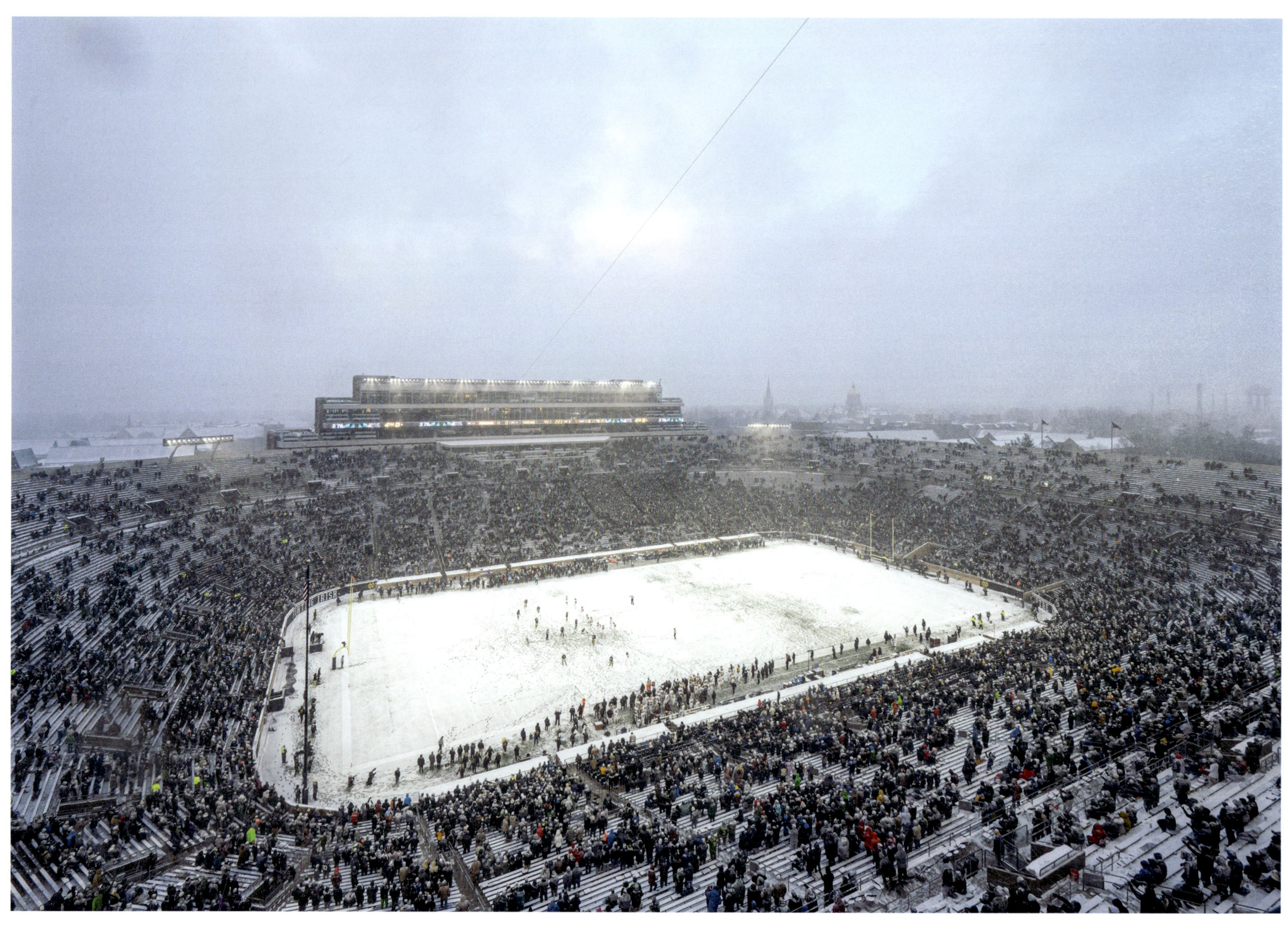

Snow falls on Notre Dame Stadium, Nikon Z7II, 14mm, 1/125 f10, ISO640

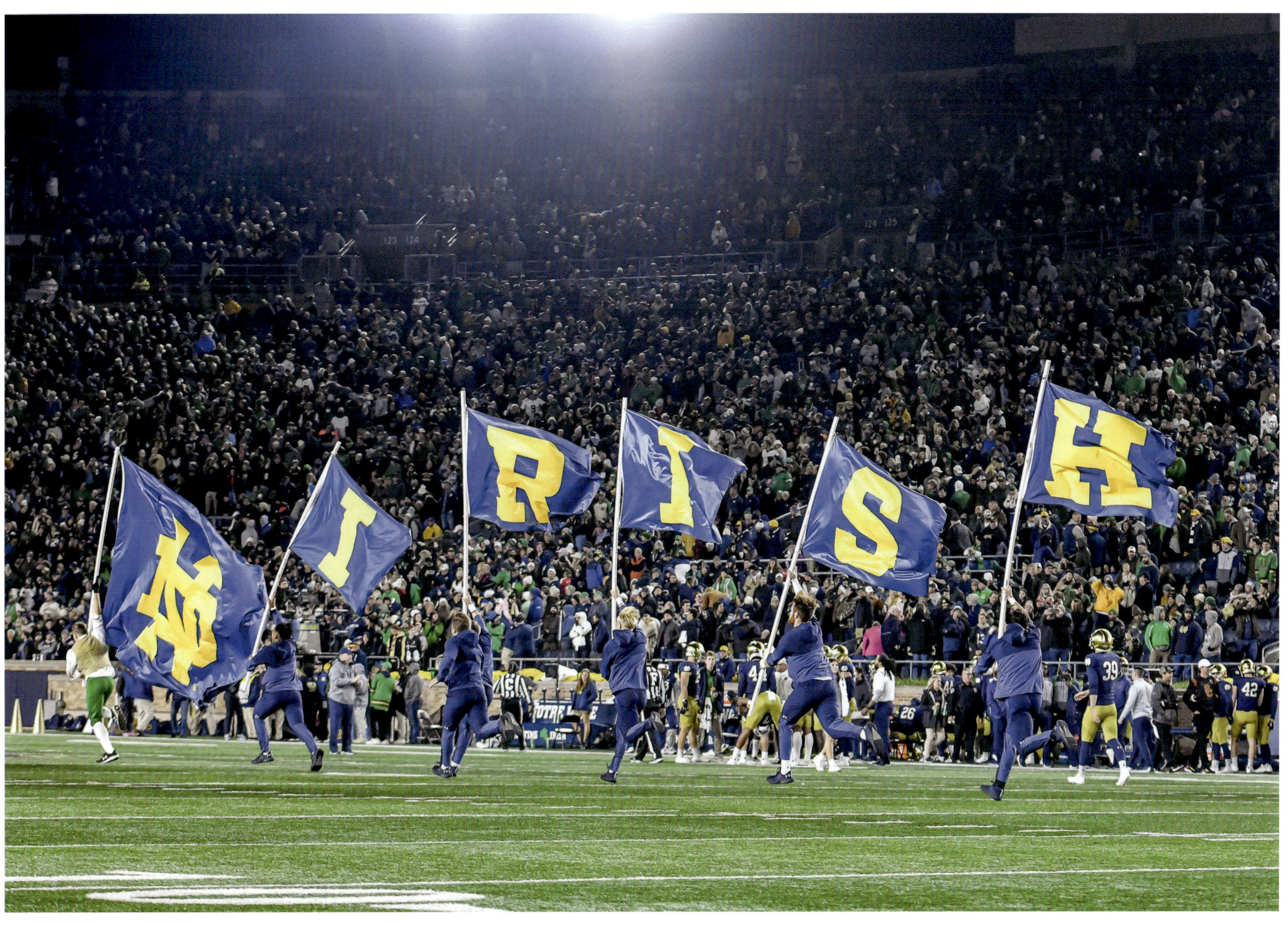

Cheerleaders celebrate a touchdown, Nikon D500, 70mm, 1/1250 f3.5, ISO1600

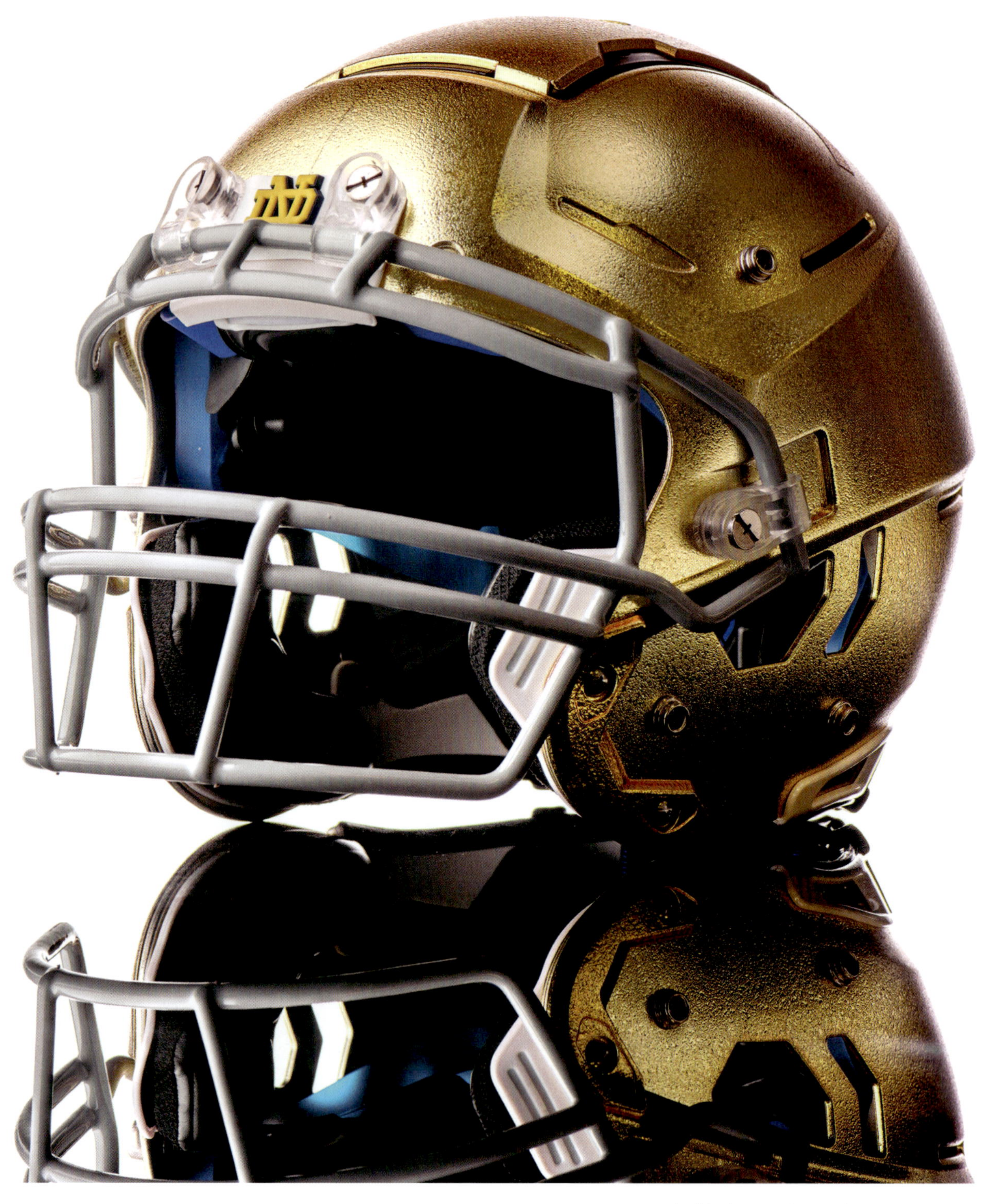

Football helmet in the studio, Pentax 645Z, 120mm, 1/125 f10, ISO200

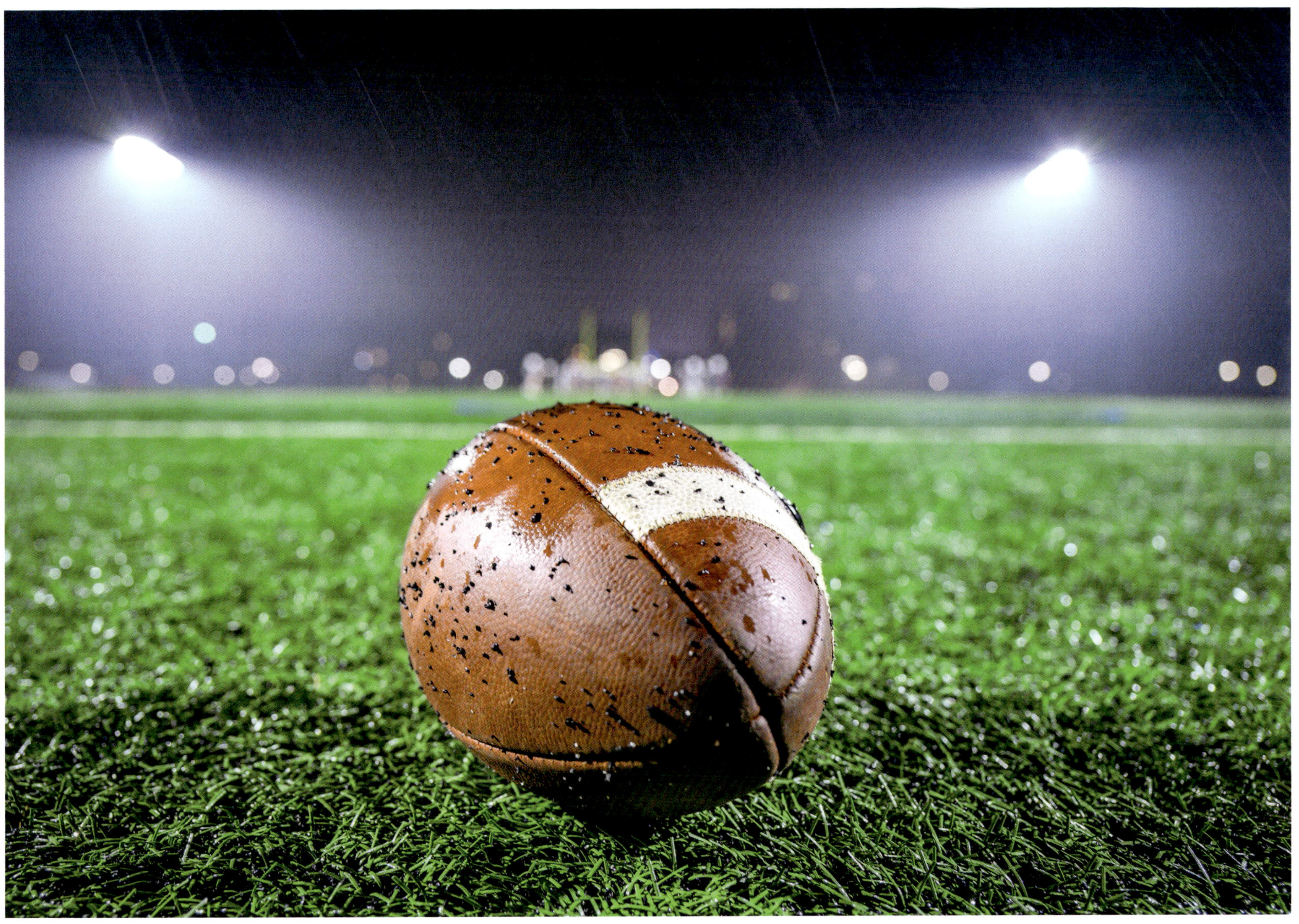

Football on Ricci Family Fields, Nikon Z7II, 24mm, 1/60 f3.5, ISO1600

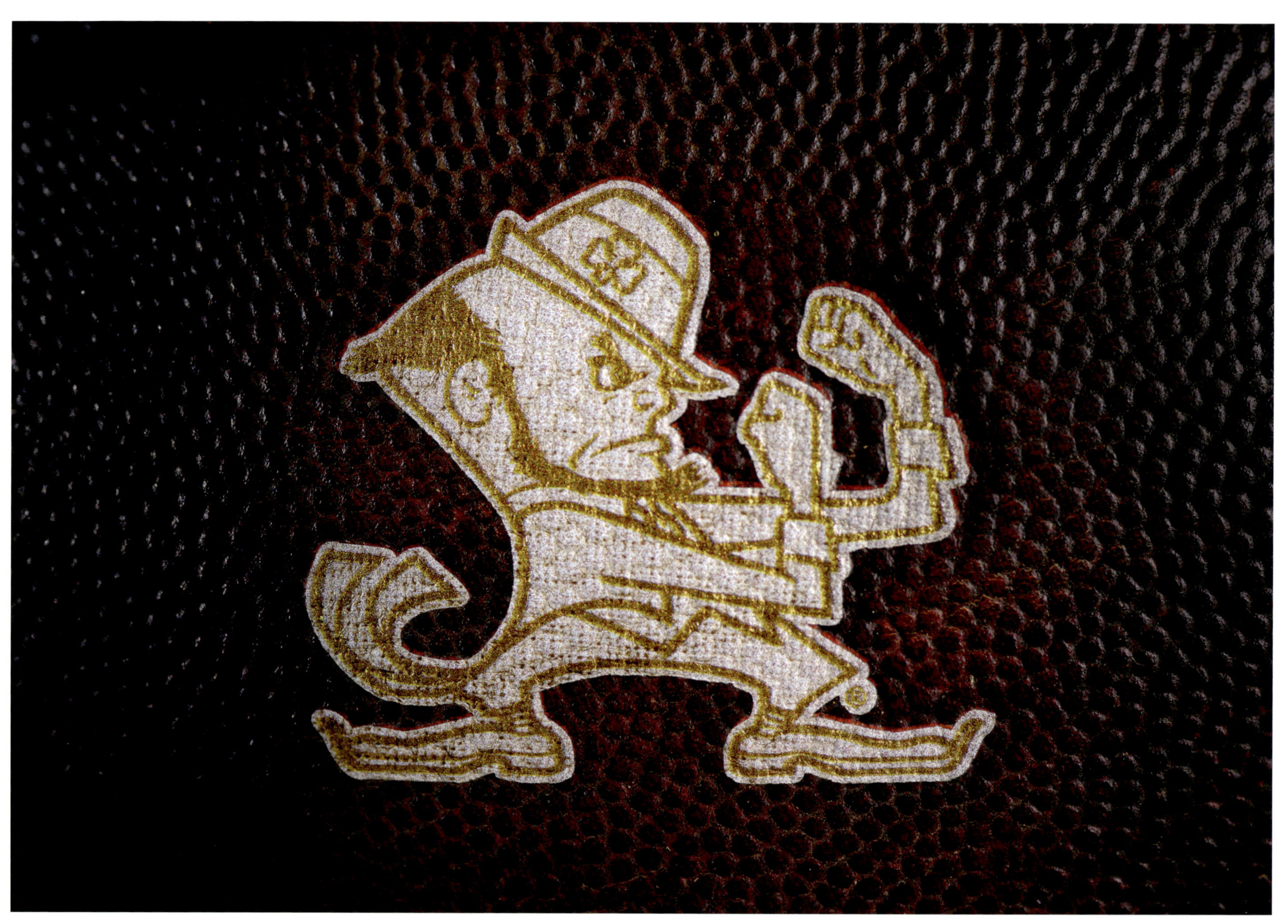

Football detail, in studio, Pentax 645Z, 120mm, 1/125 f7.1, ISO100

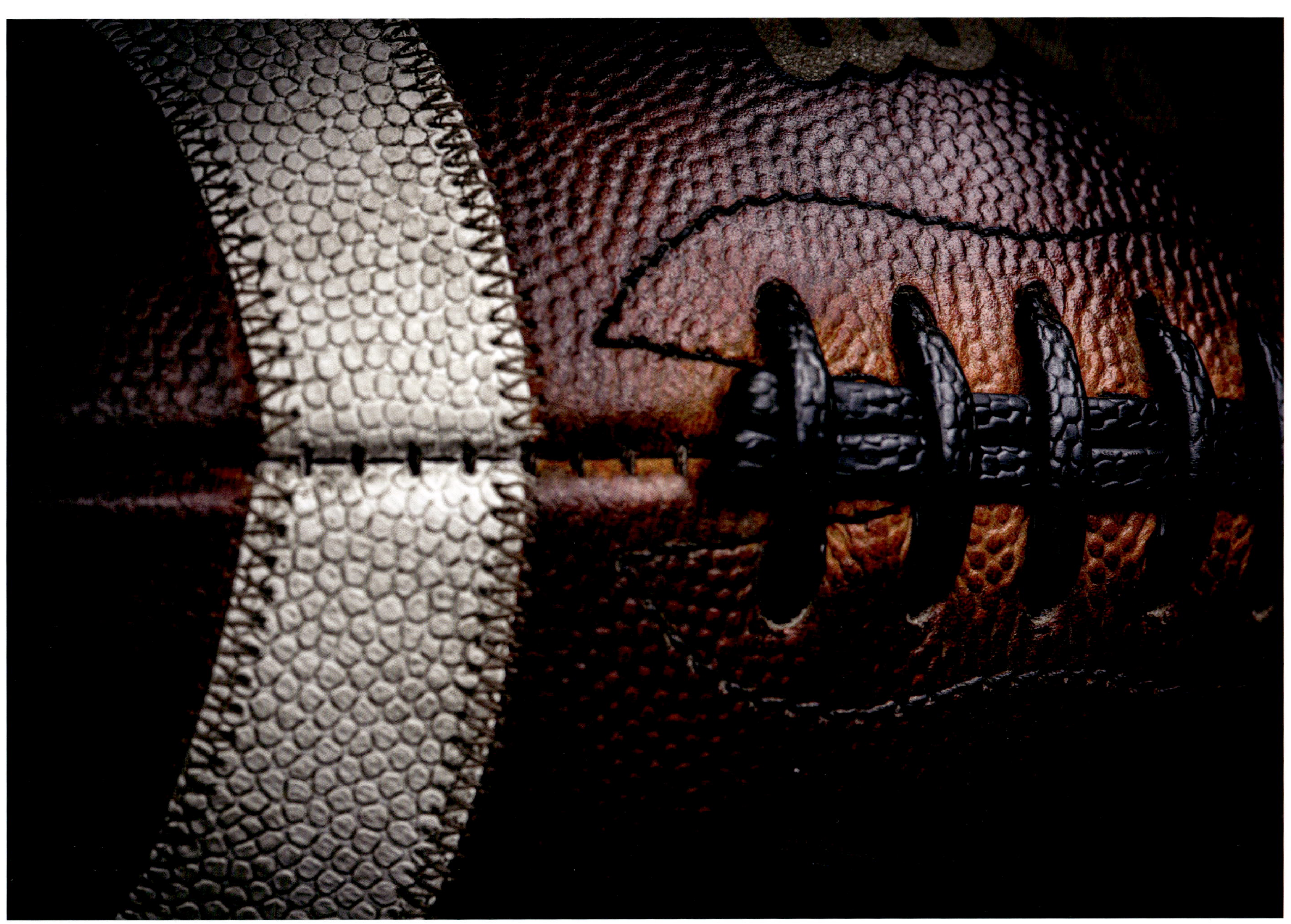

Football detail, in studio, Pentax 645Z, 120mm, 1/125 f11, ISO400

Commencement. All I have to do is show up! Spring weather, the pageantry and spectacle of the ceremonies, and the exuberance of the graduates and their families combine in a visual feast. The fun challenge is to come up with new ideas for where to go or put a remote camera. In 2019, weather moved the ceremony indoors to the Joyce Center arena. I put a remote-controlled camera in the catwalk before the ceremony, which resulted in a unique top-down look at the many colors of the faculty's academic robes.

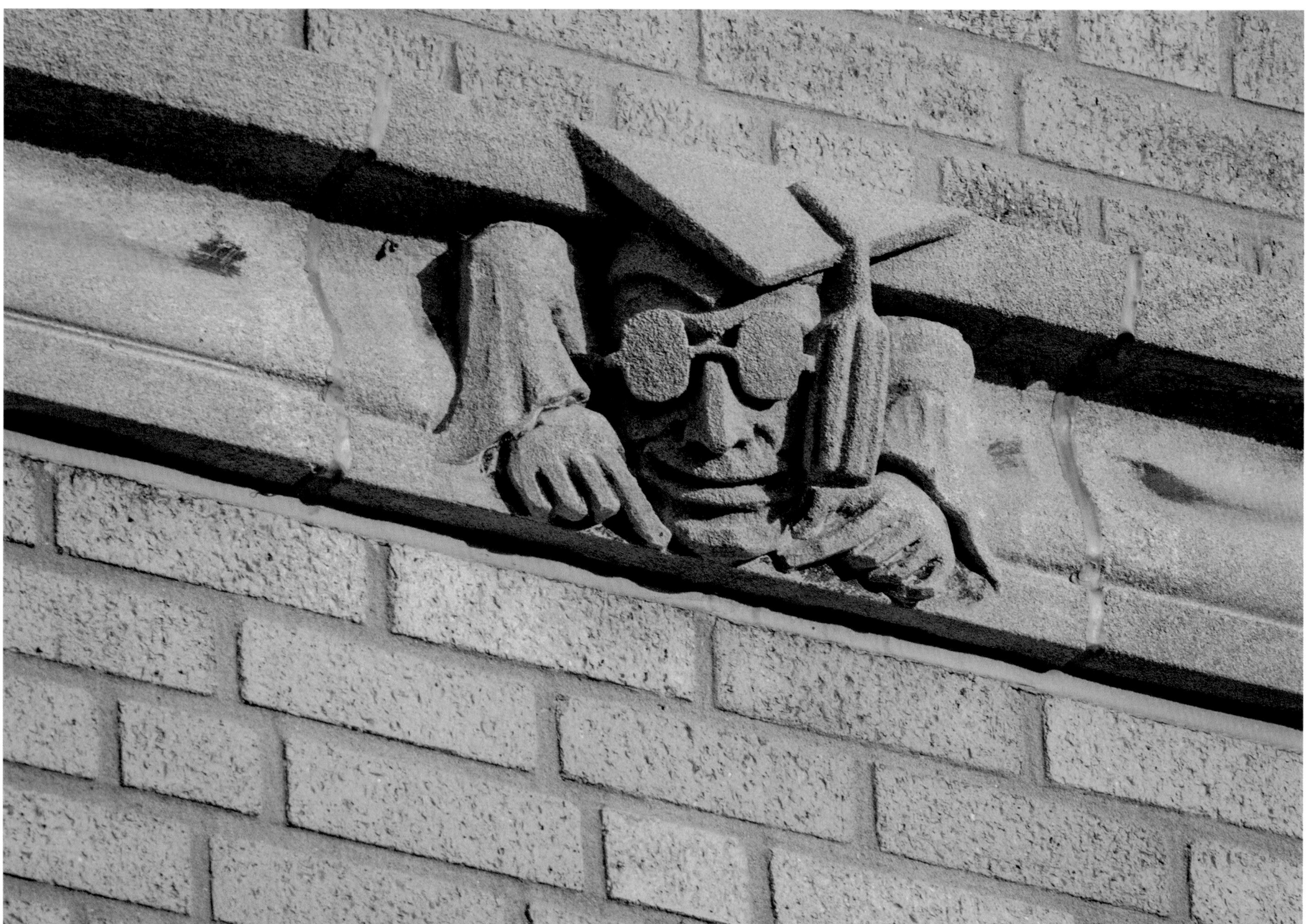

Howard Hall relief, Nikon D850, 500mm mirror lens, 1/800 f8, ISO200

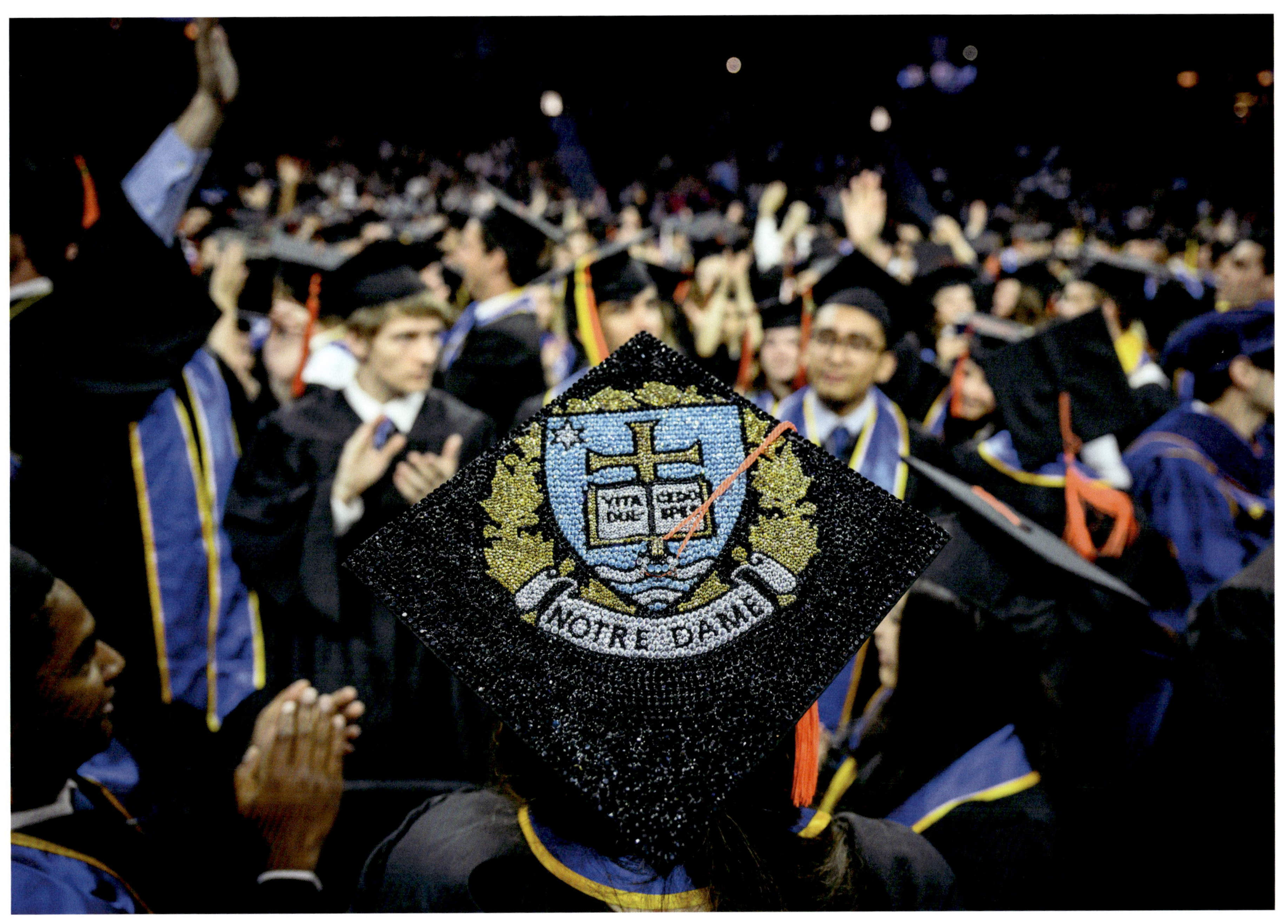

Bedazzled graduate cap, Nikon Z7, 24mm, 1/200 f3.2, ISO1600

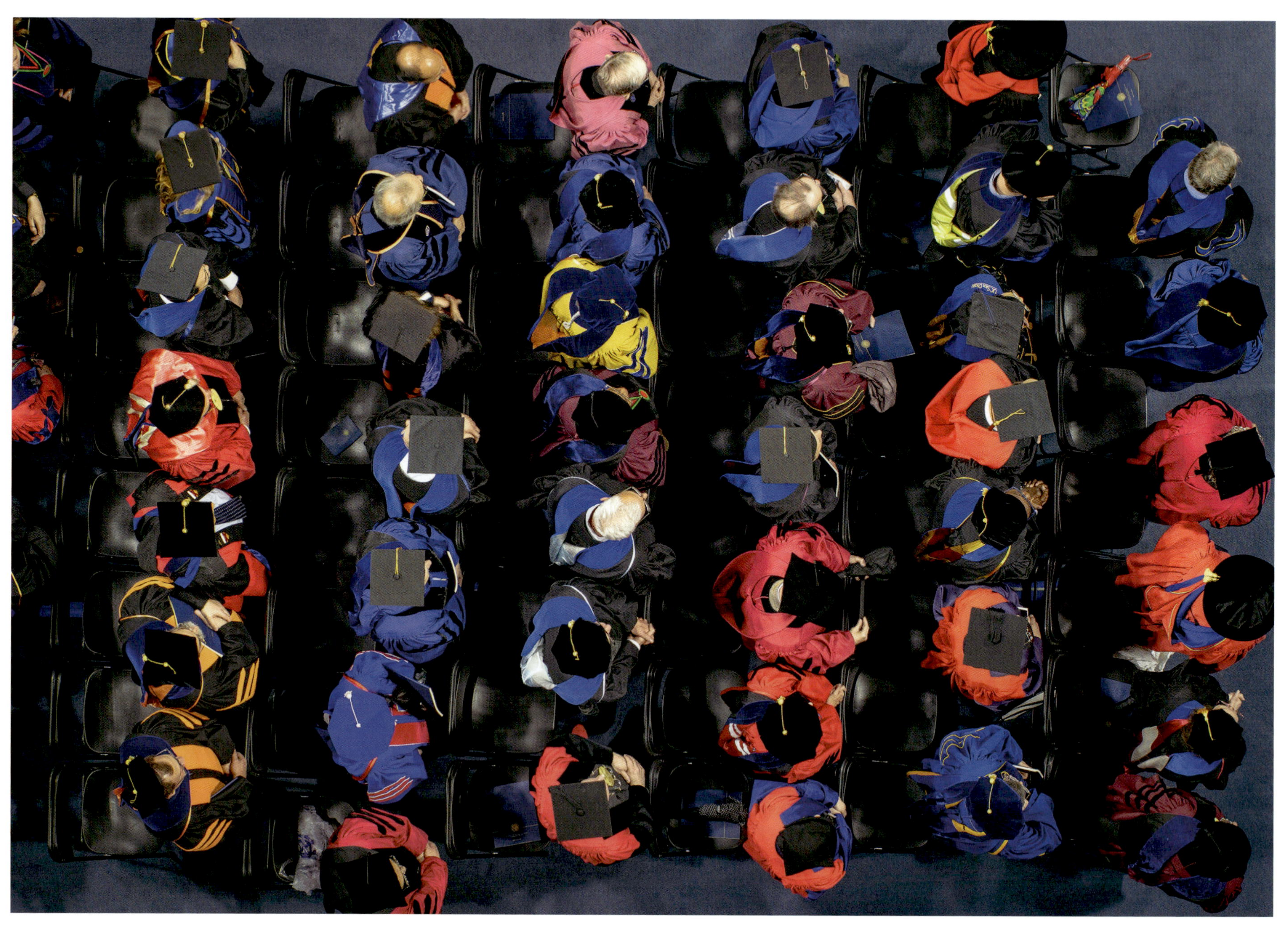

Faculty at Commencement, Nikon D850, 50mm, 1/15 f5.6, ISO320

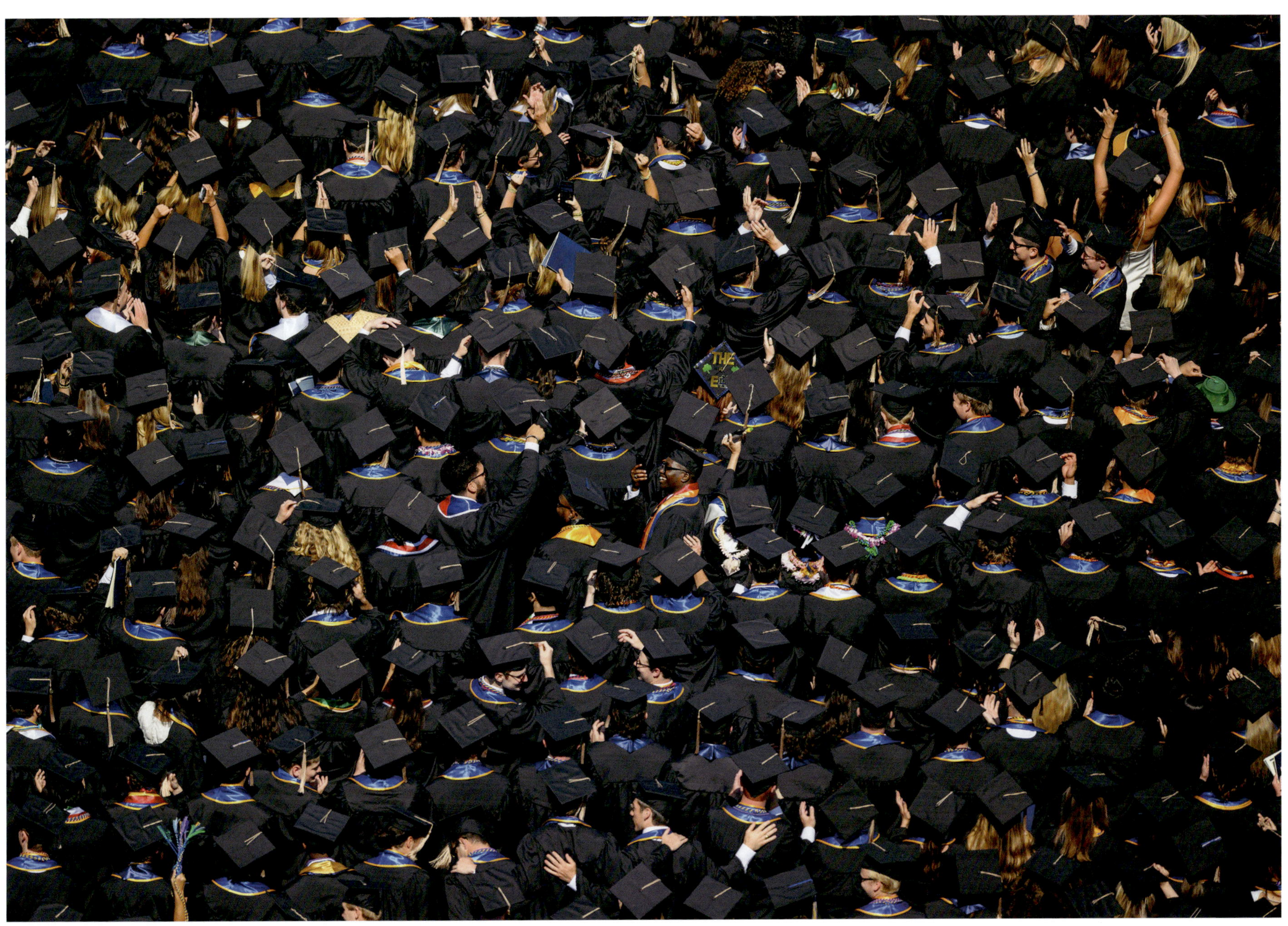

Graduates in Notre Dame Stadium, Nikon Z9, 400mm, 1/2000 f2.8, ISO64

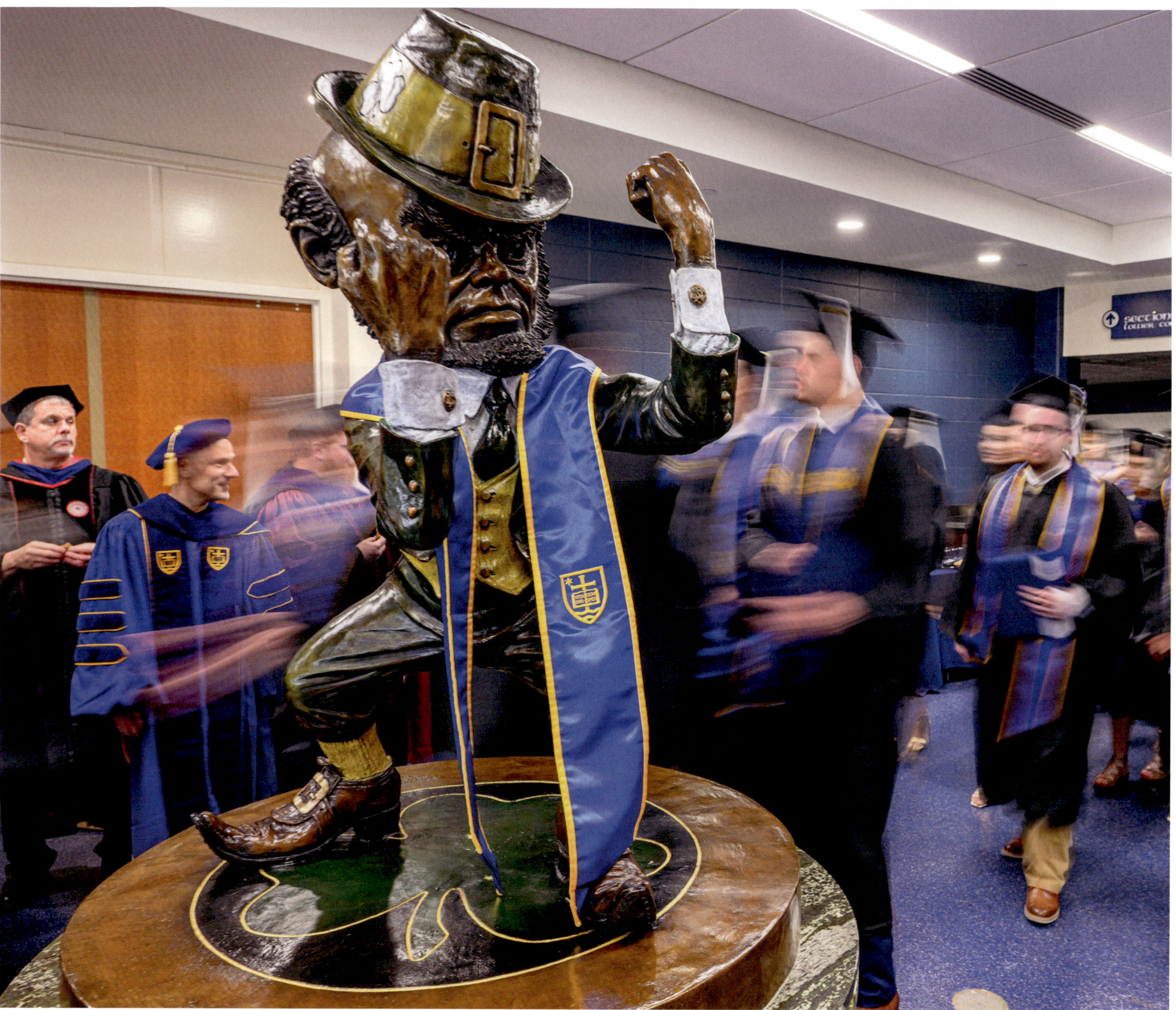

Arts and Letters grads leave the Purcell Pavilion, Nikon Z9, 24mm, 1/2.5 f8, ISO125

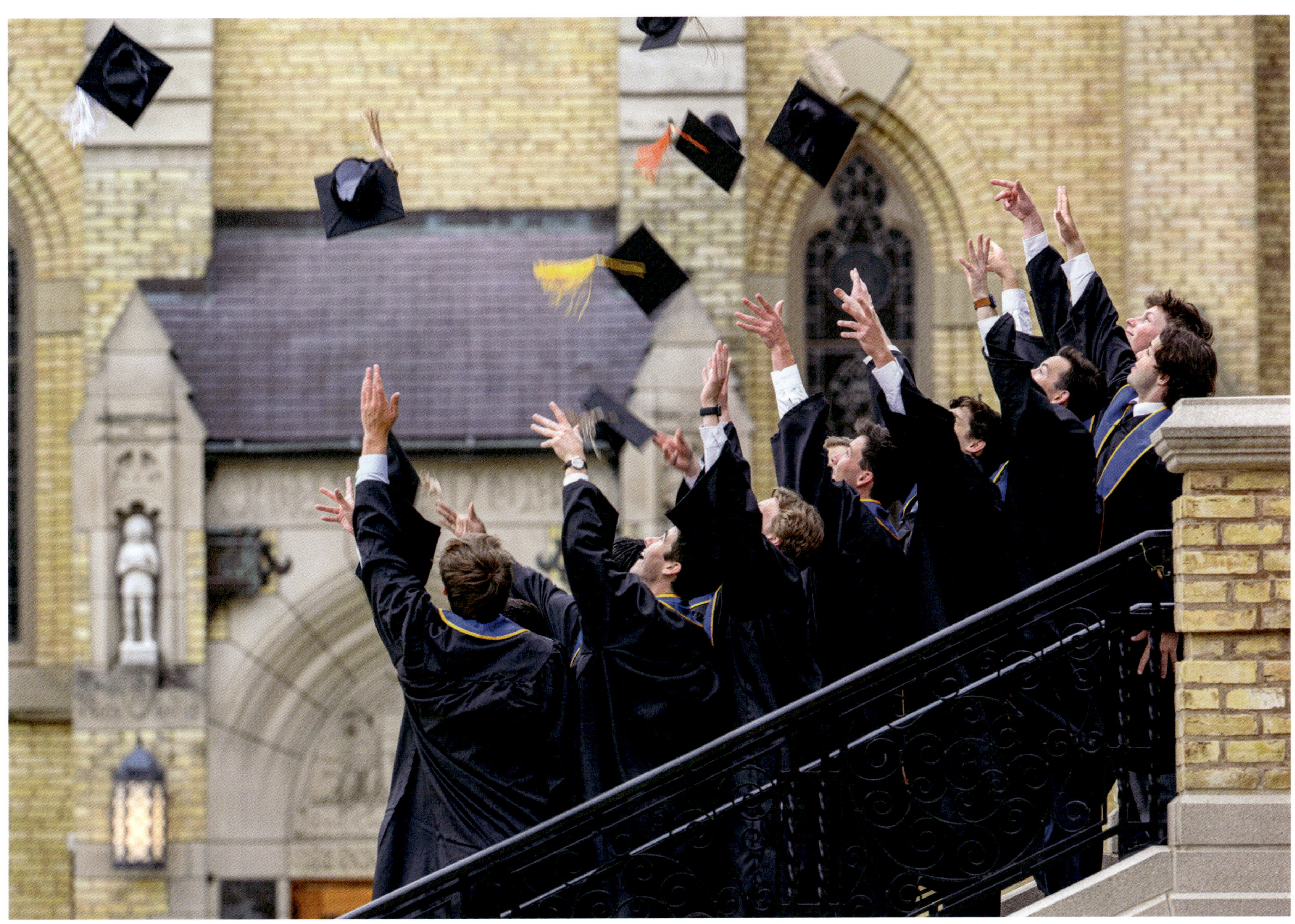

Graduates on Main Building Steps, Nikon Z9, 400mm, 1/250 f6.3, ISO250

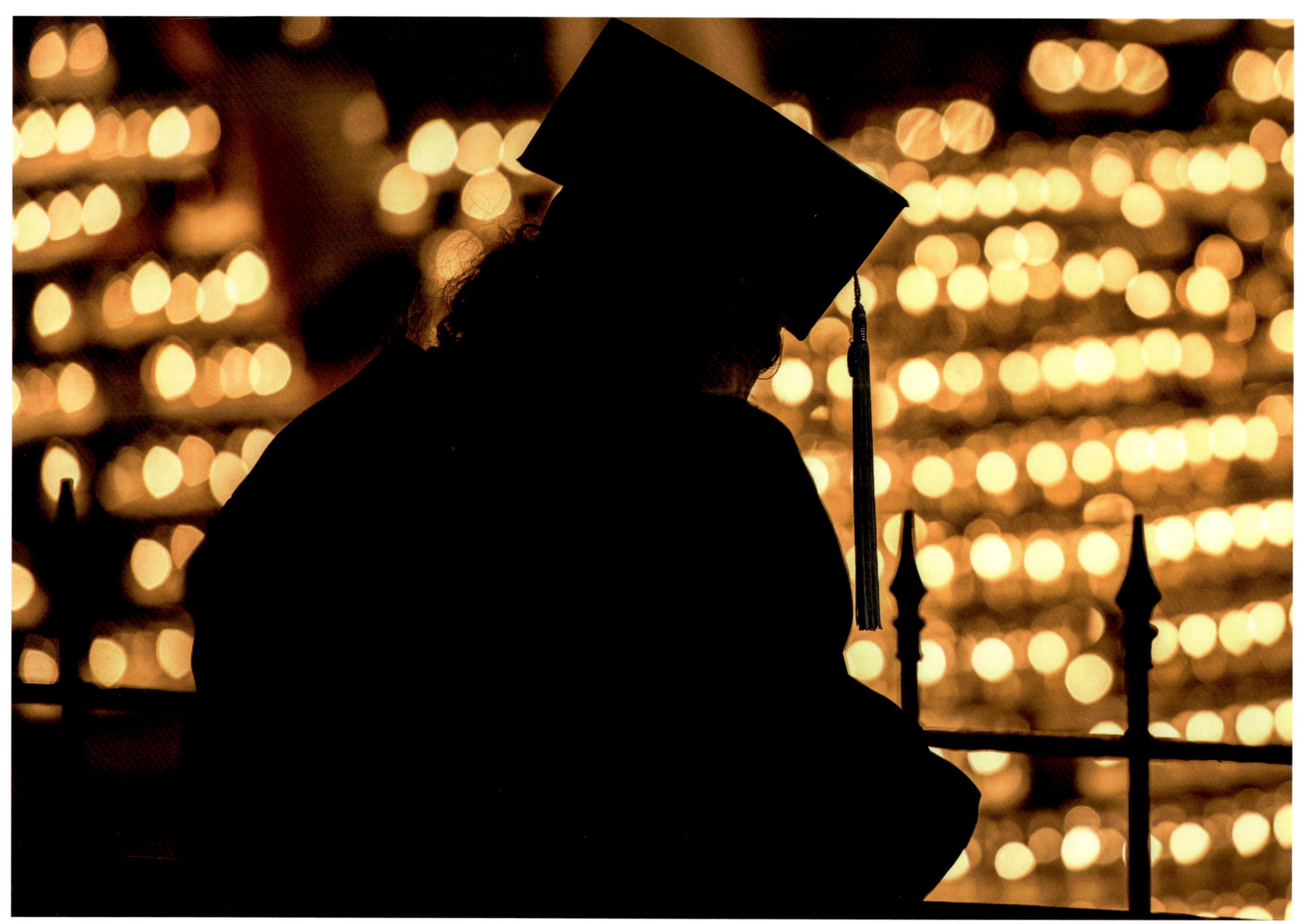

Graduate at the Grotto, Nikon D4s, 195mm, 1/125 f3.2, ISO1600

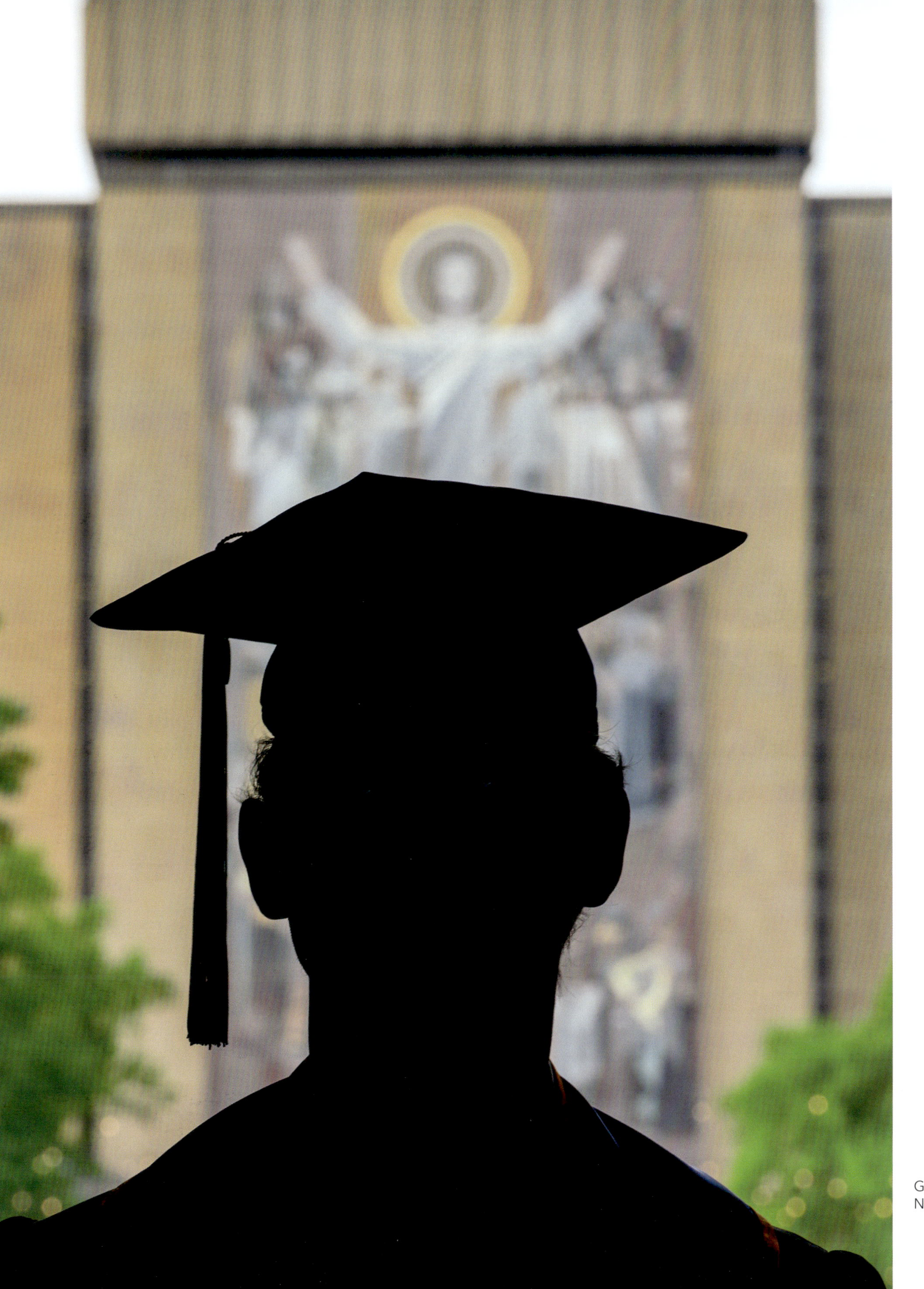

Graduate enters Notre Dame Stadium,
Nikon Z7, 165mm, 1/50 f16, ISO250

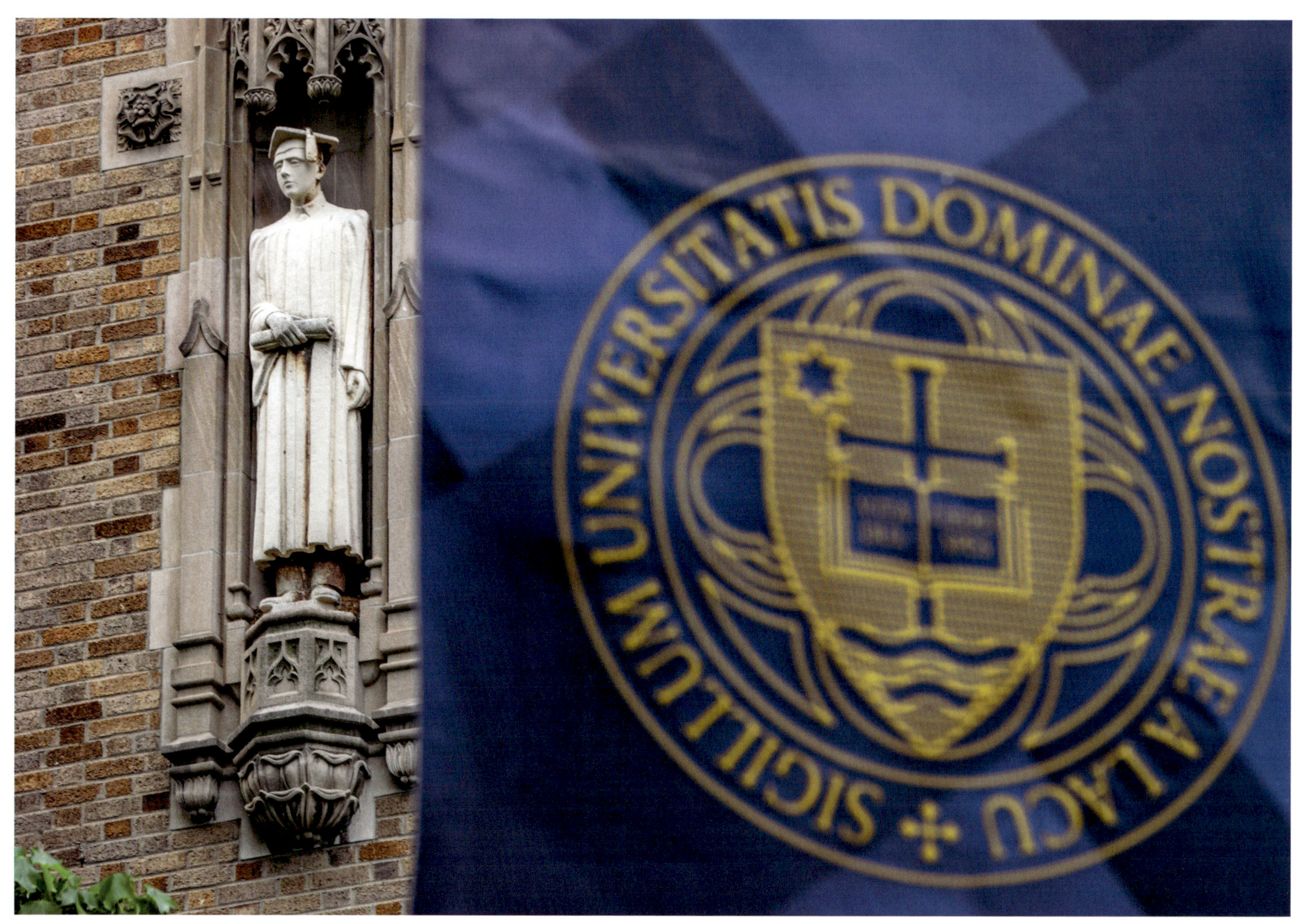

Statue on Alumni Hall, Nikon Z7, 135mm, 1/25 f18, ISO64

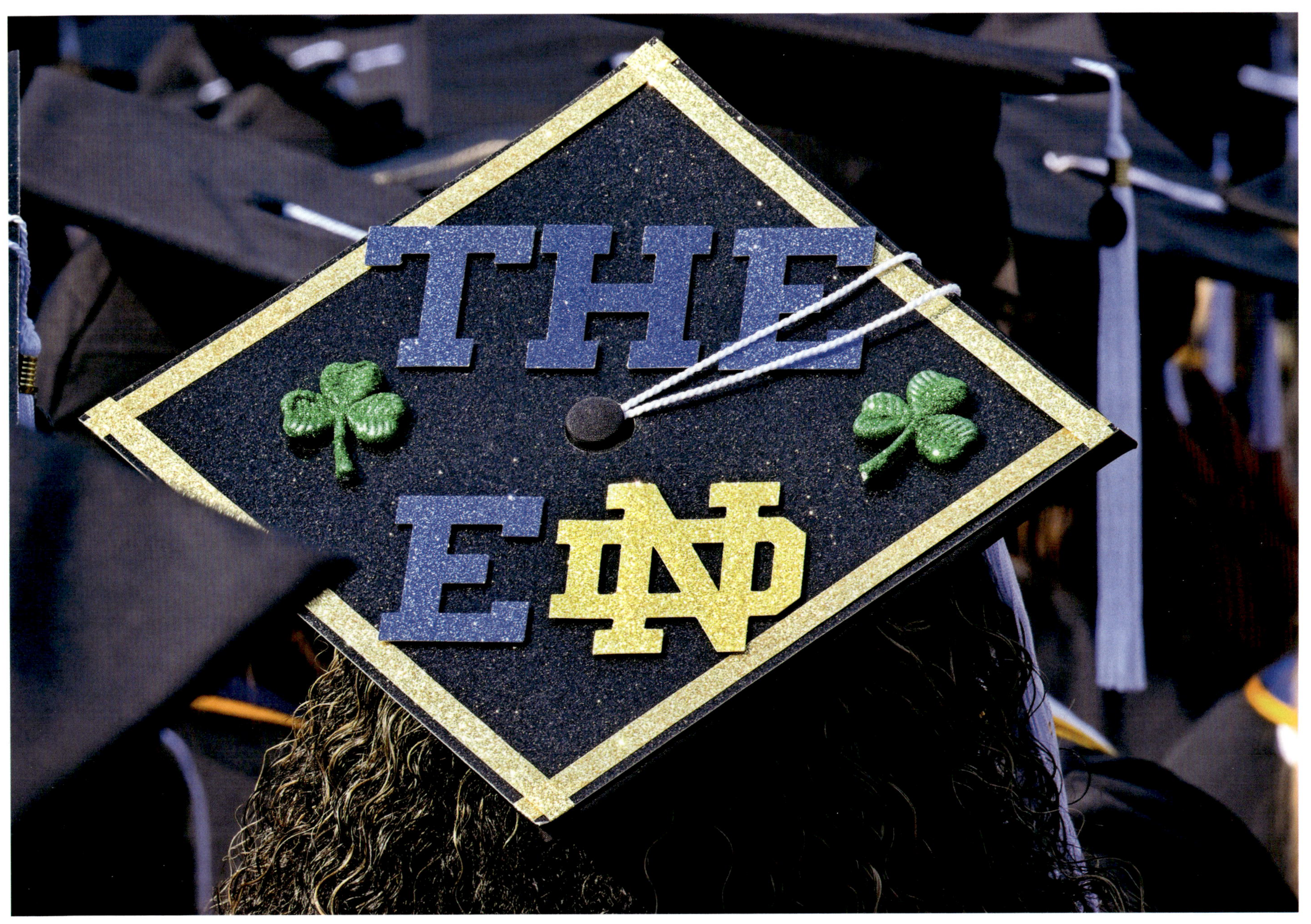

Graduate cap, Nikon Z9, 200mm, 1/320 f18, ISO500